DEBORAH,
GOLDA,
AND
ME

For Susan —

In sisterhood!

Letty Cottin Pogrebin

DEBORAH, GOLDA, AND ME

BEING FEMALE AND JEWISH

IN AMERICA

Letty Cottin Pogrebin

Anchor Books
DOUBLEDAY

NEW YORK   LONDON   TORONTO   SYDNEY   AUCKLAND

An Anchor Book

PUBLISHED BY DOUBLEDAY

a division of Bantam Doubleday Dell Publishing Group, Inc.
666 Fifth Avenue, New York, New York 10103

Anchor Books, Doubleday, and the portrayal of an anchor
are trademarks of Doubleday, a division of Bantam Doubleday
Dell Publishing Group, Inc.

Deborah, Golda, and Me was originally published in hardcover by
Crown Publishers, Inc. in 1991. The Anchor Books edition is
published by arrangement with Crown Publishers, Inc.

Portions of this book have appeared in different forms in *Ms., The
New York Times, Moment, Na'amat, Chatelaine,* and *Lilith.* An abbreviated
version of chapter 3 was first published as the Introduction to *A Mensch Among
Men: Explorations in Jewish Masculinity,* edited by Harry Brod (Freedom, CA:
Crossing Press, 1988). All copyrights are held by Letty Cottin Pogrebin.

Library of Congress Cataloging-in-Publication Data

Pogrebin, Letty Cottin.
Deborah, Golda, and me: being female and Jewish in America /
Letty Cottin Pogrebin.—1st Anchor Books ed.
p. cm.
Originally published: New York: Crown, c1991.
Includes bibliographical references and index.
1. Pogrebin, Letty Cottin. 2. Jews—United States—Biography.
3. Women, Jewish—United States—Biography. 4. Feminists—United
States—Biography. I. Title.
[E184.J5P59 1992]
973'.0492402—dc20
[B] 92-21838
CIP

ISBN 0-385-42512-0
FIRST ANCHOR BOOKS EDITION: October 1992

1 3 5 7 9 10 8 6 4 2

THIS BOOK IS DEDICATED

TO MY MOTHER,
CEIL HALPERN COTTIN,
MY DAUGHTERS, ABIGAIL AND ROBIN,
AND ALL JEWISH WOMEN,
PAST, PRESENT, AND FUTURE,
KNOWN, UNKNOWN, AND FORGOTTEN.
ESPECIALLY THE REBELS.

A question that has been raised more than once and that gives me no inner peace is why did so many nations in the past, and often still now, treat women as inferior to men? Everyone can agree how unjust this is, but that is not enough for me. I would also like to know the cause of the great injustice. . . . It is stupid enough of women to have borne it all in silence for such a long time, since the more centuries this arrangement lasts, the more deeply rooted it becomes. . . . Many people, particularly women, but also men, now realize for how long this state of affairs has been wrong, and modern women demand the right of complete independence! But that's not all, respect for women, that's going to have to come as well!

Anne Frank

Contents

Introduction

Why This Book?

NOT LONG AGO, I WAS DEEP IN CONVERSATION WITH A FRIEND WHEN he interrupted me mid-sentence.

"Wait a minute, I'm confused," he said. "You keep saying *We* this and *we* that and I never know if you mean your family, women, or the Jews!"

There's my problem in a nutshell, I thought. I have a wandering "we." My priorities are forever shifting, upstaging each other, pulling me in different directions. First comes my family, but after that I seem to be caught in a tug of war between women and the Jews.

I wondered if this "doubleness" is the lot of any woman who leads a hyphenated life, a life defined and determined by two major aspects of her identity—femaleness and something else. In my case, the hyphen links a Jew and a feminist in one human being with the gift or burden of double vision and the belief that anti-Semitism and sexism are equivalent evils. While I often feel like a double agent for two sacred causes, Judaism and feminism, neither of which necessarily believes the other deserves a place in heaven, at the same time, I've discovered that seeing double can be a useful survival mechanism. The compulsion to analyze events from varying perspectives has helped me to uncover meanings and motives, to reconcile contradictions and decode power relations.

My habit of policing two flanks did not begin with Judaism or feminism, it began when I was a child learning to please two very different parents. Accommodating to meet their contradictory demands and expectations, their polar behaviors and disparate goals, taught me to always look both ways.

As I mulled over this legacy of dualism, childhood memories flooded my mind. I thought about how certain family patterns simultaneously bred conformity and rebellion. I thought about the tension between my mother's emotional, mystical ways and my father's rational pragmatism and I considered how this heritage plays out in my adult life. There's a book here, I thought, and almost immediately started a file marked NOVEL. I could not imagine writing about myself and my family without a fictional disguise, but the novel wouldn't come. What came instead is this book—a confession, an autobiographical mystery partially solved, a narrative strung together from fragments of a life in search of its meaning.

The story you are about to read is true; the people existed, the events happened, only the conclusions are "imaginary" in that I have imagined a way to make sense of my experiences. In the process I have also sought to understand the contradictions that coexist within a Jew who is a woman and a woman who is a Jew. Try as I may to find other words for it, this book is about gender, family, religion, culture, and what the Mexican novelist Carlos Fuentes calls "a burning quest for identity."

To me, a person's identity is composed of both an "I" and a "we." The "I" finds itself in love, work, and pleasure, but it also locates itself within some meaningful *group* identity—a tribe, a community, a "we." America is too big and bland a tribe for most of us. We prefer hyphenation: Hispanic-American, Irish-American, Jewish-American. Of the more than 226 million people counted in the last United States census, only 13 million described themselves as "American"; the rest chose to assert their ethnic ancestry.

I know a woman who was born in Boston and is married to a Latvian who came here twenty years ago. All of his Latvian friends call her "the American." At first she didn't know who they were talking about. "I think of myself as a woman, a Jew, and a sociologist," she told me. "The only time I think of myself as an American is when I travel abroad."

Finding a comfortable collective identity is not as easy as it sounds—especially for people who think of themselves as independent spirits. Moreover, we are not likely to consciously identify with one of our "affinity groups" unless it means enough to us. For instance, I could legitimately group myself with native New Yorkers, nonfiction writers, or the middle-aged, but I choose to identify with the categories I find most meaningful, "women" and "Jews," two groups that manage to be simultaneously significant yet intractably marginal.

What do I mean by marginal? Neither of my chosen affinity groups is a cultural norm. The human norm is male and the American norm is a white Christian male and as long as Americans are measured against the standards of the white Christian male, both women and Jews will be seen as the Outsider—the Other—and the Jewish woman as the Other twice over. (The same is true for women of color, women of other ethnic groups, and of lesbians, whose distance from the norm can be tripled.)

Discrimination and bigotry are intrinsic hazards of Otherness; so is invisibility. Invisibility results when a word is used to describe a class of people in which you count yourself—American, for example—but you discover that the person using that word doesn't mean you. To test Jewish and female invisibility, ask the next ten people you meet to describe "an American." Chances are not one will conjure up a female of any persuasion or a Jew of either sex. Now ask any ten Jews to describe "a Jew" and I'd be surprised if any of them pictures a Jewish woman. That's what I mean by double marginality.

One advantage of living in the margins is that it allows a person to see the center more clearly than those who are in it. Because we must monitor at least two realities at once, marginalized people develop the survival skill I've called double vision. Others have described this adaptation in similar terms. In *The Souls of Black Folk*, W. E. B. DuBois speaks of the "double consciousness" of African-Americans. The novelist and short story writer, Hortense Calisher once said Southern Jews have "double expressiveness" because they occupy the feeling-states of both Jews and Southerners. Sigmund Freud, the founder of psychoanalysis, "felt doubly alienated and saw himself as a marginal man," according to Freud scholar Peter Gay. Being a Jew among Austrians and a nonbeliever among Jews "made [Freud] familiar in his youth with being in opposition and thus prepared the way for a 'certain independence of judgment.'" The critic Ted Solotaroff notes that marginality gave a "special angle of vision" to Jewish writers like Philip Roth, Bernard Malamud, Saul Bellow, Norman Mailer, Alfred Kazin, and Arthur Miller:

> *marginality had the implication of standing apart, as the American-Jewish writer was perceived to do with respect to both sides of the hyphen. Being an outsider in both the American and Jewish communities, he was enabled to see what more accustomed eyes would miss at a faculty meeting in Oregon or on the screen of a western or in the Jewish dietary laws.*

But a Jewish male can never be an outsider the way a Jewish woman is an outsider. Her Otherness is compounded by rejection from her *own* groups. With other *women* she remains The Jew, and with male *Jews* she remains The Woman; always a trifle alien, if not inferior, she is never entirely *of* them, never quite credentialed in the fullness of their "we." To be accepted by Gentile women she must act more WASPy, or less Jewish (whatever that means), or alter the aspects of herself that don't "fit" (her accent, her appearance, her politics). To be accepted by male Jews, she must renounce her "special" interests, and play by the rules Jewish men have made. If she lets second class treatment from either camp erode her self-esteem, she becomes a self-hating Jew or a woman-hating woman. Or else she relinquishes the whole idea of belonging and resigns herself to having a strong "I" but an unaffiliated "we."

For a number of years, where Jewish communal identity was concerned, unaffiliation was my preference. Then gradually, first in the spiritual domain and later in my secular life, I found ways to marry feminist transformation to Jewish renewal; I decided it was worth the effort to incorporate the nice Jewish girl I was raised to be, into the uppity woman I had become. The title of this book, *Deborah, Golda, and Me,* is meant to suggest that synthesis.

I am not so arrogant as to count myself an equal of the biblical Deborah, or of Golda Meir, the former prime minister of the State of Israel, but I do claim these women as my foremothers, one spiritual, the other secular. In seeking guidance from Jewish females who are protagonists rather than bit players, I have found the pickings mighty slim. (Even Deborah and Golda aren't perfect role models.) However, with this book title I want to assert that Jewish female archetypes, few as they are, can embody meaning to informed readers the way Christian male archetypes such as Saint Francis or Winston Churchill embody meaning to the culture at large. Hence, I use Deborah and Golda both as historical touchstones and as keystones to support the book's central themes.

My feeling for Deborah, the biblical character to whom I relate most viscerally, is explained in chapter 8, where I talk about my Bat Mitzvah. Golda Meir's significance to me will become clear in chapter 9, which tells of my political coming of age, and chapter 10, where I describe meeting Golda Meir in Israel. In this connection, let me say a word or two about the narrative structure of the book. The chapters are arranged thematically, not chronologically, and they proceed from the personal to the political. I begin in the family where all politics (i.e., power relations) start and gradually work through the history of my involvement in issues of global significance—such as women and anti-Semitism, Israeli affairs, the relationship between Jews and blacks, international feminism and the Palestinian issue.

Part One contains the family story. The next section, which I've called "Deborah," describes my rocky journey toward a religious identity that is consistent with feminist values. This is followed by a section entitled "Golda," which charts the complicated evolution of my secular identity. The last part attempts a kind of synthesis by suggesting how Jewish feminist principles are played out in my life and in my interactions with other groups. Through it all, my main objective is to illuminate in personal terms one woman's struggle to reconcile Judaism and feminism.

Finally, a word about the "me" in the synthesis. The first four decades of my life would not have predicted such a struggle. After graduating from Brandeis University I spent ten years working in book publishing while also getting married and having three children. I retired from the business world to become a professional writer following the publication of my first book in 1970. During the next decade, I became increasingly involved in the Women's Movement—as a founder and editor of *Ms.* magazine, and a writer, lecturer, and activist on behalf of a wide variety of social justice issues.

Throughout the Seventies and Eighties, I also wrote six books and hundreds of magazine and newspaper articles on subjects ranging from discrimination against women, to raising children without sex-role stereotypes, to the politics of the family, to an analysis of the many modes of friendship.

Looking back, I notice that my life and interests seem to have taken their sharpest turns as each decade gave rise to the next. At the close of the Fifties, I completed my education and assumed a high profile job unusual for a woman in that era. By the end of the Sixties, feeling that I had outgrown my career, I began to take myself and the world more seriously, finding new purpose in full-time writing and feminist advocacy. And as the Seventies segued into the Eighties, I was drawn toward the crossroads of feminism and Judaism and the politics of Jewish commitment. Thus I found myself at the start of the Nineties with a double identity, a warring, wandering "we," and a need to write this book.

Now a special word to its readers . . .

Despite its Jewish context, I believe much of the book will resonate for anyone who has felt marginalized in American life. On the few occasions when I have read chapters to mixed groups—for instance, at the MacDowell Colony, a writers' and artists' retreat in Peterborough, New Hampshire, where I wrote a large portion of the manuscript—non-Jewish women have told me they could readily extrapolate from my story to their own familial, ethnic, or political situations. Moreover, I discovered that men with hyphenated identities can relate to my feeling of doubleness because they know the strain of maintaining ethnic pride while remaining loyal to a nation that romanticizes the melting pot.

If I had to summarize this book in a sentence, I would describe it as a deeply personal account of one woman's efforts to merge the feminist ideology of equality and autonomy with the particularity of Judaism and Jewish ethics. If I had to shorten the description to a slogan, it would be *Forced choices are false choices*. The slogan proclaims that we who have a double identity will not deny one part of ourselves to serve the interests of another. It translates into "both/and"—not "either/or"—thinking. It means that I espouse *both* feminist *and* Jewish interests while accepting that, at times, one agenda might be more pressing than the other. It means working toward more Jewish consciousness in feminism and more feminist consciousness in Judaism. As difficult as this is to accomplish—for sometimes they turn out to be competing interests—I have discovered that unless I interlace ethnicity and gender, I am internally at odds with myself and externally vulnerable; I have no clarity of purpose; I cannot be sure why I am here or where I belong in the world.

Proverbs 11.1 says: "A false balance is an abomination to the Lord, but a just weight is God's delight." In the playground of life, I am the one standing on the seesaw—trying to achieve a just weight—leaning toward one side or the other depending upon which needs the extra mass. Thinking "either/or" tips the balance; thinking "both/and" holds the promise of equilibrium.

As a metaphor, the seesaw is a pretty shaky image. But those of us with divided loyalties never feel more secure than when we are free to move in two directions. At least that's been true in my life, the life you are about to enter.

PART ONE

Parents as Prologue

1

Family Secrets

SOME PEOPLE INSIST THAT IMPORTANT REALIZATIONS ALWAYS TAKE shape slowly; that understanding something "all of a sudden" happens only in pulp detective stories. But in my experience, the most profound, life-changing insights always seem to arrive suddenly, like a rash, a fever, an epiphany straight from God.

That's how I learned my family's best-kept secret—all of a sudden, on a raw, blustery day in the spring of 1951. From one moment to the next, the truth was revealed, a lie stood naked, the house of trust collapsed. The truth hung in the air, acrid as smoke. At first, I could not breathe; I could not take it in. But after weeks and months, I realized that if this deception could have been so well disguised, then the world must be full of secrets and I would have to spend the rest of my life trying to uncover and name them.

April 1951. My father's side of the family has gathered in Winthrop, Massachusetts, to celebrate my cousin Simon's Bar Mitzvah. After walking back from the service, the relatives have gathered in his parents' modest little house facing the ocean. Sea spray streaks the windows with a gritty film and a strong wind whistles beneath the eaves as the grown-ups—my parents, aunts, and uncles—steam up the kitchen with their coffee and conversation. In the living room, I am playing cards with my cousin Rita, a short, bubbly young woman of twenty-two. I am almost twelve.

Something in our card game triggers a dispute that escalates within seconds. Now, Rita and I are red-faced, arguing, flinging the playing cards, shouting, trading insults.

"You and your whole family stink!" she screams.

"You're just jealous," I counter, seventh-grade style.

"Of you? Don't make me laugh."

"No, of Betty," I say, thinking fast. " 'Cause she's older and smarter and prettier than you."

"Who cares about *her*?!" sneers Rita. "I'm still the first *real* grandchild and I always will be."

I know she's mad at me, but this makes no sense. Betty is twenty-six, Rita is twenty-two. Can't she count?

"What are you talking about?" I insist, more confused than angry. "My sister is the first-born grandchild; she's older than you."

"Your sister isn't even your whole sister!" sneers Rita, reveling in the last word. "And she wasn't even *in* this family until your parents got married!"

You've heard the expression "The mind reels"? Well, it doesn't. When presented with information too stunning to comprehend, the brain stops dead. It empties out, folds in on itself, goes blank. I stare into Rita's eyes, which are shooting sparks and smiling triumph. I cannot understand what she is saying but I know she is telling me the truth. I pass out.

When I regain consciousness, I am lying on the floor, my father and mother kneeling beside me. She is pressing a cold washcloth to my forehead. He looks angry. Rita has left the room. My parents keep saying how sorry they are. "We didn't want you to find out this way. We should have told you before. We should have told you ourselves. We're so sorry."

They help me to my feet. My legs are trembling. They suggest the three of us take a walk along the beach. Outside, my coat is as useless as a summer blanket on a winter's night. The wet April wind cuts through to my skin. My parents are huddled close, pressing either side of me like soft bookends, each with an arm around me. They are talking in hoarse, frightened voices. They are trying to explain. My mouth is dry. I am crying. I am beginning to understand.

* * *

It seems that both Ceil and Jack, my mother and father, had been married to other people and had been divorced years before they met each other. Today, this is not worth a raised eyebrow, but in the 1920s, Jewish people considered a failed marriage as shameful as a criminal record. Divorce was a *shonda*, a scandal, especially for a woman, and especially when the woman was left with a child. Ceil did not want to be looked upon as a "divorcee." She did not want Betty, the daughter of her first marriage, to be stigmatized. So in 1937, when she and Jack got married, Ceil conceived of the subterfuge that would eclipse her past. Since Jack was adopting Betty anyway, the three of them would present themselves to the outside world as a long-established family. Betty had been born in 1925, therefore Jack and Ceil would claim to have married each other in 1923. When asked about the fourteen-year age difference between Betty and me, Ceil would say she had been trying to conceive all that time and had just about given up when I, "the love child," answered her prayers in 1939.

Of course the relatives knew the ruse, which is why Rita had the information, but for public consumption—for their new friends and neighbors, for the Jewish community in Jamaica, the New York City suburb where they set up housekeeping, and eventually for *my* information—a fictional biography was created and all of us were integrated into a coherent family legend.

Having no reason to dispute this legend, I accepted it. Scrapbooks would have disclosed the lie had I viewed them critically, but what child reads her parents' script with the eye of suspicion? I never noticed that there were no snapshots of my parents together in their younger days, no wedding pictures, no photographs showing both my father and sister until she was in her teens. I had no problem with the age spread between Betty and myself; rather I felt lucky to have an older sister who was like a second mother only more fun. I remember her pageboy hairdo and saddle shoes, her college friends, her wartime beaus who came calling in their army uniforms. In June 1946, Betty became a glamorous bride and I was her flower girl. I had just turned seven. When she moved out of the house, she bequeathed to me her pink bedroom including the dressing table with its three-paneled mirror and pink organdy skirt.

On February 12 each year, my parents had celebrated their wedding anniversary with its bogus number and I had feted them with handmade presents—carefully rhymed poems, finger paintings, ceramic ashtrays, macramé key chains. In 1948, I saved my money and bought them a serious gift, a cut-glass decanter with six tiny liqueur glasses. The set cost me $9.98, more than two months' allowance, but I was happy to splurge for my parents' "silver anniversary." Although there was a number 25 on their cake, in 1948 they had been married for eleven years.

"Why didn't you tell me?" I ask my parents as we trudge along the beach in Winthrop, Massachusetts. "I could have kept the secret too."

"I was so ashamed of my divorce," my mother answers. "Betty had spent so many years in boarding school while I was single. I wanted us to be a *real* family." The tears in her eyes thickened.

"Why didn't you tell me?" I asked Betty nearly forty years later, while I was writing this chapter. "I guess I wanted to feel I was part of a real family . . ." she replied. Her sentence hung in the air with the poignancy of a child's wish.

My mother stops to kick the sand off her shoes one at a time, leaning against me, forgetting that I am the one who needs to be propped up. She is still wearing the high heels she had on in synagogue this morning and they are as caked with wet sand as a wooden spoon with raw cookie batter.

"Betty's real father is around somewhere," she says, looking down. "His name is Joe Holtzman."

The seagulls squawk overhead. I flash on the name "Betty Holtzman" written in my sister's hand on the flyleaf of her dictionary which I inherited when she moved out. When I asked her about it then, she said Holtzman was the last name of a boy she'd had a crush on in high school. She said she had written Betty Holtzman in her book to see how her name would look if she married him.

Now my mother is explaining why she divorced Joe Holtzman; something about his squandering all his money on bogus land bargains in Florida, and then refusing to get a job; something else about his mother moving into their apartment to cook for him and tuck him in at night. Ceil left Joe when he slapped her during an argument. He did not fight for custody of Betty when she was a baby and he readily gave his permission when Jack asked to adopt her.

"Your cousin Rita was dead wrong," my father insists in his lawyer's voice, and I am relieved to see that it was Rita who had made him angry, not I. "Betty *is* your whole sister. Even though she's your half-sister biologically, she's your full sister legally because I adopted her and I consider myself her only father." He wants me to understand that he did the right thing. "You know Betty thinks of me as her real father. And she considers you her real sister! You know *that*, don't you?"

His words swirl around me, cold as the wind. My ears feel like fingers, trying to sift out the lies, to trap the facts. Once I knew who was who and where I fit in. Now nothing is sure. I hear the rhythm of my breathing, interspersed with the relentless waves. The sky is as gray as slate.

"That's not all," says my father, squeezing my shoulders, his voice gentler but still urgent with the need to get the whole story out in the open. "There's more."

He stops to pick up a pointed stick that has washed up on the beach. He begins to draw lines in the sand in the configuration of a family tree. Down from the plane on which he scrawls his name and that of his first wife, he draws a line with a circle at the end of it. In the circle, he writes the name RENA.

That is how my father tells me he has another daughter.

This daughter, by *his* first marriage, is two years younger than Betty, which makes her twelve years my senior. No one knows where she is, he says, and it doesn't matter anyway because he is not allowed to see her. His first wife was a madwoman, paranoid schizophrenic. She would not give him visitation rights. He fought her in court, he says, and for a time, Rena did come to spend a few weekends with him, Ceil, and Betty, but after I was born, the ex-wife put a stop to the visits and threatened to harm Rena if he ever tried to see her again.

"Since the woman had a history of violent behavior," he says, "I had to give Rena up, for her own safety."

For a moment, I feel sorry for my unknown sister. I am sad that she had to lose her Daddy and live with her awful mother. It does not occur to me to ask how a father could abandon his daughter to a crazy woman "for her own safety." I study Rena's circle in the sand and wonder where she is and what she looks like. Then I notice that Rena's circle and my circle are on the same plane in the family tree. By blood, I am no closer to my father than she is. A thought heats up behind my eyes. If he could give her up, he could give me up. The thought becomes a question: Would he trade *me* in for a new wife as he traded Rena for my mother?

The question was prophetic; five years later, he would do just that.

My eyes sweep back and forth across my father's sand drawing. There are branches, lines, and circles going in all directions. I see my father's ex-wife, my mother's ex-husband, and my parents' initials in their little circles, and stemming from them are lines attached to each of their daughters, my half-sisters (one adopted, one invisible), and in the center of all the converging lines is the circle that is me. I am the only child who is the product of both my parents. On the diagram, my circle looks like the fruition of some Mendelian genetic experiment. But on the beach, I feel like a hybrid, unsure of her family, genus, or species. Walking between my own mother and father, I feel orphaned and alone.

For a few days after we returned home to Jamaica, I was aware of my parents watching me closely and treating me with gingerly concern. Gradually, when they were persuaded that I had survived the emotional upheaval and would not unexpectedly explode, they returned to normal. The Big Lie was not mentioned again until three years later when Rena arrived on our doorstep unannounced.

But I had exploded, or more accurately, I had imploded. The most fundamental facts of my childhood world had been turned inside out. Once it was simple. Adults told the truth; only children lied. Then it got complicated. I learned that grown-ups hide and are hidden. What is real can be as imaginary as a fairy tale. Nothing was certain any more.

The revelations of the Winthrop weekend left me embarrassed by my own naiveté and determined never again to be caught unknowing. I was nothing if not a good student. In one afternoon, I had learned lessons that would stay with me to the present day. Adults can be as afraid of the truth as children are of make-believe. Order is one sentence away from chaos. Life is not lived in plain language but in codes and symbols. Facts are slippery toads, and trust is no substitute for proof.

In 1951, I processed these epiphanies into rules. At the age of eleven-going-on-twelve, I realized "all of a sudden" that I would have to acquire certain skills in order to protect myself from this kind of pain. I remember unlocking my little leather diary with its tiny brass key and the gilt-edged pages, and writing that I would henceforth become a more vigilant observer. I would not merely live my life, I would interpret it. I would analyze people's behavior, listening between the lines instead of just hearing surface meanings. With these skills I would never again be surprised by the truth.

No other revelation would ever hurt as much as discovering that my parents had lied to me about themselves. None would threaten my world as much as the realization that my father had abandoned one daughter and could therefore abandon another. None would be as disenchanting as the discovery that my mother cared more about keeping up appearances than about living honestly. And none would ever reconfigure my identity as much as learning that I had not one "regular" sister but two half-sisters, one of whom I might never know.

Still, there were other surprises, other family secrets as well guarded as the divorce cover-up, so many in fact that I began to think of reality as a Russian doll. On my windowsill stood this brightly decorated, pear-shaped figure that seemed at first glance to be a solid, sculpted block of painted wood. But close up, one saw that it could be split at the waist and opened to reveal a hollow shell inside of which was another seemingly solid, perfectly painted doll that in turn concealed another doll, and another and another and another, until the last little doll emerged, as tiny as a plum pit.

I wondered how one could know which doll would be the last, the solid one with no hidden contents, the ultimate truth that is no more or less than itself.

In my family, kashruth was one of those realities with many layers. At home, my mother obeyed the Jewish dietary laws; she bought her meat from the kosher butcher and maintained separate sets of dishes and cookware for meat and dairy meals. However, in the homes of people who did not keep kosher, we ate meat with milk—Chicken à la King, for instance—and in restaurants we ate trayf, ritually unclean foods like pork or shellfish. If we could order lobster or Sweet and Sour Pork "out," I asked my mother, why go through the motions of keeping a kosher kitchen at home?

"Because of Grandma," she said. My mother obeyed the dietary laws so that *her* mother, who was strictly kosher, would be able to eat in our house. Okay, that made sense, but then, after going to all that trouble, why did Mommy cheat on her own rules? At the end of a meat meal, if no outsiders were present, she served my father evaporated milk in his coffee, the way he liked it. And because I was so skinny, she fed me baked potatoes with butter and sour cream alongside my flanken. Between meals, she gave me all sorts of nutritional bonuses, from cod liver oil and Hemo chocolate milk supplement, to after-school treats like double-fudge brownies and a delicious finger food she called "lamb-chops-on-paper."

My mother had a special pan in which she prepared this snack; she opened the windows when she cooked it, and she always served it to me on a paper plate which made it reasonable, if anyone were to ask me what I had eaten that day, for me to answer, in all innocence, "lamb-chops-on-paper." That way, Grandma would never know that there had been bacon in my mother's kitchen. I didn't know it either until a Catholic friend invited me to share her lunch, and when I questioned her calling a lamb-chops-on-paper sandwich a "BLT," I learned what the "B" was.

Although I had been made into an unwitting accomplice, I understood that my mother's duplicity was motivated by love. She loved Grandma enough to keep kosher. She loved my father enough to give him evaporated milk. She loved me enough to give me what the "goyim" ate. Gentiles all seemed so big and healthy; she thought maybe it was eating pig that did it. Years later she justified it to me this way: "Nobody got hurt. You gained weight. Grandma never knew. And God understood."

My mother's kashruth fraud is part of a category of family secrets that I think of as "cheating on Judaism." Among other such fakeries were our violations of the Sabbath.

Jews are not supposed to travel on the Sabbath, but my father, pillar of the Jewish community and model of pious propriety, drove to shul on Friday nights and Saturday mornings. He parked the car three or four blocks away, then we got out and walked, ostentatiously arriving by foot. (Only on the High Holy Days did we actually trek the mile or so to the Center.)

Second, Jews are not permitted to smoke on the Sabbath. But Daddy was a two-pack-a-day man. After three or four hours at services, he could hardly wait to light up, which he did about a block away from shul. If one of the other congregants approached, he quickly stamped out the cigarette beneath his shoe.

Jews also are not allowed to carry money, cook, work, or shop on the Sabbath. But it was okay for Daddy to go into his office on Saturday because he had a heavy case load. It was okay for us to carry money to buy some bagels or coffee cake on the way home from shul.

It was okay for Mommy to cook on Saturday if she hadn't prepared enough food in advance of the Sabbath. It was okay for me to go to the movies on Saturday if I was bored stiff and getting on my parents' nerves. Exceptions were made but never exactly acknowledged. They were our secret.

Besides cheating on Judaism, there was the category of family secrets that related to life-cycle events, especially sex, marriage, and death. I was in my early teens when I learned that my mother's mother—my sweet, shy, strictly kosher, God-fearing Grandma—was a runaway bride. Back in 1898 or thereabouts, in her little shtetl in Hungary, she was the victim of an arranged marriage to a man she loathed. After vows were exchanged but before the union was consummated, she ran away to the man who was to become my Grandpa. I wasn't exactly shocked when I found out about it as much as I was struck by disbelief that my meek, dour grandparents could once have been such impulsive lovers.

Also on my mother's side there was my aunt and uncle's secret marriage. At this writing, Aunt Tillie and Uncle Ralph are well past their sixty-fifth wedding anniversary. However, they were legally married for two years before their public religious ceremony. Custom required that a man not be wed until his older sisters were married. Ralph and Tillie kept their earlier marriage date a secret until their daughter discovered the license. She was ten years old.

My Uncle Herbie and Aunt Joan were the objects of family-wide pity because they were childless. "Such a shame, she's barren," everyone whispered. I was in my thirties before I discovered Herbie and Joan's secret: they didn't *want* children. In fact, Joan had had at least one abortion. But in our family, Joan had concluded, it was easier for her to pretend infertility than to assert her wish to remain childless. One of my cousins insists Joan later invented the abortion story to cover for her sterility, which was considered the worst failure of womanhood.

Oh, yes, the secret abortions. Between them, my mother, sister, aunts, and cousins must have had a half-dozen abortions, but of course I never knew about any of them. These secrets were revealed to me many years later, after I had survived an illegal abortion which I too had kept secret from my female relatives.

There were secrets on my father's side as well. Two sisters unhappily married—don't ask *how* unhappy—and making the best of it.

Two brothers who had died mysteriously, the brilliant one at eighteen of what was called a "glandular disturbance"; the other one, a vagabond, from "something infectious" which felled him in a Chicago hospital room. "The doctors told us the room had to be fumigated," said my father, and would say no more.

After circumventions about Judaism, sex, marriage, and death came the political cover-ups, a category of deceptions justified by McCarthyism. When I was about twelve years old, I learned that my Aunt Tillie on my mother's side and my Uncle Lou on my father's side were "Communists." Being let in on this secret was educational. To understand what a Communist was, Tillie sent me off to read Howard Fast's *Citizen Tom Paine*, *Spartacus*, and *Freedom Road*, and a smattering of Marx and Engels. She made me think about things few kids have much use for, like surplus labor and the redistribution of wealth. Having Communists in the family gave me a strong incentive to be well read: I wanted to be able to take part in the high-energy political arguments that raged around the dinner table when our extended family got together. Tillie, who lived next door, took on her siblings and their spouses, mainstream Democrats all; even my browbeating, eloquent father. I always thought my aunt came out the winner.

My mother supported her sister's politics but always somewhat tentatively, protecting herself against the possibility of my father's tongue-lashing. To get in on the action, I read and studied and became slightly intoxicated with Marxist discourse. The whole process was a game for me until Senator Joseph McCarthy went on his Red-baiting rampage. Then, the exotic turned terrifying and keeping our Communists under wraps became not just a family secret but a heavy burden. When the FBI came to interview my mother about my aunt, I knew enough to understand we were in danger, and when my sixth-grade teacher asked me who directed me to Howard Fast's novels for my book review project, I knew enough to tell her I had just picked them off the shelf at the Queens Borough Public Library.

Being in cahoots with my mother to protect my Aunt Tillie from the FBI seemed only slightly more perilous than protecting my mother's *knippel* from my father, which I had been doing since I was about eight. I discovered the secret purse when I caught her tucking some bills into the back of her stocking drawer. The reason she hid a small portion of the household allowance my father paid her every week was not to cheat him but to insure her own peace of mind, because he would never tell her how much he earned or how much, if anything, he was saving. Like many men, my father believed his money was his own business as long as his family was taken care of. But my mother had reason to feel otherwise.

"A woman should always have something of her own, just in case," she told me. At the time, I did not know that the woman proffering this advice had supported herself and her firstborn daughter for more than ten years, alone. To me, watching the bills go from his wallet to her *knippel* was like transferring goodies from one cookie jar to another. It was all Parent Money; what difference did it make where they kept it? Daddy would always take care of us, Mommy wasn't going anywhere, why worry? Because "Daddy isn't a saver," she told me. So she had to build this secret cushion just for us.

When she died, the dollars from the *knippel* turned up in a bank account amounting to more than $1,500, a tidy sum in 1955. She left it all to me. I received the money when I was eighteen. Since my father did not believe in supporting me beyond tuition, room, and board, it was my mother who bought me my independence. Her *knippel* taught me early on that money is freedom and a woman should always have something of her own, just in case.

Incidentally, when my father died, he left nothing. Mommy was right. He wasn't a saver.

As I recall my family's secrets, I see coherent patterns that illuminate my own behavior and relate directly to the identity search I have undertaken in this book. I see that most of our secrets were guarded by the women of the family, who revealed the information bit by bit like time-release pain capsules. While men control the history of nations and civilizations, women use family history as their negotiable instruments. And if knowledge is power, clandestine knowledge is power squared; it can be withheld, exchanged, and leveraged. For women, who traditionally were excluded from prestige-building occupations or the exercise of worldly influence, guarding secrets may have been the only power they knew.

I see too that the main stimulus for stockpiling secrets in my family was the fear of shame. The women especially worried about "how it would look" and "what people would think." Was this because the women were socialized to be more image-conscious than the men? Or because appearances assume greater importance to those who have few concrete measures of their worth? Or because keeping certain behaviors under wraps allowed the women to remain presentable yet do what they wanted to do anyway?

Most of my family's cover-ups related to "unacceptable" behavior in two areas: women's role and Jewish observance. How ironic to find in memory's attic, rattling around among the skeletons, the very same issues that have concerned me for the last twenty years: women's role and Jewish observance. Yet it makes perfect sense. In past generations even more than my own, both femininity and Judaism demanded absolute conformity to their strict regimens. So of course there were mistakes, blunders, transgressions; and of course, they had to be concealed, or how would it look and what would people think?

Rather than challenge those harsh dictates of femininity and Judaism, my family chose to hide its failures. Keeping secrets was the way they responded to the tyranny of the ideal. They wouldn't conform but neither would they admit it. I have chosen not to conform—and to confront it—both as a writer and a social activist. Yet I can not help wondering if my memory of old deceptions and wasted shame has made this forthright rebellion—my overt feminism and antiauthoritarian Judaism—all the more inevitable.

2

Mother, I Hardly Knew You

I FEEL ABOUT MOTHERS THE WAY I FEEL ABOUT DIMPLES: BECAUSE I do not have one myself, I notice everyone who does.

Most people who have a dimple or two take them for granted, unaware of how these endearing parentheses punctuate a smile. While I spent months of my childhood going to bed with a button taped into each cheek trying to imprint nature, my dimpled friends fell asleep unappreciative of their genetic gifts. They did not notice what they had always had.

Most people who have a mother take her for granted in much the same way. They accept or criticize her without remarking on the fact that there is a mother there at all—or how it would feel if there were none. I've never had the luxury of being so blasé. Since I lost my mother when I was quite young, I keep pressing my mother-memories into my mind, like the buttons in my cheeks, hoping to deepen an imprint that time has tried to erase.

She was fifty-three when she died; I was fifteen. I had less time with my mother than I've had with my children. Less time than I've known my closest friends, or many colleagues. The truth is, if you subtract the earliest part of my childhood and the darkest months of her illness, my mother and I really knew one another for a scant ten years.

I suppose I should be grateful that so little time has left so much to remember.

I think about my mother most in the spring—not just on April 20, the anniversary of her death, but whenever ordinary events, like spring cleaning, evoke everyday images of her. I remember that I would come home from school one day to find her in the midst of the annual purification of our house. She called it "freshening up." Singlehand-edly, she would take down the heavy damask draperies and put up diaphanous curtains, pack away the carpets and spread out rattan rugs, bathe the venetian blinds, costume the tweed sofa with some flowered chintz that announced the end of winter more defiantly than the first crocus, rearrange the furniture, and leave the air smelling like pine needles.

Since 1955, spring has not arrived with much fanfare in the houses of my life, but one whiff of pine-scented cleaner reminds me of my mother's domestic metamorphoses, a metaphor for her belief in new beginnings.

She also liked freshening herself up at the end of the day. After cooking supper, she would tidy the house so that my father could return from his law office to calm surroundings and never suspect the mess of daily child rearing—a reality so many men are spared by impeccable wives. Then, like a teenaged girl preparing for a date, she would dash into the shower, powder her Rubenesque body with a puff of peach-colored down, and put on a rayon or starched cotton housedress such as those sold today in vintage clothing shops at prices that would have bought my mother three winter coats.

When I see a certain kind of dress—with a tiny plaid pattern or an overall floral print—I can conjure my mother buttoning such a dress over her slip, then sitting at a mirrored dressing table like the one I'd inherited from Betty, smiling to bring out her cheek mounds for the rouge, fastening the catch on a string of pearls, scooping her hair up on each side with a tortoiseshell comb. As she dabs Shalimar perfume behind each ear, I can hear her saying: "It's good to freshen up for your husband. Makes a man glad to come home."

My father always came home for dinner, usually at seven. But no matter how lovely my mother looked, he didn't *stay* home. It wasn't another woman that propelled him out the door, it was a lifelong affair with meetings. Almost every night of the week, he went out to attend meetings—of the United Jewish Appeal or the Jewish War Veterans, or any of his other organizations devoted to the welfare of Jews or of Israel. At one time or other, he was the president, chairman, or county commander of every one of them.

My mother would beg him to stay home for my sake, to give me "a real father, a real family life." But a woman in a housedress and a noisy little girl are no match for the lure of a roomful of power and adulation.

Watching him leave the house, I lost faith in my mother's axioms for feminine success, yet she kept reciting them like a litany—not only "Freshen up for your husband," but "Don't show your brains; smart girls scare men," "Always laugh at his jokes," "Act interested in his work even if you're not." My mother lived by these bromides. She freshened up, listened, laughed, and cooked up a storm, but none of it stopped the man she loved from getting into his Dodge sedan and driving away.

Passover always reminds me of my mother. The eight-day holiday demanded attic-to-basement housecleaning to rid every surface of *chametz* (leaven products), and a complete change of dishes, and because she kept a (mostly) kosher kitchen, she had to pack away two sets of everything (meat and dairy), and unpack all their Passover equivalents right down to the can opener. I never heard her complain. Maybe the Passover makeover suited her optimistic nature, her love for fresh starts and rites of transformation. I remember how efficiently she unearthed her Passover recipe files or turned to the right section of her dogeared copy of *Jewish Home Beautiful* to double-check the traditional recipes for gefilte fish, chopped liver, chicken soup with matzo balls, potato pudding, carrot tzimmes, macaroons—all of which she would make from scratch. There was no pressure cooker or electric mixer in her kitchen, no food processor or microwave. She used a hand-cranked meat grinder and a flat metal vegetable grater. She whipped with a fork, chopped in a wooden bowl, and beat with a wooden spoon. For years, she even plucked her own chickens.

I have a sense memory of the aromas that wafted up to my bedroom just above the kitchen, but few recollections of helping my mother except when she was baking. My squeamish complaints about "yucky" raw liver and "disgusting" chicken feet must have made it preferable for her to let me stay upstairs.

To this day, I can remember the look of our seder table: the damask cloth with dim pink shadows from red-wine spills of meals past; the ceremonial plate with separate compartments for the parsley, *haroset*, gnarled horseradish root, roasted shank bone, and charred hard-boiled egg; the cut-glass bowls for salt water; three matzot in their layered satin case; two pair of candlesticks, chrome and brass; the silver goblet for the Prophet Elijah. But only in recent years have I let myself think about my mother's exhaustion. It shows on her face in our home movies of the last Passover of her life. Could she have been that exhausted every year?

On both seder nights, while she and the other women served the meal and cleared the dishes, my father reclined in an oversized chair at the head of the table, ennobled in his *kipah* (skullcap) and *kittel* (white ceremonial robe). Year after year, the Haggadah, the retelling of Israel's liberation from bondage, came to us in my father's authoritative bass voice, annotated by the symbols, songs, and rituals that he brought upstage like some great maestro conducting the solo parts of the seder symphony. It took me years to see that my father's virtuosity depended on my mother's labor and that the seders I remember with such heartwarming intensity were sanctified by her creation even more than his.

Music reminds me of my mother, especially classical music broadcast on WQXR, the station she tuned into whenever she wasn't listening to *Helen Trent, Our Gal Sunday*, and the rest of her afternoon soap operas. We never went to a live performance or bought classical records, but there was always radio music in our house.

Certain songs bring to mind my mother and me as a happy pair, with my father in the wings somewhere and my parents' fights edited out. The lullaby Mommy always sang, "Old Lady Moon," transports me back to my red-and-yellow room with her sitting at the edge of my bed, stroking my forehead. I'm even further back in childhood, curled in her lap, when I hear *"Oyfin Pripitshik,"* the only Yiddish song she ever taught me. She believed Yiddish was the language of old people and the Old Country—the language parents used to keep secrets from their American-born children, not the vocabulary of my future—but she made an exception for this song, now the anthem of my maternal mythology. Beethoven's *"Für Elise"* unlocks an image of me in long braids, sitting at the piano with a straight back and my skinny legs barely reaching the pedals, practicing the opening bars with Mommy in the kitchen humming along like a metronome. "My Yiddishe Momma" reminds me of my mother's devotion to my grandmother, who outlived her. "Try a Little Tenderness" brings tears to my eyes now as it did in 1954 when I played the record over and over again within my father's hearing, praying he would take Frank Sinatra's advice.

Music is a complicated catalyst. While these songs of my childhood elicit a rush of memories of my mother, they also evoke the larger reality of those times. As a woman, I long for the past about as much as I long for boned girdles and sanitary belts. I want to visit Memory Lane, I don't want to live there. My sentimentality is selective.

And my nostalgia is bittersweet. The bitter part acknowledges existential loss, an understanding that "only yesterday" was years ago and never to be seen again. But the sweet part glories in having lived, in possessing life by remembering its sounds and textures, and claiming the right to say, "I was there and that's the way it was." Old music and vintage clothes are precious to me because things evoke people. And, since people die, I am grateful when things—a housedress, a kiddush cup, a song—stay around.

Springtime also reminds me of my mother because of the burst of family birthdays—my husband's and son's in April, my daughters' birthdays in May, and mine in early June. Birthdays make me realize that the four human beings who are dearest to me in the world are people my mother never knew; and that they will never know her, except as I reveal her to them, filtering the perceptions of a fifteen-year-old through the language of a grown woman. Birthdays and holidays—events we would surely have celebrated with her had she lived—are the times above all others when I think about how much we've missed.

Then, quite honestly, another thought comes to mind. If she had lived I might not have this husband and these children. I probably would not have gone away to college at sixteen, then lived alone for five years, traveling by myself, becoming self-supporting, learning to take risks. More likely, I'd have stayed close to home, gone to Queens College, and married upon graduation as my sister Betty did. My mother's aspirations for me were entirely oriented toward marriage and childbearing.

But her death forced me to live a different life. And since that life has suited me, and I have made gratifying decisions without a mother's advice or counsel, I wonder irreverently, ironically, whether my mother mothered me best by dying. That sentence is bizarre, I know, yet it is what I keep thinking. The contradictions are obvious: to mourn this woman so deeply and at the same time feel grateful to her for leaving me alone to grow up by myself; to palpably miss her to this day, and yet simultaneously dread what might have happened between us had she lived.

Suppose I had rejected her axioms of femininity? What if she didn't approve of my beliefs, my habits, my choices? What if my feminism frightened or shamed her? Disturbing possibilities. I try to imagine our relationship whenever I see mothers and grown daughters playing out their scenarios not in my land of what-*if*, but in their land of what-*is*. So many mother-daughter pairs are hostile and resentful. Could Mommy and I have avoided that? Could I have wrenched free of her timidity, taking with me the person she was but rejecting her formulas? Could we have drawn energy from our differences, or would she have viewed my life as an affront to hers?

Of course I will never know.

Not long ago, a friend found an old photograph of her family taken before they left Estonia on the eve of World War II. "You were four in this picture," her mother told her, misty-eyed. "You used to spend hours at that spot overlooking the valley and you'd sing at the top of your lungs."

My friend gazed at the picture in disbelief. It showed her standing in a place that, for decades until that moment, had appeared only in her dreams.

Mothers seem able to come up with these unexpected revelations about one's child-self, or to suddenly recollect a turning-point experience that explains one's adult obsession. Mothers save precious preschool artifacts in shoe boxes at the top of the closet. Mothers remember a child's first words, and quote them in tones usually reserved for Byron. Only a mother remembers her children's landmarks as her own.

Therefore, losing a mother when you are still a child cuts short your hindsight and historiography. Without my mother's testimony, I know myself almost exclusively *through* myself. I can only reconstruct that part of the past that I can remember firsthand. Without my mother,

I have no possibility of being surprised by my own history. All I have is a *Baby Book* in which she inscribed my "Cute Sayings," traced an outline of my infant foot, entered my height and weight, and described my favorite foods, toys, and books. Tucked between its pages is a lock of my baby hair secured with a limp satin ribbon, some grade-school report cards, and a homemade Mother's Day poem which would not have predicted a professional writing career by any stretch of the imagination. These are my archaeological treasures. While my mother-in-law has conducted an ongoing dig into my husband's boyhood (and finds and remembers new things every year), all record of my existence from birth to six is in that *Baby Book*. There will be no further surprises.

My father was never much help in enlightening me about my former self, either because he wasn't paying attention or because he wasn't there. Although he claimed to adore me, and I remember him as lavishly affectionate, he was better at reminiscing about *his* childhood than about mine. If he did remember something about me, it was what *he* did with me, or how I reacted to *him*. He loved to recall how I didn't recognize him after he shaved off his mustache. He was amused that I had run from him in fear, but I felt sorry for the little girl he described—a child who spent so little time with her Daddy that she didn't know him well enough to see beyond a mustache.

My father lived for more than twenty-seven years after my mother died, yet he remains a father figure rather than a father. She is the parent I remember and hers is the life I keep mining for gold, running my sieve through the same old streams, searching for precious nuggets that might connect my memories of her to the life I have lived without her. I keep hoping that the missing pieces will turn up in my mother's past.

She was called Sarah when she sailed from Hungary in steerage in 1907, a little girl wearing paper shoes, and she never overcame her sense of inferiority at being a "greenhorn" in the New World. Soon after her arrival, she changed her name to Cyral and then Ceil, undoubtedly to glamorize and Americanize herself. It occurs to me now that the name change also may have had something to do with two of her most distinctive traits: her love of transformations and her superstitions. According to Jewish mysticism, one changed a person's name when he or she was gravely ill. This would mislead the Devil who was thought to keep track of vulnerable people by name. Maybe my mother believed that a name change would also divert the Devil from a weak and vulnerable greenhorn like herself.

She went to work in her father's grocery store straight after graduation from the eighth grade because her parents needed her help. Later, she got a job in a garment factory, doing I don't know what. She was deliberately vague about her work life until she made something of a success of it. She married the indolent first husband, gave birth to Betty, got her divorce, and sometime in the late 1920s, found work with the respected hatmaker and couturiere Hattie Carnegie where she eventually worked her way up to the position of designer. Photographs from those years show Ceil as an elegant young woman whose clothes and posture were a cut above those of the friends posing with her on the running board of some big black automobile. Despite the wonderful flapper outfits and Jazz Age look of the pictures, she told me—once I knew the truth of her life—how miserable those years were for her. No career accomplishment could overshadow the *shonda* of divorce or the disgrace of having had to send her daughter away.

I confess now that I have trouble understanding how the fiercely maternal, overprotective woman who was my mother was the same woman who could leave Betty in a boarding school at the age of three. When my daughters were three, I used to stare fixedly at them and try to imagine depositing those angelic little toddlers in some school dormitory and leaving them there all week, only to visit on Sundays. I couldn't even wrap my brain around the image. Nor did it jibe with what I knew of my mother, the kind of person she was with me. Yet it is also true that the mother I knew was a married full-time housewife with a lawyer husband, and the mother Betty knew was a struggling single working woman. In 1928, enrolling her little girl in an upstate, upscale boarding school must have made sense. What now looks like cold-hearted rejection must have been to her way of thinking an act of loving sacrifice.

Betty says it would have been easier (and free) to let Grandma baby-sit, but Ceil was determined that her little girl become a "real American," not a second-generation greenhorn. Thinking about her frequent references to "real Americans" and "real families" I can see how obsessed my mother was with what she wasn't. She believed that her parents' Yiddish accents and immigrant ways would rub off on her daughter. Rather than let such a tragedy happen, she worked long hours to pay for the expensive boarding school until Betty was twelve and my father adopted her.

As for Ceil, she spent those years polishing her English until it was pristinely unaccented. She read voraciously and informed herself about art, politics, and music. Nevertheless, she remained so ashamed of her origins and her family's poverty that the address she gave her beaus was not the Lower East Side tenement where she lived with her parents and unmarried siblings, but the home of a "rich" cousin in the Bronx. She took the subway to the Bronx so that she could be picked up there by her date and returned there at the end of an evening. When the beau left, she got back on the subway and rode home to the Lower East Side alone.

After almost ten years of single life and subterfuge (which perhaps presaged her later secrets), she married the man who would become my father. They met on Visiting Day at the boarding school where both of their daughters were enrolled. Usually Ceil visited Betty on Sundays, and Jack visited Rena on Saturdays. They had never crossed paths until one weekend, when Jack had to switch to a Sunday. Mirroring the French film *A Man and a Woman*, the two parents were introduced by Betty who, almost from the start, waged a campaign for them to marry. Eventually, she got her wish and more: Jack Cottin became her father.

Ceil could not believe her good fortune. She had married a "real American" and a good provider, a lawyer who, despite the Depression, was making a living. She quit her job. Now she could have a "real family" like every other middle-class woman she admired. No more boarding school; no more crowded Lower East Side tenement— they moved to a Bronx apartment that was even finer than the "rich" cousin's digs Ceil had claimed as her own. At last, by her lights, she was a success.

The one casualty of these happy developments was Jack's daughter, Rena. Although initially she spent some weekends with Jack, Ceil, and Betty, for reasons I will explain in the next chapter, the visits stopped. Shortly after I was born, Rena dropped out of sight altogether and the new family mythology was constructed, making me and Betty my parents' only daughters.

When I was about a year old, we moved to Jamaica, Queens, to a semidetached house with a front lawn, a backyard, six rooms, and a porch. This should have been the happily-ever-after part of my mother's story, but it didn't work out that way. Ceil felt painfully inferior to her well-educated, silver-tongued spouse—and if my father did not exactly flaunt his superiority, neither did he disabuse my mother of her low self-image. She worked hard to compensate, taking courses in oil painting, Hebrew, and Jewish history. She learned to play bridge—never well enough to still his carping ridicule. She learned to drive but he would not let her have the wheel when he was in the car. He gave her the allowance from which she squirreled away that secret cache that would become my nest egg, but she never felt secure.

Though she fought a losing battle against his meetings and organizations, she never gave up trying to lure her husband home by adorning herself, improving herself, and trying to win his heart the old-fashioned way—through his stomach. Her handwritten recipe cards attest to her efforts. In the 1940s and '50s, when most housewives thought "gourmet" meant Jell-O molds, my mother was stuffing prunes with pecans and frosting the rims of iced-tea glasses. To please me—a notoriously picky eater who was by Jewish standards "emaciated"—she created food art, making a pear into a bunny with clove eyes, almond ears, and a marshmallow tail, or getting me to eat fresh vegetables by presenting me with Salad Sally, whose celery body packed cream cheese up its middle and wore a lettuce skirt and parsley belt.

Some of my mother's recipe entries are artifacts in themselves—reminders of her everyday life in two separate worlds. Menus clipped from the Yiddish newspaper, *The Forward*, alternate with cuttings from the *Ladies Home Journal*. The recipe for huckleberry cake is scrawled on the back of a ticket for the Military Ball of the Jewish War Veterans' Ladies Auxiliary (November 25, 1942), while Beet Salad is written on the stationery of the City Patrol Corps. Both of my parents served as Air Raid Wardens during the war. I suspect Ceil volunteered for civil defense work not just as a public service but because it was one of the few activities she and Daddy could do together.

Even more assiduously than recipes, my mother collected people. Her relatives were first in her heart, time, and devotion. After the family came her many friends in the Jewish community, the women of our Temple Sisterhood, Hadassah, the National Council of Jewish Women, Women's American ORT, and the JWV Ladies Auxiliary.

She also had a group of friends who played Mah-Jongg as if it was the Russian chess championships, but without the silence. I remember iced tea with mint in tall glasses and sandwiches without crusts—cream cheese, tomato, and olives; tuna salad with swiss—and above the clicking tiles and cacophonous cross talk, I remember hearing the women complain about demanding, helpless husbands who would be lost without them. The ladies of the Mah-Jongg group could forecast doomed marriages and fatal illnesses long before the principals knew they were in trouble. I learned to recognize the gravity of a person's condition from the voice levels of the narrator. Whispers meant polio and cancer. Heart attacks were discussed a little louder, the flu at full volume. When they forgot I was upstairs with my big ears, the women talked about sex—either they had too much or too little, or they suffered from physical problems that I couldn't understand and couldn't find listed in the copy of *Love Without Fear* that I kept hidden in a zippered bolster. Compared to the other women, my mother didn't say much; she listened, and offered a "Really?" or "How interesting!" but she didn't dish the gossip.

Other than the peripatetic Mah-Jongg group, there was not much house-to-house visiting. The telephone was the preferred means of communication among my mother's friends—and it was the telephone that brought "Carl" into our lives, this mystery man from Cleveland who was planning to come to New York for a sex-change operation in the early 1950s when the transsexual phenomenon was virtually unknown. At first, Mommy's side of the conversations was a complete puzzlement to me:

"Don't worry, you'll learn to sit right once you get used to wearing dresses."

"I'm sure the doctors will fix your voice too."

"So, you won't let him touch you there until you feel comfortable."

I badgered her with questions until she finally explained what was going on. Somehow this uneducated Jewish housewife, who blushed at circumcision jokes, had become the telephone therapist to a stranger who was about to surrender his penis and begin life as a woman. She took his calls because he had been referred to her by one of her Cleveland cousins. For months, I heard her reassuring the tormented Carl, assuaging his fears, discussing his medical plans, and responding to his questions about femininity with the sort of physiological detail that would have been off-limits had she not accepted the role of the comforting confidante. One day I heard her correcting herself and calling Carl "Carol." Shortly afterward the calls ceased.

When I asked what happened, Mommy simply said, "Carol doesn't need me anymore, she just wants to get on with her life."

There were seven siblings and dozens of cousins in my mother's family, but Ceil was the one you would call if you had a transsexual friend in need. She was the organizer, the family glue, the counsel of last resort. Everyone leaned on her. And because her husband, the man of her dreams, was almost never home, she filled her life with everyone else. She took in uncles who returned from the war and cousins who had survived the Holocaust, putting them up until they could get settled on their own. When I was six, one of my aunts died in childbirth and Mommy insisted that my newborn cousin, Simma, live with us until her father could find another wife. Thus, in 1945 and 1946, I had a "baby sister." In 1950, my mother invited a friend's daughter to stay in our extra bedroom so the girl could continue to attend her own school while her parents moved out of the city for her father's health. And when my grandparents were too old to maintain their own home, Mommy performed one of her domestic miracles and transformed our basement into their pied-à-terre.

Whether it was a family crisis, a holiday get-together, a dinner to be hosted for one of my father's clients or organizations—whatever it was, if it needed doing, my mother did it with grace.

Aishes Chayil (The Woman of Valor) from Proverbs 31 is traditionally read by Jewish husbands to their wives every Sabbath Eve. So far as I know, my father never spoke these verses to my mother, but no wife deserved them more. Our rabbi, Gershon Levi, recited them at her funeral; they might have been written just for her.

> *What a rare find is a capable wife!*
> *Her worth is far beyond that of rubies.*
> *Her husband puts his confidence in her,*
> *And lacks no good thing.*
> *She is good to him, never bad*
> *All the days of her life. . . .*
>
> *She rises while it is still night,*
> *And supplies provisions for her household. . . .*
>
> *She girds herself with strength,*
> *And performs her tasks with vigor. . . .*
>
> *She gives generously to the poor;*

Her hands are stretched out to the needy. . . .

Her husband is prominent in the gates,
As he sits among the elders of the land. . . .

Her mouth is full of wisdom,
Her tongue with kindly teaching.
She oversees the activities of her household,
And never eats the bread of idleness. . . .

Ovarian cancer was the recorded cause of her death. Today, with all the talk of cancer-prone behavior and the physiological ravages of stress, I wonder if the female body's ultimate expression of feminine suffering is to develop ovarian cancer. I wonder if my mother died from too many years of self-sacrifice.

More than five hundred people came to her funeral. I heard one man say the turnout reflected my father's prominence in the community, but most people knew otherwise; these were *her* friends, the people who had claimed her love in my father's absence. And they appreciated her as he never did.

I'm quite sure my mother died without understanding how remarkable she was. Once, during the last weeks of her life, when I was sitting with her after school, she started crying. "I'm so sorry that I will never see you grown up," she said. "I hope I've raised you well, because I've been a failure at everything else."

"Everything else?" I whispered.

"Yes," she explained. "Choosing a husband is the most important decision in a woman's life, and twice I chose wrong."

She never saw herself for what she was: a brave pioneer in the new world, a female wage earner unbowed by a grade-school education, a single parent who supported and educated her child throughout the Depression, a gifted artist and designer, an intrepid student, a maker of feasts and celebrations, a relentless optimist, a nourishing mother, and a true and giving friend.

I learned what success means from this woman who considered herself a failure. In the past, I have oversimplified her lesson; I've said her life taught me what *not* to tolerate in my own. But the older I get, the more rich and complicated her legacy seems. Before she could become the conformist that I might today deplore, she had to learn a language, decipher an entire social system, make the leap from a shtetl

with wooden cottages and mud paths to a crowded city tenement—
and decide that tenement life wasn't going to be good enough. Where
did she get the vision? In a time when women tolerated all kinds of
abuse in order to stay married and economically secure, she walked
away from an insufferable husband. Where did she get the nerve?

From my present perspective, I can bemoan the years she wasted on
undeserving men, the needless humiliation she felt on behalf of her
impoverished, unassimilated family, her misguided inferiorities, the
excuses she made for having had a career in the design world that
struck her as unseemly. Again, that critique is simplistic. I see now
that my mother's brilliance lay in her ability to create a persona as
original as the dress designs she coaxed out of a few folds of fabric.
In her context, for her generation, she was a miracle worker. She
invented herself. Then she invented the family life she thought she and
her daughters deserved. Deeply, desperately, she wanted to be like
everyone else, but when the American dream didn't deliver, she made
up her own.

I have the luxury of pursuing my goals unencumbered by the
weighty bundles of a greenhorn. Still, to unlearn the constricted, self-
sacrificial, conformist kind of womanhood that my mother bequeathed to me (just as her mother bequeathed it to her), I find myself
using her survival skills and tools of invention. While she never acknowledged her strengths I recognize them in my own idealism, will-
fulness, and belief in the possibility of change. In a funny way, the
little girl in paper shoes became my role model after all.

Along with her optimism, I've also inherited her mysticism. My
superstitions are my mother's superstitions—not black cats and rab-
bit's feet, but the amulets and incantations that she learned from *her*
mother and I learned from her. I don't mean to suggest that she
intended to school me in the occult. Quite the contrary; she tried to
hide her shtetl formulas; she wanted me, like Betty, to rise above her
Old World ways. But eventually, just by living with her, I came to
know them all: Never take a picture of a pregnant woman. Be sure
you have bread and salt in a house before you live in it. When an
eyelash falls out, make a wish on it. Knock wood when speaking
about good things that have happened to you. Don't leave a bride
alone on her wedding day. Eat the ends of bread if you want to give
birth to a boy. (Betty followed this prescription during her first pregnancy, never accepting anything but the heel ends of a loaf of bread,

and she gave birth to a boy. "See, I told you so!" said Mommy. But Betty's next two were also boys even though she'd sworn off eating bread ends. Finally, her fourth child was a girl.)

The day when I first discovered menstrual blood on my panties, I called for my mother to hurry into the bathroom. My friends had been having their periods for years. At last, I had mine. I was fourteen and I was thrilled. As soon as she saw the blood, Mommy said something in Yiddish and slapped me across the cheek. Then she hugged me. I'd never been struck before by either parent. I was stunned, but as she held me firm in her embrace, she whispered into my hair, "I'm sorry, darling, but Jews have to slap a girl on her first menstruation to prepare her for the pain of womanhood. Please God, that slap should be the worst pain you ever know."

Often, Mommy would tiptoe into my room after she thought I was asleep and she would kiss my forehead three times while making odd little noises that sounded like a cross between sucking and spitting: "Thpu. Thpu. Thpu." One night, as she pulled her face away from mine, I opened my eyes. "*Mother*, what *are* you doing?" I demanded.

Embarrassed, she told me she was excising the Evil Eye just in case I had attracted its attention that day by being especially wonderful. She believed her three noises could suck out any envy or ill will that those less fortunate may have directed at her daughter.

By the time I was in my teens, I was almost on speaking terms with the Evil Eye, a jealous spirit that kept track of people who had disproportionate amounts of happiness or good fortune, and zapped them with sickness and misery to even the score. To guard against this mischief, Ceil practiced rituals of evasion, deference, and, above all, avoidance of situations where the Evil Eye might feel at home.

This is why I wasn't allowed to attend funerals or visit a house where someone had recently died. This also is why my mother did not like to mend my clothes while I was wearing them. The only garment one should properly get sewn *into*, she said, is a shroud. To ensure that the Evil Eye did not confuse my pinafore with a burial outfit, my mother insisted that I chew a thread while she sewed, thus proving myself very much alive.

Outwitting the Evil Eye also accounted for her closing the window shades above my bed whenever there was a full moon. "The moon should shine on you only in your grave," she explained. "Moonshine belongs in cemeteries."

Because we were dealing with a deadly force, I also wasn't supposed to say any words associated with mortality. This was hard for a kid who punctuated every anecdote with the verb "to die"—as in, "You'll die when you hear this!" "This boy is to die," or "If I don't get my math done, I'm dead." I managed to avoid using such expressions in front of my mother until the day she came home from an auction with a painting I hated and we started arguing about whether it should be displayed on our walls. Unthinking, I pressed my point with a melodramatic idiom.

"That picture will hang over my dead body," I shouted. Without a word, my mother ran into the kitchen, grabbed a carving knife and slashed the canvas to shreds. Not only wouldn't that painting go up in our house, it would never surface in anyone else's either. I might as well have invited the Evil Eye to tea.

I think I finally understand all this now. Just as an athlete keeps wearing the same lucky T-shirt in every game to prolong a winning streak, Ceil's superstitions gave her a means of imposing order on a chaotic system. Experience had taught her that life was unpredictable and incomprehensible. Anything that might put matters under control was worth a try. Her desire to influence the fates sprang from the same source that makes the San Francisco 49ers' defense more superstitious than the offensive team. The defensive team has less control; they don't have the ball.

Women like my mother never had the ball. She died leaving me with deep regrets for what she might have been—and a growing respect for who she was. I wish I had a million clear recollections of her, but when you don't expect someone to die, you don't store up enough memories. It hurts that I cannot remember the sound of her voice, or the shape of her hands. But her mystical practices are among the sharpest impressions she left behind. In honor of this matrilinear heritage—and to symbolize my mother's effort to control her life as I in my way try to find order in mine—I knock on wood and respect her other superstitions to the letter. My children laugh at me but they understand that performing these harmless rituals has helped me keep my mother alive in my mind.

One night when my son David was seventeen, I was awakened by the realization that the window blinds in his room had been removed that day for repair. Smiling at my own compulsion, I got a bedsheet to tack up against the moonlight. When I opened his bedroom door, what I saw brought tears to my eyes. There, hopelessly askew, was a blanket David already had taped to his window like a curtain.

My mother never lived to know her grandson, but he knew she would not want the moon to shine upon him as he slept.

3

One Man,
Two Fathers

I DON'T LIKE TO WRITE ABOUT MY FATHER.

During more than twenty years as a writer, I've poured out thousands of words about my mother, but my father, who lived until 1982, has earned only a sentence here or there. I've written extensively about my husband, my children, my colleagues, my friends, but I don't like to write about my father.

I'm afraid to read what I have to say.

I would have to start with the good things: He looked like Clark Gable and dressed like a movie star too. He carried his bills in a gold money clip shaped like a dollar sign. He wore cream-colored trousers and cashmere coats; breast-pocket handkerchiefs, white-on-white shirts, initialed gold cuff links, and a pinky ring with an onyx eye.

"Real snappy," he'd say, smoothing the brim of his fedora hat as he passed the hallway mirror. "Real snappy."

As a child, even more than watching my mother dress, I loved to watch my father perform his toilette. I remember the way he tapped a little mound of Pepsodent tooth powder on his palm, dipped his toothbrush into his hand, and then brushed methodically, uppers, lowers, left and right. I marveled at the way his straight, light-brown hair turned dark as he smoothed it down with pomade, making his hair sleek and close to his head like the men in *The Great Gatsby.*

But the main event was his shaving ritual: I loved watching him slap the straight razor, thwack-thwack, back and forth over the razor strop until the blade glistened, then swirl his bone-handled shaving brush against a cake of soap in a wooden bowl where it foamed like whipped cream. Sometimes he let me lather my face as well. Then both of us "shaved" together in front of the mirror, he with the straight razor making trailblazing paths down his cheeks, and I zigzagging through my soapy beard with an empty chrome safety razor.

"Great job, Bunny," he'd say approvingly, his praise showering me with self-respect as we drizzled ourselves with Mennen aftershave lotion and a light dusting of talc. He had nicknamed me Bunny at birth, but when I was especially adorable, he called me Sugar Pie, or *Ketzele* (pussycat), or *Kepele.* To be told I had a good *kepele*, a smart head, was the ultimate compliment; brains were all that mattered and if my father said you had a good head, you might as well be Einstein.

My father knew everything. First of all, as I've said, he was an all-American boy in a generation of greenhorns. Although his parents had barely arrived from Russia, he was born with the century on Valentine's Day, 1900, in New Haven, Connecticut, which made him, as he put it, "a regular Yankee Doodle Dandy."

Secondly, he had credentials. He graduated from Townsend Harris, a high school for gifted boys, entered City College at sixteen, whizzed through NYU law school with honors. And now, while all the other fathers were furriers, cloak-and-suiters, or men who "went to business," my Daddy was a lawyer.

Third, he really knew his history, classics, Torah, Talmud, Hebrew, Yiddish, French, carpentry, plumbing, electricity, sailing, fishing, baseball, you name it—so you can just imagine how he could talk. And he didn't just talk, he pronounced, like a sage. And he was a great teacher, though far from easygoing. I loved it when he taught me things no one else in the family had mastered, like chess, diving, Ping-Pong, or my haftarah (the reading from the Prophets recited by the child who is being Bar or Bat Mitzvah'd).

Preparing me for my Bat Mitzvah was perhaps his finest hour. He was well equipped for the task, having learned Hebrew at age six from his paternal grandmother ("a most unusual woman," he would say) and studied Talmud with his father, a man so erudite that rabbis came to him with questions. At ten, my father was reading the Torah for his synagogue congregation, reading it with perfect cantillation, the singsong litany that makes Torah reading unmistakably its own art. He attended Uptown Talmud Torah after school, then transferred to a Yeshiva on the Lower East Side, continuing his study with his father on Saturday afternoons after he moved on to high school. While attending college and law school, he taught Hebrew school for twenty hours a week and took four boys per year for Bar Mitzvah training at $150 each, a princely sum in 1920.

No wonder my father brought so much facility and fervor to my Bat Mitzvah lessons. He was in his element. He put me through my paces as if he was a rabbi, which he could have been, and as if I was a boy, which I should have been to please him although he never said it. I adored him for treating me like a son and taking me seriously. He drilled and polished my Hebrew recitation until I was the kind of virtuoso performer that synagogue legends were made of back in 1952, when girls, as a rule, did not do that sort of thing. But I did whatever my father valued. More than anything, I wanted his approval because he was my mentor and I saw myself as his intellectual heir. There was no son to make that claim. Betty was long out of the house with kids of her own, and the mysterious Rena had yet to turn up in his life. Clearly, his legacy was mine if I proved myself worthy of it.

Even when I was very young, he made me feel important just by talking to me. He spoke didactically but never condescendingly the way he sometimes addressed my mother and aunts. He talked to me as if I could be trusted to get it on first hearing. He was an intelligent man but not a patient one.

I was in heaven when he talked law or Judaism, explaining the convolutions of an ongoing case, the outcome of a lawsuit, the rationale for a particular Jewish ceremony, some intricate point of Mishnah or Gemara. I asked him a million questions and he answered them; for smart questions, he was patient.

"Daddy, why is the Mishnah called the Oral Law if it's written down?"

"Because the rabbis wanted to prevent any confusion between the Torah, which was God's law given to Moses and never to be changed, and subsequent case law, which was meant to be flexible and subject to new insights and interpretations."

"Daddy, why does the Mishnah demand twice the penalty for a slap in the face as for a punch in the stomach?"

"Because an insult is twice as destructive as an ordinary injury. A punch in the belly hurts, but a blow to the face humiliates and degrades a person."

"Daddy, why does the Talmud say judges can't sentence criminals on the same day as their trial?"

"Because if you're going to condemn someone to death, the least you can do is sleep on your decision."

I knew that if I could get him started explicating a text, he would smoke one Lucky Strike after another, meandering from midrash to midrash long after I was supposed to go to bed. I became adept at engaging him in conversations that piqued his interest while he fed me the information I needed in order to grow up and be like him.

My father's life was so much more exciting than my mother's that I thought it only logical to make him my model and my hero. He was the hero of others in our family as well. For instance, his sister Esther, college educated and married to a lawyer herself, always held up my father as the example of man-at-his-best, putting her own husband and sons under pressure to match my father's style and accomplishments. Esther's younger son, Simon, who is a musician and was always a very studious child, recalls that when my father asked him what he wanted for his Bar Mitzvah (that fateful weekend in Winthrop), he requested a baseball mitt. Simon didn't care about sports at all, he just wanted to impress my father.

Beyond the family, my Daddy seemed to be other people's hero too—judging by how many groups elected him their leader: the United Jewish Appeal, B'nai B'rith, the Zionist Organization of America, State of Israel Bonds, to mention just a few. At the Jamaica Jewish Center, where we went for services every Shabbat and holiday, my father was president of the shul. He did the Torah reading, sat up on the *bimah* (raised platform), or busied himself in the congregation, giving out *kipot* (skullcaps) and *talitot* (prayer shawls), helping people find their place in the siddur (prayer book), all the while davening (chanting the prayers) by heart with the loudest voice in the sanctuary.

There were distinct advantages to being small-daughter-of-the-Big-Macher (Big Shot). I could sit in the front row at services, set the table for the Men's Club bagel breakfast, use Jamaica Jewish Center stationery, or help operate the switchboard with its octopus cords, switches, and plugs. Best of all were the special times when my father took me along wherever he was going. I've never forgotten when we went to the Jewish War Veterans' convention at Grossinger's Hotel in the Catskills. I was five or six. My father was J.W.V. County Commander, so he sat up on the dais and I sat on his lap. Next to us was a withered old man who seemed lost inside his uniform. My father introduced him as a veteran of the Civil War; he was ninety-eight years old, the most ancient person I had ever met. As the old vet took my hand in his bony grip, he said, "Bunny, you must always remember me because you just shook the hand that shook the hand of Abraham Lincoln."

I don't like to write about my father because I don't want to have to give him credit for that memorable encounter or for any of the other special events of my childhood. He didn't go out of his way to make them happen; he never went out of his way for anyone. He got credit for so much because he himself seemed so important that just being with him made you feel important.

Somehow I learned how to be fathered by this man. I understood that if I wanted to have him at all I had to enter his world and do things his way. I learned that I was adored when I was smart and cute, but never when I was inconvenient. In my early years, I didn't notice that he wasn't around much, except when my mother cried and begged him to stay home from his endless meetings and accused him of giving more of himself to his organizations than to his wife and child. For me, it was enough to be his well-behaved little pet, his mascot, his creation.

I don't like to write about my father because I would have to describe the good memories, as I just have, and he would sound like a better father than he was. And then, I would have to set the record straight. I would have to explain what it took me years to absorb: that he gave to me, not so that I would *have*, but in order to show the world what *he* had to give. Even the Bat Mitzvah was ultimately for him. Lauded as an extraordinary lay teacher, he claimed the triumph long after it was mine. The patriarch of the Jewish community had shown that he could teach his Yentl Torah.

I would have to point out that the reason I remember everything my father did with me is because he did so little:

He read two books to me at bedtime. One was Charles and Mary Lamb's narrative, *Tales from Shakespeare*. The second was a series of stories by Arthur Train about the adventures of Mr. Tutt, an old-fashioned country lawyer who wore a stovepipe hat and smoked a pipe. I must have been seven or eight at the time.

My father administered a couple of alcohol rubs when I had a fever. I remember once during the night, I woke up sick to my stomach and he helped support my head over the toilet while I vomited. I also remember feeling ashamed that he had to see me that way.

Most of the time when I was sick my mother nursed me back to health. She read me hundreds of stories, not two. She taught me to make Alexander Calder–type sculptures from the wires that were wrapped around the caps of the glass milk bottles that were delivered to our house by Holland Farms Dairy. Together, she and I made cutout paper people, and set up my toys amongst my bedclothes in what Robert Louis Stevenson described as "the pleasant land of counterpane." She brought me magazines, puzzles, and other "sick girl presents," cups of tea and bowls of soup and toast that she'd shaped with cookie cutters to look like stars and gingerbread men. Her constant care blurs into the maternal mists while his few alcohol rubs are as memorable as if they were anointments by a prophet.

He taught me how to swim when I was five. Soon after that, he took me horseback riding and made sure I learned how to post and canter. A year or two later we went to the Bronx Zoo. In a snapshot taken that day, I am wearing a leopard-skin coat that my Uncle Herman the furrier made for me. I remember my father joking that I might be mistaken for a baby leopard and claimed by a leopard family as one of their own, and he would have to climb into the cage and rescue me. Back then, I believed he could.

I remember a summer evening in Coney Island where we rode the bumper cars and ate hot dogs for supper; and a winter outing to some park with a frozen pond where he and I went ice-skating for about an hour while my mother sat on a bench in the snow, watching us. Two or three times, he took me along with my Uncle Ralph and my cousin Danny to watch the Brooklyn Dodgers play in Ebbets Field.

My father was proud that I understood the game, but it was no thanks to him that I did. My baseball mentor was my cousin Danny, who was six years older than I and lived next door. Danny kept track of the Dodgers in bulging scrapbooks he fashioned out of black composition notebooks with spidery white designs on the cover, the kind I filled with arithmetic problems and geography homework. It was my job to paste in newspaper stories about Jackie Robinson, Pee Wee Reese, Billy Herman, and Dixie Walker; that's how I knew their names and positions. As we listened to the play-by-play on the radio (neither of us had a television in those days), Danny explained the rules of the game and taught me how to record the action on an official scorecard. He let me hang around when he and his friends played stickball in the street—and when the planets were in perfect alignment, I even had a turn at bat. To this day, I have Danny to thank for the excitement I feel when I first enter a baseball stadium. My father didn't give me that.

But Daddy did give me a feeling for ferris wheels the one time he took me to Coney Island. On the first turn of the huge wheel, my stomach dropped, my mouth went dry, and I began to cry. I wasn't sure if I was going to faint or die, but I became so terrified that I begged him to make the operator stop the motor and let me off. Daddy wouldn't hear of it. Instead, he put his arm around my shoulders and instructed me to chant one phrase over and over again to myself until the ride was over: "Uuuuup and dowwwwwn, round and round; uuuuup and dowwwwwn, round and round," he intoned in the singsong voice I knew from his synagogue davening. Focusing on his litany of calm, I did as he said and amazed myself by not only taming my fear but enjoying the ride so much that I decided to go around again. Many times since then I've used my father's mantra to cope with anxious situations. But he never again took me to Coney Island.

That's it. Those are my memories of life with father from birth to age fifteen. If I'm lucky the good days add up to a month all told. Maybe I don't like to write about my father because I'm afraid I'd discover that they don't even amount to a month's worth. Then I would have to move on to the rest of the memories which would reveal this brilliant, dashing man to be another kind of father altogether.

One man, two fathers. Daddy and the Other Father. Maybe I've been afraid that if I were to examine the Other Father more closely I would forever destroy the mythic Daddy, the man I once thought perfect. But as long as I did not write about him at all, I could keep the two images separate—grouse about the man I came to know from age fifteen onward, and keep Bunny's Daddy, the mentor Daddy, the Jewish sage, safe in the bell jar of childhood.

The Other Father was another story. I came to know him, and to be disappointed by him, during the year of my mother's illness and then all the years after she was gone. Without her there—to cover for him, to run interference, to neutralize his absences with her luminous presence, and his selfishness with her love—without her there as our go-between, my father's Russian doll broke open and little by little, layer by layer, I saw the real person inside.

Even before she died, there were a few previews of the Other Father, thanks to a strange family reunion.

Spring 1954. It is an unseasonably warm afternoon. I answer the doorbell and there on the doorstep is a young woman wearing glasses and a long braid. "Hello," she says, extending her hand. "I'm Rena."

That is how I meet my father's third daughter, my other sister, who has finally come to life from the family tree in the sand. Given the drama of the moment, the twenty-seven-year-old Rena seems subdued though not at all unpleasant. Her mission is a practical one, she says, with a directness I would soon recognize as typical. She has come for "our" father's help. She wants to move out of the apartment where she has been living with her deranged mother, whose violence has escalated so alarmingly that it is not even safe for her to go back alone to pack up her things. She needs Daddy to get a court order so that she can return in the presence of a marshal or a police officer.

After a reunion with *our* father that can only be described as sedate, and after a dinner during which my mother seems to be trying extra hard to make her feel welcome, Rena spends the next several days with us sleeping in our attic bedroom. I rush home from school every day to spend time with her, as if she is a visiting mermaid who might disappear with the next wave. One evening, she tells me almost dispassionately how her mother hears voices, hallucinates, beats her mercilessly. Once the woman nearly blinded Rena with a blow to her eyes that broke her glasses; several times her mother attempted to strangle her, and once she dangled her out of a window, bragging, "I gave birth to you, so I can kill you."

"Why did you stay?" I ask, incredulous.

She says she stayed because there was nowhere else to go, no one else to support her mother, and no one to protect her half-sister Ellen, who is about my age. But now it has become too dangerous to remain. "If I get killed myself, I can't protect Ellen any better than I can by leaving," she says. "And if I stay, I know I will be killed."

Daddy obtains the court order and helps Rena secure her belongings. She moves into an apartment of her own, but continues her regular visits, saying she wants to get to know me better. Sometimes she sleeps over for a few days at a time. Neighbors have noticed. Friends are asking questions. Mommy and Daddy tell Rena they want to acknowledge her in the community, but rather than disentangle everyone's complicated relationships at this late date, they ask if she would mind being introduced as a cousin.

To be disowned not once but twice, to be rejected after being rediscovered, to find her father more interested in the judgments of his community than the feelings of his daughter—how that must hurt. But Rena just nods and says cousin is fine.

I notice that whenever Daddy is around, Rena's voice assumes a flat, formal tone, whereas in Mommy's presence, she is chatty and relaxed. As Mommy's illness sets in and her condition worsens, Rena is helpful and solicitous, in the manner of one who has a lot of experience putting herself last. I am confused by her alternating kindness and coldness, her eagerness to visit and then her airs of detachment once she is here.

The hours I spend with her away from the house confirm that this new sister of mine is a true eccentric. She keeps her entire wardrobe piled up on her ironing board. A Bohemian-style nonconformist, she wears a long braid and no makeup when the most admired woman in America is Mamie Eisenhower. She makes obscure references to the principles of cybernetics or physiometry, and enjoys correcting people's pronunciations. ("When you hide something, you se*crete* it," she intones, though the word sounds like oozing to me.) Her arcane vocabulary sends me rushing to the dictionary after every visit to look up words like "tautology" and "anima," which she sprinkles throughout ordinary conversation—and which I will gleefully encounter months later on the College Boards exam.

"Her I.Q. is 180," says my father by way of explanation one evening after she has left. He seems proud and proprietary, as if her intelligence was entirely of his making.

Rena is an anthropologist specializing in Gypsy cultures. She has a Ph.D. She speaks twenty Romani dialects. As she reveals more and more about herself, I begin to feel like an apprentice rather than a baby sister. She brings me with her to visit with the Gypsies who live in upper Manhattan among whom she did her doctoral fieldwork. I meet the king of the tribe and learn that he has adopted Rena as his honorary daughter. I do not miss the irony of this: my father, *our* father, adopted Betty, who had wandered like a gypsy child in search of a family, while his daughter Rena found her family in a Gypsy tribe.

I realize "all of a sudden" that I am the sister of a certifiable prodigy and a Romani princess. As delighted as I am with Rena, I am still mystified by her emotional restraint. Even though Daddy did not feel able to acknowledge their relationship publicly, I cannot understand why she isn't happier to be back with her long-lost father after all these years.

"I came to him because I had no place else to go for help," she says, when I ask about her intractable coolness. "Now, my interest is in developing a compensatory relationship with you, not with him. He could live without me for fourteen years. I can live without him now."

"But he *wanted* to keep seeing you," I insist, repeating the story as I heard it on the beach three years before. "It's just that your mother threatened to harm you if he tried to get in touch or fight for you in court, so he stopped trying."

"My mother harmed me anyway," she says bitterly. "And he knew she would because she was always violent. No, that's *not* what happened. His court-ordered visitation rights were contingent on his paying child support. When you were born, he stopped paying, so my mother stopped the visits. He never fought for me. He didn't want me. He left me alone with her and I never heard from him again."

I think of Rena, twelve years old, waiting every Saturday morning for a father who just stopped showing up. I must have seemed like her replacement, her father's new toy. I think about the next fourteen years without a word, a phone call, a letter; fourteen years trapped with a demented woman; fourteen years of beatings. I cannot believe that the father who abandoned his daughter to that abuse is the same man I call Daddy. I cannot believe my father could do such a thing. Therefore, I cannot believe Rena. Soon, I will discover him for myself.

February 3, 1955. It is an ordinary school night except that my mother is not home; she is in the hospital. After supper, my father takes me into his study, closes the door, and offers me one of his Luckies. He flicks his Zippo lighter for both of us to draw from the flame. I know something terrible is coming. Until now, I had only smoked behind his back. His gesture tells me I am about to be addressed as an adult.

"Your mother has cancer," he says.

There is no preamble. He prides himself on going straight to the point. "The doctors say she has less than six months to live. You'll have to be very helpful and very brave."

That's it. And that matter-of-fact attitude marks his behavior after we bring Mommy home from the hospital to die slowly and painfully in their bedroom. During the whole ordeal, he takes care of things in his no-nonsense, efficient way. There are treatments and medications, doctors to consult, a housekeeper and nurse to hire. No time for reflection. No room for feelings, or ceremony, or despair.

"We all die sometime," he says.

But not my Mommy. Not this wonderful, giving woman who sacrifices for everyone else. Not my mother.

"No use complaining about what we can't help."

But you can help me get through this. Talk to me. Hug me.

"The best thing we can do is to go on with our lives."

And he does.

April 20, 1955. She dies during the night. There are tears in my father's eyes when he awakens me. I won't say he *cries* but they are, to my knowledge, his first tears. He says I can go into their room and kiss my mother goodbye. Then he shifts into his lawyerly mode, making phone calls, giving out assignments, complaining about how much detail work is required by death and dying. Even the modest requirements of a Jewish burial, he says, are too elaborate. "Don't do any of this for me, I just want to be cremated."

(Twenty-seven years later, he is cremated—according to his wishes, and contrary to Jewish law.)

Our week at home sitting *shiva* (the seven days of mourning) is interminable for him. He is impatient with the daytime inactivity, the constant flow of visitors, and the mountains of food accumulating on the kitchen counter. During the evening memorial service, however, he comes into his own. He leads the prayers.

One night, about twenty people are milling about the house but by Jewish computation, there are only nine Jews in our living room. This is because only nine men have shown up for the memorial service. A minyan, the quorum required for Jewish communal prayer, calls for ten men.

"I know the Hebrew." I say. "You can count *me*, Daddy."

I meant, *I want to count.* I meant, don't count me out just because I am a girl.

"You know it's not allowed," he replies, frowning.

"For my own mother's Kaddish I can be counted in the minyan. For God's sake, it's *your* house! It's *your* minyan, Daddy."

"Not allowed!" says my father.

He calls the synagogue and asks them to send us a tenth man.

May 1955. My father gives away my mother's things. Barely out of childhood, grieving, I do not think to petition for a hope chest of her clothes, or her paintings, or the books, china, or costume jewelry that were precious to her. Unmindful that I might someday have a home of my own and wish to own concrete mementos of my mother's life, my father lets the relatives pick through her closets and drawers like scavengers at a flea market. He lets them load their arms and pack their cars and take away her history.

Summer 1956. I find out that my father has sold our house and most of our furniture. He never asks me how I feel about it. He never gives me the chance to say what objects have special meaning to me. It does not occur to him that I might think of the contents of our house as mine and hers, as well as his.

Everything is sold before I know it. At first, I do not understand. And then I understand. He is getting married. He gets married. His new wife is a Southern belle with an exaggerated drawl, Jewish but unschooled in Judaism and unobservant, fifty-four years old but relentlessly girlish and charming—and self-centered to a fault. She is given to dramatic color-coordinated outfits and dyed black hair styled sleek as patent leather into a chignon at the top of her head. I am in my peasant-blouse-and-black-stockings Bohemian phase. She and I have nothing in common but our mutual distrust. Her Southern baby talk is insufferable. She manipulates my father who dotes on her, serves her, tolerates her domestic ineptitude, seems enchanted by her glamour and helplessness. She is to my mother as polyester is to pure silk. She is a phony. I hate my father's wife. It does not occur to me to hate him for choosing her.

They rent an apartment. The apartment has one bedroom. There is a daybed for me in the foyer. I am a freshman in college. I don't need a whole bedroom just for school vacations, do I? It is clear the new wife doesn't want me around. What my father wants is not at all clear to me anymore.

November 1958. I am a senior in college. I call my father at the office and tell him I must see him. I will leave after my last class and will arrive in New York around seven P.M. Where can we meet?

Since I've never before asked for a scheduled appointment and since I will be driving for four hours from Massachusetts on a weekday night, I expect he will deduce that my business with him is urgent. In a wild moment, I even imagine he might ask me to have dinner with him. But that night, as always, he has a meeting. He tells me to come straight to the Rego Park Jewish Center on Queens Boulevard, and fetch him out of his meeting. We'll have our talk in one of the empty Hebrew School classrooms and when we're done, he will return to his meeting.

I leave Brandeis at three P.M., drive for four hours, and locate him in a smoke-filled room. He excuses himself and we find some privacy in a classroom with low kindergarten tables and little chairs. I sit in a little chair. He sits on the table. I tell him I am pregnant. My life will be ruined if I don't have an abortion, but I don't have the money. (Abortion was then illegal and expensive.) I don't know where to find a doctor. I am paralyzed with fear. He assures me that he will make the necessary arrangements. No moralizing. No scolding. But also no comfort. Straight to the practical issues: who, when, where, and how much. Then he returns to his meeting and I get back into my car and drive back to school.

Late one night, a few weeks later, I go to a darkened doctor's office accompanied by my father and his new wife. I hate having her along but my father insists we may need a woman in case there are complications. She acts as if we are asking her to rob a bank. Then she plays the martyred accomplice. There are no complications. The abortion costs my father $350 but I pay him back.

It takes me five years, but I pay him every penny.

I needn't dredge up other such recollections. You get the point. That's the Other Father, the one I have to reconcile with the good Daddy before I can fully understand myself and, most particularly, my relationship to Judaism.

In the years after my mother died, incident after incident left me feeling confused and betrayed. At first, I excused my father's behavior, blaming his maleness for his mindless insensitivities, blaming his new wife for everything else. Gradually, it became clear to me that "his behavior" was who he was. I lowered my expectations. It didn't help. I began to feel the emotions that Rena had acted out during her visits with him. I withdrew. I closed up. I stopped hoping. This might have been a manageable psychological problem if it had not become an untenable spiritual one.

Somehow, father and faith had gotten all mixed up; I could not separate them. I couldn't mark where one began and the other ended. Both were male-gendered sources of rewarding power. My religion was personified by my Daddy, and I was socially enmeshed in a Jewish world controlled by Jewish men. Whatever honors I had been given or denied were granted or withheld by Jewish men. The creators of historical consciousness and the guardians of privilege were Jewish men like my father, often my father himself. When it suited his needs, Daddy had taken me into his realms; I was *his* little scholar, *his* Bat Mitzvah girl. But when it mattered to *me* to be included, he had exercised his masculine right to shut me out.

In a matter of months, this man who was once my adored mentor had revealed himself to be self-centered, unfeeling — almost a stranger. Because father and faith had been so intertwined, it was only logical that when I broke away from the enchantment of my father, I also cut off my formal affiliation with Judaism. Merge the Jewish patriarch with patriarchal Judaism and when you leave one, you leave them both.

For years, I stayed away from organized Judaism, from the institutionalized Judaism of my father. I married a Jewish man who had never been Bar Mitzvah'd. I raised a Jewish son and two Jewish daughters but did not have a Bar or Bat Mitzvah for any of them. I suppose I did not want those I loved to be covenanted in the faith of the father who betrayed me, the faith that left me out.

Over time, I reconnected to Jewish life in a process that I shall describe in subsequent chapters. But I have yet to deal with Daddy. The Other Father keeps getting in my way.

PART TWO

Deborah

Rituals and Revisionism

4

The Eternal Light

IN NEW SQUARE, NEW YORK, A VILLAGE LARGELY INHABITED BY Orthodox Jews, there is a sign advertising a Talmud course: TALMUD FOR EVERYONE—MEN ONLY.

I have a perverse fondness for this sentence. Absurd as it is, it strips away all of religious Judaism's polite rationalizations and puts the truth out in the open: Men are "everyone," women are not.

Which reminds me of secular semantics. Women are instructed to read ourselves into "man," the word for the human race. Periodically, however, the term's true meaning gets in the way. Just as "everyone" in New Square means Jewish males, "man" in Western culture often really means *men*. This line from an anthropology text illustrates what I mean: "Man's basic needs are food, clothing, shelter, and access to females."

Until recently, the message on the Talmud notice could have applied not only to study sessions among the ultra-Orthodox, but also to much of Jewish history, prayer, and ritual. Judaism equates the male with the human, and man with God. "Words create worlds," says author Susannah Heschel. "If God is male then the male is God." And the male is also the Jew. She points to a telling line in the traditional prayerbook: "Blessed be this congregation, its wives, sons and daughters." If the congregation has "wives" it is not a congregation of women. In Jewish life, the congregation is male because "everyone" is male.

Cynthia Ozick has written:

> In the world at large, I call myself, and am called, a Jew. But when I sit among women in my traditional shul and the rabbi speaks the word "Jew," I can be sure that he is not referring to me. . . . When my rabbi says, "A Jew is called to the Torah," he never means me or any other living Jewish woman. . . . My own synagogue is the only place in the world where I am not named Jew.

"Jew" means man, because males are the only Jews who count—literally. I learned this when I was most vulnerable, when I wanted to count—to be counted as a Jew. It didn't matter that I was my father's intellectual heir, my mother's daughter, an educated Jewish student, and a Bat Mitzvah girl. None of it mattered. I may as well have been a Christian, Muslim, or Druze.

A strange man was called in to say Kaddish for my mother, because he was more a "Jew" than I.

In those first weeks after losing my mother I needed to lean on my religion, crawl into its arms, rock myself to Hebrew rhythms as familiar to me as rain. But how could I mourn as a Jew if my Kaddish did not count?

The answer is, I could not.

I refused to be an illegitimate child in my own religion. I could not be a ghost in the minyan. If I did not count, I would not stay.

I mourned as a daughter, and left Judaism behind.

Six months later, in my freshman English class at Brandeis University, I wrote a story—a transparent exercise in self-pity—whose denouement formalized my departure. It told of a pious little girl who was kind, devout, and dutiful but instead of being rewarded, she was tormented by teachers, friends, boyfriends, and acne. Through it all, she kept the faith—until her mother died and she discovered her Kaddish did not count.

Burning with rage, she ran to the synagogue, burst through the doors of the empty sanctuary, and with all her strength threw her hard rubber ball at the Eternal Light that shines perpetually over the

Holy Ark—a symbol of the Jewish people's constant faith in God. The lantern crashed to the floor in pieces. The girl shoved the ball in her pocket, turned her back on the Ark, and walked out of the synagogue forever.

Thirty-five years later, I am still trying to mend that shattered lamp, metaphor of my broken faith. In this and the next four chapters you will see that I have pieced together a flickering, personal kind of Judaism that illuminates the way for me.

Excluding females from rituals of mourning seems to me the unkindest cut of all. Under Jewish law, children are obligated to say Kaddish for their deceased parents in a public prayer group three times a day for eleven months. What that means is, sons are *obligated* to say the Kaddish; daughters are not *prohibited* from saying it.

Nevertheless, daughters have been effectively prohibited. Countless grieving women have been silenced, our Kaddish made meaningless, like background noise, our bodies barred from the minyan or pushed out of sight behind the *mehitzah*, the partition separating women from men in Orthodox synagogues. We have been numbed and nullified by rabbis and autocrats who gag us with custom if not with law. Women's need to mourn has been secondary to men's need to keep us in our place.

Many Jewish women trace their religious alienation and feminist epiphanies to Kaddish experiences similar to mine. Former Congresswoman Bella Abzug remembers

> *When I was thirteen my father died, leaving no sons or brothers to say Kaddish. I went to the synagogue and I did it, though I wasn't supposed to. I learned that I could speak out and no one would stop me.*

When E. M. Broner lost her father, she wanted to spend eleven months saying Kaddish for him. Reform synagogues *would* count her in the minyan but they do not have daily services; an Orthodox shul has daily services but would not count her in the minyan. What a choice: to honor her father she had to dishonor herself. At an old Orthodox synagogue on West 23rd Street, where she was the only woman in the dwindling congregation, she conducted a war of nerves with ten angry men who kept trying to entomb her behind a *mehitzah* made of heavy drapes and opaque shower curtains. In their zeal to block her body from their view and her voice from their ears, they cared not at all if they obliterated *her* sight and hearing so that even her passive witness to the service would be impossible.

But she fought back with dignity and humor, and after six weeks, she wrote asking me and other feminist friends to stand with her at services on Sunday morning, March 29, 1987. The invitation, which is reprinted in her book *Mornings and Mourning: A Kaddish Journal*, said:

> *It's been an education for all of us in this minyan group—I who am counted or discounted as half-a-man, the others who thought they were safe on an island of males. There has been abrasiveness, insult, humiliation and, to some degree, accommodation . . . but I want them to know that where I stand, a shadow extends—women behind curtain, behind chador, in purdah. I also want them to know that now that they can almost recognize me—with the curtain more and more compressed and I peering out of it, pulling it tight and pushing it from me—that we are there, we women, and WILL honor our dead.*

When a group of us arrived to support Esther, what we found was not a Maginot Line but a limp excuse for a *mehitzah*—some flimsy fabric shoved down to one end of a cord stretched haphazardly across a row of seats—and a minyan of elderly men whom Esther Broner had converted into reluctant but respectful admirers.

Few women "win" this battle. After the death of Abraham Joshua Heschel, the beloved and highly respected modern Jewish philosopher, his daughter Susannah sought out a daily minyan so that she could say Kaddish for him. One afternoon, while en route from Boston to New York, she stopped in New Haven where she found an Orthodox synagogue but was barred from the service because there was no *mehitzah* to block her from men's view. Heschel recalls:

> *One old man said, "We can't daven as long as you remain in the room." I told them that I had to say Kaddish, and that I would stand in the back of the room or even in the hallway. But that made no difference; they told me I had to leave. So I left in tears, absolutely broken.*

"The purpose of prayer," says Susannah Heschel, "is to be brought to God's attention." What men are saying when they silence women is that men, and only men, deserve God's attention. I cannot believe that God believes that; or that God would have women silenced so that men can be heard. I cannot believe God wants less from women than we want to give. I cannot believe that the judgments of centuries of Jewish men are the judgments of God. None of this makes any sense until I remember that men have defined what sense is.

In her essay "Kaddish from the 'Wrong' Side of the Mehitzah," Sara Reguer, a professor of Judaic studies, tells of her mortification when she joined her father and brother in reciting the Kaddish at her mother's funeral, and the head of the Orthodox burial society ordered her to stop.

"I looked straight through him," she writes, "and continued in an even louder voice."

It is traditional for the closest family members to participate in the finality of death by shoveling a bit of earth onto the coffin before it is buried. At the graveside, the same man, that guardian of male prerogatives, livid now, gave the spade to Sara Reguer's father, brother, and male cousin, but not to her.

"I ignored the man, bent down to scoop up some dirt with my hands, and threw it into the grave. . . ."

But the man prevailed in the end. He prevented Sara from passing between the double rows of people who traditionally bracket the mourners as they move from the grave back into life. By insisting that a "modest woman" does not parade between rows of men, he eroticized her, assigned her sexual motives, made a grieving daughter into carnal flesh. And he prevailed.

During Sara's year of mourning, other men tried to silence her. They offered to say the Kaddish for her.

"If it offended anyone for me to say it alone, they were welcome to say it with me, but not *for* me," she countered.

Her answer reminded me of Henrietta Szold, the great Zionist leader, founder of Hadassah, and first woman student at the Jewish Theological Seminary (who was accepted on the condition that she not ask to become a rabbi). When Szold's mother died and a male friend offered to say Kaddish for her, Szold answered:

When my father died, my mother would not permit others to take her daughters' place in saying the Kaddish, and so I am sure I am acting in her spirit when I am moved to decline.

Sara Reguer was moved to respond to another male censor encountered in a Hasidic synagogue:

> . . . *one man almost shouted at me to say Kaddish silently because my chanting aloud was against the injunction of* kol ishah; *the singing voice of a woman is considered by some to be sexually arousing to men and therefore is forbidden. I asked the man whether he spoke to women in public. He said yes. I said that I was merely speaking in public also, but to God.*

That men should be shielded from women's voices is *minhag*, custom, not halacha, law. Yet in the name of custom, Judaism deems it more important to shield a man from his baser instincts than to enable a woman to fulfill her highest instincts. My question is this: If males are so spiritually superior—if they can be motivated enough to fulfill all 613 mitzvot, divine commandments—why can't they be held responsible for their own spiritual focus?

While in mourning for her mother, Greta Weiner went to a shul where she was sent behind a six-foot, thickly meshed screen that totally obscured the Holy Ark, the rabbi, everything. "It was very difficult for me to believe that my religion expected me to pray from within a cage," she writes, explaining that she let herself out and stood at the back of the chapel for the rest of the service.

The *mehitzah* is not God's cage. Scholars have determined that the women's section of the synagogue was established only one thousand years ago, not at the beginning of Judaism. Cynthia Ozick points out the great irony in Orthodoxy's devotion to the *mehitzah*:

> *These defenders of the barrier that pens women in and away from the liturgical action argue that it's the "assimilationists" who want to remove it, when the fact is that the mehitzah was first introduced by assimilationists who wanted to be like the majority culture, which was Moslem!*

What a twist: these Jewish purists who denigrate Reform congregations and despise the strangers' ways have been defending a symbol that owes its origins to *chadors*, veils, and the sex-separationist tenets of Islam.

The Orthodox feminist author Blu Greenberg had a feminist epiphany in hindsight when she remembered what happened at the funeral of her Uncle Izzie:

> *He had a special spot in his heart for his six grandchildren, especially two girls who grew up in his house. In his eulogy, the rabbi commented on this special relationship. At the end of the service, he asked the grandchildren to accompany the casket out of the synagogue. Three boys and three girls, all in their teens, stepped forward. The president of the congregation hastened over and asked the girls to be seated. The rabbi, he said, meant only male grandchildren.*

"Talmud for everyone" means men only. "Grandchildren, step forward" means boys only. "Children must say Kaddish for their parents" means sons only. Even at the age of fifteen, I couldn't swallow that.

The turning point in my spiritual life was the night I was rejected from the minyan that said Kaddish for my mother. I could point to the *shiva* experience in my living room, say that my father sent me into the arms of feminism, and leave it at that. A man did it; one of the many Jewish male guardians at Judaism's gates did it. No woman who has suffered the anguish and insult of exclusion on top of the tragedy of her bereavement forgets that her humiliation was inflicted by Jewish men. But I want to make a larger point than the obvious pain of sex discrimination: I want to emphasize that the policing of women during mourning is just one example of many instances where, *in the act of defending custom or tradition, men violate more profound precepts of Judaism.*

Custom and patriarchal rules fly in the face of far more fundamental mitzvot—instructions to pursue justice, love mercy, care for the weak, show empathy for the stranger, and practice lovingkindness toward all human beings. This glorious ethical mandate, the core message of the Exodus experience, the moral system revealed to the Jewish people at Sinai, is breached in the name of the small, base custom of controlling women's spiritual autonomy—and is breached by men who consider themselves holy.

I have serious questions for these holy men: Was it an act of halachic righteousness to harass Esther Broner or to bar three little girls from walking beside their Grandpa's casket? Were the men in

New Haven emulating God's lovingkindness when they slammed the door against Susannah Heschel? And those men who bullied Sara Reguer, were they pursuing justice? Was it mercy that made my father silence the Kaddish of his motherless child?

How can a serious Jew treat grieving women this way? How can cruelty be holy?

If, as it is said, the life of Torah is embodied in Hillel's injunction, *"That which is hateful to you, do not do unto another,"* then these men who deny women's spiritual needs are defiling the life of Torah, for surely, none of them would want done unto himself what is done to ritual-starved women in the name of Jewish law.

Ritual is the formalized, systematic enactment or expression of a culture's values and beliefs. Ritual is food to the spiritually hungry. Ritual has the potential to heal and warm; to glorify God and reify human devotion; to make objects and places sacred; to create community; to permeate the membrane between religion and peoplehood and bond one person into the whole. Ritual physicalizes the spiritual and spiritualizes the physical. Jewish mourning rites, in particular, ensure spiritual regeneration and emotional catharsis at a time of unbearable loss. These comforts should not be denied to any grieving Jew, regardless of sex. Much the same can be said of virtually every ritual in Jewish life, from lighting Sabbath candles to reciting the Torah benediction. All should be accessible to *everyone* because each has its own special potency and purpose.

Ritual is "the instrument for giving ethical ideals a grip on our conscience," write Robert Gordis and David Feldman. *"What poetry is to language ritual is to life."* (My emphasis.)

But now, imagine a world in which women are not permitted to read or speak certain poems, or where the poetry available to them is abridged or bowdlerized, or only to be read in the presence of other women, or only to be read behind a screen. Imagine that all poetry is written by men, about men, with male pronouns and imagery, and male verbs and verities. Imagine that women are enjoined both from speaking men's poems aloud and from writing poems of their own. Imagine that women who dare to read men's poetry are branded harlots and devils.

This "Handmaid's Tale" of poetic fascism is not so far removed from the denial of ritual that is experienced by many Jewish women. Such denials are especially unfortunate in the light of two simultaneous but paradoxical trends: while thousands of Jews are turning away from Jewish practices because of intermarriage and assimilation, many others are seeking ever more formalized expressions of their religious beliefs. Modern Orthodoxy is the fastest-growing segment of our faith and new shoots are sprouting on other branches as well. Conservative synagogues are establishing Torah study sessions in response to congregants' demands. Reform Jews have been reclaiming previously repudiated observances, from ritual circumcision to the signing of the *Ketubah*, the traditional Jewish marriage contract. And after decades of spurning the supernatural, Reconstructionist Judaism has restored miracles and mysticism to its prayer book. Nonaffiliated Jews who were uncomfortable in mainstream synagogues have been gathering together in self-selected *havurah* groups that conduct communal prayer, study, and celebrations. And within every sect and sub-sect, women have become more actively spiritual.

When her spirituality is stymied by religious sex discrimination, a woman can either accept the status quo or pursue the Jewish feminist route which offers two broad options: change the old rituals; or create new ones. I have tried to blend both because neither option is enough by itself.

Removing the MEN ONLY signs from Judaism is a long, hard struggle against an army of defenders sworn to protect the granddaddy of patriarchal systems. We can't forget that Judaism's worldview rests on a hierarchical paradigm (God over man, man over woman-child-animal-plant) that sanctifies male supremacy and diminishes the female in its theology, history, and daily ritual. Probably the most quoted, most devastating ritual example is the prayer an Orthodox man utters each morning in which he thanks God for not creating him a woman.

Jewish law assigns to men the responsibilities and rewards of prayer, study, and religious leadership; to woman, the home, family, and children. At first blush, this may seem to be a functional division of labor—separate but complementary. However, its inherent illogic and injustice show through when a woman who is unmarried, widowed, childless, or has grown children (who is, in other words, unbound by domestic responsibilities) is still not welcome to assume "men's roles." Why? The answer is turf. The answer is power.

It's a shock to discover that one group of people can prevent another group of people from expressing its spirituality. That's when we realize "that the spiritual is political," as Rabbi Julie Greenberg puts it, echoing the classic feminist slogan, "The personal is political." Indeed, men's power to determine women's place in Judaism, and men's protection of their prerogatives, is no different from male domination in the secular sphere, where we hear the same arguments for male supremacy: tradition, custom, natural roles, God's will:

"We can't hire a woman because a man has always done this job."

"Our clients won't take legal advice from a woman."

"Our customers prefer male sales reps."

"Men will never work for a woman."

Or, "God didn't make women to be long-distance runners," or ditch-diggers, or presidents—whatever it is men want to keep for themselves.

In Judaism, the woman who violates tradition, custom, natural roles, and God's will is often condemned, not just corrected. Name-calling is the way Rabbi Immanuel Schochet responded to two serious Judaic scholars—the aforementioned writer, Blu Greenberg, and Norma Joseph, a professor at Concordia University—when they dared to request more opportunities for women to worship God and study Judaism in the synagogue and seminary. For this crime, Rabbi Schochet read them out of the Jewish religion and labeled each a "Jezebel," a term defined as "a scheming, evil woman" and "one who is notorious for profligacy, fanaticism, and cruelty."

Rabbi Marc Angel has said that the major obstacle facing the women's movement in Judaism is not halacha, but the fear of change. The most feared change is the loss of male power. Let's not kid ourselves: power is never given, it must be taken, and since men are the ones who have it, they are the ones putting up the fight.

Although a few women have been hurt in the process of demanding change, many have met with success; they have removed the MEN ONLY signs, at least in the more liberal segments of Judaism, and have won access to ancient rites and traditions whose *tam* (flavor) and texture I love. I'm grateful, in particular, to the Jewish feminist advocates of the early 1970s who made it possible for my neighborhood congregation, the Stephen Wise Synagogue, to have a woman rabbi and a woman cantor on the *bimah* performing the Rosh Hashanah service. There the service is not just for women but for every Jew, and it is not an overflow service in the basement but the main service in the main sanctuary.

But gaining equal access to male spaces and structures is not enough if, once inside, we mouth the same patriarchal words and concepts that kept us out in the first place. At Stephen Wise Synagogue, Rabbi Helene Ferris alters the text of the prayer book as she reads aloud, changing "Lord" or "King" to "Eternal," and substituting "God— you" for "God—he" or "him." Ferris says she makes these substitutions because she truly believes the essence of God is Eternal, not gendered. However, while nonsexist God-words matter to her, she sees their limitations:

> *I am not so naive to believe that a change in liturgical language will have the slightest impact on the legal, economic, or social equality of women. After all, Sabbath "bride" and "queen" and the Hebrew prophets' references to Israel as "mother," "daughter," and "wife" have been of no help whatsoever to the status of women.*

In most Reform and Conservative synagogues, a woman now has the right to an aliyah—being called up to the *bimah* for the Torah-reading portion of the service—but when she is called up by her Hebrew name, it is as the daughter of her father (I would be "*Yafah, bat Yaakov,*" Letty, daughter of Jacob—not of Jacob and Sarah).

The right to aliyah is significant to me. I seethe when my husband and I are in some foreign shul and he is offered the honor of an aliyah although he cannot daven to save himself, while I, who have the blessings etched into my brain, am ignored or sent behind the partition. Whenever I am part of the Torah-reading service, I feel hallowed by my proximity to the holy scrolls. Other women have described similar feelings of transcendence. Alice Shalvi, founder of the Israel Women's Network and former principal of an Orthodox girls' high school in Jerusalem, burst into tears when she saw the inside of a Torah for the first time. She was fifty-three years old. She could not believe that it had taken her more than half a century to see and touch the sacred scrolls that every Jewish male could experience weekly. Michele Landsberg, a Canadian journalist, also was moved to cry when she first touched a Torah. And now, she says, "Whenever I see my daughter carrying the Torah with her calm attitude of entitlement, I am moved again even though I am not religious. It is a strong moment of affirmation for me after so many experiences of being rejected."

Those times when I have stood close to the Torah, I have experienced a shimmering kind of enchantment, almost an altered state of consciousness. Feeling this, I can imagine how hard it must be for men to step aside to let women in on it.

While I can attest that being *in* is better than being *out*, being in can also co-opt a woman, making her a collaborator in the promotion of the status quo. (It's great to be able to have an aliyah, but not if the blessings you chant are full of masculine God-words.) Unless she is willing to challenge our tradition's sexism from within, having her on the inside does not cure the intrinsic "outness" of Jewish women or correct the absence of the female perspective in religious life.

Until women have a *transformative* influence on all aspects of Jewish life, sex integration in the synagogue and in religious rituals will remain a partial victory—like that of the women who win Wall Street jobs without redefining the infrastructure that keeps them from achieving senior-most status.

Nevertheless, we must demand to be let in, and when refused, we must carry on like Refuseniks—put on the pressure, call attention to our plight, and get allies in high places to petition for *our* freedom of religion. Actually, the Russian parallel doesn't quite work. For decades, Soviet Jews pleaded for the right to *be* Jews, but now that virtually everyone is able either to emigrate or to stay and practice Judaism, female Soviet Jews are *still* not allowed to be practicing Jews in the fullest sense. Rabbi Adin Steinsaltz, the preeminent Israeli Talmudist, has opened a yeshiva in Moscow, the first in the Soviet Union in fifty years—but the school only accepts men. It appears that teaching Judaism to "everyone" means the same thing in Moscow as it does in New Square.

The second path available to women who are fed up with the status quo is to turn away from men's spaces and structures and create new ones, or reclaim the old ones but give them new meanings that permit us to transform spirituality as it transforms us.

Cynthia Ozick asserts that the biblical Hannah, mother of Samuel, "is a heroine of religious civilization because she invents, out of her own urgent imagining, inward prayer." At a time when all liturgical prayer was public and communal, Hannah prayed "in her heart; only her lips moved, but her voice was not heard." Hannah's transcendent mumbling was misperceived and she was accused of drunkenness.

I like to think of today's feminist prayer innovators as Hannah's daughters, part of a long and respectable legacy of women's spiritual communication which was initially misperceived but eventually understood to be holy.

Some of the new prayer language actively validates woman as the *pray-er*; its audacity demands attention and facilitates *kavvanah*, spiritual focus. It offers the surprise of female imagery, the shock of sensing closeness, mutuality, and nurture where before there were only remote majesty and military allusions. The new ceremonies exhibit both grit and grace; they seem to reach out and pull us in, the way energetic dancers lure the shy observer into their hora circle. All of us are participants, they insist. We don't need an audience.

I have joined several of these ceremonial circles, participating in women's seders, Rosh Hodesh celebrations (which make the new moon a woman's holiday and an occasion for study and worship), Jewish women's peace rituals, and a *tashlich* service at the Hudson River docks, where a group of chanting women toss bread into the river, casting our sins into the "living waters" in preparation for Rosh Hashanah. There is nothing quite like the feeling of community created by women for women in a Jewish context. Although I tend to approach these "women's culture" experiences tentatively, convinced that I'm not the touchy-feely, crunchy-granola type, inevitably I get seduced by the sweetness of sisterhood.

Hundreds, perhaps thousands of women have discovered such group expressions of this new spirituality. At this writing, I know of two feminist Jewish congregations in Los Angeles—Bet Schechinah (the House of God's Feminine Essence) and Ilanot Mamre (Sacred Grove). There are feminist retreats—among them B'not Aysh (Daughters of Fire), Achyot Or (Sisters of Light), and Kotchkes (Wild Ducks)—where participants discuss spirituality and social activism in the context of class, race, sexuality, ethics, and ethnicity. In Philadelphia, P'nai Or (Faces of Light), an egalitarian Jewish renewal group; and the Jewish Renewal Life Center, a new progressive yeshiva that appeals especially to nontraditional students (women, lesbians, and gay men) and offers a one-year program that combines Jewish feminist living, scholarship, spirituality, and politics.

While I find these innovations provocative and exciting, other supposedly "feminizing" adjustments seem unconvincing or unnecessary—for instance, pink *talitot* (prayer shawls), lace *kipot* (skullcaps), and beribboned tefillin (phylacteries, those cubes containing biblical parchment attached to leather straps that bind Jews symbolically to God). When a thing itself is flawed, it should be fixed. But there is nothing inherently wrong with *kipot*, tefillin, and *talitot*. True, women traditionally have not used them. However there is no rabbinic agreement as to whether wearing ritual adornments is actually prohibited by law; in fact, we know that they were worn by Michal, the daughter of Saul and the wife of King David, and by the (unnamed) daughter of Rashi, the great Torah and Talmud commentator of the eleventh century.

Phyllis Toback is one of a growing number of contemporary women who choose to wear traditional ceremonial objects to intensify the experience of the sacred. "Putting on the tallit is like taking refuge in the shadow of God's wings," she says. She loves the tallit prayer with its image of a "sheltering and embracing" God, and the bridal imagery associated with the prayer for the tefillin. "It is as though every morning you marry God." Here again, physicalizing the spiritual is an important rationale for ritual.

For Amy Eilberg, the first woman rabbi ordained by Conservative Judaism, putting on tefillin allows her to "feel Jewishly authentic in my feminist demands for equality in every aspect of Jewish life . . . a system that emphasizes obligation over rights." Eilberg takes joy in "voluntarily accepting for myself all of the same religious obligations as males, and therefore claiming all the rights and privileges that were theirs."

If I were a fully observant Jew, even a fully observant feminist Jew, I am not sure I would choose to wear tefillin because of how "gendered" they are in my mind. When a thing has come to have a sex, when an object registers on one's senses as intrinsically male as a result of years of associating it with one's father and other men, it's hard to appropriate that object for ritual use without feeling like a male impersonator. Younger women won't have that problem because of the increasingly familiar sight of females wrapped in the sanctity of ritual objects. I rejoice in the fervor of observant women. What I don't appreciate are commercial interests who exploit it, trying to sell women frilly versions of ritual objects that should have no gender.

Advertisements for these cutesy items in Jewish mail-order catalogues make me feel like a grown woman being asked to order her meal from the children's menu. I'm reminded of when Lionel, the maker of toy electric trains, tried to market a pink locomotive for girls and the effort was a bust. After years of watching our fathers and brothers play with black-and-silver Lionels, we didn't want a bubble-gum imitation; we wanted the real thing. I feel the same way about *kipot*, *talitot* and tefillin.

I have a different problem with the issue of *mikvah*, the ritual bath in which Orthodox women immerse themselves every month, after their menstrual periods. I'm glad there are observant feminists who have chosen to "take back the water," that is, to reclaim the ritual and assign it new feminist meanings, but some of their so-called reinterpretations strike me as rationalizations.

"Because a *mikvah* is a uniquely female place and a uniquely female mitzvah, it creates a community of Jewish women, an instant sisterhood," writes a correspondent to *Lilith* magazine. (Orthodox women are obligated to fulfill three mitzvot, commandments, all of them sex-role related: going to *mikvah*, lighting Sabbath candles, and setting aside the *challah*.) "*Mikvah* always seemed to me to be the most 'feminist' of mitzvot, once it is freed from the idea of the menstrual taboo. . . ."

But how do we free this ritual from the fact that for the period of menstruation plus seven days—a minimum of twelve days a month, 144 days every year—a woman is considered "ritually impure"; supposedly she has been defiled by death because of the loss of her egg, the embryo that never was. *Mikvah* feminists choose to read this as a respectful affirmation of women's biological potential. But according to Jewish law, "ritually impure" equates a normal, healthy female with a person who has had contact with a dead body or with nasty animals, or someone who has a scabrous skin disease. These feminists seem able to excuse the idea that a woman is desecrated, and can desecrate others, just by being the way God made her. They accept the fact that for nearly two weeks every month, she is unfit, not just for holy activities but for lovemaking; her husband is not allowed to touch her or even receive an object from her hand. Somehow, they can explain away nearly five months a year without sex or physical affection; five months of being labeled a pollutant, a container of death. Somehow, presumably, they also find feminist justification for the law that makes a woman ritually impure during labor (because of uterine bleeding)—which means her husband cannot touch, hold, or stroke her during the agonies of contractions and delivery. And finally, they accept that Jewish law deems a woman ritually impure for seven days after the birth of a boy, but fourteen days after the birth of a girl.

Most of the time I consider Orthodox feminist revisionists—a subgroup that sounds like an oxymoron—brave pioneers. But when they call the laws of *female impurity* "family purity" laws, they are adopting a euphemism worthy of Jerry Falwell or Pat Robertson, those Christian fundamentalists who have the habit of dubbing policies that are anti-woman "pro-family." The phrase "family purity" masks the misogyny of *mikvah* laws and allows women to reinterpret the taboos associated with their own bodies as politically correct symbols of feminine dignity. Some of these women argue that enforced sexual separation ensures that wives are not seen as sex objects (although how else does one view forbidden fruit?). Others claim that a man and woman who are prohibited from making love at certain times learn to relate as respectful friends, implying that couples who are year-round lovers cannot be respectful or companionable.

Let's suppose for a moment that the benefits of periodic sexual separation are true. Then why not separate during *any* segment of the month? Why not forbid both sexes from touching *each other*? Why link the untouchable time to menstruation, thus vilifying women's most natural process and God's gift to reproductive humanity? Is it because Jewish laws were written by squeamish men who found women's bleeding offensive, frightening, or mysterious? Might the laws of *mikvah* have been men's attempt to regain control of the powers of reproduction that originate in women's bodies? Did *mikvah* laws develop because Judaism prefers procreative sex (and the time of the month when sex is permissible happens to coincide with ovulation)? Since *mikvah* is designed to promote conception, and since women are exempted from most religious rituals on the grounds that they are too busy being pregnant and rearing Jewish children, the ritual suggests its own hidden agenda with a prescriptive inevitability and a kind of Machiavellian logic.

While *mikvah* revisionists leave me unconvinced, I am far more supportive of two other kinds of innovators: *transformational feminists* who are changing and questioning the entire Judaic canon; and *radical traditionalists* who are bending and stretching Orthodoxy so that it accommodates Orthodox women. Each comes out of a different "camp" of Judaism but together they embody the diversity and strength of Jewish feminist scholarship—the scholarship of inclusion. These are the thinkers who have reconfigured my Jewish identity.

In the transformational camp, there are historians who reconstruct the Jewish past as if women's experiences were central, not peripheral; liberationist feminists who affirm the authority of the Bible but redefine authority as partnership, not domination; writers and theologians who are creating new midrashim (imaginative writings that probe for new meanings behind the literal Bible); and poets and ritual-makers who are rewriting the liturgy and finding new ways to enact Jewish spirituality.

"The study of the woman question in Judaism is as important as the study of the Jewish question in general history," says Paula Hyman, professor of Jewish history at Yale, who is attempting to alter the fact that we know more about how other cultures have dealt with Jews than we do about how Jews have dealt with Jewish women.

The poet Alicia Ostriker begins her feminist transformations with the question, "What happens when women writers re-imagine . . . that masculine foundation of Western culture, the Bible?" Her answer is a collection of new myths that are, she asserts, "an almost inevitable outcome of Jewish tradition. For are we not told that 'there is always another interpretation' of Torah?" One of her provocative reinterpretations suggests that Noah got drunk (Genesis 9:21) because of survivor guilt.

Savina Teubal has dug deeply into biblical texts to try to reconstruct the lives of the Matriarchs and priestesses.

Tikva Frymer-Kensky has researched a biblical period in which women occupied public office and enjoyed prominent roles in the community, and has found that only after exposure to the misogyny within early Greek influences were the rabbis moved to fear women's sexual power and to interpret the law in ways that repressed Jewish females.

Leila Bronner also has unearthed evidence of more Jewish women who served as judges, prophets, and spiritual, political, and financial advisers to Jewish communities than is commonly believed.

Natalie Z. Davis is exploring Jewish women's spirituality in the Middle Ages.

Ellen Umansky mines the past for specific clues to women's relationship with God. She asks, "If Jewish women were denied access to study and public prayer, does that mean that the lives of Jewish women were not spiritual?" Of course not, is the reply, but women expressed their spirituality in their own way. "It was intuitive, emotional and personal ... an inner piety not revealed through reflection of texts but rather through personal experience and contemplation of the divine."

Umansky has made a study of the spiritual lives of elite Jewish women who functioned as unordained leaders in the late nineteenth century, and has written a biography of Lilly Montague, the founder and leader of Liberal (Reform) Judaism in England.

Faith Rogos and Sue Levy Elwell are examining twentieth century Jewish women's organizations in the light of the hypothesis that women established separatist groups to meet their educational and spiritual needs, which were being neglected by the larger (male) community.

Shulamit Magnus challenges virtually all the givens of the past. She says we teach separate courses in Jewish history and Jewish women's history "as if they were not the same subject." She favors gender-consciousness and catch-up education but warns that Women's Studies must not create "an historical *mehitzah* which permits 'business as usual' on the other side of the fence." Nevertheless, gender is her diagnostic tool; she changes our angle of vision to accentuate women's point of view. For example, she says, the "Talmudic Era" cannot be discussed as if it was a unitary experience for all Jews when it had a completely different meaning for each sex; it democratized learning for rich and poor—*if one was male*—but for women it toughened access by professionalizing scholarship and codifying gender distinctions.

Magnus wants us to revisit the rabbinic texts and historical sources to deduce women's "social reality" from every shred of evidence available to us. What were *our* ways of expressing Jewish identity and religious understanding? What were *our* rituals, child-rearing practices, healing skills, community behaviors? How was the woman of the "Talmudic Era" a Jew?

Judith Plaskow, one of the thinkers who has influenced me most, argues that Jewish feminist historians are not only revolutionizing history but are also "claiming to amplify Torah, and thus questioning the finality of the Torah we have." Our Torah is only a "partial record" of Jewish experience because it leaves out women's experience and women's "God-wrestling," says Plaskow. By discovering that other half of Jewish history, we discover "more of the primordial Torah, the divine fullness . . ."

Her logic has illuminated my own spiritual journey because she seeks not just reparations for women, but to reshape all of Jewish memory. She says feminist midrash-making is the ideal "strategy for Jewish remembrance." Utilizing the rabbinic methodology of imaginative reconstruction, women too can search out deeper meanings that help us ask new questions and find new answers in the "infinite meaningfulness" of the Torah text. The Judaism defined by the rabbis of the Talmud is only one interpretation of Judaism; alternative interpretations can have equal validity. It is our task, Plaskow says, to "reinterpret the past to meet the needs of a radically different present."

While working to unearth and reinterpret women's experiences and write these meanings forward into our era, feminist scholars also have plunged into the roiling waters of theology. Plaskow asks point-blank, "Is this the God we want to pray to?" This God who exercises power as domination? This being who is described to us exclusively by men in male terms? This lord, warrior, king? Or shouldn't we "reconceptualize God's power" in words and images that give voice to women's experience of the divine?

Images matter because they "evoke nonrational responses," says Plaskow. "God the father evokes feelings about our fathers." When God-language is not generic but gendered, it becomes a block to prayer rather than a way to God. If the ultimate being has a masculine image, how can maleness not be the ideal to be emulated and valued?

Plaskow's answer is a God-language that utilizes gentle, nongendered metaphors such as lover, friend, or companion; metaphors of "sustaining power" such as source, fountain, wellspring, or tree of life; and words like co-creator, which presuppose that God and humanity are partners in sustaining creation. To those who have trouble with the whole issue of the divine image, Plaskow advises, "Spend more time talking *to* God and less time talking *about* God."

Currently, some of the most beautiful God-talk can be found in *The Book of Blessings: A Feminist Jewish Reconstruction of Prayer*, Marcia Falk's nongendered, nonhierarchical alternatives to the blessings we Jews grew up with. Instead of the traditional "Blessed art thou, O Lord our God, king of the universe . . ."—and instead of substituting Lady, Queen, or other self-conscious feminine equivalents for these formulaic masculine phrases—Falk has created all-inclusive liturgical language that unites the human and the divine in a shared celebration of life. Because she sees God as giver rather than ruler, she has named the divinity "The source of life." Here, for instance, is her blessing over the wine:

> *Let us bless the source of life that ripens fruit on the vine as we hallow the Sabbath day in remembrance of creation.*

Hard as it is to retrain one's ears, eyes, and spirit away from the familiar, Falk is right to insist "that no single set of names and images ought to monopolize religious authority"; that we must not let traditional blessings become a kind of verbal idolatry whereby stock phrases are more holy than their subject. She expects women to share in the power of God-naming.

For the God that some feminists choose to name "Goddess," Jane Litwoman originated the word "Elilah," which evokes the Hebrew word *elilim*, meaning "small, foreign gods or idols." Her notion is to take the invective that patriarchal Judaism has used against Goddess images, and make it a positive name for a feminized God.

Rita M. Gross also favors balancing male images of God with female images even though God is clearly neither. Gross insists that using female terminology like Queen or Goddess makes people confront their resistance to the very idea of the feminine as holy.

"If it is daring, degrading or alienating to speak of God using female pronouns and imagery, perhaps that indicates something about the way women and the feminine are valued," she says, adding,

> *God language does not really tell us about God, but it does tell us a considerable amount about those who use the God language. I only wish the people who argue to retain solely male imagery were as aware that God is not really male as I am that God is not really female.*

Feminist innovators do not tamper with tradition merely for the sake of art, change, or rebellion. Each is searching for ways to enlarge women's spiritual vocabulary and intensify the faith experience for the benefit of those Jews—read women—who have felt excluded in the past. Each in her way, through scholarship or poetry, is reexamining fundamental beliefs about gender that sit unquestioned at the

center of Judaism, like sagging floo
been replaced to extend the life of a

At the same time as the feminist transforma
traditional texts and guiding us toward egalit
ishly well-educated women—whom I call "radi
are taking *possession* of the sources and using them
change. A few examples:

Cynthia Ozick draws on the most basic precepts of
halacha to argue for equal justice for women. She insists
"woman problem" is not a minor defect of Judaism but its
flaw; the central, institutionalized moral failure of our faith.

"Where is the missing Commandment that will say, from the beginning of history until now, *Thou shalt not lessen the humanity of
women?*" she asks. Why in every other category does halacha correct
for injustice, but in the treatment of women, perpetuate it?

Talmudist Judith Hauptman insists Judaism was meant to keep
evolving and she finds justification for egalitarian re-vision within the
Mishnah and Gemara which she has mastered with a depth that
would impress even my father.

Blu Greenberg, the Orthodox writer and lecturer—who has been a
frequent target of condemnation from the ultra-Orthodox—bravely
promotes Torah study for women and girls, and a greater role for
religious women in ceremony and prayer. When her feminism and her
Orthodoxy become unreconcilable, Blu opts for Orthodoxy, but the
rest of the time, she makes a sincere effort to incorporate feminist
values into her traditional community.

Chava Weissler has revived the *Techinot,* Yiddish devotional
prayers which were written by men for women in past centuries.
Some feminists say these maudlin petitionary prayers should be forgotten since they reflect men's limited idea of female spirituality, not
women's own prayerfulness. Rabbi Nina Beth Cardin of the Jewish
Theological Seminary persuades me otherwise. "We don't have to like
everything we find in women's history, but we should *know* everything," she insists. Then we can decide which parts of our past we
want to reclaim, and the rest—the unusable past—we can convert
into memory.

Rivka Haut, founder of the Women's Tefillah Network and the
Flatbush Women's Davening Group, is one of many radical tradition-

here women them-
passages normally
have sprung up in
ox they serve the
geable, observant
service that they
, and to play lead-
However, they still
their service must
male minyan.)
vice conducted in
ty with the Inter-
ll, the thousand-
n of the Wall in
oalition of Israeli
Hodesh (the new
incessant harass-
ment from the ultra-Orthodox.

This Jerusalem prayer group was first launched on December 1, 1988, by a group of about sixty women from many nations who were in Israel attending the International Jewish Feminist Conference (which will be described in chapter 15). The sixty included women whose religious affiliations ran the gamut, as did that of their leaders—Rivka Haut and Norma Joseph, both Orthodox; Helene Ferris, a Reform rabbi; Reconstructionist rabbi Deborah Brin; and Francine Klagsbrun, a Conservative Jew, who was given the honor of holding the Torah. It was the first time a service with a Torah reading ever took place on the women's side of the Wall. And the first service in which the four main denominations of Judaism prayed *together* at the Wall, or anyplace else—and it took a women's group to do it.

"In order to pray together, each woman sacrificed an important principle," says Phyllis Chesler, the psychologist and author, in her article in *On the Issues,* describing the morning service at the *kotel* [Western Wall]:

> *Women who vowed never to pray behind a mehitzah did so. Those who do not recognize women rabbis were led in prayer by women rabbis. . . . It was an inspired show of unity both as feminists and as Jews.*

Francine Klagsbrun gives this assessment:

More than ever as I carried the scroll to the Wall, the Torah became part of me and I part of it. The act of reading from it with a group of women reaffirmed that moment at Sinai when the Torah was given to all of us, women as well as men.

"The experience of praying at the *kotel,* affirming that I am a Jew, that the Torah is mine also, that I am part of the covenant that the Torah symbolizes, was very important," adds Norma Joseph. "Equally important was the feeling of shared community with the women involved. . . ."

I too was in Jerusalem that morning, but I was one of those who declined to attend the service because I had long ago vowed never to pray in sex-segregated space. As a result, I missed this transcendent service at the Wall—a great loss. By allowing rebellion to become a more compelling motivation than feminist solidarity, I cheated myself; I became the casualty of my own stored-up rage.

In 1976, the first time my husband and I went to Israel, of course we went to the Wall—I to the women's side, he to the men's. Later he told me that he had astonished himself by feeling overcome with emotion and, lacking the proper words, he had recited the only Hebrew prayer he knew: the blessing over the wine. ("God must have thought, 'There's a wino at the Wall,' " he quipped later.) I too had felt enormously moved in the shadows of the cold and massive stones, but my emotions were bruised when I noticed how much smaller the women's section was than the men's, and it troubled me to watch the women pray silently, almost meekly, while the men bellowed their prayers and danced together with the Torah.

Since women are "supposed" to pray silently and separately, and since the feminists who went to the Wall that December dawn prayed as a group, dared to pray aloud, *and* held a Torah—the *haredim* (ultra-Orthodox) felt they were being provoked. I can think of few images more peaceful and benign than women praying, yet one would have thought this group was a battalion of Iraqi commandos. The *haredi* started braying, bellowing, and shouting. They grabbed the huge metal *mehitzah* dividing the men's and women's section, and shook it violently while demanding that the women stop their prayers. One *haredi* man screamed, "A woman reading the Torah at the Wall is like a pig at the wall." One *haredi* woman kept shouting, "The Torah belongs to men." Several *haredi* women worked themselves into a frenzy, tried to grab the Torah to give it to the men on the other side of the partition. Our feminist worshipers reminded their attackers that their prayer service was in no way contrary to Jewish law, but the *haredi* harassment only escalated and turned even uglier and more physical. One angry man ran off promising to bring reinforcements—young men from a nearby yeshiva. Our women's group huddled together, finished their prayers, and left the site quickly. I talked with them immediately upon their return to our hotel. They were still elated from the beauty of their prayers but all were visibly shaken by the protest.

After the International Jewish Feminist Conference adjourned and our delegates left Jerusalem, a group of Israeli women who had been part of the prayer group constituted themselves the Women of the Wall, and they have been praying together since in numbers ranging from thirty-five to two hundred. At first, they prayed in the women's section of the Wall area, with the Torah, and with purity of intent, utter decorum, and fidelity to halacha. This did not placate the *haredi* men, who harangued them mercilessly each time they appeared. The men shouted, shook the metal partition, and even threw chairs over it, injuring several women, one seriously. Some ultra-Orthodox women threw mud and shoved the women who were trying to pray. Female security guards did not restrain the attackers but shouted at the praying women to "stop that noise." The police and the army responded when Arabs threw stones at Jewish worshipers at the Temple Mount, but when Jews bombard other Jews with mud and metal chairs, there is no protection.

When the feminists continued with their devotions, says Bonna Haberman, a member of Women of the Wall, the guards "pulled and pushed us so hard that finally we were all on the ground." Some women filed charges against the Jerusalem city government for failing to provide adequate police protection. (Two government officials, one of them Ettya Simcha, the prime minister's adviser on women's affairs, blamed the violence on the "provocative behavior" of the women at prayer.)

Yehuda Getz, the rabbi in charge of the Wall, was present during one of the confrontations, says Haberman, and he "looked on at what was going on with pride." While Getz acknowledged that what they were doing was not halachically prohibited (even menstruating women are permitted to touch the Torah), he condemned these "deviationist" devotions and pronounced women's Torah reading contrary to "tradition."

I am reminded of the words of Bernadette Mosala, a black South African clergywoman: "When men are oppressed, it's a tragedy. When women are oppressed, it's tradition." In the name of tradition, the Women of the Wall have been punched, pummeled, cursed, bitten, spat upon, dragged along the ground, and tear-gassed by police who were supposed to protect them.

At this writing, Rabbi Getz has banned women at the Wall from Torah reading, wearing *talitot*, praying in groups, and praying audibly (remember *kol ishah;* "the voice of woman is lascivious"). Women who insist on doing any of the banned activities must be exiled to the back of the plaza that faces the Wall.

"They need the Wall like I need a cross," the rabbi told the press.

What do we do with the bone-crushing, stomach-wrenching insult of that sentence? Clearly, Rabbi Getz does not need a cross because he is not a Christian. Are we to understand that women do not need the Wall because we are not Jews? Yet we know those women are Jews and Jews need the Wall. We know Jews press themselves against the Wall, Jews tuck their crumpled prayers and tiny paper wishes into the ancient cracks of the Wall, Jews flood the Wall with tears, and are so moved by its symbolic power that they recite any Hebrew blessing at all rather than profane this ancient place with the American tongue—yet Rabbi Getz has decided women do not need the Wall because . . . ?

Because women are not *Jews*, not real Jews, not *the* Jews. How much plainer can they say it? How much longer must we hear it?

The Western Wall, formerly called the Wailing Wall for the sadness its stones have witnessed over the centuries, is the only surviving section of the Second Temple destroyed by the Romans in the year 70. The Wall was sex-integrated throughout most of its history, but as soon as Israel "liberated" it in 1967, the Orthodox took over its jurisdiction and put up a partition to separate men and women.

Professor Shmuel Safrai of the Hebrew University has found evidence that women and men prayed together in the original Temple except on the holiday of Shavuot, when Jews pray all night. An Orthodox scholar himself, Dr. Safrai objects strenuously to the restraints put on the Women of the Wall by "those ultra-Orthodox who do not serve in the army and who sat by while others liberated the Wall. . . .

"No one has the right to interfere with the prayers of other Jews, much less to commit violence, not at the Wall and not at any other synagogue," he insists.

Despite several such opinions from respected authorities, Israel's Ministry of Religious Affairs has prohibited "nontraditional religious ceremonies in public places which offend the sensibilities of those who pray there." One feminist responded exactly as I would have: "If halacha permits something that offends your sensibilities, then perhaps it is your sensibilities that ought to be changed."

Sadly, the Israeli Supreme Court has thus far upheld Rabbi Getz's restrictions: At the Wall, women must not have a Torah or tallit; they must not stand in a group and must not allow their prayers to be audible. If they wish to do any of those things, they must stand far away from the Wall where they will not offend everyone—you remember "*everyone.*" Yet not everyone is offended. One day, the women were parading with the Torah through the Dung Gate when they passed a group of Moroccan Jewish tourists, each of whom reverently kissed the Torah as it passed. Those Jews focused on the Torah, not the sex of the person who holds it.

In effect, by thus far upholding Rabbi Getz's orders, the Ministry of Religion and the Supreme Court have changed the Wall from a precious remnant of ancient Judaism that belongs to the entire Jewish people to the private property of black-hat bullies who dare to call themselves *B'nai Mitzvot*, sons of God's Commandments. These same guardians of sacred Jewish geography have tolerated every manner of secular event at the Wall, from musicals to hunger strikes, to military ceremonies, to Maccabiah sports celebrations complete with fireworks and laser spotlights. Only when it comes to women's prayers is the Wall so sacrosanct that Jews, female Jews, must be silenced in its honor.

According to midrash, the *Shechina*, God's divine feminine presence, never leaves the Western Wall. When the Jews went into exile, it is said the *Shechina* accompanied them while also remaining at the Wall, so that She would be there to welcome those who were able to return. Now, I believe, She is waiting at the Wall for women to achieve spiritual equality.

The International Committee for Women of the Wall is helping to make this happen. They have pledged "to claim public sacred space as the rightful domain of every Jewish woman." They, along with the Israeli Women of the Wall and the Israel Women's Network, an advocacy group, have petitioned the High Court of Justice for equal rights at the Wall on the grounds that it is a national historic site governed by the laws of the State of Israel. They have collected funds from around the world and purchased a Torah for the Jerusalem prayer group. Several emissaries brought it to Israel where there was to be an outdoor prayer service followed by a Torah presentation ceremony at the Laromme Hotel. However, the previous day the Jerusalem rabbinate had threatened to revoke the Laromme's kashruth certificate and to issue a ban on the hotel if it permitted the ceremony to be held on its premises. Clearly, this was an unfair restraint of trade in a country where every hotel catering to Jews must keep kosher in order to appeal to observant as well as secular patrons. The American Jewish Congress sued to compel the hotel to honor its contract but the court upheld the cancellation, requiring only that the hotel's management find other accommodations for the women's service.

As the rabbis continue to wage war against women whose only crime is love of Torah, I continue to ask my questions: Is a man living the life of Torah when he denies Torah to another Jew? Is a Jew who stones another Jew in God's name sanctifying God or profaning God? Why is it a crime when Arabs stone Jews at the Wall but not when men stone women? Who is harmed when pious women wish to enact their spirituality in the fullness of ritual? Is shouting curses at prayerful women an act of lovingkindness? Would these Hasidic men want such things to be done unto them?

Attending the New York women's prayer service in support of the Women of the Wall was one of the most moving experiences of my Jewish life. Sponsored by the International Women's Tefillah Network, this service was duplicated in Jerusalem and eight other cities in the United States and Canada. Ours in New York was a completely proper, unexpurgated Orthodox service led by women, including a Torah reading beautifully cantillated by a woman. At its conclusion, every participant signed a tambourine (recalling the timbrel with which Miriam led the Hebrew women across the Red Sea) that was to be sent to Jerusalem as a symbol of our unity with their efforts.

I should not single out these special services when hundreds, perhaps thousands, of religious women meet regularly in such groups to sustain their own spiritual needs with more direct participation in the liturgy than they are permitted in traditional Orthodox congregations.

In addition to women's prayer groups, religious feminists have reclaimed Rosh Hodesh, the celebration of the new moon, as a time for women's ceremonies. When the Israelites, tired of waiting for Moses to come down from Mount Sinai, decided to build themselves a golden calf, according to midrash, the Israelite women refused to contribute their gold ornaments to the making of the idol. As a reward, the minor holiday of Rosh Hodesh was given to women.

Another women's ceremony borrowed from the ancient world rests on the practice of visiting Rachel's Tomb to pray for a worthy bridegroom or for the conception of a healthy child. Nowadays religious feminists study midrash about Rachel, make a pilgrimage to her Tomb, wrap a red thread around the holy site, and ask God to fulfill their prayers—which are as often political as personal.

Says the American feminist, Rabbi Geela Rayzel Robinson:

> *The significance of the ceremony at Rachel's Tomb is that it is a glimmer of an authentic Jewish ritual for women that already existed, and we are so starved for our own rituals, history, and tradition.*

Despite the fact that many of these new rituals take place in sex-segregated spaces, I have felt inspired and energized by them, and proud to pray alongside so many learned women. The difference between women's prayer groups and the sex segregation at the Wall or in an Orthodox synagogue rests in the *choosing* and the *doing*. For women to choose the spiritual camaraderie of other women is not the same as being ghettoized by men for *their* spiritual benefit. For us to do the praying, reading, and ceremonies is not the same as watching men do it for us.

While I am enthusiastic about this ferment in the religious feminist community, there are other groundbreaking but equally reverent innovations being created by feminists at other points along the spectrum. I'm thinking of life-cycle rituals such as the *Simchat Bat*, the baby-naming ceremony that welcomes the birth of a daughter with as much fanfare as the *Brit Milah* (ritual circumcision) accords to a son; or the adult Bat Mitzvah for women who wish to officially come of age in a Jewish context (some have paired up with their adolescent sons or daughters).

I'm also thinking of inventions that are more intrinsically feminist although grounded in Jewish imagery and Jewish values. (See the Bibliography, pages 381–382, for specific information.) These include hot-tub immersion rituals that borrow the *mikvah*'s ideology of re-dedication without its denigrating underpinnings; a newly "resurrected" eighteenth-century prayer for breast-feeding; Rabbi Julie Gordon's "Prayer After an Abortion" and Diane Solomon's Kaddish for a miscarriage; ceremonies to celebrate a love commitment, whether gay or heterosexual, to mark an adoption, or the weaning of a child; Vicki Hollander's divorce rites which include a twenty-four-hour fast, a "mourner's minyan" (ten women who witness the death of the marriage), a document that formalizes the "ritual of unbinding," and a fast-breaking meal of consolation and transition; Drorah Setel's communal circles; Irene Fine's rites of passage for middle-aged women; the "Simchat Chochma" (celebration of wisdom) ceremony originated by Savina Teubal with the help of Setel and Debbie Friedman, which in turn inspired Marcia Cohn Spiegel's "Croning Ceremony"—both rituals honoring the woman turning sixty who is ready to assume the mantle of the "wise old crone"; as well as ceremonies for changing jobs, coming out as a lesbian, saying farewell to a friend, moving to a new town, even for the onset of menstruation or menopause.

And why not? Aren't Jews commanded to instill spirituality into every detail of existence? Jewish law requires men to say daily blessings over virtually every human act in order to sanctify the ordinary and renew their consciousness of God's creation. There is even a prayer to be said after going to the bathroom:

> *Blessed art thou O God . . . who created the human with wisdom, making apertures and orifices, and if a tube or pipe that is supposed to be open is closed, or if one that should be closed is open, it would be impossible to exist for even a moment. Blessed is God the healer of all flesh, the doer of wondrous things.*

If it's okay to be thankful for well-functioning apertures and orifices, why not for timely menarche and menopause? The fact that women's biological processes do not have official sanctifications of their own (Judaism has no blessing specifically in response to childbirth) only proves how much is left out when men are put in charge of sanctifying. Says Rabbi Julie Greenberg: "You can just imagine how many rituals there would be if men had babies!"

As was true of the first option, getting women included, I embrace this second option, making feminist change, but I embrace it with a caveat: I am not ready to substitute all of women's poetry for all of men's poetry. I want a middle ground, a literature of both/and, not either/or. Revision acquires resonance when seen against the original; it is deepened by the contrasts. I want judicious editing and cross-cutting. I want old cadences and new ideas, old rhymes and new rhythms; meters both feminist and *frum* (observant). I want Then and Now in one inclusive, mutually authorized anthology. Tradition and invention. Vision and re-vision. I cannot relinquish either; I want both.

My duplicity surprises me. When I hear the old ways defended and the new ways ridiculed, I rise up like that ghost in my father's minyan, demanding equality. I want to know why it was acceptable to question halacha a thousand years ago but not now, when women are doing the questioning. If the Talmud could reinterpret the Torah, and Rashi and Maimonides could reinterpret the Talmud, and rabbis through the ages could create new midrashim, why in our time is it the task of Orthodox rabbis to stand in the path of change?

"To cast off thousands of years of Jewish history is risky business," says Rabbi Marshall Meyer. "But that doesn't mean that all of the past is right or sacred. Jews have lasted all these years because our ancestors were brave enough to change what wasn't right."

In the best of all possible worlds, we would reconvene the Sanhedrin, the central juridical authority which, from the time of the giving of the Torah until the year 425 C.E., decided changes in halacha as required by human circumstances. Where women are concerned, many special circumstances have arisen since 425. What we need now is a new Sanhedrin made up of the full spectrum of the rabbinate—including women rabbis—and the best of Judaic scholars—including feminist scholars. Ideally, they would review all the laws and customs that are predicated on the presumed inferiority of women. Following the dictates of simple justice and utilizing the genius of Judaic reasoning, the new Sanhedrin would equalize woman-as-Jew in one giant leap. But since this is not the best possible world but an ordinary sexist one, leaps seem to be out of the question.

Joel Roth, the learned professor whose responsa helped women gain admission to the Conservative rabbinate, at least takes a step in the right direction when he asserts in his book *The Halachic Process* that when laws are "to the detriment of the Jewish people, observance of the law is no longer either mandated or even desired."

Once, the great rabbis found a way to reason Judaism away from animal sacrifice and polygamy, both of which are expressly included in the original written law. Now, it must be possible for great thinkers to reason Judaism away from sexism and the diminishment of women which, although included in the written law, are clearly detrimental to the Jewish people—especially the Jewish people who are women.

Having said all this in support of change, I must also admit that when the new ways are presented as wholesale substitutes for tradition, I resist that solution as well. Not because I fear opening the gates of chaos and disorder, or changing the power balance—concerns that underlie Orthodox objections—but because I fear the loss of memory and continuity.

"I see Judaism as a huge tree that has been growing for five thousand years," says the filmmaker Susan Seidelman. "If I don't pass the religion on, one of its branches will dead-end with me."

The tree image works nicely, but I prefer a musical metaphor. I see Judaism as a sound library that has been growing for as long as there have been Jewish voices. If I don't remember the old songs and pass them to my children, the songs will die with me. But, say the makers of new sounds, the old lyrics leave women out. I know, I say, but women sang them. My foremothers sang them. I hear their echoes. I feel their emotional resonances. And by now, men's prayers are mine because I have said and sung them all my life. That's why I don't want my cantor to change the tunes to which I sing "*Shalom Aleichem*" and "*Adon Olam.*" I can't take a steady diet of New Age spirituality even if it is politically correct. I want my old-time religion. Heartstrings and viscera connect me to a Judaism of ancestral words and melodies through which I conduct my conversations with God. Unless a feminist ritual can stir up that visceral spirituality—and many do—it doesn't *feel* Jewish to me.

At a recent conference on Feminist Judaism sponsored by the National Council of Jewish Women, I present my problem to Judith Plaskow. She assures me that the sounds religious feminists are making that may seem New Age or overly intellectualized to me now will be ancestral words for the next generation. Wait fifty years, she says, and our rituals will have become so familiar, so full of associations and visceral emotion, that *they* will be too precious to change, and our daughters will say of them, "I grew up with this—this is what *feels* Jewish to me."

I suspect she's right. It is certainly true of the rituals in the feminist seder that my daughters and I have attended every year since 1975 and which they now accord the sacrosanct status of "tradition." But what about me, right now? How does someone raised on a rich, resonating Judaism turn away from the "old ways" for reasons of equality and justice if the turning leaves her in a kind of spiritual desert?

Plaskow replies, "It's always hard for the transitional generation."

Sometimes it's *too* hard. For me, therefore, the transition requires synthesis rather than substitution. Now and then I need to hear the familiar melodies, even if they leave out the women's parts. I care about reparations, but also about remembering.

There is a well-known tale of Rabbi Israel ben Eliezer, the Baal Shem Tov, the eighteenth-century founder of Hasidism, who became known as a miracle worker. When misfortune threatened, he went to a place in the forest, lit a fire, said a prayer, and the evil was averted. The next generation, faced with disaster, also went into the forest to the holy place. "We forgot how to light a fire," they said, "but we can still say the prayer." They too avoided misfortune. When the third generation got into trouble they said, "We don't know how to make fire or say the prayer, but we know the place." And they were saved as well. Then came a generation that said, "We know neither fire, prayer, or place. All we can do is tell the story." And they too got their miracle. Remembering was enough.

Whether or not we choose to enter men's places—whether I light Jewish fires the old way, or speak my father's prayers—I feel we must continue to tell the story. For me, the two options—getting women in and making feminist change—come together in a solution many of us call, not Jewish feminism but feminist Judaism. "Feminist Judaism is what feminist Jews create," says Julie Greenberg.

While it might amuse radical feminists and infuriate Orthodox Jews, this creation, this mix of soul-satisfying tradition and egalitarian invention, this amalgam of religious conviction and feminist principle, has allowed me to continue to feel and be Jewish.

I supposed I've created my own Feminist Jewish Orthodoxy because I have very strong preferences. I like pro forma Conservative synagogue services with lots of Hebrew chants and congregational participation—but I enjoy them best when the text is ungendered and

God is an equal-opportunity divinity. I believe in God (rather than trendy feminist goddesses or nouvelle paganisms), but God, the presence in creation, not the old white man with the long white beard. I like my High Holy Day services intensely spiritual but not run by the book. I attend three Passover seders: the traditional family version, a "liberation" seder, and a feminist seder which you will read about in chapter 7. I want the option to enjoy an all-women's prayer service, but not if it is my *only* option. I love new birth ceremonies for Jewish daughters, but I want those daughters to continue to be named for their ancestors, male as well as female.

Mine is a Judaism of compromise but not complacency. I struggle with my compromises but I see no other way to be a Jew; that is, I see no other way to be a Jew whose spiritual life is in tune with her integrity as a woman. From the menu of classic and innovative Jewish observances, I have chosen the rituals that nourish me best. It's not a *glatt* kosher meal, but it is a balanced diet and no one is turned away from the table.

5

The
High Holy Days

New Clothes and Bare Feet

ALTHOUGH I THINK OF ROSH HASHANAH AND YOM KIPPUR AS MY father's holidays (Hanukkah and Passover were my mother's), I still have some warm and positive associations with the High Holy Days of my childhood. First, they embodied the very essence of new beginnings; for autumn, not spring, was when everything was new: my clothes, my classroom, books, pencil box, teachers—and Jewish chronology, which decreed a fresh start, a clean slate, a chance to improve on the past.

Second, the High Holy Days were special to me because the last two digits of the new year always corresponded to my age. In 1949, for example, when the Jewish year was 5710, I was 10 years old. This annual coincidence made me feel some small connection to the incomprehensible notion of five millennia having passed since the creation of the world.

Third, the High Holies, as I called them, was the time when I consciously recommitted myself to aspire to my mother's character and my father's achievements. However Pollyannaish it sounds, that's the sort of child I was. I wanted to be his kind of Jew and her kind of human being. I wanted to think like him and act like her. Speaking from my doubled perspective, his example was a constant reminder of my intellectual shortcomings, but the heavier burden was my failure to measure up to her kindness: I had been selfish where she was self-sacrificing, vain where she was effortlessly modest. Next year I would be better.

I recognize the stirrings of those long-ago High Holy Day feelings whenever I buy new fall clothes. According to the Talmud, on the Days of Judgment, Jews are not supposed to appear serious and dowdy the way we might dress to appear before a human judge. For God, we are instructed to dress festively, in bright new garments that symbolize our cheerful confidence in spiritual regeneration. So each fall, my mother and I went shopping together, hoping to find something I would be willing to wear to services. It wasn't a pleasant process. For most of my youth, I hated my scrawny body and stick-straight legs. Long after my friends had blossomed into puberty and graduated to Junior and Misses sizes, I was still skulking into the Preteen department with my mother at my side murmuring reassurances that next year I'd finally "develop."

Patiently, she sat on a bench in my dressing room bucking up my spirits as I tried on one outfit after another until I made a few grudging selections: a taffeta dress with a lace collar, a blue corduroy jumper and white eyelet blouse, a plaid pleated skirt with a wool sweater set. When it was her turn to try on clothes, I sat in her dressing room but never patiently. I was overheated. I was irritable. I hated department stores. I wanted to go home.

We went home by subway—forty minutes on the E or F train to Jamaica—weighted down with boxes from S. Klein on The Square, or Ohrbach's or Macy's, with me fussing and squirming—until I could collapse on the living room sofa. Nothing perked me up faster than my father's inevitable demand for a fashion show. He wanted to see his "girls" dressed up to do him proud. So, after an exhausting day, we unwrapped our new purchases and modeled them for him. He always raved about how we looked and what we had bought. Whether he truly approved, I will never know. It didn't matter anyway; his praise was my reward for enduring a day in the stores.

On Rosh Hashanah, I got dressed early and walked the mile to synagogue with my father. Mommy would come later, after she had made the beds and prepared the lunch we would expect when we came home from services, or the dinner—always dairy—that we would devour after the twenty-four-hour fast of Yom Kippur. I did not stay home to help. On the High Holies, I was my father's daughter. I went to shul with him, running to keep up with his rapid strides, swinging my little-girl purse, with a Chap Stick and a linen hanky tucked inside.

My father carried his tallit in a blue velvet pouch with a Star of David embroidered on it in gold threads. He never turned the pouch toward his body or hid it in a paper bag as other men did but carried it openly, inviting the gaze of our Gentile neighbors, advertising his Jewish star the way men flaunt their designer labels today. His confidence established my comfort level. Of course I had no tallit, but around my neck, I wore a slender gold chain on which hung my Jewish star.

Inside the sanctuary, my father blessed his tallit, kissed it, and flung it around his shoulders with the unconscious grace of one who had performed the gesture countless times before. When I sat beside him, I would drape one end of the silky shawl across my shoulders, enjoying the swing of its fringe against my arm. Maybe I did it to feel closer to him. Maybe I did it to wrap myself in the comfort of his Judaism. All I remember is wanting to have a tallit of my own.

IT'S NOT JUST TALLIT ENVY proclaimed a button circulated at a long-ago Jewish feminist conference. But for me, it *was* tallit envy. What I wished for was not a boy's sex but his tallit and tefillin and his significance in Jewish life—especially life at the Jamaica Jewish Center.

The Center was my second home. I saw it the way we "see" any familiar environment, noticing nothing in particular until something in it has changed. On the High Holy Days, the grand ballroom was changed, from an all-purpose space where we danced Israeli dances and watched Jewish National Fund films, into a lustrous sanctuary big enough to hold all the congregants who showed up at this time of year if no other. How well I remember that room: The Holy Ark was set in the center of the stage with huge vases of gladioli on either side. On that very stage I had played in the school Purim production; now it was hallowed ground. Also flanking the Ark were two ornate candelabra taller than I was. There were throne chairs for the VIPs (where my father sat during the years when he was president of the shul). And standing like sentries at the borders of the stage were two flags, the stars and stripes, and the white flag with the blue Star of David which we called "the Jewish flag" before there was an Israel. In the auditorium, rows of gilt chairs with red velvet seats were lined up neatly. Balconies swept around three sides of the room—not for women's separatism (we were a Conservative synagogue with mixed seating) but for come-lately members of our huge congregation.

I remember the people too: the rabbi and cantor, looking as pink as popes in their special-occasion white robes and satin crowns; the ushers (all men), who seemed so important because they dispensed prayer books, mediated children's disputes, and controlled our coming in and going out like the guards at the gates of Oz.

My Hebrew School friends, who made their way to the seat locations their families reserved year after year—the way society families reserve a box at the opera—signaled to me when they were going to take a bathroom break and wanted me to meet them outside. Most of the time, I stayed put and followed the service. I had learned very young to daven in Hebrew, rocking back and forth on my heels as my father did and as I sometimes do today, no matter how much it bemuses the synagogue elders. I took the High Holy Days seriously. They were my time of reckoning. During the silent devotion, I began my soul-searching, concentrating all my thoughts on my behavior over the previous year. I enumerated my sins. I resolved to remedy my faults and prayed hard that I might be written in the Book of Life for the coming year.

But the hours were long and sometimes my eyes led my mind astray: to Bobby Rabin or Bobby Malkin or whichever boy had set my heart aflame that year. To counting the light bulbs in the ceiling fixtures. To imagining how I would look in Marsha Smilen's bangs or Dena Pinsky's bottle curls. To the fur stole draped around my mother's chair, skinny foxes joined head to tail, their beady eyes intact. Then, ashamed of my meanderings, I would return to my meditation and repentence.

The audio portion of these memories contains two tracks: one carries the deep chorus of a thousand congregants praying aloud, the other the rustling murmur of them whispering to each other so loudly that the rabbi had to interrupt the service to ask them to stop. Both kinds of clamor sound Jewish to me: the monologue addressed to God and the dialogue between Jews. Both provided the background music of my introspection, a mix as comforting to me as the sound of my parents' voices in the next room at home.

My *kavvanah* (spiritual concentration) was at its best not during private prayer, the province of children at bedtime, but during the public litany of confession whose text could have been written today. In this prayer, every member of the congregation—woman and man, child and adult—admits to collective wrongdoing, in unison, in the first person plural. *We* had sinned. (The discovery that adults had been bad was both unnerving and reassuring.) *We* were imperfect. There was no room for individual disclaimers. All of us had committed these infractions: we were stubborn, spiteful, and jealous; we were liars and talebearers. We had broken our promises. We had been greedy and mean-spirited. We were in this together, supplicants at the same well of mercy.

After my mother's death and despite my many spiritual detours, I never failed to attend shul on Rosh Hashanah and Yom Kippur. The Jewish New Year was the real new year; January First some pagan imitation.

So every autumn—even though these were my father's holidays, even when I felt angriest at him and at patriarchy, even when I lived alone in New York and answered to no one, even when I married my nonbeliever husband—I paid for a single ticket and went to stand with other Jews on the Days of Awe. Any synagogue would do, as long as it did not have a *mehitzah*. All I needed was a Jewish space in which I could give strict account of my deeds, ask forgiveness from a God I felt owed me a favor, and say Kaddish for my mother. Every Rosh Hashanah, I put on my new fall clothes and took my place in some overflow service in some synagogue basement and ten days later, after Yom Kippur, this wandering worshiper disappeared from the Jewish community until the same time next year.

All this changed in 1970 when, in the oddest place for the oddest reasons, I reentered the Jewish community, catapulting from my anonymous seat into, of all places, the pulpit. I became a *chazanit*, a cantor, singer of Hebrew liturgy in a "house of prayer" in Saltaire, Fire Island. What began for me as an act of community service for the landed (or sanded) Jewish gentry eventually sent me on a much more personal quest to undo my defiant alienation. In plain words, it brought me back to Jewish life.

Fire Island is a narrow, thirty-two-mile-long barrier beach about two hours east of Times Square. From Memorial Day to Columbus Day, it attracts sun-loving city folk of various social persuasions—swinging singles, groupers, gays, and nuclear family types—who leave their cars and their everyday lives on the mainland and migrate by ferry across the Great South Bay to whichever of the fifteen distinctive Fire Island communities best suits their tastes.

Our little village of Saltaire is a family enclave; weathered American Gothic, not Brighton Beach. In 1968, when my husband and I and our three small children first started spending weekends and vacations there, one could get bagels at the village market but lox and herring required a special order. A few years before that, there would have been few requests for either. Saltaire had been tacitly restricted since its founding in 1910 and the two or three token Jews who'd slipped into town over the decades had kept a low profile. Gradually, in the early Sixties, an undeclared change of policy opened the harbor to a steady influx of Jewish renters and homeowners, and today, estimates of Jewish households range from 20 to 30 percent.

But who's counting? Religion is not an issue in Saltaire. Residents are more concerned with beach erosion and Lyme disease than with questions of theology. Today we are a restricted community in only two areas: we exclude "groupers" (individuals renting shares in a group house) and we restrict motor vehicles in favor of bicycles and little red wagons (for pulling baggage and freight from the ferry to our homes). On those issues, Saltairians of every faith are unanimous.

Yet for all its secular character, one fact about this 400-household village could not escape the alert observer. Rising out of the beach grass are two churches of quite respectable size, the brown-shingled Episcopal sanctuary situated hard by the softball field, and the white-washed Roman Catholic minicathedral which backs on the marshes of Clam Cove.

From ocean to bay, from one horizon line to the other, there isn't a synagogue in sight.

When I first arrived in Saltaire, the Jews used to kid each other about starting a building fund. What would the town elders say if we put up one of those fund-raising thermometers near the Village Hall, or stood outside the Saltaire Market with a *pushky* (collection box) labeled HELP MAKE OUR TEMPLE A REALITY? Taking a cue from the Protestant church, St. Andrew's by the Sea, we could name our synagogue Bait Andy by the Shore, or we could echo the Catholic church, Our Lady Star of the Sea, and call it Our Levi, Star of David. The kidding around rested not only on the town's past policies but on our assessment of ourselves. Which of us felt like a displaced person because no shul was near? How many attended Sabbath services back home? Did any of us care that we were a people without a "church"?

I doubt it. We were the Woodstock Generation and those were the God Is Dead years. In the late 1960s, when my tale begins, Saltaire contained a microcosm of secular American Jewry one or two generations removed from their immigrant forebears; most were assimilated young professionals, Wall Street types, teachers, writers, hippies, housewives, and businesspeople whose ethnic roots were acknowledged but not affirmed. Some Jews were negative about all organized religion, others hostile toward "bourgeois Judaism" or whatever Judaism they grew up in. They were more apt to be active in the antiwar or civil rights movements than in organizations concerned with Soviet Jewry, Israel, and other Jewish causes. If you'd asked me then how the majority felt about their religious identity, I would have answered, "They're just Jews."

However, even "just Jews" tend to go to synagogue on the most solemn days of the Jewish calendar. Often this meant forgoing a golden autumn weekend at the beach and staying in the city to attend services. For the totally lapsed, it meant coming out to the beach but feeling guilty.

Two women had found a way to keep the faith while remaining on the Island. Adele Seltzer and Peggy Schuman hiked two miles further east along the beach to the neighboring Fire Island village of Seaview where a friend of theirs held impromptu services on her deck. In 1969, inspired by this example, the Schumans and Seltzers decided to borrow ten prayer books and perform their own service in Saltaire. Adele's husband, Hal, gathered a flock of worshipers by strolling along our boardwalks cadging everyone he knew (or suspected) to be Jewish. Thirty-two people ended up in the Seltzers' living room sharing the ten books.

"We didn't know what we were doing," remembers Hal.

Earl Schuman, a lyricist, was the rabbi though he couldn't read Hebrew. His brother Alden, a composer, was in charge of the record player. He put on a few minutes of Richard Tucker's service and then we recited English passages from the prayer books and made up a few things of our own. For the first time in years I wasn't embarrassed about my lack of religious training. I felt at home in Judaism.

In a way far different from Hal's, I too had not been feeling at home in Judaism. That's why, when I heard about the impromptu Saltaire congregation, I decided to try it out the following year instead of spending the High Holy Days in yet another overflow service in some synagogue basement.

This time the planning was spearheaded by Larry Weber, a New York stockbroker best known as Saltaire's most gung-ho volunteer fireman. To be sure he hadn't missed any Jews and to make Gentile friends feel welcome, Larry didn't just rely on word-of-mouth, he posted signs about our service at the market, the ferry dock, and on the lifeguards' shack at the ocean. Many people were intrigued and enthusiastic. Some volunteered to bring wine and honeycake for the kiddush. I offered to help plan the service and to select some Hebrew songs to be sung by a children's choir. Judy Weber and Adele Seltzer began rehearsing the choir in August. Other people contributed money toward expenses. And suddenly, we had expenses. Larry, our de facto rabbi, went to Bloch Publishers in lower Manhattan to buy twenty-five more *mahzors* (High Holy Day prayer books) and a shofar (ram's horn), the quintessential symbol of the Jewish New Year.

To avoid having to charge sales tax, the clerk said he would need the name of Larry's congregation. Our fireman-stockbroker thought quickly and replied, "B'nai Saltaire" (which means Sons of Saltaire).

Back on the Island, Larry soon discovered that none of the sons could read Hebrew well enough to do it aloud. I took one of the prayer books home, thumbed the pages, and mouthed the words I had been saying in synagogue every year since I was a toddler. The liturgical chants flooded my memory like a medley of old love songs. The next day, I told Larry I would read or sing part of the service in Hebrew, confessing to him, and myself, that I thought certain prayers would be irreparably diminished if they were recited in English. I did not realize it at the time, but when I stepped forward in this way, when I chose to take responsibility for the traditional sound and texture of the service, I was beginning a journey toward a new place for myself within Judaism.

My ascension into the pulpit happened without protest or fanfare. Back then, at the dawn of the 1970s, the women's movement was still in its infancy, and Jewish feminism was not even a gleam in its founders' eyes. It would be a year before *Ms.* magazine was founded, two years before the first woman rabbi was ordained by the Reform branch of Judaism, three years before Conservatives counted women in a minyan, five years before any synagogue in America would see a Reform woman cantor, and the mid-Eighties before the Conservatives finally accepted women rabbis and cantors.

I'm not comparing myself to a trained cantor nor B'nai Saltaire to a real synagogue; however, as a community of Jews who accepted a woman prayer leader, we were a predictive phenomenon. Our unconventional service presaged the growth of the Jewish renewal, and the breakdown of gender barriers in the pulpit—and we brought others besides myself back into the fold.

Once we had prayer books, a shofar, and a self-anointed rabbi and cantor, we were ready to set up our "sanctuary." At the front of the Seltzers' living room, we stacked two end tables on top of each other and covered them with a cloth to create an altar for a kiddush cup and a pair of candlesticks. Tall reeds and dense blueberry bushes pressed against the railings outside, while inside about fifty people pressed against each other, sharing prayer books and balancing kids on their laps. I imagined us as members of the lost tribes taking refuge at an oasis in the Negev.

The conventional Rosh Hashanah service can last more than four hours, but Larry and I were afraid of overwhelming our congregants so we selected only ninety minutes' worth of excerpts from the *mahzor*. Everyone participated eagerly. The shofar blasts brought a spontaneous roar of appreciation, and the children's singing was as sweet as the honey and apples awaiting us on the sideboard. It was an efficient little service, stripped bare and mottled with mistakes, yet I was moved by the beauty of it and by a new sense of belonging. Others must have felt the same way for the crowd around the kiddush table badgered us with one demand: "When are Yom Kippur services next week!?"

Yom Kippur services were held in the late afternoon, October 10, 1970. This time, our oasis was the outdoor deck of the Weber house and Japanese pines were our witness. Again, we attempted very little, just Yizkor (memorial services), and Neilah (the concluding service of the High Holy Days). As I finished chanting the seven-times-repeated litany that ends the service, the sun slipped behind the trees like a magnificently timed special effect, setting on the old year right on cue.

Looking back, I could say the sun was also setting on an old habit, my tendency to equate being Jewish with practicing Judaism my father's way. In Saltaire, the High Holy Days had become my holiday as much as his. Here, I had abandoned all pretense of doing it "right" and still it felt right; more than that, it felt real. For the first time, I began to think about finding a way to rejoin the Jewish people, a way to be a Jew not just at home or in my head but publicly and communally, though it would take me years to determine what that way would be. It is ironic that feminism, a profoundly secular movement, is at the root of the most seismic changes in my Jewish life. Although I couldn't have named it at the time, I left Judaism essentially because of a feminist issue—my exclusion from the Kaddish minyan—and I returned to Judaism because of a feminist issue: my acceptance as the cantor of a prayer group that grew twenty times larger than a minyan.

News of our services spread quickly and by the following summer so many people asked about services for the upcoming Rosh Hashanah that it was clear our 1971 congregation would be too large for anyone's living room or sun deck. Happily, a senior pillar of the Episcopal community offered us the use of St. Andrew's church which could comfortably seat 110. We wanted to accept but secretly feared humiliation. Would we fill those pews? What if the novelty had worn off? What if we gave a High Holy Day service and nobody came?

With trepidation, we accepted the offer and hoped that our lost tribe would double. If so, we were ready for them. As people entered St. Andrew's wood-beamed chapel on Rosh Hashanah Eve, they heard a hidden tape recording of Jan Peerce singing liturgical chants. They found that the church had been "converted" to Judaism. Although we couldn't do anything about the Christ scenes depicted on the stained-glass windows, we did remove other signs of Christian worship—a banner, brass cross, and chalice—and replaced them with our own symbols, a silver kiddush cup, our shofar on a stand, and a stained-glass Star of David made by Syd (Sadie) Weiss, a local artist.

Ushers escorted the congregants to their seats. Each person received photocopied sheets containing the prayers we had excerpted from the *mahzor*. Larry and I stood in the anteroom behind the altar peering through a crack in the door—he in a business suit and I in a long-sleeved, floor-length white cotton dress that would have to pass for cantorial robes. We watched people fill the pews, then inch closer together to squeeze an extra person in each row. Minutes later, the aisles were jammed. I stopped counting at 220 people. Rosh Hashanah in Saltaire had become standing-room-only.

In appreciation of the use of their chapel, the Jewish community gave the Episcopal church a pair of candlesticks on which we engraved a quotation from Isaiah: THY HOUSE SHALL BE A HOUSE FOR ALL PEOPLE. But perhaps the real message had been exchanged without words: the days when Jews were unwelcome in Saltaire belonged to a dim and distant past.

Although still a minority, we have become an accepted and visible constituency and our annual services—which attract a standing-room crowd every year—have become a village "event." A week or so in advance of the holidays, the announcement case in front of the church spells out HAPPY NEW YEAR and lists the schedule of our services. Passersby do a double-take trying to reconcile the announcement out front with the cross on the bell tower. The Saltaire market and private individuals donate sacramental wine for our kiddush, and various people contribute *challah* (braided loaves of bread) and honey cake, flowers from their gardens, and *kipot* they've collected from Jewish functions attended during the year (stamped THE BAR MITZVAH OF JONATHAN SCHWARTZ or THE COHEN-FEINBERG WEDDING).

After a few years, our photocopied prayer sheets were dog-eared and dwindling. It was time to prepare a more permanent little *mahzor* and luckily we had a printer in our midst to help us do it. A Jew who happens to be the publisher of Catholic periodicals contributed 300 spiral-bound booklets with a cover painting by Chaim Gross—a bright watercolor of the blowing of the ram's horn. Somehow, with our own prayer books, I felt we were a permanent institution. This feeling solidified the following year when a motel in Kismet, the community just west of ours, ran an ad in the travel section of *The New York Times*. Alongside large notices for the Concord and Grossinger's, the motel's little headline said, JOIN US FOR THE HOLIDAYS. RELIGIOUS SERVICES NEARBY. They meant us.

Each year, from 1970 through 1983, I entered my metaphorical telephone booth, shed my secular identity, and emerged as the cantor of this flock that materialized out of the mists like Brigadoon. In 1984, I passed the cantorial robes to another woman, Laura Nowak, a finance professor whose girlhood yeshiva schooling makes her over-qualified for the job. During Laura's tenure (with a whole new group of volunteers) the congregation has remained large and loyal even after the original Seaview prayer group a few miles down the beach actually built themselves a synagogue and hired a rabbi and a cantor.

There's a famous joke about the two Jews marooned on a desert island who erect three shuls. Why three? One for Morris, one for Abe, and one that neither one of them would be caught dead in. The few diehard traditionalists who wouldn't be caught dead at B'nai Saltaire went to the Seaview shul. Although Seaview permitted mixed-sex seating, their Orthodox-leaning congregation did not permit women to play an equal role in their services until 5750 (1989). The progressives and the renegades come to us, looking like a Chaucerian pilgrimage as they arrive by bicycle and tricycle, on foot, and pulling wagons full of children. The fashion aesthetic ranges from sweat suits to nautical chic, with men in crew-neck sweaters and khaki pants, and women in white ducks or gauzy shifts and kids in everything from a Superman outfit to a well-pressed sunsuit—apparel as removed from the new fall clothes of my childhood as my wavering soprano is from the baritone of Cantor Moishe Oysher. And to complete the look, everyone wears sandals, sneakers, or Fire Island's most common footwear: no shoes at all.

For thirteen years, my favorite sight was the tableau of suntanned children walking down the aisles, barefoot in shul.

Thirteen years. An interesting number, come to think of it. If the thirteen years until my Bat Mitzvah charted my original coming of age within Judaism, the thirteen years of my cantorial duties marked another kind of spiritual and religious maturity—one that has been more organic, more creative, and certainly more conscious. The first coming-of-age tested my mastery of dogma and absolutes; the second developed my capacity to synthesize and question:

What do I mean when I call myself a Jew? Can I, in the words of Ismar Schorsch, "translate nostalgia into commitment"? What do I really *believe*? How do I experience the divine? Which ceremonies move me to a higher spiritual realm, and which do I want to perform for the sake of Jewish continuity whether they move me or not? Is my Judaism less authentic if I experience it as metaphor more often than faith? How do I reconcile the contradictions between Jewish tradition and feminist ethics? If I am unwilling to fulfill most of the religion's formal obligations, can I still create some distillation of Torah ethics and ritual that adds up to a "Jewish way of life"?

I began dealing with these questions in all seriousness when I "came out" as a cantor. The issue of obligation, for example. Though worlds away from the 613 commandments required of the Orthodox male, I had taken on *one* Jewish obligation—to serve the congregation at the beach. Yet at times I felt burdened even by that—by having to meet in the dog days of summer to plan each year's service, to discuss the sermon, assign text readings, and organize the volunteers. It wasn't always convenient to carve out time to review the Hebrew text in the midst of a busy work week, or to appear on the *bimah* on schedule regardless of what was happening in my household. It would have been a lot easier to buy an anonymous seat in a synagogue and just show up.

But fulfilling these obligations clarified for me how the demands of the Jewish calendar impose a cyclical orderliness on an otherwise fleeting, undifferentiated year, and how this heightened consciousness keeps God in the ordinary and reminds human beings to reaffirm the covenant. I began to see that throughout the fifteen years when I had felt utterly disconnected from Jews and Judaism, my decision to keep lighting Sabbath candles and keep observing the High Holy Days, Hanukkah, and Passover had been an acceptance of obligation and an act of commitment whether I realized it or not. My conscious reason for doing it was to honor my mother, but in the process I was remaining a Jew.

Realizing all this did not answer the most confounding questions. Can God and I forgive one another? Can I forgive God for the unspeakable cruelties of the Holocaust, slavery, the torture of children? Closer to home, can I forgive God for taking my mother at such a young age? Can God forgive me for shattering the Eternal Light, for turning away, for complaining so incessantly, and for taking so much of Judaism into my own hands?

On the eve of Yom Kippur as I stood in the pulpit ready to intone Kol Nidre (All Vows), Judaism's most holy and haunting invocation, I saw once again the magnitude of my own impertinence. Inevitably, even in the thirteenth year, a wave of fear coursed through me. Who was I to worship in this crazy, heretical way? Even though my congregation couldn't care less, I was no stranger to the rules: the cantor is the *shaliach tzibbur*, the messenger of prayer for the whole congregation. The cantor prays for those who may not be conversant in prayer; therefore the cantor must have the same obligations as the people who listen (legally, if even one man is present only a male can pray on his behalf). Also, there is the custom that prohibits men from hearing *kol ishah*, the lascivious voice of women raised in song, a custom that has come to have the force of law. Because I knew all this,

I also knew that it is harder for Judaism to accept women as cantors than as rabbis, whose task is to teach, advise, interpret Jewish law, and comfort the sick, none of which is prohibited to women.

Whether or not a Jewish man actually observes all 613 commandments, being male would be credential enough for him to be standing in my place. Conversely, being female was curse enough. A woman cannot pray on man's behalf. Her prayers are empty. She is nothing but a potential distraction. I could not believe God intended such a double standard to apply to human beings who are also created in the divine image; therefore, I concluded, the inequity was not God's law but men's—and could be ignored.

So I lifted my voice and sang through my fears, although I always paused after the first two words to see if God might prefer to strike me dead rather than endure another round of supplications from this strange quarter—a church with a Star of David on its altar, where a woman with a thin soprano and no spiritual authority had the audacity to sing Kol Nidre.

Writing this, I am reminded of a tale told about that same Rabbi Israel ben Eliezer, the Baal Shem Tov, who worked miracles with the fire and the prayer in the forest. This story tells of a dull-witted boy who could not read but only was fit to tend sheep. When he was thirteen and of age according to God's laws, his father took him to the Baal Shem Tov's house of prayer on the Day of Atonement in case the boy might otherwise eat on the fast day because he knew no better.

"Just listen to the prayers," said the father, and the boy did as he was told.

After sitting at attention throughout the morning, the boy pointed to the shepherd's pipe in his pocket and whispered, "Father, may I play?" Horrified, the father flatly forbade it.

When the afternoon service began, the boy again said, "Father, please permit me to blow my pipe," and again the father said no, this time placing his hand firmly over his son's pocket.

The day lengthened and as the closing prayer began, the boy asked a third time for permission to blow his pipe and again the father refused and gripped the pocket more firmly. But just as the service was ending, the boy could contain himself no longer. He pushed away his father's hand, pulled out the pipe, and blew a very long, very loud note.

"All were frightened and confused," writes Martin Buber in his

Tales of the Hasidim. "But the Baal Shem went on with the prayer, only more quickly and easily than usual. Later he said: 'The boy made things easy for me.' " Another version of the same tale concludes, "At the end of the Day of Atonement Rabbi Israel declared that with his pipe the boy had sent all their prayers aloft to heaven."

The Baal Shem Tov believed that how Jews prayed or where they prayed was less important than *that* they prayed. He believed that passion and heart spoke to God more urgently than ritual correctness. I am the polar opposite of a Hasid, but I do have a Jewish heart, and deep within it, where I keep hopes that have no logic, I hoped that my singing, like the blast of the boy's whistle, by its very strangeness would engage God's ear and carry *our* prayers aloft to heaven.

Often, in "real" synagogues, I had experienced the Kol Nidre as a performance more than a plea. I responded to male cantors who sang sweetly and mournfully but felt alienated by those who sang in stentorian tones, as if mimicking God. Their voices seemed too majesterial for confession; in contrast, my little Kol Nidre could be said to express the common voice of ordinary humanity—powerless, supplicating, humble. I liked the idea that, for a change, the voice of "the Jewish people" was a woman's voice. I liked having my children and everyone else's children see a woman on the *bimah* leading the worship of hundreds of people. I was glad that, before any woman was officially ordained within organized Judaism, the kids who grew up in Saltaire took it for granted that a woman could be a religious leader (such as I was), and before Hebrew Union College or the Jewish Theological Seminary determined that a woman could count in a minyan, the children of Saltaire saw that in our House of Prayer, girls counted as much as boys and mothers counted as much as fathers.

It is my position throughout this book that every feminist breakthrough is good-for-the-Jews—for *all* Jews, not "just" Jewish women. In Saltaire, I was the feminist breakthrough but I was also the bringer of tradition: rebel and conservor in one.

I have wonderful memories of these seaside High Holy Days where community and spirituality were braided together like a havdalah candle, as tight as the families in a tiny Jewish shtetl in tsarist Russia.

I love the potluck dinners we've shared at the home of Gloria and Gerry Franklin, where we come with wagonloads of food never before exhibited on the boardwalks of Saltaire—stuffed cabbage, tzimmes, *cholent*, kasha *varnishkes*, and a few versions of *kugel*.

I loved the time when Sheldon Secunda, son of Shalom, the song-writer, sang a selection of his father's best-known compositions, in-cluding "Bei Mir Bist Du Schoen," which was one of my mother's favorites.

And I love the fact that the *challah*s provided for our communal *motzei* (blessing over the bread) have so often been baked by men—either George Meluso, an Italian Catholic, or Gerry Franklin, a Prot-estant married to a Jew, or Dick Newman, a Jew. One year, after we recited the blessing over the huge, braided loaves, an unidentified guest appropriated the knife and said it looked as if we needed about 200 pieces. While the rest of us gaped in amazement, he proceeded to slice the *challah*s with the speed and style of a Samurai swordsman. "I used to be a caterer," he said.

I even love our crises—like the time when the fire alarm sounded just as we were set to begin Kol Nidre. Larry, the fireman-rabbi, trembling with indecision, resolved his conflict of interests in favor of human life and we postponed the start of services until the fire was out.

Best of all are the uncommon sermons delivered each year by vol-unteers. Most speakers have chosen conservationist themes—Judaicized paeans to the unspoiled beauty of our Island, testimonials from speakers who find God in the wind and tides, the beach plums and bayberries, the sand crabs and seagulls. But there have been other memorable messages: One woman underscored Jewish progress in America by contrasting today's religious coexistence in Saltaire with her personal reminiscences of more hostile times. A man's stirring condemnation of anti-Semitism helped us cope with news of the mur-der of eleven Israeli athletes at the Munich Olympics. More contro-versial was Victor Kovner's rousing protest against Israel's 1982 invasion of Lebanon. And in 1989, Barbara Barrie read a chapter from her book, *Lone Star*, a memoir of growing up Jewish in a small Texas town where Jews were as scarce as skyscrapers.

But everyone's all-time favorite seems to be Hal Seltzer's sermon addressed to "twice-a-year Jews."

"No need to apologize for coming to services only twice a year," he reassured the congregation.

I think it's great that you show up here at all! Because what you're saying is you're a Jew . . . and on this holy day, if on no other day, you want to go to shul, pray to God as Jews have prayed for over four thousand years, and restore yourself and your faith.

Are we restoring our faith, or are we simply providing a way for people to avoid Jewish guilt by making an appearance in a temporarily consecrated Jewish space? I have to think that something more profound is going on. What happens among Saltaire Jews on the High Holy Days is faith at its most rugged and indestructible. Against all likelihood, these people, lapsed and casual, believers and agnostics, fallen-away and prodigal though they are, want to gather together and proclaim that they are Jews. Why? For what? It is more than our hand-crafted icons, makeshift prayers, or idiosyncratic sermons that draw them to us. When we are together in that "converted" church, we seem to arouse in one another a kind of atavistic Jewishness, a basic, primal identification that is often lacking anywhere else, even in the most beautiful temple prayer service.

Do we feel this because we created B'nai Saltaire against the odds of a secular slide, or because we have sustained ourselves all these years without the imprimatur of officialdom? Is it because we established a Jewish presence in a Christian community, and did it with dignity and pride? Do we value our little congregation because it is so self-selected, the way people seem to value friends over relatives because friends are *chosen* rather than inherited?

Certainly, this brand of Judaism is easy to take. It's come-as-you-are and donate-if-you-feel-like-it. Contrary to Jewish law, we ride bikes to services and play music on the Holy Days. We blow the shofar and perform *tashlich* (casting our sins upon the waters) even when Rosh Hashanah falls on the Sabbath. We skip great portions of the liturgy and when we're finished, the kids go back to the beach and the grown-ups to the tennis courts. On Yom Kippur, as far as I can tell, only a few of us fast all day.

I can't help the fact that on the other 363 days of the year most of our congregants are still "just Jews." But I like to think that for many of them, the twice-a-year affirmation of faith may be what *keeps* them Jewish at all. Those two days in our "shul" may innoculate them against "the stranger's ways," triggering some sort of "racial memory" of their Jewish heritage and giving them a few rituals that touch them deeply. Those two days may solder the links in a chain that would otherwise have rusted away long ago, a chain of historical continuity that tethers them to the togetherness we call the Jewish community.

Abraham Kook, the chief Ashkenazi rabbi of Palestine and a prophet of messianic Zionism, distinguished between "external holiness," the pious performance of rituals, and "internal holiness," the feeling of being linked to the Jewish people, the Jewish heart, and the Jewish destiny. Our seaside services don't do much for external holiness, but twice a year we add fuel to the flames of internal holiness keeping these particular Jews Jewish, in the peoplehood sense, for another twelve months.

B'nai Saltaire is a long way from the Jamaica Jewish Center. Had my father ever felt interested enough to attend our service, I'm sure he would have pronounced it "kindergarten Judaism," and so it is, even by the most Reform standard. Still, I refuse to call what we do a cop-out. The ultimate cop-out is to drop out and to disengage from the Jewish community. I know, because I took that route for fifteen years. Religious purists may prefer the all-or-nothing approach but it would take a lot of hard proof to persuade me that doing nothing is better for the Jews than doing something—or that God is offended by our efforts. If the alternative is silence, I'll take the shepherd's pipe every time.

6

My Hanukkah

I WASN'T ONE OF THOSE JEWISH KIDS WHO ENVIED CHRISTIANS THEIR Christmas. I never even wished for a Christmas tree—and not because I didn't know what I was missing. Every Christmas Eve, my Irish-Catholic friend Sue, who lived across the street in a semidetached brick house identical to mine, invited me over to help her family trim their tree and share in the frenzy of present wrapping before the family went to midnight Mass. We sang Christmas carols and nibbled Christmas cookies, and the grown-ups drank beer and eggnog as we worked for hours stringing the colored lights and garlands of tinsel around the pine branches, and hooking shiny ornaments and candy canes onto the limbs. When we finished, Sue's father climbed the kitchen stepladder and placed a sequined star on top, and then, around the base of the tree, we spread Ivory Flakes "snow" and on it set a manger scene that reminded me of my dollhouse. I was never too sure of the events it symbolized but I knew a baby named Jesus was the hero, and I knew he was a Jew.

Never having read the New Testament, I got my information about Christianity straight from Sue. She told me her priest said Jesus was born a Jew and died at the hands of Jews, which made me vaguely uncomfortable although it didn't seem to affect her or her family's feelings about me one way or the other. There was always a little something for me tucked into one of the fuzzy red stockings hanging from the mirror.

All this hoopla made me feel excited and happy but never jealous. I had my Hanukkah, Sue had her Christmas, and all seemed right with the world. And when she came over to my house to share in my family's festivities, I felt I was offering her not a second-rate Christmas, but a holiday with its own magic and its own glow. In fact, if I remember correctly, I felt a little sorry for Sue: her holiday was over in twenty-four hours while mine lasted for eight glorious days.

In our house, the antique silver menorah gleamed at the center of a table covered in white damask and placed in front of a window. The candelabrum had eight little silver cups for oil lined up along its base, and a ninth little cup hooked onto the top of a hammered-silver backplate. Rather than oil, we used candles the color of orange peel; we lit one for each night plus the *shamash,* or caretaker candle, which we used to kindle each of the tapers and then placed in the topmost cup. Tiny lead dreidels (spinning tops) were scattered on the table along with Hanukkah *gelt,* chocolate coins wrapped in gold foil, the prizes for our dreidel game. From the ceiling, my mother and I had hung dreidels, menorahs, wine goblets, and six-pointed Jewish stars that we'd cut out of construction paper. My crayon drawings of the Maccabee soldiers, whose heroism the holiday commemorates, decorated the walls and my HAPPY HANUKKAH poster was tacked out front on our entrance door.

In the living room, a mountain of presents accumulated for weeks before the holiday, each gift-wrapped by my mother in blue and white, the colors of the Jewish flag. Along with surprises for everyone in our extended family, there were eight presents just for me. This wasn't like a birthday when you blew out your candles and got a nice gift. At Hanukkah, you *didn't* blow out the candles and you got a present every night for a week and a day.

Like Passover, Hanukkah was created by my mother but sanctified by my father. He said the blessings and led us in Hebrew song, but she made it *feel* like Hanukkah; she altered reality and made it transcendent. In the same spirit in which Jews beautify the vestments for the Torah, or elaborate on the artistry of the kiddush cup to enhance the holiness of the rituals associated with those objects, my mother beautified everything associated with Hanukkah. She individualized her gift wrappings with drawings and ribbons. Together, she and I made quirky menorahs and dreidels out of clay, endless paper chains that looped around the chandelier and snaked from room to room, and handwritten songsheets (before the Age of Xerox) so that everyone could sing along. On the first night of Hanukkah, she invited friends and family (even second cousins) to dinner, set a beautiful table, and produced the smells and tastes that made this celebration unmistakably itself.

I cannot even imagine a Hanukkah without potato *latkes,* pancakes fried in oil—calories made sacred. Oil was the theme motif of the holiday story, a story that, like Christmas, is part history, part tradition, and part apocrypha. I loved hearing how Judah Maccabee and his brothers defeated the vast armies of the Syrian-Greek king Antiochus who had taxed the Jews heavily, forbidden their religious practices, forced them to adopt Hellenistic ways, taken over the Holy Temple, and instituted pig sacrifices on the altar.

In 164 B.C.E., after three years of struggle, the Maccabees recaptured the Temple. Joyously, they purified the altar and prepared to light the Great Menorah; however, they could find only one cruse of oil, enough to fuel the lamp for a single day. A party of desperate soldiers rode off to fetch more but it took them eight days to pick and press more olives and purify the oil. Amazingly, the few drops from the cruse lasted for eight days.

In my child-mind, I'll admit, the Hanukkah story and my eight presents were intertwined. As the pile of gifts dwindled, I had a clear metaphor for the dwindling oil that put my ancestors into a panic. But beyond the material rewards of Hanukkah, I learned that the legend of the long-lasting oil symbolizes Jewish continuity, and Judah Maccabee's victory should set an example for every generation to resist domination and assimilation.

Midrash teaches that the Maccabees' rebellion was instigated by a respectable Israelite named Judith who was fed up with her people's assimilation, especially their willingness to let the Syrian Greeks claim manor rights—sexual use of Hebrew women. To protest, Judith stripped off her clothes and paraded naked through the streets. When the Jewish elders were outraged, she said they had forfeited their right to define Jewish morality. Then the men realized things had gone too far, and decided to undertake the rebellion. Because Judith started it all, Jewish women are supposed to rest while the Hanukkah candles are burning. (Some rest! Those skinny candles are gone in minutes.)

Whether commemorating the actions of Judith or Judah, we Jews have been celebrating the Festival of Lights for more than two thousand years, beginning on the twenty-fifth day of the Hebrew month of Kislev (which falls in December). When we kindle the Hanukkah candles we remember the miracle of the oil but also the message: by remaining true to our own beliefs, Jews have survived as a people long after our conquerors have been forgotten.

Like Saint Nicholas's celestial sleigh ride, the miracle of the oil is the part of the story that kids love best, and the miracle is confirmed "in writing" by the Hebrew letters imprinted on the four sides of every dreidel. *Nun, gimmel, hay, shin.* The initials stand for the words "A great miracle occurred there." (Israeli dreidels say, "A great miracle occurred *here*.") When I was a kid, my mother made it reoccur every year in my own house.

A lot of things happened to change this idyll. My mother died, and neither my father nor any of my aunts or uncles took up her role of holiday-keeper and family-gatherer. I went away to college where I retreated further from formal Jewish practice. I don't remember how or if I celebrated Hanukkah from 1955 until 1959 when I moved to Manhattan and had my own apartment.

I was dating a young man, a Columbia Law student, who was half-Jewish but had made Christmas his holiday of choice. Since he lived in the dorms, he wanted us to buy a big tree and decorate it at my place. I simply could not do it. To me, a Christmas tree wasn't just another evergreen, it was a religious symbol—Sue's symbol, not mine. But in 1959, I was into pleasing men. So, I honored the boyfriend's request, sort of: I bought him a six-inch statue of a predecorated tree and put it on the mantelpiece.

But I also bought a supply of tiny birthday candles and a six-inch chrome menorah for myself. (My father's new wife had inherited my mother's silver one.) And from then on, regardless of the spiritual proclivities of my boyfriend of the season, and eventually of my husband, I made Hanukkah happen for me. Bert—that child of left-wing, utterly secular parents—expressed bemused wonder when I packed for our Caribbean honeymoon in December 1963. Into a separate suitcase went my little chrome menorah, plus candles for eight nights and eight wrapped Hanukkah presents for Bert. Rebellion was one thing; giving up the Jewish holidays was something else. I wasn't going to let my alienation from my father's religious institutions cut me off from the rituals I loved, rituals I associated with my mother and the home-based Judaism in which my heritage seemed most present and most real. I would choose my own ways to link up with the chain of memory and assure my children a connection to the Jewish people.

So I wrapped the presents and decorated the house and taught my children Hanukkah songs and dreidel games and cooked the special dishes my mother had taught me. And, because of my Jewish education, I also took on my father's part—the Hebrew blessings and the retelling of the miracle. When my children were in their twenties and living on their own, one of my daughters told me she had never had reason to envy Christians their Christmas, and she wondered why any Jew would want to imitate another group's ritual.

This is not true of many Jews, including several of my friends. In 1978, I gave a lot of thought to my Hanukkah when *The New York Times* published an article, "Christmas Comes to a Jewish Home," in which Anne Roiphe discussed how and why she, her husband, and their daughters celebrated Christmas. After confessing some feelings of guilt—in consideration of her ancestors who had been killed by Christians in the name of the babe whose birthday is observed on December 25th—Anne went on to describe how much she and her children loved decorating the tree, watching *Rudolph the Red-Nosed Reindeer* on television, and giving an annual Yuletime party, at which someone always recited Dylan Thomas's "A Child's Christmas in Wales."

She justified this on the grounds that her wealthy parents had supported Jewish causes but gave her "no religious energy"; they had permitted their German maid to fill Anne's childhood home with the sparkle of a Bavarian Christmas. When Anne grew up, she decided that the Jewish "Jehovah was too cruel." She blamed God for the war between the Maccabees and King Antiochus and scolded: ". . . the proper miracle would have been to have created Romans without the need to conquer and avoided the bloody war altogether."

Anne's essay upset me deeply and I was far from alone. A follow-up note in the *Times* said the editors had received an unusual number of reader responses—mostly negative. Many of these respondents felt as I did—sorry for any Jew who could experience this holiday as at all inferior to Christmas, sad that Jewish children had missed out on Judah and Judith, the Temple, the menorah, the dreidels and *latkes*. I was lamenting too on behalf of generations of ancestors who might suffer to hear Jewish children singing "Silent Night" instead of "Rock of Ages." I was sorry that the tall, broad redwoods of Jewish history could so easily be cut down in favor of the short-lived glory of a Christmas pine. Besides its spiritual rewards, I had always treasured the civil liberties lesson of Hanukkah—that a minority must be free to practice its beliefs within a majority culture—a lesson with direct contemporary application to both Jews and feminists.

Anne endured an onslaught of hate mail and phone calls ("I hope your children get leukemia"), but she also received invitations to enlightenment from observant Jews, rabbis, and scholars, some of whom were instrumental in her subsequent intense pursuit of Bible study, history, and Jewish mysticism. Since then, she has written several books on Jewish subjects including *Generation Without Memory,* the moving story of her own journey into learning and spirituality; *Lovingkindness*, a powerful novel about a mother and daughter torn apart by the daughter's romance with Hasidism; and *The Pursuit of Happiness,* a rich and evocative Jewish family saga.

More than a decade after the *Times* essay was published, Anne wrote in *Tikkun* magazine:

I was now tied, by a love beyond understanding, to the fate of the Jewish people. I began to understand the meanings behind the rituals, and I found that I was amazed and proud of what it meant to be Jewish, of the ways Jews have approached intellectual issues, of the ways we have survived, of the ways our rituals blend into the seasons and bind us together in a past that finds its purpose in the future.

Today, Anne is a devoted Jewish feminist, a friend of Israel, and a frequent colleague in Jewish causes. But it was her 1978 essay that put me in touch with my grievances about Christmas—feelings suppressed in the name of interreligious harmony and Women's Movement solidarity. The truth is, I am in distress every December. It isn't just a matter of the commercialization of Christmas, it's that this is the only time of the year when I am made to feel like an alien in my own country. When the president of the United States flicks the switch to light up the Christmas tree on the White House lawn, that house ceases to be an American symbol; it becomes a Christian symbol. Growing up, that's how I knew which were the Christian families in Jamaica—by the Christmas decorations on their house or the Christmas tree ablaze inside. That's when I understood how outnumbered we were.

December is the one time when my sense of Otherness as a woman in a man's world—a perennial dull ache—is compounded by this sharper Otherness of the Jew in a Christian world. All year, women tolerate various expressions of the cultural assumption that Person equals Male. (For instance, advertisements that instruct the airline customer to "Bring her along.") Come Christmastime, we Jews have to live with the culture-wide assumption that Person equals Christian. ("Merry Christmas," they say to us as we go home to light our Hanukkah candles.) 'Tis the season for Jewish women to feel their double marginalization like the crosscutting of two icy winds. Christmas is the winter of my discontent.

From the day after Thanksgiving, I feel assaulted by images of the Christian "master story" and the incessant repetition of religious songs about people and events in which I do not believe or may have reason to find discomforting. Christmas is not all tinsel and merriment to those of us with a memory long enough to remember Jewish history. I cannot forget the inquisitions, pogroms, blood libels, Nazis who were good Christians, or popes who looked the other way. I feel no hostility toward individual Gentiles but I do have a problem with the casual secularization of a religion whose moral infrastructure has permitted so much violence to be committed against Jews through the ages.

I don't want to replace every wreath with a dreidel, nor do I suspect Gentiles of trying to convert me through Lord & Taylor's Christmas windows. But I am offended by the assumption that, as a shopper or worker, I would feel welcome in a store, school, or office displaying Three Wise Men, a Holy Virgin, and a Messiah I do not accept as my own. Although I relish being a part of the private celebrations of my Christian friends, that doesn't mean I want to encounter someone else's holiday everywhere I turn. Moreover, despite the Supreme

Court's 1989 decision in the Pittsburgh City Hall case, I remain unconvinced by the argument that Christmas trees (or menorahs for that matter) are merely neutral tokens of the season.

"Christianity's early use of the Christmas tree was based on a legend that on the night Jesus was born, all the trees of the forest bloomed and bore fruit despite the ice and snow that covered them," writes Rabbi Helene Ferris, quoting Christian sources to refute the neutrality claim. "Today, religious Christians believe that the tree is meant to symbolize the resurrection and immortality of Jesus, as well as the wood used for the crucifixion." Even the decorations have religious meanings, says Ferris. The star on the top of the tree reminds Christians that Christ came from heaven. "The tinsel signifies 'angels' hair' and recalls the 'heavenly hosts' who attended the miraculous birth of Jesus." The mistletoe symbolizes Christ as the everlasting Tree of Life, and the holly wreath represents "the crown of thorns which Christ wore on the cross, the little red berries symbolizing the drops of blood."

That does not sound secular to me. What's more, if Christmas trees and symbols are so nonsectarian, why aren't they used to decorate Muslim homes and mosques, or the lobby of my synagogue? If they're so neutral, why don't we find them displayed not just in Bethlehem and other Christian quarters but all over Israel, a country that is quick to adopt every other secular Western symbol? If the Christmas tree is just a cold-weather decorative symbol, why not display it in February as well as December?

Sorry, I remain unconvinced and ill at ease, and I resent the suggestion that there's something wrong with *me*.

Why should Jews be required to spend six weeks a year immersed in Christian imagery? No one would ask black people to tolerate whole cities festooned with Confederate flags and pictures of the Battle of Bull Run and paeans to Generals Robert E. Lee and Stonewall Jackson. We understand that a South that flaunts the Confederate flag is disregarding the sensitivities and perspectives of black Americans. Why is it so hard to understand how a nation that flaunts Christmas does not fully belong to the Jews?

All this explains why you'll find me each December muttering under my breath while everyone else is admiring the store windows— or fuming when a secular meeting hall is decorated for Christmas, or switching radio stations for the tenth time to escape "Hark the Herald Angels Sing." And if I squirm at this saturation exposure in the outside world, you can imagine how I might feel about encountering signs of Christmas in a Jewish home. When it happens, I let my mother's breeding triumph over my father's temper. I praise the tree. But what I want to do is beg these people to remember their intrepid forebears whose courage allowed Jews to live to see another Hanukkah, and ignore it. I mourn the death of memory and the deprivation of those Jews who do not know the potency of their own heritage. I want to rail against the assimilation that has brought so many Jews to "normalcy" and with it a preference for the majority's "normal" holiday.

At the same time, of course, I cannot blame Jews who choose Christmas because no one exposed them to the meaning or pleasures of Hanukkah. I can only hope that something happens in their lives to make them reconsider, as something happened to another writer, Judith Viorst.

In a 1970 issue of *Redbook*, Judy published a story entitled "My Jewish Christmas Tree." She too was bombarded with angry letters. At first, she was defensive. "See what religion does to people," she said. "It makes them intolerant; it makes them hate." Then she sat down and reread the letters and saw that what she'd thought was hatred was really a cry of pain.

"I began to understand what was involved for these Jews in isolated little towns to keep Judaism alive all by themselves," Judy tells me one summer night twenty years later as we schmooze over bowls of chocolate-chip ice cream.

In cosmopolitan cities with sizable Jewish populations, it's easy being Jewish. You can call yourself Jewish and not have to do anything about it. But in little Midwestern towns where the Jewish kids ask their parents, "Why can't we have a tree like everyone else?" and the parents are struggling to maintain Jewish traditions against all the pressures to just go along with the majority, it's really hard to have someone like me say it's okay to forget all that and have a Christmas tree.

Once she was able to get beyond the bruising tone of the letters, Judy was moved enough to let their logic "convert" her. She decided to try to switch to Hanukkah. She called a family meeting and read some of the most persuasive letters to her husband, Milton, and her three sons who were all under age ten at the time. Then she put the issue to a vote: were they willing to give up the tree, learn about Hanukkah, and celebrate their own holiday?

The yeses were unanimous and the Viorsts proceeded to get books about Hanukkah. While they were at it, they learned about Passover and other holidays, too. "It's rare for readers' letters to have such an effect on a writer but this, in fact, is what happened to me and my family," says Judy. Slowly, the Viorsts taught themselves to be Jewish, more Jewish than the families they came from, and today they observe many traditions in their home and belong to a temple, which is more than either of their parents did before them.

"Milton and the boys have become very sanctimonious about having Hanukkah and condemning Jewish houses with Christmas trees," Judy concludes. "Usually, I'm the queen of the self-righteous, but I try to understand the kind of past that would result in a tree in the middle of a Jewish living room."

So do I try to understand, but I still would prefer my fellow and sister Jews to keep the candles burning. That's why when our kids were young, we gave an annual Hanukkah party to which dozens of friends (including the Roiphes) contributed a performance—a song, poem, skit, reading, or musical recital—something "enlightening" in the spirit of Hanukkah.

My children's annual contribution was a short skit enacting the Hanukkah story, complete with Antiochus (Bert in a toga), the cruse of oil reincarnated in a salad cruet, and dialogue you won't find in the Hebrew sources.

> *There was a Jew, Mattathias,*
> *Who was strong and undoubtedly pious;*
> *He had two special sons,*
> *Judah and Simeon,*
> *Who ate* latkes, *fruit and papayas. . . .*
>
> *This story was pretty near right*
> *Regarding the Judaean fight;*
> *Forgive all the liberties,*
> *I took with the Maccabees,*
> *And enjoy the rest of the night.*

I was pleased that the kids found the events of two thousand years ago exciting enough to dramatize, because in the process they educated our guests, most of whom had no idea of the origins of Hanukkah and the splendors of the Festival of Lights. I was pleased too that my mother's home-based Judaism—passed through me to my children—had spawned their deeply felt little production.

I only wish she could have lived to see the show.

7

Wandering
in the Desert

En Route to the Feminist Seder

AS I LEAP FROM THE HIGH HOLY DAYS TO HANUKKAH AND NOW TO Passover, you may be wondering if my spirituality is to the topography of Judaism what the famous *New Yorker* map is to the standard globe. Saul Steinberg's cartoon shows the Hudson River nearly abutting the West Coast to create a graphic representation of the parochialism of Manhattanites. My spiritual map reveals a similar truncation of Jewish tradition. But I know what I'm leaving out, and why.

I'm short-changing all the other holidays because they are way stations for me, not major stops on memory's route. They have synagogue resonances but not deeply personal ones. I remember waving my apple-topped Jewish flag on Simchat Torah when we completed the Torah reading for the year and began again at the beginning. I remember ratcheting my noisemaker to drown out Haman's name during the reading of the Megillah on Purim, the Festival of Queen Esther. On Sukkot, I helped to erect the temporary dwelling in which Jews are supposed to live for a week under the stars. We built our sukkah up on the roof of the Jamaica Jewish Center, and though no one slept in it, my parents and I came there after dinner for wine and cake.

One year, on the open porch over the garage behind our house, we built our own sukkah with a latticed roof woven out of maple branches and walls decorated with gourds, dried flowers, and paper chains. Eating meals there with my parents was like playing house with grown-ups. Why we did that once and never again I have no idea—and there is no one left to ask.

These holidays get short shrift here not for lack of respect but due to a shortage of deposits in my memory bank. This is not the case with Passover, where the memories are earning interest. I have described my mother's marathon of preparations—how she scoured away the *chametz* and cooked for days—and my father's star turn as leader of the seder wearing his white *kittel* and reclining in his chair at the head of the table. But what about *my* Passover?

I must confess that as a child I hated the interminable hours we spent at the seder table reading every word of the Haggadah, the story of the Exodus which is rendered in legends, rabbinic discussions, prayers, parables, blessings, and songs. Our seder began after the family, maybe twenty-five of us, had settled ourselves at a long, pieced-together table and each of the males above Bar Mitzvah age had stood up one by one to recite the kiddush over the first cup of wine. The wives of the married men rose with them, standing silently at their sides like ladies-in-waiting—and they waited, like well-behaved ladies, for their husbands to speak to God on their behalf. When one of the men faltered or mispronounced a word, I had to hold myself back from correcting him. But no female, not even a yeshiva girl, imagined it was her right to say the kiddush.

After the men finished, my father held up the matzah and spoke the opening line of the seder: "This is the bread of affliction that our forefathers ate in the land of Egypt," and as the tale began unfolding yet again, I felt like shouting, "We know this already! What's the point of going through it all over again!?"

It took me a long time to understand that going through it all over again *is* the point: that an event has no meaning until human beings invest it with meaning. Retelling the Exodus story year after year is what has turned event into symbol, and symbol into a liberation ethos that invests the Jewish people with a clear sense of purpose. I had to learn why we are instructed not to merely recall those four hundred years of slavery but to feel as if we *ourselves* had been slaves in Egypt. In the 125 generations since Moses led the children of Israel to Mount Sinai, Jews have been reiterating that we are descended from a slave people, not from kings and queens or gods and goddesses. Remembering our oppression helps us identify with the oppressed. Recalling that "we were strangers in Egypt," we are enjoined to care for the stranger in our midst.

Long after I knew the story by heart, I kept uncovering layers of its meaning until I now see the Exodus as a radical paradigm—the first "master story" that renders spiritual issues political. The revelation of Jewish law at Sinai brought the covenant into history, as Michael Walzer puts it in his book *Exodus and Revolution*. In other words, the contract between God and the Jewish people requires Jews to imitate God, and since God intervened with Pharaoh to liberate the Hebrew slaves, Jews are expected to intervene in the political world to free the oppressed. Exodus teaches us that history is not incorrigible. For as long as Jews take our mandate seriously and imitate God's liberation model, we can affect events. We can be the vehicle for social progress and world redemption.

Lately, I have also become quite taken with the Exodus as a framework for black-Jewish understanding (see chapter 14). Both blacks and Jews have known Egypt. Jews have known it as certain death (the killing of the firstborn, then the ovens and gas chambers). Blacks have known it as death and terror by bondage (the Middle Passage, Gory Island, Jim Crow, and the lash). As a rule, blacks try to forget their slavery because enduring it *obliterated* their identity as a free people; Jews choose to remember our slavery because escaping it *gave* us our identity as a free people.

Our experiences differ most profoundly once our peoples left bondage behind. Blacks of both sexes escaped from their Egypt but have not yet crossed the Red Sea. The pharaoh's soldiers are still at their heels. Their Moses has been murdered. They are still awaiting their miracles. As for Jews, the men heard the revelation at Sinai, and entered the Promised Land where they are now living less than perfect lives. But Jewish women are still wandering in the desert, awaiting inclusion in the covenant, awaiting their Sinai.

It took me a long time to notice that when Moses spoke to the Israelites to prepare them to receive the Law at Sinai, he addressed only the men: "Be ready on the third day and do not go near a woman" (Exodus 19:15). Why not "Husbands and wives do not go near each other?" Weren't women there? If we were not addressed when God's contract with the Jews was forged, and if we cannot undergo circumcision, the physical sign of the covenant, then we must ask whether we are included in the arrangement. And if not, was the original oversight God's or man's? And how long must we keep wandering?

When I was growing up, the seder elicited none of these thoughts; it was simply hours of nonstop davening and too much food. My cousins and I passed the time at the children's table giggling, or sitting among our elders complaining and fidgeting. Happily, our misery was relieved by several beloved rituals which, mercifully, are well distributed throughout the Haggadah, maybe for just that reason—to keep the children interested.

My seder was made endurable by the Four Questions, the Four Sons, the Ten Plagues, Elijah's visit, "Dayenu," the *haroset* and hard-boiled egg; the ransoming of the *afikoman* (the broken half of matzah hidden early in the evening by the seder leader), and finally, the after-dinner songfest.

I loved the Four Questions and the *afikoman* because these rituals were explicitly reserved to us kids and they were the most consequential events of the evening. Without the Four Questions, the seder could not begin, since the Haggadah provides the answers (and how could one have answers before questions?). And the seder could not end unless the children who had "stolen" the *afikoman* were willing to return it for a suitable ransom (in my family, the price was one silver dollar per child), since everyone had to eat a piece of this special "dessert" matzah before the final grace could be said.

I asked the Four Questions for an inordinate number of years, not because I was always the youngest at the table—a criterion dictated by tradition—but because for a long time I remained the youngest child who could chant the Hebrew. The English translation was recited by my junior cousins as soon as each one learned to read.

I was also the ringleader of the *afikoman* thieves because I had made it my business never to let my father out of my sight. I watched where he put the piece of matzah that he had wrapped in his napkin and tucked away while trying to distract us with jokes, funny faces, and other diversionary tactics. The instant he left the dining room for the ritual hand-washing, I sprang into action, retrieved the special matzah, and after a quick and raucous consultation with my cousins, rehid it in a new location.

The story of the Four Sons was of no interest to me except as a kind of lottery: Which of us kids would be dealt the worst parts? We roared when my father called on one of us to read the passage about the Simple Son who asks stupid questions, or the Wicked Son who ridicules Passover, or the Son Who Does Not Know How to Ask anything. Each of us wanted to be the Wise Son with the right questions. I don't remember noticing that there were no daughters, wise or simple.

Reciting the Ten Plagues had the appeal of a good horror movie. It gave me the chills but at a comfortable distance. *Blood. Frogs. Lice. Noxious beasts.* Each ominous word, which the whole group uttered portentously in unison, was accompanied by the dipping of the pinky finger into one's wine and tapping the tainted drop onto one's plate. *Pestilence. Boils. Hail. Locusts. Darkness. The slaying of firstborn boys.* Some did their dipping left, right, and center but I liked to be neat about it. My Plagues, ten little fingerprints of red wine, circled my plate like a Limoges border design. The trick was *not* to absentmindedly lick your pinky when you finished, thereby ingesting locusts and lice. We kids thought that idea was hilarious. My father squelched our laughter by reminding us that the reason Jewish people recite the Plagues is to remember the Egyptians' suffering, not to revel in their punishment. This was a powerful mandate to put at the tip of a child's pinky, especially one who, at eight or nine years old, failed to see the merits of sympathizing with her enemies.

It was also a powerful ritual—and always a child's honor—to open the door for Elijah, the prophet who was said to visit every Jewish home to sip from the goblet reserved for him in the center of the seder table. Legend has it that Elijah would be the forerunner of the Messiah, so the wine was there to signify every Jew's readiness for redemption.

At the proper moment, one child went to open the outside door while the rest of us remained in our seats, eyes glued to Elijah's cup, straining to see the wine stir as his spirit took a sip—a special effect I later learned was accomplished by an adult yanking discreetly on the tablecloth.

Singing was another thing that made the long seders tolerable. I particularly loved "Dayenu," whose chorus wound around itself like a hooked rug, and whose verses rested on a seductive literary device. If God only had given us the Torah, *dayenu*, it would have sufficed.

And if God only had given us the Sabbath, *dayenu*, each gift would have been enough for anyone. And still, there were more. Secretly, I rewrote the song and dedicated it to my cousin Pris. "If Pris was only pretty, *dayenu*. And if she was only a good jacks player, *dayenu*." And so on into infinity—with choruses in between.

The eating of the *haroset*, a sublime combination of chopped apples, walnuts, cinnamon, and Manischewitz Concord grape wine, carried me through another stretch of boredom. The mixture, which we spread on pieces of matzah, was a dual symbol: first, of the mortar made by Jewish slaves under the Egyptian lash, and second, of the sweetness of God who remembered the Jewish people and put an end to such labors. The bitter/sweet contradiction confounded me. When I asked my father how one thing could represent such opposites, he answered that it typified Jewish experience and I'd better get used to it. Being the Chosen People didn't mean we were chosen for the best.

I loved my father's exegeses; his wisecracks and midrashim reminded me of the elucidations of the great rabbis. When I was very small and my grandfather ran the seder, we weren't supposed to interrupt. But my father encouraged questions, so I asked him whatever popped into my mind—even though my cousins gave me dirty looks because his answers lengthened the service considerably. I accepted his view of the *haroset*, but later, when I helped myself to extra servings, I willed it to be all sweetness and no mortar.

The arrival at the table of a bowl full of hard-boiled eggs signaled the end of the first part of the service and the beginning of the seder meal. Although not officially prescribed, dipping the egg (symbol of rebirth) into a small bowl of salt water (the tears of our enslaved ancestors) is a common practice and one that I took to heart. I used to dip my egg into the water with a quick and gingerly flourish so as not to let it absorb too much sadness. My father, on the other hand, always mashed his egg with his fork, making a soup of life and tears, clouding his salt water with white and yellow lumps. The sight disgusted me—so much so that I had to look away. At the same time, it reaffirmed my childhood view of my father as a man who tempted the fates but came up lucky. His egg seemed to conquer suffering, incorporating it into an earthy stew, while my egg was afraid of the brine.

After a belt-bursting meal, when waves of adult conversation threatened to inundate us children, my mother—always aware of everyone's needs—would come to the rescue. She would excuse us from the table, and send us up to the bedrooms or down to the rumpus room until it was time to negotiate for the retrieval of the *afikoman*. This transaction accomplished, most of my cousins wanted to take their silver dollars and run. I wanted to sing, and sing, and sing: "Chad Gadya," "Eliyahu Hanavi," "Addir Hu," "Echad Me Yodayah," "Ki Lo Noeh"—everything in the book.

Those exuberant hymns and story-songs seemed to express what the seder had been driving at all night; they made the whole evening worth the price of endurance. I was grateful to the men who stayed at the table bellowing every last word with me. I had no use for the women. Why were they puttering around when they could be singing? Why hadn't they learned the words after all these years? I never considered the mountains of dirty dishes in the kitchen. I was too busy speed-singing the intricate lyrics in competition with my uncles and male cousins. I was too busy feeling like an honorary son.

The years have seen some dramatic changes in our family seders brought about by births and deaths, the aging of three generations, a new brood of kids, and the influence of feminism. We still use a traditional Haggadah but we revise the male language as we go along and supplement the printed text with special readings about anti-Semitism, sexism, the Holocaust, Soviet Jews, Ethiopian Jews, and other groups in trouble. Nowadays, the men of our family help to serve or clear, and the women read and sing Hebrew and recite the kiddush for themselves.

Our seder leader is still a male, my brother-in-law, Bernie, but he is a reluctant "master" and I suspect he would gladly abdicate if I or any of the other women volunteered to take the job. I have not offered because the tradition-loving side of me still wants one "old-fashioned" seder led by a man wearing my Grandpa's *kittel*. (This white linen robe enfolds an Orthodox man when he is a groom, a seder leader, or praying on the High Holy Days. It is also supposed to serve as his shroud, but my Grandpa wanted his *kittel* to stay among us, so he gave it to my father who passed it on to Bernie.)

Bernie is almost twenty years older than I. Someday, when he is ready to retire from the head of the table, I will probably take over. But I'm not ready yet. Once I ran a seder for my husband's side of the family, and I've taken key roles in the other seders of my life. But I'm not ready for the *kittel*.

In recent years, we've often had our family seder on the second night of Passover. On the first night, my husband, children, and I attend a wildly unorthodox ceremony conducted by Sarah and Victor Kovner for fifty or sixty of their friends and relatives. The Kovners open their doors to "orphans" who have no family seder of their own, to Jew, Christian, Muslim, or Hindu. In the past, they have invited people as disparate as Victor's cousins Abba and Vitka Kovner, the heroes of Vilna ghetto, and Maryam and Edward Said, the Palestinian rights activists, as well as a changing parade of visitors from foreign lands. One year I sat next to the first lady of Bangladesh, who was making her seder debut. I hastened to inform her that the Kovner seder was not typical. Stewart Mott, a Protestant and a great fan of seders, uses his desktop publishing equipment to print up a program and an annotated list of participants. He also contributes the *haroset*, which he embellishes with dates, figs, raisins, and, one year, crumbled Ritz crackers. I tried to explain that Ritz crackers are a rather overt violation of the dietary requirements of the Festival of Matzot, but given the evening's other idiosyncratic practices, it sounded as if I was nit-picking.

Peter Yarrow, of Peter, Paul and Mary, who lives in the Kovners' building, is there every year with his guitar, his children, and his mother. Between courses, he leads us in singing folk songs of the Spanish Civil War, the civil rights struggle, South Africa, and Nicaragua—and if we're lucky, a verse or two of "Dayenu." Victor, who leads the seder, uses one of the New Jewish Agenda's boldly politicized Haggadot, one that draws some uncomfortable parallels between the oppression of the Hebrews under the Egyptians and that of the Palestinians under the Israelis. I like to add an excerpt from an "alternative" feminist Haggadah—one composed by either Aviva Cantor, Rebecca Alpert, Esther Broner, Lynn Rosen, the Twin Cities Women's Minyan, or the Women's Equality Task Force of the Union of American Hebrew Congregations.

While most people accept these embellishments as catalysts for healthy disputation, some Jews have found the Kovners' seders too radical, particularly when the readings give the Palestinians equal time with the Israelites. A few people have come once and not returned. Two of my kids, who are hardly religious fundamentalists, worry that the history of the Israelites is being lost in its modern allegorical applications; Abigail and David would prefer that Peter Yarrow concentrate on traditional Passover songs. They are their mother's children: the past matters to them. Yet their mother feels okay about this counterculture event. Mentally, I have removed it from the religious category and repositioned it in the realm of political ritual where I can accept it as an extension of the Exodus paradigm and enjoy it on its own terms. Besides, I always have my third seder.

Now, nobody *needs* three seders. God seems to think two are enough. Yet I have come to feel that the holiday is incomplete without the all-women ritual that I have attended on the third night of Passover every year since 1976.

Why is this night different from all other nights?

Because on this night, twenty to thirty women sit in a wide circle on pillows on the floor with a cloth spread like a table before us, and we ask the Four Questions of women. On this night, for a change, we speak of the Four Daughters, female archetypes yearning to know their past. And on this night, the goblet usually set aside for the prophet Elijah belongs to the prophet Miriam.

At the feminist seder, Miriam comes alive to me as a rebel (her name means "rebellion"), a leader and a visionary. A famous midrash says that when Pharaoh condemned Jewish babies to die and Miriam's father lost all hope for the future, it was Miriam, then seven years old, who dissuaded him from divorcing her mother Yocheved. It was Miriam who convinced her parents to stay together and continue having children. It was Miriam who rebelled against death and argued for life. The result was the birth of Moses. Then it was Miriam who watched over her baby brother in the bullrushes and, when the Egyptian princess found him, it was Miriam who put forward Moses's own mother as his wet nurse. Years later, after the crossing of the Red Sea, it was Miriam who led the Hebrew women with timbrel and song, acts recognized as a sign of prophetic power. (Only four women in the Bible are given the title prophetess: Miriam, Deborah, Huldah, and Noadiah.) The traditional telling of the Passover story barely mentions Miriam. Our feminist Haggadah makes amends and gives the prophetess her due.

On this night, we use the Haggadah that Esther Broner wrote with Naomi Nimrod, who runs a parallel seder in Israel. Esther writes,

We were told that we were brought out of Egypt from the house of bondage, but we were still our fathers' daughters, obedient wives, and servers of our children, and were not yet ourselves.

On this night, we become ourselves. We speak with grammar of the feminine plural and invoke the *Shechina*, the feminine essence of the deity, whom you'll remember from the Western Wall. On this night, the ritual hand washing is not a solitary act but a rite of collective nurture. We pass a pitcher of water and a basin and each woman washes the hands of the woman sitting beside her. On this night, one by one, we name our mothers and grandmothers, the women who cleaned, cooked, and served at family seders while the men reclined against their pillows retelling Jewish history—*his* story, the story of Jewish men.

On this night, we give *her* story equal time. We remember the five disobedient women to whom are owed the life of Moses and the destiny of the Jewish people: his sister Miriam; Shiphrah and Puah, the midwives who disobeyed the pharaoh's order to murder all first-born Jewish sons; Moses's mother Yocheved, who defied maternal desires and gave up her baby so that he might survive; and the pharaoh's daughter, a righteous Gentile who disobeyed her father's decree and adopted a Hebrew baby marked for murder. At our seder, we do not praise good girls and polite ladies; we honor rebellious women.

We also remember the unsung heroines of the rabbinic period: Rachel, who labored for twenty-four years so that her husband could study (what man has done that for what woman?). Beruriah, an esteemed teacher of Torah, whose husband Rabbi Meir insisted on proving that women are weak and thus tested her virtue by sending one of his students to seduce her, again and again and again, until she succumbed—and then killed herself. The daughter of Rabbi Gamliel, a wise woman who does not even have a name of her own. And Ima Shalom, another feisty intellect, descendent of Hillel, daughter of a scholar, wife of the head of the Sanhedrin (governing body), the man who left us such aphorisms as "It is better to burn the words of the Torah than to give them to women."

On the third night of Passover, the words *belong* to women.

Esther, our seder leader, wears her embroidered *kipah* and luminous spirituality with the grace of a high priestess. When she calls on us to read or when she explains the rituals, it is not in a commanding voice like my father's but in lyrical tones that ennoble every word.

Phyllis Chesler, the psychologist and author, also sits at the head of the table, crosslegged like a wise Buddha. Each year, her inventive rituals and the symbolic objects she brings for all to touch infuse our service with Cabbalistic magic and mystical rightness.

Lilly Rivlin, a writer and filmmaker, adds sweet intensity and the power of a perfect quotation to illuminate our theme. One year she filmed the seder, and the resulting short feature, "Miriam's Daughters Now," was shown on public television.

Artists Bea Kreloff and Edith Isaac–Rose and journalist Michele Landsberg bring humor and candor to the proceedings, but more important, they contribute strong ideas and political content that ensure ours is not just a women's seder but a feminist one.

These six women and myself constitute the Seder Sisters, Seder Seven, Seder Makers, or Seder Mothers. Whatever we call ourselves, our job has been to bring the event into being, to plan the service, invite the guests, organize the potluck meal, and choose the seder theme.

Last year, the theme was "Omission, Absence, and Silence." Under that heading, we asked participants to undo men's silencing of women and women's self-censorship. My assignment was to create a feminist midrash on Jephthah's Daughter, a character in the Book of Judges. Jephthah, a military general, promised God that in return for the defeat of the Ammonites, he would sacrifice the first thing that emerged from his house upon his return. The first to open the door and welcome him was his (nameless) daughter, whose perspective on the ensuing tale, unrecorded in the Bible, was the subject of my recitation.

"I am here to break the silence of Jephthah's Daughter," I said.

Now the questions begin. We ask God, Why did you allow an innocent girl to be sacrificed in your name? You stayed Abraham's hand and Isaac lived. Why did you save the son and let the daughter die? Why to this day have you forgotten all the daughters destroyed by their fathers, neglected, abused, exploited and violated by their fathers?

The questions I posed to God, the Israelites, and Jephthah challenged us to reexperience a Torah event from the Daughter's point of view, and in so doing reframed the moral of the story.

Through the years, I've kept notes on our seder themes, menus, and guest lists, but my recollections would be dim without the supplementary details in Esther's as-yet-unpublished chronology, "The Telling," an archival gem. Between the two of us, future historians will know the names of the women who have been part of our seder, who hail from both the secular women's movement and Jewish feminism. They will also know that we took in "the stranger"—non-Jewish women, white women and women of color—such as writers Kate Millett and Mary Gordon; Sonia Johnson, the Mormon woman who was excommunicated for her support of the Equal Rights Amendment; educators Amina Rahman and Betty Powell.

In 1976, we started small. At our first seder, thirteen of us sat in a circle at Phyllis Chesler's apartment and introduced ourselves as we would every year thereafter, by our matrilineage: "I am Letty, daughter of Ceil, who was the daughter of Jenny." (Few of us could name a woman who predated our grandmothers.) Esther asked us who our *real* mothers are, who comforts and nurtures us now? One woman said Martha Graham, the dancer, mothered her goals; another credited her art teacher; I named my husband, Bert, realizing quite suddenly that his unconditional love had replaced my mother's. Then we recited the Ten Plagues, *our* plagues, the afflictions of women: the plague of being unwanted daughters and taken-for-granted mothers, the plague of voices silenced and minds unused, the plagues of poverty, dependence, and discrimination, of rape and battery and sexual exploitation, of defamation and subordination and lost dreams. And we opened the door for the prophetess Miriam . . .

The second year we brought our daughters with us, and they would attend every seder from then on. Esther's daughter Nahama, then seventeen, my twins Abigail and Robin, who were almost twelve, and another little girl named Maya Helman went scurrying through the Broner loft with a feather and a candle, searching for *chametz*, which we burned together. In 1977, the mothers blessed the daughters. None of us could have known that a dozen years later, these young girls would bless us with a seder of their own.

My notes for the seder of 1978 remind me of how ambitious we were that year. We invited thirty-six women to fulfill our theme, which drew upon the ancient legend of the *lamed vavniks*. This legend holds that the world survives because of the deeds of thirty-six "just men" whose identity is God's secret. We asked each invitee to tell us about a "just woman" who might be a *lamed vavnik* for our age. They brought us stories of Ernestine Rose, Emma Goldman, Henrietta Szold, their mothers, aunts, and colleagues.

Also at this seder, we gave the *afikoman* a new meaning. "We spoke of that breaking of the matzah as a breaking in our own tradition, the hiding of our past from ourselves, the need to redeem it, to create a whole from the broken halves," remembers Esther. To ransom this stolen past would take many more seders and more than a silver dollar.

My 1979 seder list shows that Susan Brownmiller brought the sponge cake; Eve Merriam, gefilte fish; Gloria Steinem, kosher wine; and Bella Abzug, chicken. But I will always remember 1979 as the year of the veil. In response to the Ayatollah Khomeini's rise to power, Phyllis Chesler, our resident symbolist, brought us a *chador*, the head-and-body covering worn by Afghan women. The only opening in this heavy black garment was a small, tightly woven mesh window for the eyes. Each seder guest took a turn wearing the *chador*, felt the weight of its concealment, then each recalled those times when she was figuratively veiled, constricted, made carnal and ashamed. One woman put on the *chador* and found what we least expected: freedom. She said she felt liberated beneath the veil because men could not see her, touch her, evaluate and judge her. We wondered at women's dilemmas—to be hidden or harassed.

We began our 1980 seder by holding up our matzah and proclaiming: "This is the bread of affliction and poverty which our foremothers ate in Mitzraim (Egypt), and every place that has felt like Mitzraim."

The 1981 seder focused on our mentors, those who had influenced our development as women or as Jews. We brought photographs, artifacts, excerpts from their writings. We brought memories and gratitude.

Our seventh seder was a numerological feast. Each woman came with her Sevens: the seven-branch candelabrum, Seventh Heaven, the seven seas, deadly sins, lively arts. Some brought the biblical sevens—the seventh day when God rested; the seven weeks between Passover (liberation) and Shavuot (revelation). The seventh year is the sabbatical year when slaves must be freed and the land must lie fallow; the Jubilee year comes after seven-times-seven years; Jacob labored seven years to win Rachel, and seven more after he found Leah in his bed; tefillin is bound seven times around the arm.

Phyllis remembered Joseph's dream. She brought us seven ears of corn to get us through the lean years, the Reagan years.

During the seder of 1983, she wrapped us in a "sacred *shmatte*," a rope of knotted lavender scarves that symbolized our bond, our covenant with each other. It would soon be taken to Israel where it would be wound around Jewish, Christian, and Muslim women in an interfaith peace ceremony. (Five years later, at our Bat Mitzvah seder, Phyllis proposed to burn the sacred *shmatte* as a sign of our coming of age. Horrified, I plucked it from the fireplace. Symbols of women's power are too rare to be destroyed, I said, even for the right reasons. The sacred *shmatte* is a part of feminist history. It is still with us.)

For our ninth seder and in honor of the nine months of gestation, we returned to the theme of mothers and daughters. We invited more mother-daughter pairs, talked about daughters leading the mothers as Miriam led the way for Yocheved. That year, Phyllis brought tablecloths and bedspreads and we raised a tent over our heads to shelter mothers and daughters from the sandstorms of sexism.

The tenth was our outreach seder. Black women came from the Black-Jewish group of which several of us had been part (see chapter 14). Esther rewrote "Dayenu": "If women bonding, like Naomi and Ruth, were the tradition and not the exception, *dayenu*." And Phyllis rewrote the Ten Commandments: "IV. Love and cherish your mother and all men who are good to her."

1986 was a hard year for the Seder Mothers. There were misunderstandings, quarrels, betrayals. Would the seder survive? Could women rise above their hurt feelings? It would and we did. The theme for this, our eleventh seder, was "conflict resolution." The symbol Phyllis brought for us to pass from hand to hand was a stone, hard and cold, like the angry heart.

During the following year, several of us experienced the death of someone close: Bella's husband, Martin; Esther's father; my friend Toby who died of a brain tumor the year she turned fifty. So we dedicated our twelfth seder to "Loss and Continuity." As we wept, our daughters dipped their parsley into salt water and promised us a future.

In 1988, our thirteenth seder theme was "Coming of Age." Our Bat Mitzvah year was also the year Israel turned forty, entering middle age in the shadow of the *intifada*, the Palestinian uprising in the occupied territories. We worried about the Jewish soul. As a mark of our own maturity, the Seder Mothers decided we were ready to let go. Next year, the torch would pass to the daughters.

On April 23, 1989, the fourteenth annual feminist seder took place at the apartment that my daughters, Abigail and Robin, were then sharing on West 86th Street, three flights up. It felt strange to just show up with my pillow and a bottle of wine. After so many years encumbered by lists and chores, at last the Seder Mothers were carefree.

Everything had been taken care of by the daughters. Who could have imagined that those little girls tiptoeing around with their candles and feathers searching out *chametz* would so soon become these strong, self-assured, glowing young women who now welcomed us to their seder? Yet, here they were instructing us: this year a beaker of whisky would represent women's *chametz*, the stuff we have to get rid of before we can "pass over" into freedom. Along with our customary introductions ("I am Robin, daughter of Letty, daughter of Ceil, daughter of Jenny") each woman was to name her *chametz* and pour some whisky from the beaker into a large pan to get rid of it.

"My *chametz* is shyness," said one woman.

"My *chametz* is loneliness," said another.

And the list grew and the whisky flowed: Jealousy. Hurtful gossip. Obsession with body image. Passivity. Fear of failure. Addiction to pleasing men. When the pan was full, Robin put a match to it and set the liquid ablaze, burning the detritus of femininity.

Then we could begin. Laurie said kiddush in English, Michal, a young rabbinical student said it in Hebrew. Naomi asked the Four Questions from the Haggadah, then all the daughters posed questions to the "elders": What do you want to pass on, and what don't you want us to inherit? Are you ready to let go, not just of the responsibility, but of the power? Will you let the daughters be Jews and feminists in their own way?

The young women worried that passing it on meant we were giving it up. They worried that they might not do justice to our legacy; that they would just glide along on the road we paved for them. They felt guilty about being feminists for themselves but not in the context of a movement. They wanted to know: Could they keep their mother's traditions and also change them? At what point does feminist orthodoxy become as oppressive as any other orthothoxy? Could we have an ongoing dialogue between the generations instead of a linear lesson? Mothers who are good role models also are a tough act to follow. We made them strong, now would we set them free?

Naomi broke the middle matzah for the *afikoman*: "What is broken with questions will be made whole when we have the answers."

A question was posed to everyone: Which one are you: Sarah, the self-abnegating wife, Miriam, the smart but unheralded daughter, or Deborah, the fearless leader? Which one are you?

Immediately, controversy raged: "Biblical models are too limiting." "My mother is a Sarah; I can't reject Sarah without rejecting *her*." "Why does a Deborah have to end up alone?" "We all have in us parts of all three women." "Let's synthesize them." "Let's create new paradigms." "Let's continue the seder," said Robin, and we poured the third cup of wine.

Michal talked about the traditional meaning of three of the symbols on the seder plate—matzah, *maror* (bitter herbs), and *pesach* (shank bone). Then we discussed women's equivalents. For the matzah, Nahama held sand, a reminder that we are still in our desert. For the shank bone Robin held a key, symbol of separation and connection; even independent daughters have the key to their mother's door. To symbolize women's bitter herbs, Abigail brought out a wire hanger (a reminder of death from illegal abortion) from which she had hung a toy soldier, a hair curler, a pot scrubber, a 59¢ coin (then the wage gap per dollar between women and men), a TV remote control (our enslavement to media), and pictures of Vice President Dan Quayle (a political adversary) and convicted murderer and batterer Joel Steinberg. The mothers stared. Those were our pharaohs. That was our Egypt. All this we do not pass on.

After communal hand washing, *haroset*, hard-boiled eggs, and a fine meal, it was time for closure. "We have broken the *afikoman* with the daughters' questions and now we choose to restore it with the mothers' answers," said Nahama. "We ask you to help us make it whole again."

But the mothers had no answers. And that, I believe, was our legacy. We said they must find their own answers. We told them to never stop asking questions. We told them that we do not have it all figured out; we only appear more secure because we made our revolution together, with passion and anger. That was our way; they would find theirs.

The truth is, I do have one answer for them: Just as Jews are instructed to remember slavery as if it had happened to each one of us, daughters should remember their mothers' oppression—that wire hanger with its grotesque symbols—as if it had happened to them. Because it could happen to them. Women's Exodus is not complete. Our Sinai is still to come.

8

A Bat Mitzvah Sermon

IN 1987, MY NIECE AMY ASKED ME TO DELIVER THE SERMON AT HER Bat Mitzvah. I had attended many such ceremonies, but this was the first time I would be directly involved in one since my own Bat Mitzvah thirty-five years before.

More than when I learned to drive, more than my first sexual experience, more than going away to college, my Bat Mitzvah was my most intoxicating rite of passage. It was a conscious farewell address to childhood and I was wearing a black velvet dress—the first time my superstitious mother had let me wear black. How clearly I can recall the ecstasy of standing before the whole congregation and reciting my haftarah, a portion from the Prophets, then delivering the speech I had written describing my continuing commitment to Jewish life and my gratitude for my parents' love.

Now I looked forward to my niece's moment in the sun. Yet when it came time to write the sermon, I found myself laboring over every line and spending twice as much time on the research as I would for the toughest article assignment. It became evident that the problem was emotional, not literary. Beneath my initial pride at being asked, and beyond the aroused nostalgia for my youth, was a poignant subtext of regret: I should have done this for my own children.

Since my husband had no religious training, it had been up to me to establish the standard of Jewish practice expected of our kids. But in the 1970s, as Abigail, Robin, and David each approached the age of thirteen, I was involved in the Women's Movement and was still grappling with the demons of Jewish ambivalence.

I did offer the children the opportunity to go to Hebrew school, but my invitation was desultory and lackluster, like a casual "Let's have lunch one of these days"—the right thing to say, yet patently insincere. All three refused my offer, contenting themselves with the vicarious pleasures of their friends' Bar or Bat Mitzvah celebrations. For them, giving up a day in the spotlight and a party with lots of presents was easier than electing years of Hebrew study. And for me, letting the demons rage inside me was easier than negotiating a public settlement. We all took the easy way out, and they missed their official initiation into Jewish life.

My children *felt* Jewish but had little sense of being part of a historical constituency. Apart from my lighting Shabbat candles and observing the major holidays at home and in our ad hoc Fire Island congregation, they were strangers to religious services. We belonged to no synagogue then, they attended no Hebrew school, and their roots in the Jewish past went only as deep as my impromptu holiday narratives and homegrown rituals. So their adolescence came and went without my having to confront religious sexism and patriarchal Scriptures on my children's behalf. I finessed the whole problem by opting out.

Like many of my antireligion decisions, I have come to view this as a grievous error of judgment. Because I had a feminist axe to grind, I cheated my children out of a Jewish education and allowed them to reject a rite of tribal inclusion whose significance they were not equipped to evaluate. I denied them the capacity to make their own choices *and* the tools to fight religious sexism with the best weapon of all: knowledge.

Now in their twenties, all three of them are casualties of my rebellion. Yes, they are relatively unscathed by Jewish sexism, but they are paying for my commitment to their pain-free nonreligious childhoods with the shallowness of their ethnic foundations. Both Robin and Abigail seemed to compensate for this by taking college courses in theology, Hebrew, Jewish literature, and history. David, who was grateful to be at liberty when his friends were receiving Bar Mitzvah tutoring after school, has wondered aloud whether he should have been among them. At least he would have had a deeper grounding in his faith and could make his own decision about what to embrace or reject.

In addition to nostalgia, regrets, and second thoughts, I brought to my sermon assignment strong feelings about my niece, who'd had a difficult and complicated childhood. Hearing impaired since birth, she had been mainstreamed in school and had struggled valiantly to keep up. Her parents were divorced when she was a baby. Since then, she had shuttled between their two homes. Shortly before her Bat Mitzvah, her mother had given birth to a baby girl as a single parent. Her father had remarried a woman with two teenage boys. Through it all Amy showed a cheerful sense of humor and a gutsy spirit of accommodation.

In my sermon, I wanted to say something that would acknowledge her strengths and inspire her to keep aiming high both as a woman and as a Jew. I decided to do what I had avoided doing with my own children—to opt *in*, to confront Judaism's male-supremacist bias while highlighting our unsung women heroes, to blend tradition and innovation. I wanted to write a new feminist message with an old Jewish pen.

As a matter of fact, I was going to write my sermon with a fountain pen—the marbleized black Scheaffer pen that my father had used since the 1930s. To look at the pen now, etched with his name, is to see it in my father's grip, his thick fingers with their neatly manicured nails executing what he called "chicken-scratch penmanship" as he wrote my Bat Mitzvah homework assignments on his yellow legal pads.

When my father died I inherited this fountain pen, and I've tried to use it several times, most recently in the writing of Amy's sermon. I thought it might call up his presence as I remembered him training me for Bat Mitzvah—the only time in my life when I had his company night after night. I thought it might create some mystical link between his authority as my teacher and mine as Amy's. I wanted to think of it as a scepter passed from him to me, along with the right to impart this sacred ritual. I filled it full of ink but after a word or two the point ran dry.

I wrote the sermon on my computer. Still, the idea of the pen stayed with me in echoes of that quintessential Bar Mitzvah joke, "Today I am a fountain pen," which derives from both the number of fountain pens boys once received as gifts and the portentous rabbinic send-off, "Today you are a man."

On July 11, 1987, at Congregation Rodeph Shalom in Denver, Colorado, I told Amy, "Today you are a woman."

It was as if I had uttered a forbidden incantation while trespassing on hallowed ground. When a boy is Bar Mitzvah'd, we speak to him in the tone I had just used, a life-cycle–landmark tone that conveys the profundity of what is happening. The "son of the commandment" is presented with a tallit and a set of tefillin, for from this day forth he will be counted in the minyan and will assume the obligations of an adult male in the Jewish community. No longer is his father responsible for his transgressions; now, he must answer for himself. He has become "a man"—a person in his own right.

For a boy, the Bar Mitzvah is both a holy and a holistic experience. It establishes his place in the sanctum of Jewish prayer and in the march of Jewish history. It formalizes his bond with his forefathers. No matter which reading from the Torah or haftarah falls on the Sabbath of his Bar Mitzvah, the excerpt invariably recounts the exploits of men. Looking around the synagogue, the boy sees the rabbi, the cantor, the president of the shul, in most cases, all men. Also, those called to the Torah for an aliyah, those given the honor of opening the Ark, those who hold the Torah, remove its crown and velvet mantle, unroll the scrolls; those asked to read it, carry it up and down the aisles, and then hold it up high in the posture of Moses—most if not all of these "stars" are males, his own kind. No wonder, then, that when a boy hears "Today you are a man," he has a clear image of what it means to be a man and to count in the Jewish community.

Not so for girls. While the Bar Mitzvah ceremony is more than six centuries old, there was no comparable female ritual until 1922 when Rabbi Mordecai Kaplan, the founder of the Reconstructionist Movement, conducted the Bat Mitzvah of his daughter Judith. Reform congregations soon followed suit, and the Conservative branch came around in the early Fifties in time for me to have my night on the *bimah* in February of 1952 when I was twelve. (Today Conservative and Reform congregations perform the Bat Mitzvah ritual when girls are either twelve or thirteen years old.) The Orthodox moved the proposition forward with the alacrity of the ice age, devoting years to internecine disputation—the ultra-Orthodox accusing the modern Orthodox of "licentiousness" and "aping the Gentiles" for simply advocating tame, restricted forms of Bat Mitzvah such as a celebration in the home—until finally in 1982, Rabbi Yaakov Yehiel Weinberg, a leading Talmudic authority, issued what is perhaps his most famous *teshuvah* (ruling): Discrimination against girls has no basis in the law. Moreover, it's bad for the Jews.

"In the past it was not necessary to give girls a Jewish education; every Jewish home was filled with Torah and reverence for God," said Rabbi Weinberg. "But an immense change has taken place in our time; the influence of the street removes from the hearts of boys and girls the enthusiastic attachment to Judaism."

Bottom line: the Bat Mitzvah is now sort of acceptable in many American Orthodox congregations.

Meanwhile, acceptance of the Bat Mitzvah in Reform and Conservative Judaism did not automatically bring about equality in related religious matters, such as the right to put on the tallit or tefillin, count in the minyan, say a "legitimate" Kaddish, or perform the honorary roles in the service. Nor did it assure girls equal access to the sanctuary.

In 1987, my niece Amy's Bat Mitzvah was part of the Saturday morning service, but when I was growing up, Saturday belonged to the boys. Bat Mitzvah girls were assigned to Friday evenings when the crowd was usually smaller and there was no added attraction of a Torah reading. (Maybe this was a blessing, since most of the Scriptures are so oppressively male-dominated, so focused on male heroism and male begat-ing.) I was pleased that Amy's haftarah, from the Book of Micah, included that simple, eloquent formula "to do justice, and to love mercy, and to walk humbly with thy God."

At my Bat Mitzvah, great good luck dealt me as my haftarah the story of Deborah—prophetess, military commander, and the only woman among the Bible's thirteen Judges. The Torah portion for that week from Exodus described the parting of the Red Sea including the lines about Miriam leading the women to freedom. Miriam and Deborah on my Bat Mitzvah Sabbath day. The two most autonomous women in the Bible. God was telling me something.

The Bible describes Deborah as a "a mother in Israel . . . a prophetess; she led Israel at that time"—which was about 1200 B.C.E. Scholars say she functioned as a chieftain or queen and exercised her power with the consent of the governed. (The word Deborah means "bee," which was also the title for priests of the period.) Deborah dispensed justice from under a palm tree in the hill country of Ephraim and says the Bible, "the Israelites would come to her for decisions," including halachic decisions. Although it was not uncommon for religious mystics to sit under trees, some have said Deborah did her adjudicating outdoors because it was unseemly for men to visit a woman in her house. Nevertheless, there is no small irony in the fact that the biblical Deborah could be a revered ruler and judge, while in our time a woman cannot even be a witness in a religious court case because rabbinic law accords adult females the same legal status as children, deaf-mutes, and idiots.

In the thirty-one centuries between Deborah and Golda Meir, Israel had only one other woman ruler, Queen Shlomzion, who inherited leadership from her brother. Her reign lasted for nine years during the time of the Second Temple and the tempestuous religious feuds between the Pharisees and the Sadducees. But Deborah was not just a ruler, judge, priestess, and prophetess, she also was the Bible's only woman military commander. (More than three thousand years would pass before the people of Israel had another woman general, Amira Dotan, promoted to that rank in 1986.) Commander Deborah led the Israelites in a battle against the Canaanites that was as important to Jewish unity and as decisive in Jewish history as Joshua's battle of Jericho or the Maccabees' revolt.

Deborah ordered a warrior named Barak to organize a resistance force against the huge Canaanite army and its brutal general, Sisera, although she warned Barak, "There will be no glory for you . . . for the Lord will deliver Sisera into the hands of a woman." Barak had such confidence in Deborah's ability to motivate the vastly outnumbered and disorganized Jewish tribes that he refused to proceed to battle without her.

"If you will go with me, I will go. But if you will not go with me, I will not go," said Barak, in an extraordinary gesture of male deference. Deborah went, and the Israelite forces overpowered the Canaanites, sending the exhausted General Sisera slinking off to take refuge in the tent of a Kenite woman named Yael. It was Yael who gained Sisera's trust, gave him warm milk, covered him with a blanket, and then killed him as he slept—rather grotesquely at that—by hammering a tent spike into his head, thus fulfilling Deborah's prophecy that he would die at a woman's hand.

Modest for herself, the remarkable Deborah praised God and paid tribute to Yael in a song that has been described by many commentators as the oldest and most glorious verse in Hebrew literature, although Rabbi Adin Steinsaltz notes that it also is "one of the most bloodthirsty." Extraordinary too is the notice Deborah's song pays to the suffering of Sisera's mother, who is described peering through her window and worrying about her son who is late returning from the battle. Deborah remembers that even our enemies have mothers.

After the Israelite victory, Deborah returned to her palm tree to counsel her people and preside over forty years of peace.

I find great symbolism in coincidences. Having Deborah be the subject of my haftarah in the thirteenth year of my life is too fortuitous an accident to ignore. In retrospect, when I trace the origins of my feminism, I give this event mystical weight. But back in 1952, nobody suggested that I could *be* a Deborah. And certainly no one told me, "Today you are a woman."

In those days, to say a girl had become a woman would have meant only one thing: her body was ready to reproduce. Unlike the male's rite of passage, a female's coming of age did not signal her transformation into an autonomous adult. It meant becoming biologically fertile, which was unmentionable, or it meant becoming marriageable, which Jewish-American thirteen-year-olds were not. By definition then, a Bat Mitzvah girl could not be called a woman. Instead, her coming of age marked the beginning of the Era of Waiting— waiting to grow up, waiting to be noticed, waiting to become a wife, make a Jewish home and stay in it with her children.

In my day, womanhood *was* motherhood. Nobody wanted a daughter to become a judge, a prophet, or a conqueror. Heaven forbid. But that is what I wanted for my niece. When I told her, "Today you are a woman," I had in mind a fuller kind of womanhood—an activist womanhood, which I illustrated with several precedents from the sweep of Jewish *her*story.

I told Amy about Deborah, my personal favorite, and then I went on to distill the best message I could from the lives of other biblical women. It wasn't easy. Many of these women achieved their fame by virtue of being the wives or mothers of famous men, or by conniving, falsifying, manipulating others and exploiting their sexuality. Still, given their options—given the utter powerlessness and invisibility of all women of the time, not just the Israelites—many of these women were remarkable for having believed they could have *any* impact on events, and then indeed, for leaving their mark on history.

Because Esther is the name of one of Amy's grandmothers, I wanted her to know about Esther, the Jewish queen of Persia. But I also wanted Amy to know that Esther became queen because her predecessor, Vashti, refused the order of her husband, King Ahasuerus, to dance naked before his court. The king, in his cups after a seven-day banquet, was incensed. His advisers persuaded him to have Vashti banished, for fear that her insubordination would infect the other women in the court. After issuing a directive that "all wives will treat their husbands with respect . . . [and] every man should wield authority in his home," the king called for a bevy of virgins from which to choose a new wife.

The winner was Esther, who did not reveal that she was a Hebrew. (Oddly enough, the Jews of the time did not seem to object to this intermarriage.) Once installed as queen, she was able to save her people from the wicked anti-Semite Haman, the royal adviser who had convinced King Ahasuerus that Jews were dangerous subversives. When Esther learned of Haman's plan to exterminate her people, she ignored the rule that wives must not bother their husbands or interfere in state business and she successfully petitioned the king to revoke Haman's evil decree and to have the madman killed.

On the festival of Purim, when Jews read Esther's story, we celebrate not only the survival of our ancestors but the assertiveness of their queen.

Amy's other grandmother, Leah, bears the name of one of the four matriarchs of Israel. The matriarchs—Sarah, Rebecca, Rachel, and Leah—are a problem for many feminists. Some dismiss the young Sarah as a passive beauty who let herself be "pimped" by her husband Abraham to save his life, and the older Sarah as a nagging wife and cruel mistress of Hagar; others see Sarah as a priestess.

Rebecca, on the one hand, was a deceitful woman who plotted to gain for her favored son, Jacob, what rightfully belonged to his brother, Esau. On the other hand, more positive interpretations point out, she was the first woman to be asked to consent to her own arranged marriage and the only matriarch to whom God speaks directly.

The verdict is no less complicated on Rachel and Leah, sisters who between them bore Jacob eight of the twelve sons who founded the twelve tribes of Israel. (Their two maidservants gave birth to the other four sons as part of the sisters' can-you-top-this competition for birthing boys.) The fierce sibling rivalry between these two Jewish fore-mothers cannot help but poison our view of their characters. Each was consumed by envy of what the other had: Leah envied Rachel for being beautiful and deeply beloved by Jacob, while the barren Rachel envied the homely, "weak-eyed," and unloved Leah for being effort-lessly fertile. Despite these faults, admirers of Rachel praise her beauty and self-sacrifice (and excuse her penchant for keeping idols) while Leah's fans laud her piety and forbearance.

I wanted my niece to winnow out the best of the matriarchs' leg-acies while disavowing their jealousy, duplicity, and relentless need to affirm themselves through childbearing. I wanted Amy to understand the matriarchs as prisoners of their own time, and to remember that their stories have come down to us filtered through male storytellers and male sensibilities.

"We don't have to accept men's version as the whole truth," I told her. "We can dig beneath the text to find the real story and try to understand the social forces that made such women act as they did."

Judith was another meaningful name to my niece. Judith Kaplan, the birth name of her own mother, also happens to be the name of the first Bat Mitzvah girl in America. But I also wanted Amy to know about another Judith—the one you'll recall from the Hanukkah leg-end whose Lady Godiva act inspired the Maccabean revolt, who is also said to be the Judith who saved the Jews of Bethulia from Holof-ernes, a Greek general whose army was trying to force them to sur-render and live as Greeks. This Judith of the Apocrypha insisted the Jews hold out while she hatched a plan as elaborate as a James Bond mystery. She infiltrated the general's quarters, concocted a diversion-ary story, got him drunk, and when he fell asleep, cut off his head with his own sword. Upon discovering the murder of their leader, the Greeks panicked and the Jews were able to recapture the city. When Judith's grateful people offered her the enemy's spoils, she dedicated the bounty to God and to the poor.

"May you grow up to be, not as violent as this Judith, but as clever and as generous," I told Amy:

And while you consider the small but brave pantheon of biblical wom-anhood, remember that these women were disabled by the powerless-ness of their gender. They were handicapped by the stigma of being Hebrews. They were held back by slavery, ignorance, historical invis-

ibility, or incessant childbearing—and still their lives mattered, your
heritage to claim at will.

It was important to me that Amy have Jewish female role models for
social protest, so I told her about Shiphrah and Puah, the midwives
who risked their lives by disregarding Pharoah's order to kill all the
Hebrews' boy babies, and about Miriam, the best of those splendid
disobedient ones, and about Ruth, a Moabite whose devotion to her
mother-in-law, Naomi, set a standard of loyalty unmatched in most
families to this day. Most of us know Ruth's famous vow to Naomi:
"Whither thou goest, I will go" (notice how it resonates with Barak's
lines about following Deborah into battle). Ruth's unique woman-to-
woman commitment inspired one of the few *female* supremacist statements in the Bible when the Israelite women tell Naomi, "Your
daughter-in-law who loves you ... has proved better to you than
seven sons." But we forget that Ruth went on to say, "Thy people
shall be my people, and thy God my God." If today's ultra-Orthodox
rabbis succeed in redefining Who Is a Jew, this loyal "convert" would
not qualify as a Jew or a citizen of Israel, and neither would her
great-grandson—King David.

Speaking of our glorious disobedient foremothers, I reminded Amy
that King David's first wife, Michal, defied her father, the mad King
Saul, in order to save her husband's life during his early years. Yet
most of the world knows Michal's brother Jonathan as David's only
ally—honoring male friendship but taking a wife's loyalty for granted.

For all the wisdom of Miriam, Ruth, and Michal, I wanted Amy to
look beyond sisters, daughters-in-law, and wives, to find her paradigms for Jewish womanhood not just in the family but in the public
sphere. So I told her about the revered prophetess Huldah, whose
advice was sought by the top emissaries of Josiah, King of Judah,
when he was trying to determine the validity of a scroll discovered
during renovations in the Temple. Huldah identified the scroll we
now know as Deuteronomy, the fifth book of the Bible, and she
instructed the people about God's will, wrath, and mercy. Or one of
the many *anonymous* women identified by the names of their fathers
or husbands, whose achievements are mentioned only in passing; for
instance, the nameless woman who prospered after the prophet Elisha
set her up in the oil business; the daughters of Shallum who were
among the stonemasons who rebuilt the walls of Jerusalem; or the five

daughters of Zelophehad—the first women who ever demanded their property rights when their father's inheritance was distributed to others just because he had no sons. Their request led to a new law, the first quasi-feminist legislation: "If a man die, and have no son, then ye shall cause his inheritance to pass unto his daughter." To this day, however, Jewish women do not inherit equally when there are living male heirs.

Glorious as it is, the Bible has its limits when it comes to the feminine ideal. So I gathered minibiographies and combed recent history for some role models from other eras. For instance, the third-century scholar Beruriah—the only woman whose halachic teachings are reported in the Talmud. Dona Gracia, sixteenth-century business-woman, patron of the arts, benefactor of the city of Tiberias, and rescuer of Jewish victims of the Inquisition. Gluckel of Hamelin, married at fourteen, mother of thirteen children, writer of memoirs, Yiddish stories, and parables that acknowledge women's contributions; well read, well traveled (especially for a Jewish woman of the seventeenth century), and a partner in her husband's gold business. Penina Moise, born in 1797 in Charleston, South Carolina, a popular Southern poet and the first Jew of either sex to publish poetry in America. Rebecca Gratz, who established the Hebrew Sunday School Society, making Jewish education available to all. Ernestine Rose, the ardent abolitionist and women's rights leader of the nineteenth century. Lillian Wald, who organized the settlement house movement.

I wanted Amy to know about labor leaders like Rose Pasoda of the ILGWU; or Clara Lemlich, who led the first successful large-scale strike in the garment industry; or Rose Schneiderman, who organized the Triangle Shirtwaist Factory workers. Henrietta Szold, the founder of Hadassah, who was the first woman student at the Jewish Theological Seminary. Rachel Bluwstein, the Russian emigré who went to Palestine to work as a laborer and, using only the name Rachel, wrote luminous Hebrew poetry extolling the Zionist vision. Emma Goldman, the anarchist and pacifist, a true daughter of Miriam. (It was Emma who said, "If there's no dancing, it is not my revolution.") Nadine Gordimer, the white South African anti-apartheid writer. And Golda Meir, the founding mother of the State of Israel and later its prime minister—often called "the girl who made Milwaukee famous." (A recent ad for Bank Leumi was headlined DISOBEDIENT MILWAUKEE GIRL MAKES GOOD.) If Golda had not been a rebellious kid who ran away from home, there might not be an Israel.

In a kind of fast-forward, I ended my litany with a list of contemporary American Jewish trailblazers: Dorothy Schiff, the newspaper publisher; Rosalind Franklin, the molecular physicist who helped unravel the structure of DNA; the poet Adrienne Rich; Judith Resnick, the martyred astronaut; Beverly Sills, the opera star; actress-producers Barbra Streisand, Goldie Hawn, and Bette Midler; Rosalyn Yalow, the Nobel Prize-winner; Louise Nevelson, the sculptor; Helena Rubinstein and Estee Lauder, who made their fortunes in the beauty business; Liz Claiborne and Diane von Furstenberg, designers and entrepreneurs, and a passel of activist women rabbis and cantors who continue to fight for women's rights and dignity.

While doing research for my sermon, I read my list of biblical and historical women to some of my best-educated Jewish friends. Except for the most well-known current personalities, surprisingly few names were recognizable to them. For a people whose ethos, whose very identity, is founded in *remembering*, we have forgotten too much about Jewish women. For a community that calls itself "the people of the book," we have left too many pages blank. The Jewish educational establishment has left us ignorant of Jewish women's past. Writers and historians have underdocumented our women's achievements. The Jewish press has not done justice to women, with the exception perhaps of our actresses and organizational superstars.

Recognizing the importance of memory and documentation, the historian Simon Dubnov commanded on his deathbed: "Jews, remember! Jews, write!" He feared that the record of the Holocaust would be blotted out. We have already witnessed the record of Jewish women blotted out, for the politics of memory are sexual politics and the writers of books are not equal-opportunity historians; they cycle in an orbit of self-perpetuation. The group entrusted with history-making remembers itself. Those who keep the books determine who is authorized to write in them and what is worth writing about. Authority means being the author of one's own reality as it is recorded for posterity. Remembering is not a neutral act.

"We do not remember objectively, from no standpoint at all," writes another historian, Michael L. Morgan of Indiana University:

> *Rather we remember subjectively, from a particular point of view. . . . Hence, memory depends upon, and valuably reinforces, the identity of the rememberer. . . . By remembering we both acknowledge*

*that we are continuing subjects and we add content to who that
subject is.*

Selective memory benefits certain groups, elevating their experience
above others and calling it our "heritage." Until now, it is men who
have established the common mythology and decided who is in,
who is out; who shall people our visions and who shall remain
unseen.

Writing the Bat Mitzvah sermon made me reconsider my own Jewish schooling, which included ten years in afternoon Hebrew school,
from kindergarten through Hebrew high school graduation, and two
years at the Yeshiva of Central Queens. In total, "they"—the keepers
of memory, the transmitters of history—had me as a student for
twelve years and in all that time they taught me about fewer than a
dozen Jewish women; barely one woman per year of study. A disgrace. A *shonda.*

Why was I allowed to believe that the history of an elite group of
men was the history of the entire Jewish people? How could my
teachers have dared to give me such a one-sided view of my religious and cultural legacy? How could adults teach children about
"Jews" as if Jewish women had never existed? Our sages paid careful attention to *naming,* to maintaining those long lists of man-to-
man begats—as if babies came from the thigh, the rib, the head of
man. If the "sages" were so smart, why didn't they think to ask
who the women were and what they were doing while the men were
chronicling their own achievements? I question whether any man
ought to be called a great thinker if the other half of the Jewish
people slips his mind.

Ellen Umansky, professor of religion and modern Jewish thought,
saw on the wall in a synagogue in Atlanta a time line charting Jewish
historical figures from Abraham to Ben Gurion, and *not one* was a
woman. When she attended a recent American Academy of Religion
convention, Umansky picked up a Macmillan Publishing Company
promotion piece announcing an upcoming multivolume *Encyclopedia
of Religion.* She checked the Table of Contents to see what Judaica
would be included. Of one hundred Jewish personages deemed worthy of biographical treatment, *not one* was a woman. At Umansky's
urging, Macmillan agreed to include Henrietta Szold; Lilly Montague,
founder of Liberal (Reform) Judaism in England, who had her own

congregation for sixty years; and Sarah Shenera, founder of the Bais Yakov movement which educates Orthodox girls.

Michael Morgan writes: "It is one of the central tasks of Jewish thought or theology to confront and justify the recovery of the past for the present." Confronting and justifying the recovery of Jewish women's past is long overdue. Women's past is part of the *Jewish* past. Or put another way, the omission of women's past makes Jewish history false history, and as Hebrew University Professor Yehuda Bauer points out, "False history establishes false consciousness and creates false myths."

The most outrageous false myth in Judaism is that women were not doing anything important. By whose definition? Even if most women were denied the opportunity of study, prayer, leadership, and conquest, that doesn't mean they were not *being Jews*. Their spirituality and religiosity found expression in ways that kept them and their children affirmatively Jewish in every imaginable alien culture. They were doing hard work, vital work—God's work—creating Jewish life and nourishing Jewish families. If women had written the Bible, we would know about *that* work, and *that* work would be deemed "important." Even without the male standard of importance, where is the bare-bones record of women's existence from generation to generation? Where is women's Bible? Who decided that everything female was unimportant, even our names?

We may not be able to give names to the wives-of and daughters-of and other anonymous women who flit like shadows across the pages of the written record, but, as I have noted, Jewish feminist scholars are trying to undo the damage on behalf of some women who have escaped invisibility. We must insist that the fruits of such research filter down to our young people, and that teachers make a particular effort to sift women's reality from the cast-off crumbs of memory and literature, and help young women like my niece to find sustenance in the gleanings.

My sermon was one such attempt. I asked Amy to take energy from the spirit of all those women who struggled and triumphed before her, and to view herself as their direct descendant. I concluded with these words:

You come from a tribe of feisty foremothers. It's up to you to walk in their footsteps and continue their journey. On the occasion of your

Bat Mitzvah I give you the bright, hope-filled guarantee that from now on anything is possible. And everything is possible, Amy, because today you are a woman.

Mazel tov, *and God bless you.*

My daughters could not fly out to Colorado for the Bat Mitzvah, but I gave them my text to read. The truth is, I had written it for them as well as for Amy. I owed it to them. My son might feel cheated of a Bar Mitzvah, but at least he can say he followed his father's example because Bert also missed out. But my daughters have the sad distinction of having been denied by their mother what she had herself. That I reversed the age-old tradition of Jewish parenthood by giving my children *less*, not more, than I enjoyed as a child, fills me with shame. That women of all ages (even a ninety-year-old) have taken great pains to become Bat Mitzvah'd to remedy a loss dictated by past exclusions, while I elected to deny Robin and Abigail what was theirs by right, leaves me sick with regret. It is no comfort to recall that, at the time, I believed I was sparing them the humiliation and rage I had experienced in Judaism. The principles were mine; the loss is theirs.

I wish I had written a sermon like this while my daughters were young enough to learn from it. I wish I had sent them to Hebrew school. I wish I had discovered my current synthesis of ritual and revisionism early enough to fuel their growing identities as Jewish women. But none of us can relive our children's childhoods. I can only hope that when they are parents, they will revert to the tradition of giving their children what they did not have themselves. Maybe then, there will be some Bar Mitzvot and Bat Mitzvot in my future.

PART THREE

Golda

Searching for a Secular Self

9

When You're Okay the Whole World's Jewish

STRIP AWAY THE DEBORAH PART OF ME—THE SPIRITUAL SELF WHO has been at center stage in the previous five chapters—and what remains is a writer and activist who lives most of her life in the secular world. I think of this self as my Golda part, not because Golda Meir was a feminist (which she clearly was not), but because she was a highly political woman and a Jew whose strengths and failures have helped me clarify my own identity.

Oddly enough, what happened to give new shape to my secular identity was strikingly similar to what caused the shake-up in my spiritual life in that both changes were precipitated by an event with feminist connotations: In the spiritual sphere, it was my rejection from the minyan; in the secular world, it was a confrontation with anti-Semitism in the Women's Movement.

Both transformations have something else in common: they inspired private journeys whose public expression would not have registered on the casual observer. There were no outward signs of struggle. During my fifteen-year hiatus from the Jewish religious "we," I still gave the appearance of a self-identified Jew because I went to synagogue twice a year and observed the major holidays at home. You would have had to know my history to understand what an amputation twice a year represented. You would have had to read my mind to know my anger and alienation. I looked, as one friend put it, "Jewish enough"; only I knew how disconnected I felt.

Likewise, until other people's hostility propelled me into Jewish secular consciousness, you would not have known that I did not feel like a Jew in the world. I didn't know it myself. Until my brush with anti-Semitism, being Jewish was something I took absolutely for granted, something so intrinsically *me* that I never gave it a second thought. Comfort had given rise to unconsciousness. I felt so at home in America as a Jew that I was able to concentrate on feeling displaced in America as a *woman*. I had the "luxury" of ignoring my ethnic self.

But comfort and luxury disappear when Jews are under attack. The anti-Semites remind you of who you are. Adrienne Rich writes that "to be able to ask even the child's astonished question *Why do they hate us so?* means knowing how to say 'we.' " But to give the "we" meaning beyond the things "they" hate us for, Jews must choose our Jewish identity knowledgeably, affirmatively, and publicly in the secular world. Today, I describe myself as an American feminist who tries to function with the moral and ethical consciousness of a Jew. But this sentence was a long time in the making.

Growing up in Jamaica, New York, I didn't think about being Jewish because I didn't have to. For me and my friends at Public School 131, or at the yeshiva or at Hebrew school, being Jewish was just another word for being ourselves. We were Jewish the way we were nine or twelve years old; we just were. As for the adults, religiosity didn't make them Jewish—something in their personalities gave them pungency and flavor. They were self-mocking, effusive, and argumentative. They had the keen eyes of the outsider and the workhorse hearts of perennial survivors. They filled my head with irony and one-liners.

In my life, *everyone* seemed to be Jewish except for my best friend Sue who lived across the street, the cops on the beat, and our pleasant Catholic neighbors who tacked Christmas wreaths to their doors but were careful to wish us "Happy Hanukkah." Only in retrospect do I recall how rare was a house without a wreath. At Halsey Junior High School in Rego Park, where I was bussed to a class for gifted children (no one ever objected to that sort of bussing), and later at Jamaica High School, whose district covered a wide range of neighborhoods, there must have been hundreds, even thousands, of Gentile students, but I never felt outnumbered, and those who became my friends never made me feel in the least bit conscious of my Jewishness.

Unless there were anti-Semitic vandals in her neighborhood or kids who refused to play with her, what would make a little girl think twice about her "identity"? Why question what it means to be a Jew if you can just *be* one?

In *The Counterlife*, Philip Roth's quintessential novel of Jewish-American identity conflict, the main character writes a letter to his brother in South Orange, New Jersey, that captures the significance of being mindlessly Jewish in America:

> *It may be that by flourishing mundanely in the civility and security of South Orange, more or less forgetful from one day to the next of your Jewish origins but remaining identifiably (and voluntarily) a Jew, you were making Jewish history.*

I suppose it was a sort of milestone for Jewish children to feel *that* comfortable in a Gentile land. But I wasn't thinking about history; I was "flourishing mundanely" until the spring of my junior year when my mother's cancer killed her. My sister Betty and her husband Bernie, who had four children under the age of seven, decided that I should accelerate my schooling and promptly go away to college where I could live in a supervised dormitory rather than come home to an empty house. A school dormitory was preferable to life with Father or rather life without Father, which was more likely.

Jamaica High didn't have much of a college counseling program and no one in my family seemed to care which school I chose. Had my mother lived, she might have insisted that I stay close to home, probably go to Queens College which was twenty minutes away and happened to be the school where Betty met Bernie. Now it was up to me. I picked Brandeis University, which had been founded seven years before (the same year as the state of Israel) by Jewish refugees who did not have an alma mater of their own. My father applauded my choice but I didn't choose Brandeis for him, I selected it because of my mother. From the school's inception, she had been a member of the Brandeis Women's Committee, a volunteer group that took responsibility for filling the shelves of the college library, and in this capacity she'd been receiving Brandeis newsletters which I had studied like someone who pores over travel brochures long before she qualifies for vacation time. I was seduced by those mailings. The spanking-new buildings, the stone castle, Bohemian-looking students in black turtlenecks with green book bags slung over their shoulders, and professors like Leonard Bernstein, Max Lerner, and Herbert Marcuse made the campus irresistible.

By 1955 Brandeis already had a superb academic reputation, and when the university accepted me at sixteen I was happier than if I had been recruited by Harvard or Yale. I loved being the youngest student at the youngest university in the country. It also happened to be one of America's most ethnically unbalanced nonsectarian universities: about 85 percent of the students were Jews. I hadn't done it purposely but there I was again, comfortable and untouched by anti-Semitism. Although I dated a few Christian boys, mostly athletes, the major love interests of my college years were Jews and my women friends were Jews, and no one gave me cause to ponder the meaning of being a Jew in a Gentile society.

When you're okay the whole world seems Jewish. I'm not saying I was oblivious to the reality of our minuscule numbers, or the proliferation of anti-Semitism, or the overwhelmingly Christian cast to Western culture. It's just that this reality was academic; it had never affected me personally.

After graduation, I moved to an apartment in Greenwich Village—a haven for many Jewish intellectuals—and began a career in book publishing, a field which also seems to attract a disproportionate number of Jews. Actually, one could say the same about New York City in general; almost as many Jews live in the greater metropolitan area as in the state of Israel. In Manhattan most offices empty out on the eve of Yom Kippur, and during Passover, I've never felt self-conscious eating a matzah sandwich at work.

When I moved from the book business into magazine publishing in 1971, things changed slightly; at last I was working with some people who were Irish- or Italian-Catholics and white, Anglo-Saxon Protestants. Of the five women who founded *Ms.*, two of us were Jewish, two were Christian, and one was half-and-half, and as the staff size increased to about forty employees, my sense is that the 50:50 ratio held firm at the magazine for the seventeen years I was there. All this was immaterial anyway. What bound us was our womanhood. The very few times religion or ethnicity came up among *Ms.* editors and writers was in conversation about an article assignment, say a piece on lesbian nuns or women rabbis or abortion and the Church. I'm not suggesting that I hid my religious or ethnic origins. On the contrary, I always felt proud to be a Jew and lucky to be born into a culture that reveres learning and turns its own suffering into humor. I loved movies with Jewish themes. I was not above using Yiddishisms when English was wanting, nor did I hesitate to take time off on the Jewish holidays. But otherwise, being a Jew was irrelevant to anything I was doing professionally or socially. It played no role outside of my head and household. It didn't matter one way or the other.

Understand that the overview I've just given you represents a hindsight analysis, not my awareness at the time. In those days, I never even thought about who was or wasn't Jewish except on Ash Wednesday when people showed up at work with smudged foreheads, or at Christmastime when the Gentiles wore tiny Santas on their lapels and set up the office Christmas tree. Otherwise, I was as oblivious and as comfortable in the publishing world as I had been in Jamaica or at Brandeis. In short, except for the disturbing discovery that my friend Sue's priest blamed "the Jews" for the Crucifixion, I cannot remember a single moment of personal disquiet until 1975 when I noticed for the first time that being Jewish *mattered*.

A few years earlier, at a women's conference, I wandered into one of those "identity workshops" where they post around the room signs that say HUMAN, WOMAN, MOTHER, WIFE, WORKER, WHITE, BLACK, AMERICAN, CHRISTIAN, JEW, etc.—and they ask you to stand under the word that most fundamentally describes who you are. That day I made my choice without hesitation: I placed myself beneath the sign that said WOMAN.

After 1975, I would not have been so sure, but before then—even while the private me was wrestling with religious misogyny—the public me was going about her business with no Jewish identity whatsoever. I wrote dozens of articles during those years, none on "Jewish issues." In my lectures, I never mentioned Jews. I was a universalist feminist. I was working for equality for *all* women, so why single out any one group? My activist energies went into women's organizing and general feminist consciousness-raising. I belonged to no Jewish organizations or synagogue, and felt only the most distant connection to "the Jewish community," a phrase I probably did not even understand. If asked to join, I probably would have said, No thanks, I have my hands full being a woman.

Yet when I think about how broad was the purview of feminism in the 1960s and 1970s, I can't explain why I felt no special curiosity about the status of Jewish women or the problems that Jewish girls might be facing in less hospitable environments than those in which I grew up. Likewise, since I had been directly victimized by the men of the minyan, I don't know why I wasn't motivated to investigate religious sexism or to integrate some of my private spiritual insights into my general feminist framework. Even if I did not choose to act as a Jew in the Women's Movement, why didn't I at least act as a feminist among Jews? Why didn't I join forces with Jewish women who were fighting for gender equality in the synagogue, where I was well aware of the gender inequities? Why didn't I do battle *within* the Jewish organizational establishment which I knew to be so oppressively male?

I can only guess that I steered clear of these issues to avoid opening a Pandora's box of political contradictions. Perhaps I was afraid to loose my fury upon my own people. Because individuals tend to hold their own group to a higher standard on every score, I probably knew I would take greater offense at Jewish sexism than at any other kind. Some combination of repressed resentment and unconscious protectiveness may have cauterized that part of me that might have claimed itself a *Jewish*-feminist had I been able to imagine what such a hyphenated identity entailed.

Or perhaps I still was rebelling against anything that reminded me of my father and his Judaism—and without a doubt the Jewish establishment reminded me of all that. The men who ran these organizations were just as authoritarian and egotistical as he, and the religious and communal institutions were just as masculinist as the Jamaica Jewish Center and my father's other organizations. Furthermore, how could I join those very causes that had been my rivals for my father's attention?

Of course, rebellion is a great dumping ground for life's scrap ironies. It didn't take a genius to realize that in fighting for my mother's rights I had become my father's daughter. Although my arena was the Women's Movement rather the Jewish world, I too had been asking my family to live with my organizational commitments and to forgive my absences. And it didn't take a political scientist to tell me that although being an ad hoc cantor was a nice antidote to exclusion, unless women like myself joined together and challenged the principles underlying this exclusion, our individual advances would never add up to permanent progress for Jewish women.

When I recall my former assumptions that being Jewish wasn't relevant and "didn't matter," I'm reminded of a story of Otto Kahn, the wealthy Jewish banker, who was out walking on Fifth Avenue with a friend who had a hunchback. As the two of them passed Temple Emanu-El, Kahn looked up at the synagogue and said, "You know, I used to be Jewish."

The friend smiled up at him and answered, "And I used to be a hunchback."

Many Jewish women choose not to be Jewish-identified just as many choose not to be woman-identified because they believe they have the option to behave as if peoplehood or gender "doesn't matter."

Golda Meir felt that way about being a woman. Her autobiography makes clear that she thought her femaleness didn't matter even though it was the reason her parents would not let her go to high school. ("It doesn't pay to be too clever," said her father. "Men don't like smart girls.") She thought gender didn't matter even though in the early years of her marriage her husband forced her to leave Merhavia, the kibbutz that she loved and where she had become a promising leader. She writes that "he refused to have children at all unless we left Merhavia," because he opposed collective child rearing. He wanted Golda to be a traditional wife and mother—yet she does not acknowledge the coercions of male supremacy or the tyranny of sex-role imperatives; instead, she tries to fit the feminine mold.

"To put it very bluntly," she writes,

> *I had to decide which came first: my duty to my husband, my home and my child or the kind of life I myself really wanted. . . . I realized that in a conflict between my duty and my innermost desires, it was my duty that had the prior claim. There was really no alternative other than to stop pining for a way of life that couldn't be mine.*

After giving birth to her two children, Golda was offered an important job in the Women's Labor Council, a job in which she would have the power to advance her passionately held Zionist ideals. She agonized over her decision: "I had to face up to the fact that going back to work would spell the end to my attempts to devote myself entirely to the family." She takes the job knowing it means a mutiny against her husband and the end of her marriage, for which she blames herself: "I had to be what I was, and what I was made it impossible for him to have the sort of wife he wanted and needed."

Looking back, she also worries that she did not do enough for her children:

> *I was always rushing from one place to another—to work, home, to a meeting, to take Menachem to a music lesson, to keep a doctor's appointment with Sarah, to shop, to cook, to work and back home again. And still to this day I am not sure that I didn't harm the children or neglect them, despite the efforts I made not to be away from them even an hour more than was strictly necessary. . . .*
>
> *I stayed up at night to cook for them. I mended their clothes. I went to concerts and films with them. We always talked and laughed a lot together. But were [my sister] and my mother right when they charged me for years with depriving the children of their due? I suppose that I shall never be able to answer this question to my own satisfaction. . . .*

Rather than recognize in her situation the untenable pressures and contradictions that plague virtually all achieving women, she attributes her strains and sacrifices to her private feminine or maternal failures. Faulting her own aspirations, her uncontrollable love of political work, and her burning ambitions for the Jewish State, she does not generalize to other women's feelings and experiences, or translate her tortured feminine role conflicts into a politicized response to women's situation. Instead, her regrets remain strictly personal. The conflicts that tore her apart and the harrowing guilt she carried throughout her life helped her to passively sympathize with the "heavy double burden" of working mothers but did not inspire her to politicize that sympathy and identify with feminist goals when she was Israel's prime minister. She did not concentrate on child-care policy, or concern herself with the problems of working women, or use her influence to equalize gender arrangements in the home.

Essayist Elisabeth Bumiller says of the late Indian prime minister, Indira Gandhi, that she too "transcended sexual categories," ignored those of her own sex, and made no special effort to promote other women. As far as I can tell, the same could have been said of Margaret Thatcher. And when Prime Minister Benazir Bhutto was ousted as

Pakistan's premier, *The New York Times* included among the failures of her regime that she had not worked to repeal Islamic ordinances demeaning to women.

I think of those four national leaders almost as female impersonators—women on the outside but not on the inside; women who look like us but act like traditional men. Perhaps these leaders eschewed even the most tepid feminist advocacy in the belief that such activities would remind their populations that their prime minister was "nothing but a woman" after all. Or did they fear that advocacy of women's interests might suggest neglect of men's interests? Or perhaps these women came from some mutant species devoid of the usual empathic skills most women develop—which may be why they were allowed to rise to become leaders in the first place. Or maybe they just enjoyed being the only woman in the Cabinet room or summit conference, and they didn't want any female competition.

In any case, when Golda Meir stepped down in 1973, Israel was no more economically or politically hospitable to women's needs than it was before she took office four years before. Her tenure did not advance the potentiality of female leadership beyond showing the world that *this* woman could run her country. She did not use her power to empower *other* women.

Golda's blind spot for her own gender was only exceeded by her blind spot for the other Semitic people who lived and festered within Israel and the occupied territories. With her disingenuous insistence that "there are no Palestinians," and her rejection of peace feelers from the Egyptians, American government, American Jews, and the United Nations, she pursued an obstinate, short-sighted course that denied a people's national aspirations, miscalculated the durability of their rage, and bequeathed to future generations a legacy of bitterness and violence that culminated in the outbreak of the *intifada* in 1987.

I will have more to say about Golda in the next chapter where I describe meeting her in Israel, but here I want only to establish that, although she was the most elevated Jewish female figure in the world, ultimately she was not a worthy role model. She ends her autobiography with the assertion that Jews "who have tried to opt out of their Jewishness have done so . . . at the expense of their own basic identity." I would submit that the same is true of women like Golda Meir who acknowledge their Jewishness but try to opt out of their womanhood by denying its relevance.

Thinking one's gender or peoplehood irrelevant does not for a moment change what *is*. Ultimately, somewhere down the line, the world will not allow a woman to say, "Being female doesn't matter," nor a Jew to say, "I used to be a Jew." The Jewish woman who does not take possession of her total identity, and make it count for something, may find that others will impose upon her a label she does not like at all.

That is what I discovered in 1975, when the delegates meeting in Mexico City at the first of three United Nations International Women's Decade Conferences passed a resolution that effectively identified all Jews as racists. The "Zionism is racism" resolution—called the Declaration of Mexico—took me by surprise. I could not believe that supposed feminists who had been entrusted with the inauguration of a ten-year commitment to improving the status of all the world's women—and who were pledged to address the monumental problems of female infanticide, illiteracy, high mortality rates, abject poverty, involuntary pregnancies, domestic violence, and so on—could allow their agenda to be hijacked on behalf of this unspeakable PLO slogan.

The following year, I was part of a group of women invited to Israel to look Zionism in the face and meet with our Israeli counterparts. If the Declaration of Mexico was the initial "click" that started me on my life as a *Jewish*-feminist, that first trip to Israel was the opening act of commitment, the first step in my journey toward a conscious advocacy of secular Jewish interests. It helped me start training the muscles of a different kind of Jewish identity—not the one that belonged to God, prayer, and synagogue, nor the sentimental kind associated with nostalgia, Yiddishisms, and chicken soup, but new political contours that were so robust and sinewy they made everything else in my wardrobe too small.

Although it was ostensibly the Israelis who had been attacked as racists, I knew the arrow also was meant for me. I could stand under any damn sign I pleased, but to feminists who hate Israel I was not a woman, I was a *Jewish* woman. The men of the minyan might not consider me a Jew among Jews, but to many of those delegates in Mexico City, that's all I was. Now the question I had to answer was, *Why be a Jew for them if I am not a Jew for myself?*

Theodor Herzl, the founder of Zionism, was inspired to identify affirmatively with his people after witnessing French anti-Semitism in action at the infamous Dreyfus trial. In the context of feminism, my experience mirrored his. I'd like to be able to claim a more positive impetus for my reawakened Jewish persona—an impressive mentor or persuasive literary argument—but it was only feral Jew-hating that forced me to reconsider what I was and what I wanted to be. While I had believed that feminists fight side by side *as* women, *with* women *for* women, it seemed as if some of my "sisters" were not out to get the patriarchal militarists, multinational pornographers, or capitalist imperialists—they were using the resolutions of the United Nations and the foot soldiers of international feminism to get the Jews.

I know Zionists who are racists, just as I know racist feminists, but that didn't make Zionism racism any more than a few bigoted women made feminism racism. Moreover, one could say that Zionism is to Jews what feminism is to women. Zionism began as a national liberation movement and has become an ongoing struggle for Jewish solidarity, pride, and unity. Similarly, feminism, which began as a gender-liberation movement, has become an ongoing struggle for women's solidarity, pride, and unity. Just as feminism has been maligned and misunderstood by those who do not bother to understand it, so too has Zionism been maligned and misunderstood by its enemies. And just as Zionism has been misrepresented by some of its own practitioners for unjust ends, so too has feminism been distorted by some of the women within. Yet at the heart of the matter, Zionism and feminism are directly analagous in that both movements are fueled by the fires of self-determination. Calling Zionism racism makes Jewish self-determination sound like an attack on non-Jews, which is comparable to calling feminism "anti-male," as if female self-determination were an attack on men.

The difference in the two "isms" is this: many women resist identifying as feminists because it means espousing their own interests and they've been taught that appearing "selfish" is unfeminine, whereas apart from a few ultra-Orthodox sects and rebels on the extreme left, there are relatively few Jews who do not identify as Zionists. Hence, virtually every Jewish woman at the gathering in Mexico City and every Jew reading about the conference at home considered herself a Zionist and suffered deep injuries from the impact of that anti-Zionist statement. I was accustomed to hearing Israel defamed at the U.N., but not in a gathering where *sisterhood* is supposed to be powerful. What was going on? Why was all that womanpower being directed against Jews?

Whatever the reason, I felt it was just as important for feminists to resist the trashing of Zionism as it had been for women to fight the defamation of feminism.

The second U.N. women's conference, the mid-decade meeting, was to be held in Copenhagen in 1980. Many Jewish women were skittish about returning to the same body which had terrorized them and left Israelis to twist in the wind. Because there had been so much public criticism of what happened in Mexico City, we kept hoping that in the intervening five years, solidarity and good sense would have overtaken global politics and Jewish women would be treated *as women* and not held any more accountable for Menachem Begin's policies than American feminists were for the policies of Ronald Reagan. However, this was not to be. Instead, the Copenhagen conference became an even worse quagmire. Jewish women of every nationality were isolated, excoriated, and tyrannized. When I interviewed many of the returning American delegates, they trembled as they told their stories:

"In Copenhagen I heard people say that Gloria Steinem, Betty Friedan, and Bella Abzug all being Jewish gives the American women's movement a bad name," said the Mormon activist Sonia Johnson, who added:

I heard, "The only good Jew is a dead Jew." I heard, "The only way to rid the world of Zionism is to kill all the Jews." The anti-Semitism was overt, wild, and irrational. My roommate, an Israeli, came in every night in real pain.

Paula Doress, a Boston-area health activist, told me:

I heard a Danish woman tell an American, "I was handing out PLO leaflets and my Jewish friends saw me. I was so embarrassed." The American answered, "My Jewish friends saw me too, and I don't give a damn."

"We organized a Jewish Women's Caucus to answer the attacks," remembered Barbara Leslie of the International Council of Jewish Women, continuing:

Everywhere we went we were scared to death. In Amnesty International's workshop on the torture of women prisoners, women from

Ireland and South Africa talked about being tortured horribly in their prisons. Then a Palestinian said, "I was never a prisoner but here is how Israelis torture our women."

Tamar Eschel, a member of the Israeli parliament and chair of its subcommittee on police and prisons, demanded, "Name names! I visit the prisons all the time. These preposterous accusations remind me of Goebbels's technique of the big lie—just keep repeating it and some are sure to begin believing it."

Eschel was shouted down with cries of "Liar! Liar!" When I tried to speak, a woman in front of me turned and pushed her fist into my face. . . .

Each evening the official American delegation briefed us on the conference proceedings. One night an American black woman rose to accuse our delegation of deferring to the Jews. She said she couldn't understand what was wrong with saying Zionism is racism. Women of all races applauded her statement. The Jewish women in the room sat stunned. Then former congresswoman Bella Abzug stood up. "I'll tell you what Zionism is," she said. "It is a liberation movement for a people who have been persecuted all their lives and throughout human history."

Phyllis Chesler recalled:

At the panel on refugees, we heard these heart-stopping tales about exiles from Chile, about Afghan women refugees, about the rape of the boat women, about Polisario women and children starving. But when Simcha Chorish, an Iraqi Jew, spoke about her husband being shot without charges or a trial, and about having to escape to Israel with her children, the place turned savage. "Cuba, si! Yankee, no! PLO! PLO!" they shouted. "Israel kills babies and women! Israel must die!"

"One day I was carrying a canvas bag with American Jewish Congress written on it," said Chiae Herzig, an officer of that organization.

Other Jewish women warned me not to carry it. "Don't be a lightning rod," they said. To my shame, I hid the bag. I was completely unprepared for my fear. In my community in Baltimore, I am vulnerable as a feminist; in Copenhagen, among the supposed feminists of the world, I felt vulnerable as a Jew.

Esther Broner, the author of our feminist Haggadah, was devastated by her experiences in Copenhagen:

A U.N. staff person said to me, "Denmark is wonderful but the Germans take it over in the summer, and I hate them. They only did one thing right; they killed the Jews."

I made choking sounds.

"Oh, did I hurt your feelings?" the U.N. woman asked. "Are you German?"

Esther sighed deeply, then continued:

One night I heard an Egyptian and a Thai talking with a U.N. official. "You women should make peace for your countries," said the official.

"Never," said the Thai. "The Israeli woman is not a human being. She is poisoned by the worm of Zionism. She can only be reached with the sword."

The Egyptian woman agreed: "You must speak to an Israeli with the dagger. You stab her under the table. You stab her over the table. You do not sit down with her."

A few days later, Shulamit Aloni, an Israeli member of parliament and peace activist, was interviewed by the Danish press. Would she extend her hand in peace even to Leila Khaled, the PLO skyjacker? a reporter asks.

"To anyone who will help make peace," Aloni answers.

The press finds Khaled and asks the same question. "I extend my hand with a gun," she replies.

In these accounts I heard distant rumbles from the 1930s when the Jew-hating in Germany was "just words" and the iron fist had not yet struck. The venomous words of the Copenhagen conference entered my bloodstream and sickened me. Then I had a thought so obvious but so disturbing that it took my breath away. I realized that in struggling to empower women throughout the world, *feminism might be helping to empower some women who hate Jews.*

For a moment, I felt betrayed. But by whom? The "movement" was all of us. It was every woman who used gender as an analytical tool;

it was any woman who counted herself an advocate of equality. Nobody had promised me that each one of these women would automatically embrace every other woman's human-rights objectives. Certainly, black women understood that without constant prodding, white women would not necessarily include white racism in their agendas for social change. Why should I assume that Gentile women would feel Jewish fears and see the world through Jewish eyes unless Jews made them do it? I had to get into the act. I had to decode those Copenhagen experiences and help to make sure they never happen again.

The decoding exposed many bizarre contradictions:

• The official U.N. Women's Conference was a meeting of government representatives, so of course it mirrored the distinctly anti-Israel complexion of the United Nations itself. The Forum, on the other hand, was the unofficial body of the conference—a diverse gathering of nongovernmental women who represented grass-roots feminism and international sisterhood—yet the Forum is where the anti-Semitic harangues overrode daily activities and workshops, and the Forum is where Jewish women found not sisterly support but terror.

• The nations in which women are the most repressed were in control of the official world conference, whose mandate was to address the well-being of women—and these women were directing more attention to Israel's treatment of the Palestinians than to their own governments' treatment of female human beings.

• At a conference whose goals included the pursuit of "peace," PLO terrorists Leila Khaled and Randa Nabulsi, killers of innocent people, were official delegates.

• Women from nine countries, seven of them Arab, voted for the first time in their lives at this conference. They would return to their own countries where they have no voting rights. How did they use their once-in-a-lifetime franchise? They used it to condemn Israel, the only democracy in the Middle East, and the one state that grants voting rights to women, including Israeli Arab women.

• Many Western and Third World black women sided with the Arabs despite the long history of black slavery in Saudi Arabia, Kuwait, Yemen, Oman, and Sudan. The women forgot, if they ever knew, that no Israeli Jew has ever kept a black person enslaved.

• The official U.N. document that served as background material for the conference reviewed the history of the founding of Israel without once mentioning the Holocaust. It condemned Jews for populating Israel but never noted that after World War II, virtually every country turned away Jewish refugees. It blamed Zionism for all the problems of Palestinian women, from illiteracy to unemployment, but other than a casual reference to Arab traditions that restrict her "freedom of movement," the document contained no discussion of the subordinate role of women in Muslim culture, not even a word about the "honor killings" by Arab men of women who become pregnant out of wedlock.

• While the official document excoriated Israel for its treatment of its minorities, other nations with far worse records toward their own women nationals escaped comment. There were no attacks on the neocolonialist oil sheikhdoms, no comment about the anti-women backlash in Iran under the ayatollahs, or the polarization of rich and poor women in Arab petromonarchies, no outrage that Saudi Arabia cared so little about its women that it did not even send a delegation to the conference. Only Israel was castigated and only Jewish women were abandoned to the mob. Said the writer Ellen Willis: "The real test of our fabled 'Jewish power' is how powerless Jews were in Copenhagen."

The Declaration of Mexico woke me up, my first two visits to Israel poured strong coffee down my throat, and the Copenhagen Conference held me under a cold shower. Until 1980, I had been napping. When I came to, I was no less a woman but much more a Jew. It was a rude awakening. So this is what it meant to be a Jew in the world. Real life wasn't Jamaica or Brandeis or Manhattan, or *Ms.* magazine; it was a U.N. conference where so-called sisters plot to stab you under the table.

I asked myself why U.N. sponsorship brought out the worst in Third World women. At the same time, there was no avoiding the fact that a number of *American* women had either participated in the attacks or failed to intervene on the Jews' behalf. Could it be that anti-Semitism was the dirty little secret of the U.S. sisterhood? To check it out, I undertook a large data-gathering project. For hundreds of hours, I talked with Jewish-American feminists to find out if they had ever suffered as Jews within the women's movement. My results were published in *Ms.* magazine in an essay entitled, "Anti-Semitism in the Women's Movement." Chapter 11 will discuss the main points raised in the hundreds of letters elicited by the piece. Here I want to highlight the one letter that commented, "I've been reading you for years and until now, I never knew you were Jewish."

It may have been desirable to have such a thing said about a newspaper or television news reporter who is pledged to be "objective," but I had always been an *advocacy* journalist. My readers knew I was pro-woman, pro-choice, pro-child; why hadn't I let them know I was pro-Jewish?

After Copenhagen, and after evaluating the results of my anti-Semitism survey, I saw the importance of being a public, affirmative Jew—even when ethnicity or religion "didn't matter." As much as I might wish for a world of universalist values and deemphasized differences, I would no longer tolerate a Women's Movement in which Jews are the only group asked to relinquish their own interests while other women were allowed to push their private agendas, and subvert feminist ideals when it suited them. I would no longer assume all women were my sisters. My sisters were the Jewish women who were ambushed in Mexico City, banished from the international community in Copenhagen, and betrayed in America by the promise that feminists would do things differently. From 1980 on, I would just as likely stand under the word JEW.

The final conference of the U.N. Decade for Women was to be held in Nairobi in 1985. Eager to avoid another Copenhagen, and especially to avoid situations where Jewish-American women and African-American women would be on opposite sides of the Zionism issue, I helped co-found two Black-Jewish Women's Dialogues in New York City, an intimate discussion group of six women, and a group made up of about thirty black women and Jewish women dedicated to preparing together for the Nairobi conference. Although the larger group only lasted for less than two years, that was long enough for a few black women and Jewish women to create personal alliances that helped soften the anti-Israel attacks that would indeed resurface in Nairobi (the alliances helped press for resolutions opposing South African apartheid as well). Despite incessant disruptions by Palestinian militants, the end-of-decade conference achieved some feminist unanimity and the release of a summary document that did *not* contain a condemnation of Zionism. This time Jewish women came home battered but not broken.

As for my evolving secular self, the change has been subtle but sure.

I began excavating more of my Jewish foundations by educating myself, traveling to Israel, joining Jewish organizations that do the direct-action work I believe in, and writing and speaking on Jewish issues. Emotionally, I grew to accept my Otherness as a Jew the way I had accepted my Otherness as a woman—with pride and purpose, and a willingness to create a positive "we" where no category had existed before.

Not long ago, the *The Jewish Week* reported that "increasing numbers of *ba'alei teshuvah* (returnees to the faith) are back on the secular streets again, and their defection suggests second thoughts about the much-touted success of the *ba'alei teshuvah* phenomenon." According to experts in such phenomena, the problem seems to be that these born-again Jews were trained only in Orthodox ritual observance and personal spirituality. They had recaptured the Jewish "I" but were indifferent to the Jewish "we," to Jewish collectivity. No matter how devout they were, privatized Judaism could only hold them for so long. Without the connection to Jewish peoplehood—Jewish cultural, historical, and emotional linkages—they found religion but not a deep-rooted Jewish identity.

The Israeli novelist A. B. Yehoshua comes closest to capturing my own notion of what it means to have a deep-rooted secular Jewish identity. He calls it "total Jewishness" and defines it broadly (to say the least): "Everything that happens is our responsibility and reflects our Jewishness," he says.

> *Jewish identity here in Israel is expressed by the size of our prison cells, the nature of our unemployment payments, our foreign policy— whether or not we sell weapons to South Africa. Everything we do determines our Jewishness.*

Outside of Israel, Jews cannot reflect their Jewishness quite so totally since we alone do not control our nation's institutions. But we can express our Jewishness in our individual and collective actions in the secular sphere. Blacks and Asians bear their racial identity on their faces. My gender identity is apparent on my person. But if I want my Jewish identity to be known, I must *enact* it. Wearing a Jewish star around my neck won't do; having a Jewish identity is not merely about religious pride. It is about deciding each and every day what Jewishness *means* and how I will actualize it in my life. Being Jewish-identified doesn't only relate to how I worship, what I eat, whom I marry, or where I live. It finds more concrete expression in my ethical standards, the groups I join, where I give my charitable dollars, my particular way of supporting Israel, how I interact with non-Jews, and how I live my politics.

I still have universalist dreams—visions of one world without the rancors of nationalism, tribalism, and patriarchy—but now I dream them only when fully awake, and I take my inspiration not from some naive UNICEF greeting card but from a pluralist feminism founded on a mutual respect for each other's "identity politics," which include the particularities of culture, peoplehood, and history.

My identity politics, my way of living "Jewishly," positions me in the prophetic tradition which esteems justice, rather than in the rabbinic tradition which esteems order. Under the canopy of justice, Jewish values can make a marriage with feminist ideals. In the pursuit of justice, Jews and feminists can unite in the same struggle, and I can unite the Jew and the feminist within me.

The hard part is making the marriage work.

10

———◆———

Gatekeepers
and Gate Crashers

Israel Through Feminist Eyes

THE STATE OF ISRAEL WAS FOUNDED WHEN I WAS NINE YEARS OLD, yet the first time I went there I was thirty-seven.

Since that trip in 1976, I've returned five times, made meaningful friendships, and become involved in two Israeli movements that dovetail with my most deeply held Jewish and feminist values: advancing the peace process, which I will take up in chapter 16, and improving the status of women, the subject of the present chapter.

In a moment, I'll venture a guess as to why I was in no hurry to visit Israel myself, but I cannot explain why my parents did not take me there as a child to see the nation they helped build. Maybe we never went because we couldn't afford it—although in 1948 my father bought a new Dodge and my mother got a Persian lamb coat. Maybe it was because my mother was so grateful to be living in America that she couldn't bring herself to leave, even temporarily. More likely, I suppose we didn't go to Israel because we didn't go anywhere, a vacation being an utterly alien concept to my parents. Except, that is, for the time when my father went to Palestine, alone.

Ostensibly, he went there to "settle the affairs" of his father and mother who had emigrated early in the 1930s. His mother, Yetta—I was given the name Loretta in her memory—had died in Tiberias a

164

year or so before. Then, in the spring of 1939, his father, Menahem Mendel, was murdered during an Arab raid.

I'm sure that my father felt the loss of his father and I'm sure there were "affairs to settle." But it has never been clear to me that he had to go *when* he did. He and my mother had been married for only two years, yet he went alone. More important, he left when she was in the seventh month of her pregnancy and he didn't come home until just before I was born. Why leave then? He hadn't rushed off to Palestine when his mother died, although in that instance, he might have been of some comfort to his father. This time, there were no family members left to console. Why rush off now?

Emotional catharsis? My father, as I have indicated, was the furthest thing from sentimental. His feelings about death were relentlessly, mercilessly matter-of-fact.

Ritual reasons? Impossible. By the time he could reach Tiberias by ship, his father would have been dead for weeks, the funeral and burial long past; and my father never visited anyone's grave anyway. To his way of thinking, the body was a meaningless remnant, and interment a waste of good land.

Was it the urgency of winding up his parents' affairs that propelled him to Palestine? *What* urgency? My father's photograph album reveals that he meandered around Italy and Egypt before making his way to his destination. He was no accidental tourist but an enthusiastic, methodical explorer of historic places. The snapshots capture him riding on a camel looking dapper in his white shirt, white trousers, and white beret with the Sphinx in the background, visiting the Pyramids, touring Alexandria, stopping in Pompeii, enjoying Amalfi and Capri, and finally, all points of Jerusalem, from Moses Montefiore's windmill to the Allenby Bridge. Tiberias was his last stop.

Yet urgency was the reason he gave my mother and the one she put out to the world while she was alone at home counting the days to her due date. Seeing him smiling in those sepia snapshots, I feel between my heart and lungs the hurt my mother must have suffered, realizing her husband had forsaken her for a pleasure trip. What if she had needed him? What if there were complications? Suppose he had missed my birth?

Although he would skip out quite regularly in the ensuing years, it occurs to me that my father started leaving me behind even before I was born. His trip to Palestine must have struck me as his original sin.

And since so many of my decisions make sense retroactively as unconscious reactions against something my father did or stood for, I
suspect that I avoided going to Israel because it was where he went the
first time he abandoned my mother and me for something more interesting. Later, it was the place that won his attention night after
night as he gave himself to the Zionist cause. While I needed him, he
was taking care of his other baby, his favored child.

Whether or not I'm right to trace my resistance to Israel to this
resentment, the fact remains that I did not pay that part of the world
much mind until I was well into my thirties. While I followed the
major Israeli news stories I was far more involved in the fate of
Vietnam than of Israel. I thought of myself as an antiwar activist, not
a Zionist. I believed Jews deserved a homeland but in those days I
thought Zionism required one to make aliyah (emigrate to Israel) or
at least proselytize for all Jews to settle there, and I was not about to
move. Moreover, I could have listed six countries I preferred to visit
first.

With this attitude, it might have been decades before Israel turned
up at the top of my political consciousness or my travel itinerary but
for the intervention, yet again, of feminist fate—or God herself. How
else to interpret those times when an equality issue or a woman's
event has determined a major change in my relationship with my
Jewish self? As I have already suggested, the feminist event that was
instrumental in changing my relationship with Israel was the 1975
U.N. International Women's Decade conference held in Mexico City
(described in the preceding chapter). While I hadn't thought I was a
Zionist then, the anti-Zionists made me one. Their racism accusation
forced me to focus on the basic ideology of Zionism and the policies
and principles underlying the Jewish State. In the writings of Israel's
forefather Chaim Weizmann, I found the words "There must not be
one law for the Jew and another for the Arabs," a precept embodied
in the Israeli Proclamation of Independence, which in the absence of
a constitution, has served as the country's Magna Carta:

> *The State of Israel will . . . promote the development of the country
> for the benefit of all its inhabitants; will be based on the principles of
> liberty, justice, and peace as conceived by the Prophets of Israel; will
> uphold the full social and political equality of all its citizens, without
> distinction of religion, race, or sex; will guarantee freedom of religion,
> conscience, education, and culture. . . .*

I began to feel comfortable calling myself a Zionist despite my father, or should I say, in all honesty, because of him. Ultimately, my commitments have come to resemble his so closely that they might have been genetically imprinted. When I subtract my childhood jealousy of Israel for being dearer to him than I was, what remains within me is his legacy of love for the country and its significance to Jews.

In this respect, I am a living example of how profoundly the personal is political. Having had to share my father with his Zionist cause, I conflated Zionism with my other childhood deprivations. Extending the metaphor a step closer to the bone, if Israel was my Daddy's favored child, that made her my sibling (another secret sister). Sibling rivalry, then, might explain my rejection of Israel all those years. It might also explain why, when Israel was under attack at the Mexico City conference, I finally was moved to acknowledge the intimacy of my relationship with her.

The "Zionism is racism" equation enraged me not just because it was vicious, wrongheaded (think of the ingathering of black Ethiopian Jews), and implicitly anti-Semitic, but because it so cynically co-opted a feminist event for anti-Israel activity. When psychoanalyst Erika Freeman circulated a protest petition among American women leaders, I was quick to sign and to register strong verbal protests in and outside the women's movement. I did nothing more. But some months later, to my amazement, Erika called and asked if I would like to participate in a full-scale, high-level tour of Israel to be planned and subsidized by the Israeli government as a gesture of appreciation to those who had signed the petition. Spouses were welcome.

That's how Bert and I found ourselves en route to Israel on December 19, 1976—the first time for both of us. I remember almost every detail of that trip in ways I do not remember my visits to France, Morocco, Korea, China, or anywhere else. Each experience I had in Israel, each separate conversation, drove itself deep into my memory, like pilings in the earth which together can support a structure of enormous weight. That first trip now supports the weight of my personal history, reverberations of father and faith, much of my political awakening as a Zionist and a Jewish feminist, and all the revelations and strains of my subsequent visits, including the *Ms.* magazine tour of Israel which I began organizing as soon as I returned to the States.

On the first trip, Bert and I and other petition-signers made up a delegation of sixteen. We were lawyers, elected officials, writers, businesspeople, activists, and media types—whites and blacks, Gentiles and Jews, twelve women and four men. Although the government clearly intended to show us the best of Israel's institutions, we were free to depart from the formal itinerary and talk to anyone at will. Wherever we went, I asked questions, wandered off track, opened closed doors, and found a second home. Everyone I met was new and at the same time achingly familiar. Everything was exotic yet I was completely comfortable from the moment our plane dropped beneath the clouds on its approach to Ben Gurion airport and the El Al loudspeaker broadcast the song "*Haveynu Shalom Aleichem.*"

The passengers sang along lustily, like revelers at a Jewish wedding, and the song ended at the moment we touched down on the runway, inspiring a spontaneous burst of applause which I sensed was not for our singing or the pilot's prowess. I found this collective effusion peculiar but when my feet first made contact with the ground, the actual *land* of Israel, tears flooded my eyes.

If I was surprised by that primal reaction, I was flabbergasted by what happened next. In the airport lounge, officials served us coffee along with the news that the government had just fallen. Prime Minister Yitzhak Rabin's coalition had collapsed in the wake of a dispute about whether or not American F-15 jets had arrived after sundown on the Sabbath, thereby violating Jewish law.

Back then I hadn't realized that Orthodox rabbis could make or break governments. However, I did know the rabbinate had sole jurisdiction over marriage, divorce, and child custody laws and therefore could make or break a woman's happiness. I also knew that the Jewish National Fund posters on the walls of my Hebrew school had not told the whole truth about Israeli women. They were not all strong, suntanned pioneer women in work shirts and fatigue shorts, driving tractors or tanks, liberated by socialism to plant and fight side by side with men. Like a superficially perfect marriage that unravels in bickering bitterness before one's eyes, Israel has revealed itself as a false utopia in which women's equality was largely myth. Over time I have distinguished three intransigent forces that stand like iron gates barring women's path.

The first gate was and is *the primacy of the security issue.* The constant threat of attack from within and without makes women's complaints seem pale in comparison. Someone is always asking, Can't you feminists postpone your demands until the "larger issues" are settled? How can you talk about women's salaries when we have the military budget to worry about? How can you mention domestic violence in the face of Arab terrorism? Why criticize women's status while we're getting such heat about the status of Palestinians? Can't your issues wait until the nation is safe and sound?

In 1976, long before the invasion of Lebanon and the Palestinian uprising known as the *intifada*, it was harder to use national security as a club to beat back women's demands. At the time, Ora Namir, a member of the Knesset (parliament) and chair of the Status of Women Commission, said something that proved prophetic:

> *It's a quiet period now, so women can insist that our issues be taken seriously. But something happens to this country when there's a war. You have to live here to understand the way priorities suddenly change. Just about every woman you meet has a husband or son in the army. Even feminist wives and mothers are wives and mothers first when the shooting starts. Then we worry more about their dying than about our civil rights.*

Deena Goren, professor of communications and another commission member, protested:

> *We shouldn't have to choose between women's freedom and national freedom. A mother of two children doesn't have to choose which one is more precious. All children and all freedoms are precious.*

Fifteen months later, in March 1978, when I returned with the *Ms.* group, our bus was traveling on the coastal highway at the moment when another tourist bus a few miles ahead of us was attacked by Arab terrorists (see page 335). The next day, sociologist Rivka Bar Yosef proved Ora's prediction correct.

"Today my son is in the army in the area that is in the news, and I have not heard from him," Rivka said, visibly drained.

> *So today I find myself caught in the dilemma of the Israeli woman. Everything that is connected with politics seems trivial and it is difficult to talk to you about my involvement in furthering the status of women.*

The second gate barring women from equal humanity was and still is *the power of the religious authorities*, especially their monopoly over marriage and divorce. Even if a couple is Reform, Conservative, or secular, they must obey Orthodox laws of personal status which decree, among other things, that it is the husband who creates the marriage and only he who can end it. His wife is his property. If she wants a divorce, she must ask him to physically hand her a bill of divorcement, called a *get*, in the presence of a rabbinic court. Thus, the dissolution of the marriage is literally in the hands of the husband. He can refuse to hand her the *get* until she accedes to his demands for money or child custody. He can keep withholding the *get* for as long as he likes, tormenting her, blackmailing her, punishing her. A woman in such a situation is considered an *agunah*, a chained wife—like Ora Avraham whose husband has refused to give her a *get* for thirty-seven years because she will not pay the ransom he demands. Or like Iris Levy who waited eighteen years to be divorced from a husband who beat her, gambled away their earnings, and demanded $50,000 to set her free. Or like Aliza Shmeuli, whose husband molested their children, committed a murder, was convicted and sentenced to life imprisonment, and still will not give her a *get*.

Some experts estimate that there are as many as ten thousand *agunot* in Israel, each of them prohibited from remarrying or having children with another man—for such children would be considered *mamzerim* (bastards) and would themselves be prohibited from marrying anyone but a non-Jew or another *mamzer*. (But if the husband has an extramarital affair, the children resulting from *his* union would be considered legitimate so long as the woman who gave birth to them is Jewish and not married to anyone else.)

Aware of the corruption and tragedy associated with laws of the *get*, Maimonides, the twelfth-century doctor-philosopher-rabbi, said that the rabbis should order a recalcitrant man to be flogged until he "willingly agrees to grant his wife a divorce." Modern rabbinical courts have the power to compel a husband to divorce his wife but they have been reluctant to use it. Only thirty such compulsion orders were issued between 1953 and 1987. Moreover, if the rabbinical court does issue a compulsion order and the husband ignores it, there is no civil authority to which the wife can appeal. Even if her husband is insane, even if he abandons her and disappears, even if he is incarcerated, she still cannot be divorced without his permission, and in no case has a chained wife been allowed to remarry before her *get* is in her hand.

The religious courts have shown greater willingness to interfere when it is the wife who refuses to accept the *get* from her husband. Labeling nearly one hundred such wives "rebellious," the rabbis have allowed their husbands to take new wives without penalty.

In death too, Jewish men control their women. When a husband dies leaving his wife childless, she must either marry his brother or get the brother's permission to marry someone else. (Many brothers-in-law have used this law to extort money or property from the widow.) And if her brother-in-law is younger than thirteen, she must wait until he is of age to release her. On and on it goes, this incredible catalogue of ancient inequities that burden the lives of Jewish women to this day.

The third gate standing between women and equality is the *Golda Meir syndrome*, a widespread belief that any woman can get to the top if she wants to ("Look at Golda!") and that the only reason Israeli women haven't achieved more success in politics or business is that they don't want it. This myth is compounded by the behavior of a number of so-called Queen Bees. "These are women who make it and feel no responsibility to other women," says Galia Golan, professor at the Hebrew University (who was Gail Green and a Brandeis graduate before she made aliyah—emigrated to Israel—in the early 1960s). "Golda was a perfect example of Queen Bee behavior. She made it much more difficult for us."

Besides insisting that anyone can succeed because Golda became prime minister, the common wisdom holds that most Israeli women want to be, not Goldas but middle-class housewives; that they don't wish to work outside the home and aren't looking for political power; that they want pretty clothes and nice homes and are content to do nothing but rear their children.

Altogether, the contradictions are maddening. The triple mythology—the pioneer woman, the happy housewife, and Golda—creates a muddled picture of female reality and the refusal to acknowledge that Israel has a "woman problem" at all.

Conceptualizing the problem as three barrier gates—security, Orthodoxy, and mythology—with feminists acting as gate crashers, has helped me make sense of my experiences in Israel, however puzzling or disconnected they may have seemed when they happened.

Even Yad Vashem fell into place as a piece of the security picture. I thought I was prepared for the devastating images and awesome statistics housed in this memorial to the victims of the Holocaust. It's a story we all know too well. Still, I fell to pieces before a photograph of children's shoes piled outside a gas chamber, a picture that spoke of Nazi savagery more definitively than a stack of corpses.

Looking at that hill of little shoes, each pair a life gassed away, I realized how any problem short of another Hitler might seem frivolous. If issues of war and security obsess the average Israeli, I could imagine how much more fearful must be the generation of Holocaust survivors who had lived through such scenes in the flesh. I could not blame them for caring so passionately about Israel's power and continued viability as a national refuge for Jews. At Yad Vashem I understood that feminists must honor Jewish fears while insisting that the empowerment of women *adds* to Israel's strength, and that peacemaking offers an alternative route to Jewish safety.

As obvious as that conclusion may be, it struck me with the force of a fist, just as other epiphanies have beamed clear and strong from the great and the humble, and especially from the women I visited on other trips to Israel during these last fifteen years.

I will always remember Chaika Grossman, a former member of the Knesset, because she so vehemently argued that strong Jewish women were essential to a strong Jewish people, and cited her own experience as proof:

> At age nineteen, I fought with the Partisans against the Nazis. In the Resistance, no one cared whether you were a man or a woman. Only your will and your work counted. Before 1948, it was the same in Israel, but since then women have suffered a deplorable setback. We are indeed the second sex. Even in the Knesset, we're expected to deal only with social and domestic problems.

Grossman spent a lifetime working for women's rights and peaceful coexistence with the Palestinians. In 1988, she retired as deputy speaker of the Knesset and head of the Labor and Social Affairs Committee.

As I write this, only seven women are serving in the Knesset, less than 6 percent of the total and the fewest in Israel's forty-two-year history. Among elected officials at the local level, female representation is barely 8 percent. (Women compose only 5 percent of the U.S. Congress but more than 14 percent of state legislators.) In the twelve Israeli governments since 1948, only four women have been cabinet ministers, including Golda. Currently, there are no women in the cabinet.

The walls of the Ben Gurion archives at Kibbutz Sde Boker were lined with photographs of the former prime minister accompanied by the most powerful and celebrated people of his time—all men, except for Golda. "We used to call her the only real man in the cabinet," quipped an archives spokesman. It was the third time I'd heard that line in three days.

One night, at the home of Shlomo and Ziva Lahat, the mayor of Tel Aviv and his wife, we met with a convivial group of journalists, theater people, politicians, academics, and industrialists. Given the diversity of the crowd, I was surprised at everyone's ignorance of Israeli women's status, with which we visitors seemed more familiar than they, and by some Israeli women's simplistic assessment of feminism. Opinions ranged from "Who needs liberating, we're the privileged ones!" to "Of course, I'm for equal pay for equal work, but . . ."—a range I might describe as spanning from A to B. By the time Ziva Lahat assured us that "If Golda could do it, any woman can do it," I was so sick of hearing that remark that I asked, "So why hasn't anyone else done it?" Everyone laughed. I longed for a reality check. Where were the feminists?

A few turned up at a luncheon given by the Commission on the Status of Women. This time, several Americans snickered when one of the commissioners said as if she'd invented the idea, "Golda Meir proved that it can be done."

To our relief, another commissioner barked, "Nonsense, Golda has been an alibi so that nothing need be done."

"She's also been an excuse," shouted another angry voice, adding:

Israeli women who are not interested in being prime minister think the alternative is being nobody. They're like parasites living off her fame. Just because we had one Golda doesn't mean we can't have a thousand more.

A woman in the back of the room called, "Yeah, but if you want to be a Golda, you'll have to divorce your husband and abandon your children like she did."

I met the subject of their crossfire on December 24, 1976, when she came to have breakfast with our delegation. Regardless of her feminist blind spots and what I consider moral and political misjudgments on the Palestinian issue, I was excited to meet this modern Deborah, this international symbol of Israeli independence and Jewish pride. In my secret fantasies, she also happened to be the woman I had imagined as my mother's alter ego—the woman Ceil might have been.

Golda was only two years older than my mother. Golda was born in Kiev, Russia, instead of Pilipits, Hungary—but like Ceil, she came to America at the age of seven. Golda helped out in her mother's grocery store; Ceil helped out in her father's grocery store. Golda was unhappily married; so was Ceil. Of course, the parallels are forced; still, I played them out, imagining my mother breaking free of her low self-image and man-pleasing neediness to become a passionate Zionist like Golda; going to Palestine like Golda, choosing leadership, travel, conferences, speaking out, fund raising—leaving domesticity behind while she worked to create a nation.

Golda, my fantasy mother, was by no measure a better mother than Ceil. But she was a more delineated woman, she had clearer boundaries, she had a purpose. In those ways, Golda, my fantasy mother, reminded me of my father.

At the point in her life when Golda goes to Palestine, the Ceil/Golda parallels fade out and the Jack/Golda parallels pull into focus. In the space between reverie and dreams, I merged my father's Zionist devotions with Golda's; I made his leadership career match hers as a model train resembles the original—scaled down but chugging around its own miniature track at full throttle.

Again, doubleness. Again, alternatives skewed by love for Mommy and admiration for Daddy. Golda, his female incarnation, is the woman I might have been if I grew up to be my father's daughter. Again, impossible dualities: Ceil, who is there for her family but absent to herself; and Golda, who abandons her family but is present in the world. Mommy or Daddy. Ceil or Golda? The lady or the tiger?

She arrived at our hotel trailing a phalanx of secret service men like an unruly tail on a stately old dog. A stocky woman with strong dark brown eyebrows and flashing eyes, she wore her wiry gray hair brushed straight back and fastened in a bun—the coiffeur of a Lower East Side landlady. When I stood beside her I was taller, and I am only five feet four. Yet this old woman in a simple suit, yellow blouse, amber beads, and absolutely no makeup was obviously more than somebody's grandmother. Her matronly appearance did not belie a kind of regal bearing as she shook each of our hands, a pocketbook hanging limply from her arm. With all those men in attendance upon her, she needn't have carried anything, but it struck me that the purse was the perfect homely accessory to humanize this powerful woman whom everyone, even the busboy, called Golda.

"How did it feel to always be the one woman among many men?" asked a member of our delegation as the two shook hands. "That's easy," said Golda with a half-smile, glancing at the few men in our group. "What I don't understand is how to be a man among many women."

Everyone roared. Instantly I understood how she must have tamed those monumental male egos who were her political colleagues and adversaries through the years. Maternal appearance, self-effacing humor, and supreme confidence were a formidable combination.

Once seated around the breakfast table with Golda at its head, we the petition signers introduced ourselves to her one by one. I was amused to see who embellished his or her credentials for Golda's benefit and who didn't. Regina Ryan, a free-lance book editor, didn't: "I'm an editor interested in Jewish affairs and women," she said.

"In that case," shot back Golda, "you have two problems."

Mary Anne Krupsak, who at the time was lieutenant governor of New York State, ended her introduction by proffering personal regards from then congresswoman Bella Abzug, whose name elicited obvious affection from Golda. Her reaction surprised me. Bella's politics were so much farther to the left, what could the two women have in common besides their feistiness and their willingness to talk back to power? Maybe that was enough.

Introductions out of the way, Golda announced, "Speak freely; I'm here to answer questions. I know I never get a meal for nothing."

Although charmed by her I took her invitation seriously and asked what I had come to find out: "Why, do you think, in all your years in power you never inspired more women to follow in your footsteps?"

In a strong voice the former prime minister countered:

I'm not to blame for that. Women in Israel have always been less excited about me than women outside Israel. But our women have been active; nothing is done in this country without our women. Maybe they don't want to be elected, but they do want to participate in every aspect of life. Of course, there should be many more women in the Knesset; that is a problem for each political party. But we have so many parties and so many men here.

Laughter again. Still, her answer was disappointing, a diplomatic dance of blame and flattery capped by another joke. I and others in our group were not satisfied; we had expected more when she held office, and more from her now.

Mary Anne pressed the point. As if to say, suppose *we* could make up for your failures, she asked: "What can those of us in decision-making positions do with our power to open society?"

"Change isn't easy, you know, especially in Israel," answered Golda, understanding that the question was still about her.

We have here an extreme religious faction who believe the Messiah will come and arrange everything. They think we have a lot of nerve trying to change things ourselves.

"How do you feel about the Zionism-racism resolution?" someone asked abruptly. After all, that's what brought us here.

"If the U.N. accepts a resolution that the world is flat, that doesn't mean the world *is* flat—and we don't intend to volunteer to go off the edge of it," said the former prime minister, showing her steely side.

Enid Roth, an *NBC News* director, wondered why Golda had left Milwaukee in the first place. The former prime minister replied:

I didn't leave because of anti-Semitism. I left to help build a nation of our own. In any country where Jews are a small minority, you cannot live fully as a Jew. Your language, history, holidays, are those of the minority culture. You don't need a pogrom to feel unwanted. As one of my friends said, "Jews have believed for two thousand years in what they did not have." Now we have it. Our past and our present are in one place. For instance, my grandchild came home from school after learning about the Exodus and he asked his mother if she was with Moses when he left Egypt to come here.

Golda seemed to be free-associating, transforming our group into a family spellbound by its matriarch's reminiscences. Rather than press her to answer to feminism, it was clear we would have to defer to her Zionist agenda. She continued musing:

> *I've been to the Wailing Wall three times in my life. Once in 1921 when the Wall was wedged in among dirty buildings and crowded streets. I am not an observant Jew, so I went without sentiment. But there were Jews praying there and putting shreds of paper with their wishes into cracks in the Wall—and I felt I belonged.*
>
> *The second time was in 1967 after the Six Day War. The Wall area still was not opened up to the light as it is now. Jerusalem had been freed on Wednesday. This was Friday morning, and there were still a few snipers around. It had been a fierce battle with many dead because we didn't allow our army to put its guns on Muslim or Christian holy places and that put us at a disadvantage. Anyway, the soldiers were running to the Wall, throwing their guns on a kitchen table that was set up there, and just embracing the Wall's stones and weeping until they and the wall became one. I remember one soldier who came over to me. I don't think he knew who I was. He just needed a mother. He put his head on my shoulder and wept.*

(Pictures from that day show Golda and the soldiers at the Western Wall together. Today, religious men who played no role in liberating the Wall would insist on barring Golda's presence on the "men's side" and thus would prevent that motherly embrace from taking place.)

> *The third time, the Wall area was cleared and in the open space I could see this big demonstration of Russian Jews demanding that their relatives be free to emigrate. I said to myself, "Here is another dream come true. I have lived to see Russian Jews at the Wailing Wall."*

(What if she had lived to see the Women of the Wall demanding that they and their daughters be free to pray there? Would Golda have celebrated their efforts? Would she have helped make their dream come true?)

Finally someone asked, "What about peace?"

> *Our dispute is not between those who want peace and those who want war. It's that some feel the cease-fire lines must remain; others believe*

*in territorial compromises as long as we have safe borders, and still
others want to give everything back. I'm a realist. I once said we will
have peace when [President] Nasser has a sleepless night—not over
Israel but over his hungry Egyptian children. Then he will make up his
mind that to both fight us and feed his children is not possible. We
know that Egyptian and Syrian mothers weep for the death of their
children exactly as Israeli mothers. When Sadat understands this, then
we will have peace.*

(Less than a year after Golda uttered these words to us, Egyptian
president Anwar Sadat went to Jerusalem, and a year after that, he
and Prime Minister Begin signed the Camp David accords.)

A member of our delegation asked about the Palestinian refugees
from the 1948 war who were still living in deplorable conditions in
camps in Jordan, the West Bank and Gaza.

Her answer was curt:

*We absorbed Jewish refugees from the Arab countries, but the Arab
countries wouldn't accept their own refugees. Why must Jews be the
only Christians of the world?*

She let the question hang in the air and then she sidestepped the
refugee issue.

*Some of my best friends are prime ministers, and they tell me that the
oil nations have eight hundred million pounds sterling in their banks.
I'll never forgive Moses. It took him forty years to lead the Jewish
people to the one place in this whole area where there is no oil.*

This was her closing joke, a nice, innocuous way of winding up our
meeting. But I had one more question: What lies ahead for Israel?

*My friend Pincus Sapir used to say every country has its list of
priorities—one, two, three. In Israel, everything is number one. We
must absorb our immigrants, we must develop the land, we must
educate all our people, and we must remain alive.*

She left as she had come, looking simultaneously ordinary and very,
very important. Although I wished she had been able to reframe her

experiences in a way that offered something universal or generalizable for all women, I could accept her for what she was—sui generis, a Jewish woman who had made it to the very top and the only woman in the pantheon of Israeli secular giants. Dartmouth Professor Arthur Hertzberg calls her "Queen Golda the First of Blessed Memory." Israeli author Ze'ev Chafets dubs her "the quintessential Zionist earth mother." Today, some feminists claim her as their own simply because she was a national leader and a woman. Others, myself among them, find her a complex and contradictory figure, eminently quotable ("Don't be humble, you're not that great" is her best line), but ultimately disappointing for her limited vision and for failing to use her power to greater effect. In any case, I doubt she would have cared what we thought.

I want to honor her for her place in history: Meir was only our third Jewish woman leader after Deborah and Queen Shlomzion. Yet I don't like to see her deified as a feminist heroine, and I deplore the mythology that is perpetrated in her name. The Golda syndrome— "Golda proved women can be anything, so we don't have to prove anything ourselves"—is a cover for apathy, and apathy is the self-defense of the powerless. The antidote to the Golda syndrome is an active women's movement with a concrete agenda for change.

The women I know who are carrying that agenda forward tend to be wonderful trailblazers, troublemakers, and spokespersons for the feminist cause; they are also Jewish. I am aware that they have many Arab counterparts but I must admit that, until the experiences with Arabs that I describe in chapter 16, Palestinians were merely faces in the background as I went about my business in Israel and the West Bank. As a Jewish-American and as a woman, I could try to understand what it is to be seen as a suspect minority and an inferior, but all I could do was to imagine how it felt to be treated as a despised enemy in a land one considers one's own. Some of my Jewish friends described the Palestinians' living conditions in the Occupied Territories and reported chilling examples of their second-class citizenship, including the lack of due process and the denial of their economic and educational rights, but it would be years before I would really focus on the lot of the Palestinians as opposed to Israeli Arabs living inside the Green Line, Israel's pre-1967 borders.

Oddly enough, the first Israeli Arab I ever met was a member of the board of Na'amat, the women's unit of the Histadrut, the union that represents 90 percent of Israeli workers.

"I'm a strict Muslim and I believe the man must be the dominant power at home," said Enam Zu'bi, sounding like a charter member of the Phyllis Schlafly brigade. "We Arab women cannot fight our men; it is not suitable to our own lib. We know that Muslim men do help out at home. It's just that if a neighbor comes along, our husbands sit down so as not to be seen in disgrace." While Enam's remarks rankled, they also tested my belief that pluralism requires us to listen not to what we want to hear but to what women have to say. Beneath the most retrograde words may lie clues to future understanding and effective strategy.

Enam continued:

I'm pleased that Na'amat takes Arab men to the factories where women work, so they can see that their women are safe. This is how it must be done, slow but sure.

Later, I heard Israeli feminists say that Na'amat moved *too* slowly; that it functions as a substitute institution in which women act out their political frustrations without gaining much power; that it is a barrier to participation in official decision-making structures; a complacent arm of the establishment whose reformist tactics and busy-work programs give tacit consent to the exploitation of women workers; that it did not speak out forcefully enough on many feminist issues.

Maybe these complaints were once true, but in the years since I first sat in Na'amat's boardroom, I've been greatly impressed by the organization whose current leaders—including its secretary general, Masha Lubelsky; head of its Status of Women Division, Haviva Avi-Gai; and leading women's rights attorney, Sharon Shenhav—are up-front and tireless advocates of women's advancement.

Na'amat represents nearly 800,000 Jewish, Arab, and Druze working women, including housewives. By far the largest women's organization in Israel, it has trained women for agricultural and technical jobs, established child-care programs, sponsored abortion rights laws, and helped Palestinian women who are political prisoners. Currently, it lobbies, runs leadership training programs, legal aid bureaus, and battered women's shelters, and provides free counseling for prevention of domestic violence. And it does great things for kids. Na'amat runs nearly 500 child-care centers, residences, and community centers serving Jewish, Arab, and Druze children.

At one of their residences for orphans and children separated from parents who are prisoners or drug addicts, I watched dozens of preschool kids dancing and singing Hanukkah songs in a room festooned with handmade decorations like those I used to make with my mother. Our guide, Yocheved Amir, pointed to one dark-skinned little girl with a bright smile:

She's from a Moroccan Jewish family. After she was born, her father broke into the hospital room and killed her mother for giving birth to a fifth daughter. The father is in prison for life, but he won't let any of his daughters be adopted. Despite having murdered their mother, he expects the girls to love him and no one else.

Yocheved said Na'amat maintains each child until age seven, when most are placed in foster homes or put up for adoption. She said giving parents sex education and family planning services is Na'-amat's most challenging task:

It's difficult to suggest contraception. Although large families reinforce the poverty cycle, for Arabs, children represent honor and financial support in old age and for Jews, children bring family pride and guarantee Israel's future. For the state, a high birthrate serves the need for more people to work, develop the land, and defend it. That's fine. But we still want women to know they have choices.

The burgeoning Arab birthrate was mentioned often in my conversations with Israelis. Many considered it a demographic time bomb. They felt trapped between their democratic principles and their Jewish patriotism. On the one hand, they were committed to one person, one vote; on the other hand, population experts were projecting an Arab majority within sixty years (this was before the influx of Jewish fundamentalists with large families, and the flood of Soviet immigrants) and they were worried that Arabs could use their vote to put an end to the Jewish State. In spite of this fear, no one suggested that Israel institute different contraceptive or abortion policies for Arabs than for Jews.

At the Beersheba Women's Health Collective, one Jewish woman who was pregnant with her third child said contraception is a volatile subject because of Israel's experience with personal loss:

> *If I were living in Canada or the United States I would probably stop at two children. But I cannot stop with two sons because the reality and fear of death are very strong.*

After five wars, many Israelis are worried about replenishing the Jewish nation. In 1986, the Ministry of Health allocated $3 million dollars to help six thousand infertile Jewish couples to conceive. Childless women are pitied. The average woman has 2.7 children. Those with "only" two kids feel defensive. Arabs, kibbutzniks, and ultrareligious Jews average five or six children per family.

This explains why family planning clinics are as hard to find as a doctor who makes house calls. Commenting on the paucity of contraceptive information, one woman told me: "Most Jews believe pregnancy is internal aliyah; it is women's duty to build the Jewish population and the next generation of soldiers."

No wonder the religious parties have been successful in their efforts to limit abortion. Today, the right to abortion is contingent upon the approval of one of the official "abortion committees," which are not accessible to all areas of the country and which restrict abortions to women under seventeen or over forty; pregnancies resulting from rape, incest, or an unwed relationship; pregnancies revealing a defective fetus; or those that endanger a woman's life.

That is also why, even at the height of the abortion rights campaign that I witnessed during my first visit, while Israeli feminists felt comfortable talking about a woman's right to control her own body, few dared to couple abortion rights with the right to voluntary sterilization as we do in the States. To Israelis, sterilization recalls Nazi concentration-camp experiments, and it probably always will.

The biblical command "Be fruitful and multiply" might as well be the slogan of today's social agenda in Israel. Marriage and childbearing are central to the Jewish ethic and the nation's political priorities. There are only 60,000 single-parent households. Israeli society is overwhelmingly family-centered (98 percent of the Jews marry and only one marriage in six ends in divorce) and motherhood is the one female role accorded real respect. Childlessness and lesbian life-styles are distinctly unpopular. The more children a woman has, the higher her status. Early on, the state awarded a prize of 100 Israeli pounds to every woman who bore ten children. The payouts were discontinued in the late 1950s when someone noticed that the prize was going only to Arab women. People still remember Ben Gurion's saying,

> *Any Jewish woman who does not bring into the world at least four healthy children is shirking her duty to the nation, like a soldier who evades military service.*

Na'amat has no position on family size but its counselors use creative ingenuity to lure uneducated women to its reproductive health programs. Yocheved Amir explained:

> *We offer free use of our laundromats, so the women bring in their wash and while it's in the machines, we give them a free lecture and some coffee and cake. Everyone sits around and smokes and talks and makes friends. When the husbands find out there's more than washing going on, some of them come at us with sticks. So once a month we make a beautiful dinner for both husbands and wives. Famous people, politicians, writers, professors, come to speak and exchange ideas with the men. They feel flattered to have their opinions sought by such leaders. After the dinner, somehow the men let their wives come back to the laundromat.*

At a training center in the Arab quarter of Jerusalem, run by the Women's International Zionist Organization (WIZO), I saw twelve Arab women sewing in one pleasant, airy room and a half-dozen more making handicrafts in a smaller back room. What enabled these women to work (besides their husbands' permission of course) was a kindergarten next door operated by WIZO from seven A.M. to seven P.M., meals included.

The teacher, Regina Drori, spoke fluent Arabic, Hebrew, and English although her formal education stopped after high school. She had never had a child psychology or educational methods course. She had never heard the term "nonsexist education" before I explained it to her, but she knew instinctively that block-building, counting, and cooking are developmentally important for both girls and boys. Regina told me her philosophy:

I believe the person who loves and cares for children can actually help change the world. Here I have the child of a family that lives in a cave. And here I have little girls who are brought to me because they are not valued enough to be taught at home with their brothers.

Some of the children in Regina's class belonged to the women working next door; others were orphans dropped there each day by neighbors or relatives. I saw two blond, blue-eyed boys and a girl with a pug nose and freckles as well as several dark Middle Eastern faces. But every child was an Arab—and Regina Drori is a Jew.

At first it was difficult, but I am accepted now. I have never missed a day. Even during the 1973 war, when my own son was off fighting Arabs, I came every morning to these children. I want them to know they can count on me. And maybe when they grow up they will not be able to hate all Jews because they will remember Regina.

I have always promised the parents and relatives that I will speak only Arabic in class and that I will teach no Jewish history or customs. But a few parents asked me to teach their children some of the most popular Israeli songs. Maybe they are beginning to believe we will be living together for a long time.

If Jews had saints, Regina would be beatified by now. She was a one-woman social revolution, a psychoanalytic genius, a wise soul. The Talmud says, if you save one life it is as if you have saved the world. Most people will never know how many lives Regina Drori has saved and how many she has changed, even when it meant putting herself in danger.

Once I stepped over the bounds. A woman who had six daughters came crying to me that her husband was going to take a new wife because he wanted someone to give him sons. The woman was heartbroken. She loved her husband, but under Muslim law he could take three wives and she couldn't stop him. She threatened to kill herself.

I asked her if I could talk to him—even though it is unheard-of for a woman, especially a Jewish woman, to approach an Arab man. Still, I picked up my courage and one morning when he brought his daughter to school, I told him that his wife had confided in me how much she loved him, and that she couldn't bear to share him with someone else. He was flattered but firm. Since this wife couldn't make boy babies, he had to try another. I told the man that having only daughters was his fault.

At this point in the story, I held my breath. Would Regina be brash enough to lecture him on genetics?

I told him he was wrong not to be satisfied with his lovely daughters who honored and adored him. But if he insisted on having a boy, then the way to have boy babies is to be very kind to his wife. Only a good and devoted husband is rewarded with a male child.

He promised to try out my theory. Several weeks later the wife became pregnant again. I prayed day and night for the whole nine months! During that time, the wife came and told me that her husband was a changed man. What had I done to him, she wanted to know, to make him such a wonderful husband? I bit my lip and I waited.

Thank God, her seventh baby was a boy. And now the eighth baby is a boy too. The woman is full of joy. The man thinks I'm a prophet. And he has honored me by bringing me his first son who is now two years old. The father has told me that I may have both his sons in my day nursery until they are five because, he says, "They are your children, Regina."

When our group met with the Commission on the Status of Women, I remember thinking that this was another version of the laundromat, or Regina's classroom. Although its members were drawn from an elite group of academics, businesswomen, and political leaders, the Commission's activities also were directed toward women's advocacy and empowerment. That day, for instance, they discussed the fact that Israel's equal-pay laws were meaningless as long as there was a short school day (public school children are dismissed at one P.M.) and not enough child care to free mothers to work. Nearly 60 percent of Israeli working women have part-time jobs to accommodate their family obligations. As a result, they cannot compete with men in the workplace.

In employment status, in 1991, Israeli women were where American women were thirty years ago. Although they constitute 40 percent of the Jewish work force, Israeli women constitute only 1 percent of management in private industry and 6 percent in the public sector.

A woman with a high school diploma makes as much as a man with a fourth-grade education. Israeli women earn an average of 70 cents for each dollar earned by men. American women suffer a larger pay gap, but in Israel those willing to fight the status quo are few and far between.

Since the State of Israel was founded very few women have brought discrimination charges in the courts, but when they *do* it is often with the help and counsel of Dr. Frances Raday of the Israel Women's Network and the Hebrew University law faculty. Like an unseasonably warm day in the dead of winter, Frances gladdens me in the midst of so much injustice. Right now, for instance, I'm following her lawsuit against El Al Airlines which has barred ground hostesses from the management training courses that lead to senior positions. The developments around this case have been downright comical. El Al made a ludicrous settlement offer—to accept five women of their own choosing into the course—and when the women refused, the judge publicly scolded their "unwillingness" to compromise. Even more laughable was a countersuit by male employees at El Al who claimed they would be damaged if women were allowed equal opportunity to compete with men after all these years.

I met Frances Raday and most of Israel's other feminist activists either because they surfaced in the course of my own activities in Israel—it's really a very small country—or by tracking them down in preparation for the *Ms.* tour, a Zionist-feminist journey that took place in March 1978. After the magazine ran a full-page ad announcing, "*Our* sisterhood is going to Israel," we signed up fifty-two women and four men (all husbands of participants) who hailed from twenty states, ranged in age from a Bat Mitzvah girl to a seventy-five-year-old veteran of World War II, and included women who were therapists, entrepreneurs, homemakers, an ex-prostitute, a flight attendant, health-care specialists, an actuary, and a bull cook from Alaska. The great majority were Jews, some religious, some not, and all were feminists—including the men.

The sexes were separated only twice on the *Ms.* trip, once involuntarily at the Western Wall—where a few of our women threatened to integrate the men's section but settled for slipping revolutionary notes into the cracks in the ancient stones ("Pray for the ERA," said one). The second time was the night we went for a "feminist *mikvah*" at the hot pool at the Jerusalem Turkish Baths. This collective immersion—learning each other's personal backgrounds while physically exposed—was my idea of a shortcut to sisterhood, and it worked. It started us off in high spirits and instant intimacy. (The four husbands went to the Baths the next night, so equality was reestablished.)

Unlike the tour organized by the Israeli government, I had created an itinerary with a strong emphasis on feminist themes, projects, and leaders in addition to the usual historic places and establishment politicians. This emphasis allowed us to see the universality of women's concerns—abortion, domestic violence, rape, child care, health care, nonsexist education, employment equality, sexual harassment—and to link up with our Israeli counterparts on whatever issue each of us cared about most.

Health care was on the minds of several women who had heard negative reports of the Israeli medical system—that it does not encourage preventive testing including mammograms and Pap smears, that prostate treatment was more readily available than breast examinations, that most doctors do not give women a gown to wear in the examining room, and that women doctors are routinely discriminated against in hospital assignments and promotions. We wondered whether Hadassah women back home were aware of any of the problems we discovered during our visit to the Hadassah Medical Center.

Three *Ms.* women who were health-care professionals talked their way into the emergency room and were appalled to find only the most basic equipment. A rescue helicopter and three ambulances were similarly inadequate; only one had decent stretchers, the others only makeshift ones. The staff complained of severe overwork and personnel shortages.

When one of our women asked if Hadassah should send American nurses in addition to everything else they send from the United States, a chief medical officer answered that Israel has plenty of nurses. "The problem is that they get married, have children, and like nice Jewish girls, they stay home," he said.

"Pay them decently and maybe they'll stay on the job," said one of ours.

"Do you offer child care so they can continue working after they have a family?" peppered another.

"Don't you have any male nurses?" asked the third.

I think the doctor was sorry he'd opened his mouth.

Even though the kibbutz movement has never attracted more than 4 percent of Israel's population, I was eager to see these legendary socialist experiments in collective living and gender equality.

Mishmar Ha'emek, a verdant settlement founded in the twenties, was the pride of two residents who showed us around: Yaakov Padan, a seventy-three-year-old Jewish leprechaun wearing leather sandals, and Yoneh Golan, a tall seventyish woman in a wool cardigan. Although their kibbutz had sent several of its members to the Knesset and the cabinet, Yaakov and Yoneh were prouder of their community for having reversed the Jewish socioeconomic pyramid and turned intellectuals into farmers.

"We recognize the importance of labor in every human life," Yoneh said, adding:

> *Here, no one wants to retire. One of our old women is picked up each day and brought to the sewing factory to work for two hours. She refuses to stop contributing her share. Everyone's children live, eat, study, and sleep together in our children's houses, but we don't see the collective as a replacement for the family. Parents and children spend about four hours a day together and that's undisturbed quality time because the parents have no work, cooking, or shopping to distract them.*

I asked Yoneh why we saw only women working in the children's houses.

"Men are needed for the hard physical work," she answered as if there was nothing inconsistent about sex-role stereotypes rearing their ugly heads in a socialist Eden.

Years later, Edna Politi's documentary film *Anou Banou: The Daughters of Utopia* included an interview with a woman who had also come to her kibbutz in the 1920s attracted by its dedication to hard work and equal education. Now, the woman reported dejectedly, the schools on her kibbutz channel girls into family roles and child-care jobs; and women who choose nontraditional specialties are ruthlessly harassed by male co-workers.

When I visited Kfar Blum, a kibbutz in the upper Galilee, a male resident was similarly distressed at the failure of egalitarianism there:

> *It was obvious at the beginning that women could do anything men can do. But over the years, we've regressed. Now very few women are in the technical trades. And recently, the parents voted to discontinue the children's houses so that women again have the responsibility for their children.*

(Studies completed in 1990 have shown that where the children sleep at home, only 19 percent of the women participate in governing the kibbutz, compared to 35 percent where the children sleep in group dormitories.)

When Kfar Blum was founded more than six decades ago, there wasn't a tree for twenty-five miles, the land was under water ten months of the year, malaria was as rife as the common cold, and everyone lived in tents. Somehow, the early pioneers managed to grow tomatoes, and tomatoes were what they ate—tomato soup, tomato stew, tomato pudding.

"A chicken was a gourmet delicacy," said one old man who had seen it all.

"And when a kibbutznik ate a chicken," his friend chimed in, "you knew that either the chicken was sick or the kibbutznik was sick."

Although the sinkhole they described had become a green and bustling paradise, I left feeling depressed by the possibility that problems of ideological retreat might prove more intractable than flooding and malaria.

At Kibbutz Gonen, situated on the old Syrian border, I met Paula Polansky, who had arrived in the early Seventies from the West Side of Manhattan. Despite her enthusiasm for Gonen's 1,000 acres, two factories, cotton, alfalfa, turkeys, and 140 members, the life she described struck me as the worst of both worlds. She had chosen socialist self-denial in the shadow of Syrian missiles, *plus* she still had the same family chores she'd performed under capitalism.

In the 1980s, research showed that 85 percent of all Israeli kibbutz women work in the kitchen, laundry, or children's houses. Girls reared on kibbutzim have lower self-esteem, career aspirations, and math scores and list more disadvantages to kibbutz living than do boys who were reared communally. From what I had seen myself, I was not surprised that many kibbutz women preferred nuclear family setups where at least they control their own drudge work. In 1990, I read that 65 percent of those who leave kibbutzim are women. Who can blame them?

At the Lebanese border on a wet, gray day well suited to hostile territory, we found a bleak military outpost with machine-gun emplacements and a handful of troops on duty. A drafty galvanized tin hut served as the only shelter. Inside were two male soldiers talking and smoking cigarettes while two female soldiers peeled potatoes.

My husband Bert, who sees the world through feminist eyes, asked one of the men, "Do you ever peel potatoes?"

Grinning, the soldier replied, "Only when there are no women here to do it."

Contrary to general belief and despite the frequent sight of gun-toting women soldiers, Israeli women are not men's equals in the army. Men serve three years of active duty and stay in the reserves until age fifty-five; women are drafted for only two years and finish their reserve obligation by age twenty-four. In World War II, women like Chaika Grossman fought in the Resistance and thousands more fought in the Palmach, the Jewish underground, and the Haganah, the militia of pre-state Palestine. Today, Israeli women can train male soldiers but they themselves are barred from combat. Most hold support jobs doing clerical work or peeling potatoes. Married women are exempt from the service altogether.

I've never been comfortable advocating nonsexist militarism or arguing for women's equal right to die in war, especially while simultaneously insisting that violence is no solution to national conflicts. However, as long as there are armies—most particularly the Israel Defense Forces (IDF), whose centrality in Israeli life is undeniable—I believe women must be treated as equals within them.

Amira Dotan, head of the women's corps from 1982 to 1987 and the IDF's first woman brigadier general, proved that technical skills are sex-blind when she succeeded in opening up to women such prestige specialties as tank instructor, computer operator, and flight controller. Nevertheless, 40 percent of the women in the IDF still hold clerical jobs. This takes its psychological toll. Professor Galia Golan found that women in the less prestigious positions are more demoralized and have lower career ambitions than those who perform technical jobs or fill command positions.

There are several reasons why it is important for women and for Israel that female soldiers be mainstreamed and evaluated on the merits. The Israeli obsession with security leaves many women feeling diminished by their reduced army role. They want to do more. They want to share in the national pride and gratitude associated with the IDF. Although one in seven Israeli families has had at least one close relative killed in action since the founding of the state, the Israel Institute for Military Studies found that 90 percent of high school students are enthusiastic about military service and consider the army a place of high status and prestige. For the young women, though, it is the place where they feel like second-class patriots. Those who advocate first-class equality want strong females to have at least the same combat eligibility as physically puny males.

Furthermore, says sociologist Dafna Izraeli, "the army and the political parties are the only paths to real power. And the top levels of both are effectively closed to women." Since the army is known to function as a leadership training course and an old boys' network, women's second-class status in the IDF predicts their inferior role in both public and private life.

"Men are used to women being mostly secretaries who will serve coffee and do auxiliary tasks," says Ora Namir en route to a larger point.

> *For as long as Israel's security situation remains difficult, men think they are the only ones who can handle it, and it's convenient for them to leave us to run day-care centers.*

Current gender arrangements in the army also train men to expect a continuation of male privilege at home. Having someone else peel your potatoes can be habit-forming. Women who feel they have not done their share for the nation's defense can be guilt-tripped into overindulging their husbands, sons, boyfriends, and bosses who have been on the front lines. Or to play the feminine caretaker role in society. Or to have babies on the grounds that those who cannot *be* soldiers ought to *produce* soldiers.

A favorite line is, "Men fight for the Jewish state, women populate it." The idea of women in combat is anathema to most Israelis be-

cause it inevitably raises the specter of nice Jewish girls getting cap-
tured, tortured, and raped by the enemy, especially the Syrians, known
for their barbarism in previous wars. The fact that nice Jewish boys
have been tortured and raped is somehow less terrible—an odd attitude given Jews' traditional preference for male children.

After childbearing and rape avoidance, there's another justification
for barring women from combat: Orthodox Jews object to anything
that blurs the role distinctions between women and men.

Once, while I was in Jerusalem, the Knesset was debating whether
to allow Orthodox women an automatic exemption from army service. Emotions ran high. The chief rabbis declared that wearing a
uniform or carrying a weapon is for a woman the equivalent of pros-
titution, idol worship, and murder. In the *Jerusalem Post*, a Hasidic
rabbi summed up the religious position with ineffable logic: "A Jewish woman is better dead than in the army."

Five months later, nearly thirty years of Labor government came to
an end and as part of his coalition agreement with the ultrareligious
party, Menachem Begin's Likud party granted an automatic exemption to any woman who declares herself "religious." (About 30 percent of female draftees now make that claim, and are not required to
perform alternative service.) From there it was only a matter of time
before the Orthodox parties would mount their full-court press on the
body politic.

Since my first hour in Israel when the government collapsed because an airplane violated the Sabbath, I have never been surprised by
the religious establishment's intrusions into civil affairs. Not in 1977,
when the religious parties succeeded in getting the women's army
exemption and repeal of abortion reforms in return for joining the
right-wing coalition. Not in 1984, when a religious member of the
Knesset said he would not sit in the cabinet with a woman and neither
of the unity government's leaders, Yitzhak Shamir nor Shimon Peres,
uttered a word of disapproval. Not in 1988, when Colette Avital, a
twenty-five-year veteran of the Foreign Ministry, was denied the post
of consul general in New York because the Orthodox establishment
had threatened a boycott if the consulate were headed by a woman.
Not when the religious parties tried to barter their way into a governing coalition in 1988 in return for a change in the Law of Return.
Not in 1989, when the rabbis prevented groups of women from praying together with a Torah at the Western Wall. Not in 1990, when an

eighty-eight-year-old Lubavitcher rabbi in Brooklyn—who has chosen not to set foot in Israel until the Messiah comes—destroyed the Labor Party's efforts to build a coalition because he decided God did not want Jews to trade "one inch" of land for peace; or when religious politicians introduced the so-called bacon bill, which would outlaw sales of pork products in Israel, plus bans on most public transportation on the Sabbath, plus strict limits on "indecent" advertising (bathing suits and blue jeans), and restrictions on legal abortions.

Anyone who was paying attention could have seen all this coming. Why should the rabbis draw the line at controlling women? Why shouldn't they assert their will and impose their theocratic absolutism on everyone? (You remember *everyone*.) And since Israel is a Jewish state, why shouldn't it be a *glatt* kosher state run by and for its Orthodox citizens?

The answer is, of course, because it was founded as a *democratic* state by a Proclamation of Independence that guaranteed civil rights to its diverse population—which includes a preponderance of secular Jews, plus 700,000 Arab and Druze *citizens*—and to its women. Without constant monitoring, and without feminism, the rights of Israeli women might disappear altogether.

Since every issue is connected—peace, pluralism, and equality—women's struggle is a crucial part of the rescue operation for the life and soul of the Jewish state. Or as Theodor Herzl put it nearly a century ago, "A nation striving to be recognized as equal among nations can ill afford not to recognize women as equal among men."

One evening during my 1976 visit, when most of our group had an official meeting with then defense minister Shimon Peres, seven of us went to the home of the architect Rachel Ostrowitz to participate in a strategy meeting of Israel's nascent feminist movement. Years later, when Peres became prime minister, my husband asked if I regretted choosing the feminists that night. The answer is unequivocally no. I was hungry for unadulterated, unpackaged reality and that is what we got at Rachel's house. It was the difference between processed meat and fresh fruit.

When we arrived, some twenty women from Jerusalem, Haifa, and Tel Aviv were sitting on couches and floor pillows, drinking wine, eating nuts, and passing around flyers and pamphlets. The subject under discussion was whether or not to form an independent Women's Party and run a list of feminist candidates in the upcoming Knesset elections. They knew that organizing around their gender interests would open them to charges of divisiveness; undoubtedly they would be stigmatized as lesbians, old maids, man haters, and the like. Still, most argued that anything was preferable to the continuing benign neglect by the major parties.

Their organizational problems were dizzying—petitions, deadlines, authenticating signatures, writing the platform, identifying women willing to rise above factional loyalties, reaching factory women, housewives, Israeli Arab citizens, women living in isolated settlements and kibbutzim. After a short debate over reformist versus revolutionary goals—whether to make change from within, or to overthrow the establishment and start fresh—the meeting ended with Israelis and Americans marveling at the similarities between our two movements, ideological splits and all.

A few weeks later, the Women's Party took shape with a twelve-woman slate headed by Shoshana Elings and a platform full of feminist planks: parental leave, equal pay, housewives' rights, improved women's health care, equal education, lesbian rights, tougher penalties for crimes of violence against women, and so on. In the 1977 elections, the Women's Party garnered 6,000 votes. Though far short of the 18,000 needed to win one seat in the Knesset, it was an impressive showing for such a small country with such a young feminist movement. However, the fact that so few women in the electorate were willing to vote their gender interests explains why the major parties can afford to keep ignoring women's demands. Until women are willing to behave as a cohesive constituency, politicians know they don't have to placate us, answer to our leaders, or compete for our votes.

The Women's Party has disappeared, but "The Woman Question" refuses to go away. For instance, take the issues of rape and sexual harassment. Although many Jews still believe that Jewish men are all mild, gentle, and loving, according to 1987 police data, every day in Israel ten women are violently raped. A Na'amat survey of 1,200 Israelis found that one out of every three divorced women had been assaulted by her husband. One out of four Israelis knows a battered wife. One out of five thinks wife beating is justified for infractions ranging from infidelity to poor housekeeping. Thirty percent believe that abusive husbands are mentally disturbed, when in fact male supremacy is so socially acceptable that "showing her who's boss" and beating her bloody are differences in degree, not in kind.

A Haifa judge who found a man guilty of beating his wife and daughter stated in his verdict, "I would have forgiven him had he only beaten his wife." Israeli feminists want the criminal justice system to provide judges who will treat domestic abuse and sexual assault as serious crimes. They want mandatory arrests for batterers, and they want people who worry about the endangered Jewish family to start worrying about the endangered Jewish woman inside that family. If one Hedda Nussbaum could shock us, try to imagine 150,000 of them because, according to a 1990 study, that is the number of battered women in Israel.

Israeli groups like Women Against Insulting Advertising have charged that demeaning media images of women have contributed to the climate of ridicule and disrespect that leads to violence. They point especially to TV shows that portray women as sex objects and dummies, advertisements that use female nudity to sell everything from grapefruit to men's clothing, magazine illustrations that are as raunchy as hard-core pornography, and violent pornography that trades on eroticized Holocaust scenes so ghastly and dehumanized that one cannot believe they come off Israeli printing presses and not the presses of the Third Reich.

Rachel Ostrowitz, an architect who also writes media criticism, mounted an exhibit of ten Hebrew newspapers of a random day, underlined every reference to a woman, analyzed the contents, and found that most women mentioned were the "wife of" or "daughter of" some man, and that their looks received more comment than their achievements. The overwhelming majority of stories focused on female victims of crime and sexual molestation—an emphasis that contributes to the stereotype of women as powerless victims.

Stories of sexual harassment are commonplace. When a woman student at the Hebrew University told her male professor that she didn't have enough money to buy the course textbook, he told her to "go out and turn a couple of tricks to get the money."

At a management training seminar, a male psychologist from Tel Aviv University, Dr. Uzi Barak, had the bright idea that female students and workers should be educated on how to cope with sexual harassment.

"What about educating men not to do it?" shouted a woman from the audience.

Her response reminds me of the one overtly pro-woman story I've ever heard told about Golda Meir. While she was prime minister, there was a rash of rapes in one area of the country and local officials responded that women should be put under curfew for their own safety. Said Golda: "Men are doing the raping; let them be put under curfew."

In the army, a male officer accused of molesting a female subordinate said in his own defense that the plaintiff's mere presence in the army was proof that she was already "a loose woman." Not that it matters, but 64 percent of male recruits and only 42 percent of the women have already had sexual intercourse by the time they enter the army. What matters is the prevalence of the attitude that the women who serve their country are "loose" while the men are heroes.

Still, not all the news is bad. I take comfort from the accomplishments of Israeli feminist visionaries and the alternative institutions they have established and nurtured—from the women's center founded by Joanne Yaron in Tel Aviv; to *Noga*, the Hebrew-language feminist magazine edited by Rachel Ostrowitz; to the Second Sex Publishing House established by Sara Sikes and Ilana Golan; to the battered women's movement spearheaded by Ruth Rasnic of Herzlia; to the vigorous Israel Women's Network, a multi-issue, bipartisan coalition of women activists led by the remarkable Alice Shalvi; to the feminist publishing projects of Barbara Swirski; to the nonsexist curriculum materials Shoshanna Ben Tsvi-Mayer has developed for the Israeli public schools.

These women have chosen to work from the bottom up and the outside in. Other women have tried to be agents of change from within the establishment, and though some refer to this approach as "yuppie feminism," one can argue that every little boost helps. And there have been a few little boosts. For example, in 1978 the Commission on the Status of Women issued a report that documented the effects of sex discrimination in virtually every corner of Israeli life and made 240 recommendations for change. In 1988, a follow-up study conducted by the Israel Women's Network found that only 70 of the Commission's 240 recommendations had been implemented. But that probably is 70 more than would have been the case without the Commission.

In 1984, a 120-member National Council for the Advancement of the Status of Women was established under the leadership of Professor Marilyn Safir, founder and director of the Women's Studies program at the University of Haifa. With the right budget priorities, the Council could be an effective force for change.

In 1986, the Ministry of Education hosted a groundbreaking conference for educators—religious and secular, Jews and Arabs—to develop strategies to improve educational opportunity for girls. The following spring, the ministry banned sexism in nursery schools, ordered new textbooks that feature women in expanded occupational roles and men doing more at home, and directed teachers, among other things, to stop reading stories that depict girls as "weak, passive, or waiting for a boy to rescue them."

A new law equalized men's and women's retirement ages—thanks to the litigiousness of Naomi Nevo, a social anthropologist at the Jewish Agency, who filed suit when told she had to retire at sixty though men could keep working until sixty-five. The lower court ruled against Nevo, arguing that early retirement for women was based on *distinction*, not discrimination. (One judge volunteered, "Perhaps it is better that a woman retire at sixty so she can care for her husband and family.") However, while the case was on appeal, public pressure forced the Knesset to pass a law in 1988 that gives women the option of retiring early or staying on until age sixty-five. (In December 1990, Naomi Nevo won her appeal in Israel's Supreme Court and now both sexes are protected against discriminatory retirement policies.)

Also in 1988, the Knesset passed an Equal Employment Opportunities Act that prohibits discrimination in recruitment, hiring, working conditions, promotion, training, and termination of employment. The law included sexual harassment as a form of job discrimination, and changed maternity leave to *parental* leave, making it possible for mothers *or* fathers to take time off from work to care for a newborn, adopted, or ill child. This important act passed not because the Knesset suddenly decided to care about women and families, but because of the relentless advocacy work of women's rights groups. Now Israeli feminists have to get women to *use* the law, and men to *take* the time off and do the child care.

In 1990, the right-wing administration of Yitzhak Shamir issued policy guidelines that include Item 10:

The government will view the advancement of the status of women as a socioeconomic goal . . . salaries and employment will be equated to that of men, and women will be integrated into senior levels of the administration.

For years, Israeli women of all political stripes have been demanding that the parties institute target quotas to increase female representation from the branch level to Knesset party lists to the Cabinet. They are asking for between 20 and 40 percent of their parties' lists. The only party headed by a woman is Ratz, the Citizens Rights Movement party whose leader is the courageous M.K. Shulamit Aloni, a lawyer, peace advocate, and someone I consider the conscience of the Knesset. Although numerical representation does not necessary translate into political clout, many analysts believe women have to become a critical mass before they can be taken seriously.

"The mentality is still male," says Knesset member Ora Namir, offering an insider's perspective on the problem of being a female in politics. "People who meet me are later asked, 'Was she nice?' They don't ask that about a man. Did I come to the Knesset to be nice?"

If refined behavior was a job qualification for a seat in the Israeli parliament, few of the current members would be there, secular or religious. Yet female niceness and "modesty" are special concerns of religious Jews, most of whom believe that the Knesset is no place for a woman. (Orthodox M.K.s do manage to sit in parliamentary committees with women, as long as they are not *their* women.)

Of all the religious parties, which together controlled eighteen Knesset mandates in 1990, only the National Religious Party is open to females or has ever elected a woman to the Knesset. NRP women usually rise in the party by way of its women's organization, Emunah, made up of 80,000 volunteers who sponsor child care and educational institutions. "Women are left out of the deals," says Ivria Levine, president of World Emunah and member of the NRP central committee. "We are not a large enough voting bloc, and the party feels we'll never desert them." When Emunah did desert the NRP to protest women getting no top slots on its Knesset election list, the party threatened to cut off funding for their day-care centers.

I cannot imagine how observant women, with their elaborate Sabbath and holiday labors and large families (and sometimes paid jobs), have any time left for politics. And frankly, if all they did was parrot the patriarchal views of their men I'd prefer that most of them stay out of the running. However, I'm deeply grateful to the religious women who have been courageous trailblazers for social justice; for example, the remarkable Leah Shakdiel.

Orthodox Jew, teacher of Hebrew and Judaica, devoted feminist, advocate for Bedouin rights and Israeli-Palestinian peace—Leah Shakdiel became the first woman ever nominated to a religious council. *New York Times* correspondent Thomas L. Friedman likened her act to Rosa Parks's refusal to give up her seat on the bus, when the chief rabbis and the minister of religious affairs contested her nomination, and Shakdiel petitioned the Supreme Court and won. Since religious councils are state-financed municipal bodies that make no halachic decisions but only oversee such institutions as synagogues, kashrut, the marriage office, and ritual baths, the court found no reason to deny a seat to a woman. One chief rabbi warned that the court's ruling could paralyze the nation's religious councils; another said it was against halacha for reasons of "modesty"; another insisted that learned rabbis would not sit with a woman on the same council. Leah responded, "If they have a hard time sitting with me, okay, don't be there."

When I was in Israel in 1990, Leah mentioned feeling eager for news of American feminism, so during her visit to New York a few months later, I gave a women's dinner (kosher) in her honor to which I invited a dozen writers and political activists. After each American gave a brief summary of her current concerns and activities, Leah—hair covered by a soft beret as decreed by religious law—talked about the challenge of making Orthodoxy more responsive to people's economic and social problems. She described her dedication to her neighbors in Yeroham, an impoverished development town in the Negev. She argued that women should work at community building as well as feminist struggle. "To repair the world," she said, "one must offer help and comfort, not just intellect and politics."

Regarding her groundbreaking tenure on the religious council, Leah said that the rabbis' threats had proven hollow and she had been able to do the job unimpeded. However, her victory has been exploited by nonobservant Jews who are now challenging *their* exclusion from the religious councils.

My first reaction was, Great, let's open up the whole process. But Leah was more of a purist. "Now women are no longer the issue," she protested. "Everyone is off on another battle—about Reform and Conservative Jewish representation on the councils—and it has nothing to do with us."

Although synagogue and state remain intertwined in so many arenas, there may be some relief for the *agunot* who are victims of religious divorce law. The minister of religious affairs has proposed that a husband who is unwilling to grant his wife a divorce be charged civil penalties such as loss of his right to vote, revocation of his driver's license, and denial of his check-writing privileges. In addition, this legislation would require every betrothed couple to make a prenuptial agreement covering the future disposition of their property and custody of the children in the event of divorce. It would also set up national alimony insurance and provide for compulsory mediation between the spouses.

The Israel Women's Network wants civil courts to have even greater powers: to order a division of property before the divorce is final, to award money damages for the wife's suffering, and in extreme cases, to impose a prison sentence as well. WIZO, the Israel Women's Network, and women of all religious orientations have made the plight of the *agunah* a coalition-building issue. Pnina Peli, a religious feminist and widow of a renowned Orthodox rabbi, founded an organization called Mitzvah which advocates for women in rabbinical courts. And Daniella Valency, herself an *agunah* for fourteen years, heads the Organization to Help Agunot, a group of women who have been refused a divorce, who demonstrate outside the Jerusalem and Tel Aviv rabbinates, gather data on *agunot*, and evaluate the records of individual rabbinical judges in such cases. Observant women say they are not challenging Orthodoxy's control of personal status, they merely want the rabbinate to use its prerogatives, the powers given to them by halacha—such as shunning, coercion, and physical force—to compel husbands to alleviate the misery of their chained wives.

Secular Israelis have tolerated the rabbinical courts' monopoly of marriage and divorce laws since 1953. No matter how many thousands of wives were being blackmailed or chained, there was little outcry and no organized effort to create a civil mechanism to ameliorate religious law. Why? Because divorce laws only hurt women. But now that men are hurting—now that the Orthodox have held the national political system hostage once too often and the men in power are feeling vulnerable—we hear talk of "creeping fundamentalism" and the "mortal threat to democracy." Where there have been precious few calls for divorce reform, now there are massive demonstrations for electoral reform and passionate arguments about the need for a constitution and a bill of rights that would protect secular Jews against Orthodox domination. Israelis have freedom *of* religion; what they want now is freedom *from* religion, that is, from Orthodox interference in the civil affairs of the nation.

Nothing in American political discourse prepared me for the intensity of debate in Israel about this and every subject. I will never forget the New Year's Eve Bert and I spent in Jerusalem at the home of Galia Golan and her husband David Gild. They and their guests—two union people, an army officer, a single-parent advocate, a housewife, and a women's rights lawyer—were debating at a fever pitch by the time we arrived. Whether the subject was Palestinians, the IDF, feminism, or Torah, I found their disputation so totally diverting that for the first time in my lifetime of New Year's Eves, the stroke of midnight passed unnoticed.

Initially, ignoring the clock and calendar seemed to me a symbol of Israeli pessimism: what good is a new year if it brings all the old problems? But on second thought, making conversation *the* priority struck me as a symbol of Israeli optimism—a sign of the indefatigable hope that talk can make things better.

"Two Jews, three opinions" is more than a joke in this Babel of politics and religion; it's a way of life. As Shuki, the Israeli journalist, notes in Philip Roth's *The Counterlife*:

> *Have you ever noticed that Jews shout? Even one ear is more than you need. Here everything is black and white, everybody is shouting, and everybody is always right.*

I'm not intimidated by loud voices. I love the passion. Only when Israelis stop talking, shouting, and caring will I worry that the forces of repression have won.

But at a certain point, talk must translate into action, and the action Israel needs now is social equalization, democratization, and a complete change of gatekeepers. Everybody is *not* always right. As long as Orthodoxy is the only legally recognized form of Judaism, as long as the army remains the perceived savior of the nation, and as long as men reign supreme in the state, synagogue, and military, complete freedom is impossible for those who are not Jewish, not Orthodox, or not male.

11

Special Jewish Sorrows

Women and Anti-Semitism

IN MY TWENTY YEARS AS A WRITER, ONLY ONE OF MY ARTICLES HAS won and lost friends and influenced people so dramatically that it could be called a cause célèbre.

I started working on the piece in the fall of 1980, in response to the anti-Semitic incidents that had besmirched the United Nations conference in Copenhagen. As I've said, I wanted to discover whether those outbursts were peculiar to women operating in an international context, or whether some comparable form of anti-Semitism existed among feminists in the United States. So I spent eighteen months doing in-depth interviews with more than eighty women from all parts of the country and writing the piece entitled "Anti-Semitism in the Women's Movement" that eventually appeared on eleven pages in the June 1982 issue of *Ms.*

The minute the magazine hit the newsstands, I was invited to discuss anti-Semitism on television and radio, at universities from Yale to U.C.L.A., and at public forums sponsored by Jewish groups ranging from the New England Anti-Defamation League to the Jewish Center of Dallas. The article was reprinted twice and was photocopied innumerable times as a catalyst for friends and enemies to discuss the problem in classrooms, meetings, and living rooms from Anchorage to Miami, from Toronto to Jerusalem.

The article also elicited an unprecedented volume of reader mail. Although there were some loony hate messages ("Watch out, you commie, kike, cunt, dyke, nigger-lover!") and one death threat, the overwhelming majority of letters were from readers who wanted to add their own stories to my survey ("It happened to me too"), to express relief ("I thought I was the only one feeling this way"), and to demand action ("What can we do about the Jew-hating in our midst?!!"). Out of nearly three hundred letters, about twenty were critical.

The reader mail caused considerable dissension among the magazine's editors, of which I was one. Most of the other editors, including the Jewish women, wanted to publish only the critical voices. Since I'd presented Jewish women's charges at such length, the magazine should now give equal time to opposing views, they said. I argued that to run only negative letters unfairly misrepresented the proportion of supportive responses and discredited all those other women who had experienced bigotry. Besides, we had never before published only one view of a controversy in the Letters space. I was outvoted.

The magazine published three long critical letters. More brouhaha followed. Many Jews were newly upset by the one-sided Letters column, and some pointed to this as more evidence that the movement is indeed riddled with anti-Semitism. While all this was happening I was feeling slightly battered. In time, however, I saw how many positive byproducts and progressive efforts resulted from the whole controversy. It allowed Jewish women to ventilate suppressed anger and bitterness and make a positive claim on their Jewish identity; it exposed some feminists' anti-Semitic feelings and inspired movement activists to analyze this behavior constructively in workshops and conferences, and to confront antifeminist vultures who swooped down to declare the Women's Movement dead just because I had found gangrene in one hand.

What was all the fuss about? See for yourself. Despite some 1980s political references, time (unfortunately) has not invalidated the essay, so I include it here, slightly abbreviated, before proceeding to my current thoughts about the public reaction to it and about the impact of anti-Semitism on Jewish women's self-definition.

Anti-Semitism in the Women's Movement

Why now? Why write about anti-Semitism in the Women's Movement when we have the Moral Majority and Ronald Reagan to worry about?

Because, very simply, it's there. And because I am a Jew who has been finding problems where I had felt most safe—among feminists.

• On hearing that I planned to write about anti-Semitism, one feminist asked, "Won't *Ms.* have to give equal time to the PLO?" Incredible. When did Palestine Liberation Organization interests become the other side of this issue? Wasn't it obvious that people who are against anti-Semitism are against Jew-hating? The opposite is not to be pro-PLO. The opposite is to be *for* Jew-hating.

• A white civil rights activist proudly described having organized interracial groups of women in Little Rock, Arkansas. "We went out in teams," she said. "A black woman, a Jewish woman, and a white woman." She never noticed that she had made Jews a race apart.

• Midge Costanza, President Carter's women's issues expert, gave me a view from the inside:

Because I'm known as an Italian-Catholic, Gentile women feel they can say anti-Semitic things to me, like "Why should we carry the Jews on our backs," as if Jews are responsible for the energy problem, or "That one's a Jew so there's no arguing with her." But the worst was at the 1980 Democratic Convention when a bunch of women were tossing around names to speak on various platform issues. I was amazed when both Jews and non-Jews discarded certain Jewish names because they thought having a Jew associated with an issue would hurt.

• A month or so before the United Nation's Women's Conference in Copenhagen in 1980, I asked a black friend to sign a petition warning against PLO exploitation of the event for anti-Zionist purposes.

My friend told me the Copenhagen conference was a hot topic in the black community. Trade-offs were being negotiated; an anti-apartheid resolution might be passed in return for American blacks' compliance on a Palestinian agenda item.

"Please understand," she said. "I can't afford to sign."

I understand that large numbers of Jewish women, far out of proportion to our percentage in the population, have worked for civil rights, welfare rights, Appalachian relief—issues that did not necessarily directly affect our own lives. What I do *not* understand is how much we must live through before our non-Jewish sisters can "afford" to make anti-Semitism their concern.

• When American Jewish women returned from the Copenhagen conference stung by anti-Semitic experiences, some women here at home chose not to believe their stories or called their reactions "Jewish paranoia."

I cannot think of any feminist context in which a woman's testimony—whether about sexism or racism—would be disregarded or labeled "female paranoia." Why the gap when women speak bitterness about anti-Semitism?

Are Jewish women overreacting? Evelyn Tornton Beck, professor of women's studies at the University of Wisconsin at Madison, thinks not:

At one community conference, our posters advertising a full-day workshop on homophobia and anti-Semitism were torn down— and this happened in locations that sponsored feminist activities, in women's bathrooms and women's bars. At the university where I teach, posters for my course on The Jewish Woman were ripped and defaced. I heard someone say that Jews were "taking over" the local chapter of the National Lesbian Feminist Organization in Madison.

After the great outcry against Israel's annexation of the Golan Heights, I heard a woman joke, "Israel is Hitler's last laugh on the Jews"—as if Menachem Begin's ultranationalism would ultimately destroy the Jewish people better than Hitler could. I do not think criticism of Begin is automatically anti-Semitic any more than criticism of Ronald Reagan is anti-American. However, such criticism, often under the rubric of "anti-Zionism," is sometimes a politically "respectable" cover for anti-Semitism. Jews learn to call it as we feel it. I felt the woman's "joke" was anti-Semitic, but I said nothing. For the first time, I felt afraid. I worried about my feminist friends' commitment to Jewish survival and about their opinions of events in the Middle East.

I wondered why Jewish women *are* applauded by the Women's Movement when we trudge through Judaic subcultures ruffling beards with our feminist demands but not when we bring Jewish consciousness back the other way into feminism; or why we are cheered when we critique the Bible for its anti-woman bias but not when we criticize feminists for their anti-Jewish jokes.

I thought of how often I had noticed Jews omitted from the feminist litany of "the oppressed." And I began to wonder why the Movement's healing embrace can encompass the black woman, the Chicana, the white ethnic woman, the disabled woman, and every other female whose struggle is complicated by an extra element of "outness," but the Jewish woman is not honored in her specificity? Will feminism be our movement only so long as we agree not to make Jewishness an issue? *Must we identity as Jews within feminism with as much discomfort as we identify as feminists within Judaism?*

Of course, it should not surprise us to find anti-Semitism in the Women's Movement. Unless one consciously explores the connections between all forms of oppression, it is possible to, say, work for black rights and still be a sexist or work for women's rights and still be a racist.

Racism among feminists has long been admitted, or at least given lip service, when women assemble anthologies, courses, or conferences. My point is that anti-Semitism has not yet risen to the level of concern or talk, much less action. Maybe this is because we Jews have not made it an issue; or because Jewish women are perceived as influential within the Movement and often in the nonfeminist world as well. But are we? Or is this perception part of the stereotype and thus part of the reason why anti-Semitism remains the hidden disease of the Movement?

To cure it, we need to examine the five problems basic to Jews and sisterhood.

P R O B L E M 1
Failure to See the Parallels

Time and again in my interviews, I heard women use the phrase "Jews are the women of the world," or its converse, "Women are the Jews of the world." Feminism has never systematically analyzed the similarities between anti-Semitism and sexism the way that racism and sexism are understood as twin oppressions. Yet the parallels are striking:

• Just as Woman comes in two opposing archetypes, Madonna and whore, so is the Jew split in two: victim (Anne Frank) and victimizer (Shylock).

• The myth of "female power" (our sexual or maternal omnipotence) recasts the male in the vulnerable role and thus justifies discrimination against women; the myth of "Jewish power" recasts the Christian majority as pawns, and helps justify repression of the Jews.

• "Jews really control the press," "White women really control the wealth," and "Black matriarchs really control black men" are three equally inaccurate clichés invented to mask the overwhelming concentration of power and money in the hands of *white Christian men*.

• The existence of some leisured women and some affluent Jews is claimed as proof that *all* members of both groups are privileged.

• Woman (wife, prostitute, secretary) serves as a buffer between the capitalist system and the exploited male worker; thus sexism absorbs men's economic frustration by buying them off with privatized patriarchal power. Similarly, Jew (landlord, teacher, homemaker-employer) serves as a buffer between the dominant class and the underclass, thus deflecting underclass rage onto a convenient scapegoat.

• All-purpose inferiors, both women and Jews are reminded incessantly of how we differ from the "norm." We are, interchangeably, the "quintessential Other," says historian Paula Hyman. Each group is hated because it demands "the right to be both equal and distinctive"—whether that distinctiveness refers to women's culture or Jewish culture, women's physical differences or Jews' religious differences. We make the "superior" group angry because we want to maintain our uniqueness without being penalized for it.

• Both women and Jews have to struggle to have their oppression recognized, even by its victims, because neither misogyny nor anti-

Semitism always results in economic privations. Instead, these hatreds are their own weapons honed by age-old mystical fears. The mystique of the *intrinsic* sexual-psychic evil of both women and Jews makes plausible periodic purges of Jews and bizarre accusations against women.

• "Women are too powerful" was the underlying impetus for the slaughter of 9 million "witches" and the advancement of a repressive patriarchal religious establishment. "Jews are too powerful" was the argument Hitler used to promote himself as the champion of the working class against rich "Jewish bankers." (Similar anti-Semitic innuendos are used today to mobilize nationalism in Poland, Czechoslovakia, Germany, and Japan, countries with only a handful of Jews but a deep reservoir of Jew-hating.)

Jewish women concerned about anti-Semitism are often scolded for raising "side issues," and are asked to wait until "larger" inequities are solved. Here too, there is a parallel: those who would berate us for mentioning anti-Semitism at this time—for "holding the interests of Jews above the interests of women"—ignore the fact that some of all women are Jews and half of all Jews are women. Like those who berate feminists for "holding the interests of women above the interests of blacks," or poor people, or any group, such critics ignore that half of *every* group is women. In short, asking Jews to blur themselves into womankind as defined by non-Jews is like asking feminism to blur itself into humanism as defined by males.

The failure to see these parallels and make them integral to feminist theory has meant that anti-Semitism and we who care about it are not yet taken seriously in the Women's Movement.

PROBLEM 2
The Big Squeeze: Anti-Semitism from the Right and from the Left

In the current climate, Jewish feminists have a special need for the Women's Movement to be a safe harbor from two raging storms. On the lunatic right, overt anti-Semitic violence, vandalism, swastika-painting, and desecrations have increased. The Ku Klux Klan, Neo-Nazis, White Solidarity Movement, and National States' Rights party burn crosses and curse Jews, blacks, and feminists in one fiery breath. Such groups accuse the Women's Movement of forcing Christian women into the workplace and the military where blacks and Jews are conspiring to commit lesbianism and miscegenation. The purpose of the Equal Rights Amendment, they say, is to "destroy the white Christian family and discourage the birth of white children." (In the 1990s, Jews are being accused of promoting abortion in order to thin the ranks of the Christian majority, and Jews who take a pro-choice position are equated with Nazis who fomented genocide.)

To build opposition to the ERA, the extremists appeal to anti-Semitic feelings that the Harris and Yankelovich public opinion polls have found present in one-third of Americans. At the Houston Women's Conference (a huge national conference underwritten by the Carter administration in November 1977), I remember banners saying "Kikes for Dykes" and "Abzug, Friedan, and Steinem are all anti-Christian Jews." Comedian Maxine Feldman got police protection when she performed at the conference. "There were three hundred KKK in the audience carrying placards that read KILL ALL DYKES, KIKES, COMMIES, AND ABORTIONISTS," she recalls, "and I was three out of four."

In Illinois, flyers bearing a picture of a mutilated woman warned that if the ERA passed, women would be drafted to fight in Israel and would end up similarly hurt. A broadsheet sent to each state senator lists "Zionist names" connected to the ERA plot to wreck Christian homes by "pitting wives against husbands." It cautions: "Wake up, Americans! Roll back Zionist one-worldism before . . . the ruling Jews take all the honey, leaving only the wax for you Christian Goyim."

Lyndon LaRouche's U.S. Labor party and Willis Carto's Liberty Lobby hammer at three themes: the Jews killed Christ; the Holocaust is a hoax; and Zionism is racism.

These cranks used to be easy to ignore, but the proliferation of vandalism and assaults in "respectable" neighborhoods makes the fringe seem less remote. What's more, the lunatics have made it seem reasonable and tame when Birchers or fundamentalists call for a "Christian America" or disingenuously stigmatize Jews.

Reverend Bailey Smith, president of the Southern Baptist Convention, followed his claim that "God Almighty does not hear the prayer of a Jew" with this comment in a subsequent sermon: "Why did God choose the Jews? I don't know why. I think they've got funny-looking noses myself." He later said he was misunderstood.

The Rev. Dan C. Fore, former chair of the New York Moral Majority, told *The New York Times*: "Jews have a God-given ability to make money. . . . They control the media; they control this city."

Confounding the landscape on the right are:

• Neoconservative Jews like Norman Podhoretz and Irving Kristol who, along with Reagan Republicans, are smugly anti–affirmative action and antifeminist.

• Anti-ERA, antichoice Orthodox Jews, such as the organization of rabbinical wives who invited Phyllis Schlafly to be their dinner speaker.

• Fundamentalist Christians like Jerry Falwell who claim to support Israel, but whose support is not founded on any dedication to Jewish survival but rather on a biblical prophecy that says a Jewish state must exist in order to set the stage for Jesus's Second Coming—after which all Jews must convert or be damned.

While the right plays news tricks with American Jews, the problems on the left are old and familiar. Much leftist anti-Semitism stems from radicals' inability to understand that individual Jews' economic success is not the same as Jewish political power, let alone the power to assure one's own group's safety.

Karen Lindsey explains:

The black struggle fits fairly comfortably into a leftist economic analysis: most U.S. blacks are poor or working class, with little access to good jobs or the education that might lead to them. . . . But the oppression of Jews does not so easily lend itself to a simplistic class analysis.

(As noted, neither does the oppression of women.)

Ellen Willis goes further:

The oppression of Jews is not economic oppression, it is the dynamic of anti-Semitism. It is when anti-Semitism exists and people do not admit it exists and accuse the victim of paranoia.

Another painful phenomenon on the left is the guilt of Jewish children of families who made it into the middle class; their disavowal of their parents' values and fear for their leftist credentials prevent them from identifying with other Jews. In the civil rights years, Lindsey recalls, these young people "identified themselves more as white oppressors than as Jewish oppressed, and their Gentile co-workers did nothing to discourage this view."

This sort of guilt-tripping and radical myopia is even more blatant in connection with Israel. "I've never recovered from hearing a woman at a feminist meeting scream, 'Golda Meir is not my sister, she's a fascist,' " says Elenore Lester. "By making Israel a macho imperial stand-in for the world's male supremacy, the Women's Movement threw me into the arms of Judaism."

Somehow, leftists who espouse one-world transnationalism make exceptions for "national liberation" struggles and independent nation states in Latin America, Africa, or anywhere *but* Israel.

Israel is supposed to commit suicide for the sake of Palestinian "liberation"; Jewish women are supposed to universalize themselves so that Palestinian women can have a national identity. Zionists have no standing on the left. Palestinians are all assumed to be have-nots and Israelis the affluent hosts—the parents who made it.

"Anti-Israeli leftists have no idea of who Zionists are," says Sharone Abramowitz. "They don't know that the majority of Israeli Jews are dark-skinned, poor, and uneducated refugees from Arab and North African countries."

Asked to justify their PLO support, many leftist feminists say that they are taking sides in a clash between European imperialism and Third World anticolonialism. They do not see the Israeli-Palestinian problem as a conflict between two national movements with complex historical origins. Pressed, they show ignorance of even the vaguest outlines of Jewish experience.

"I try to give feminists a thirty-minute crash course in Jewish history, but they don't want to know," says Judy Dlugacz. "It's just not cool to be a Zionist. It makes you a pariah in radical feminist circles."

Many Jews believe that pro-PLO women in America are expressing their anti-Semitism as surely as pro-Afrikaner whites in South Africa are expressing their racism:

• Barbara Seaman faults the Southern women's health center that displayed pro-PLO posters on the walls—as if anti-Zionist Third World solidarity went hand in hand with justice in health issues.

• A British feminist said anti-Zionism turns into anti-Semitism because people define "Zionism as a racial characteristic instead of a cultural phenomenon."

• Three New York women protested when the 1981 International Women's Day forum sponsored by a "Committee Against Genocide" paired a speaker decrying apartheid with a speaker decrying Zionism—implying they are comparable evils—and when *Womanews*, a feminist paper, chose to list the forum as an important *women's* event.

• Phyllis Chesler is tired of hearing women say that Israel's Law of Return is racist. (Mindful of the time when Jewish refugees were the "Boat People" of the world, the Law grants automatic Israeli citizenship to any Jew.) "I am saddened and angered by feminists who would never call a separatist coffeehouse or women's center sexist but who are quick to call the Law of Return racist," insists Chesler.

And I agree. If feminists can understand why history entitles lesbians to separatism, or minorities and women to affirmative action, we can understand why history entitles Jews to "preferential" safe space. To me, *Zionism is simply an affirmative action plan on a national scale.* Just as legal remedies are justified in reparation for racism and sexism, the Law of Return to Israel is justified, if not by Jewish religious and ethnic claims, then by the intransigence of worldwide anti-Semitism.

Because nations tend to be capricious about protecting Jewish rights, our survival has been tenuous through the ages: think about the Babylonian exile of Jews from Palestine in the sixth century B.C.E.; the crushing defeats by the Romans in the first century; think about the Crusades, the Spanish Inquisition, the nineteenth-century pogroms that drove Jews out of Eastern Europe, Stalin's purges, Hitler's "final solution" or the fact that both the Pope and Franklin Roosevelt were silent after receiving graphic early reports on the fate of European Jews in the concentration camps, and remember all the "ordinary" French, Italians, and Poles who turned in their Jews to the Nazis.

Given virtually every country's record of treating us as surplus citizenry, the survival of Israel is vital to the survival of Jews. It's that simple.

Like many, I cling to hopes of a two-state solution that does not demand Israel's suicide. I long for a PLO counterpart of the Israeli peace groups so that rational dialogue may begin. But PLO moderates, rare as they are, seem to have been silenced by their own violent hard-liners; I have heard that many—including some peace-seeking women—fear for their lives. In the absence of peace initiatives and open sisterhood, I am left to assume (according to PLO sentiments expressed in Copenhagen) that the average Palestinian woman would wish me dead. Until this changes, I have no tolerance for anti-Zionists even if they are feminists. Again, like many Jews, I have come to consider anti-Zionism tantamount to anti-Semitism because the political reality is that its bottom line is an end to the Jews.

Andrea Dworkin put it brilliantly: "In the world I'm working for, nation states will not exist. But in the world I live in, I want there to be an Israel." To those leftists who excuse their anti-Israel position because of the rightist Begin administration, Dworkin answers:

I resent the expectation that having been oppressed, Jews should exercise a higher morality running their country than anyone else. The idea that suffering purifies is Christian, not Jewish.

Some assert that anti-Zionism has become the left's socially acceptable response to "the uppity kike" the way antifeminism is the response to "the uppity broad." Ellen Willis cites the case of Vanessa Redgrave who

exemplifies a mentality that has flourished ever since 1967, when Israel became the prime metaphor for the powerful Jew: [Redgrave] hates Bad Jews—Zionists—and loves Good Jews—victims, preferably dead. . . . But the power of Jews as emotional symbols would mean little if they were not hugely outnumbered and so in reality powerless. It is that combination that makes anti-Semitism so appealing: to kill a gnat, imagining it's an elephant, is to feel powerful indeed.

Where does all this leave us? Caught in the big squeeze. The Moral Majority uses its pro-Israel position as proof that it likes Jews. The left insists that its anti-Israel position doesn't mean it *doesn't* like Jews. "Attacked from the left for being too well-off and from the right for being too left-wing, Jews lack even the contingent power of dependable political allies," says Willis, describing our double bind. To the Third World, we are white oppressors, but to our fellow white oppressors we are Jews. No wonder so many Jewish women are finding it harder and harder to find an ideological home. And no wonder we so badly need to create a feminist politic flexible enough to absorb differing views of Jewish women's issues, but firm enough to resist anti-Semitism with a single voice.

P R O B L E M   3
The Three I's
What women experience as anti-Semitism varies from *invisibility* (the omission of Jewish reality from feminist consciousness) to *insult* (slurs, Jew-baiting, and outright persecution) to *internalized oppression* (Jewish self-hatred, which some call the most pernicious anti-Semitism of all).

Invisibility. Andrea Dworkin calls it "being insensitive to genocides that are immediate to me." When the reality of the Holocaust is denied or trivialized or labeled "Jewish self-centeredness," Dworkin feels the chill of anti-Semitism.

My whole family in Eastern Europe was almost totally wiped out. I grew up among the few survivors. I understand when someone says, "My great-grandmother was a slave," but I don't feel the same understanding from others when I say, "My aunt was in Auschwitz."

Evie Beck described invisibility as a form of oppression that works against both Jews and lesbians. "When you're invisible, you lose your voice," she says. "But becoming visible opens you to attack. I found it easier to tell straight people I'm a lesbian than to tell some feminists that I'm Jewish."

T. Drorah Setel, a student rabbi and coordinator of the Feminist Task Force of the New Jewish Agenda, laments:

I am unseen as a feminist among Jews, and unseen as a Jew among feminists. Had I been black or Latina, my commitment to my community of origin would have been acceptable and my attachment to my people would have been honored.

Miriam Slifkin, a scientist and former president of North Carolina NOW, remembered a conference in her state at which some women insisted on an opening prayer that was

full of Our Fathers and Christ's name. It never occurred to them that there were Jews in the room. I asked that the prayer be struck from the record in respect for non-Christian women and the chair, Libby Koontz, made it official.

Other complaints of invisibility focus on scholars overlooking the latent anti-Semitism that fueled the nativism of suffragists who objected that ignorant immigrants could vote while native-born *Christian* women could not. Or on women's courses and conferences that always include suffragists, slaves, Christian temperance workers, but not always Jewish garment workers, labor organizers, or ghetto social workers.

Insult. Women's testimony about anti-Semitic insults is more complex. "Everyone's so laid back out here," says Phyllis Katz of Boulder, Colorado.

When someone attacks you as an "outspoken intellectual female from New York," you're not sure if they're putting you down as a feminist, a Jew, or an Easterner.

"I'm perceived as intimidating and overbearing; in other words, Jewish," says Philadelphia's Evie Litwok.

Well, my style is a result of my being the child of survivors of the Holocaust. I was brought up to take risks. That style is a threat to some women. They've tried to destroy the behavior I need to survive.

Insults often result from an ironic overlap between the typecasting of Jews and feminists: both groups are characterized by outsiders as loud, pushy, verbal, domineering, middle-class. Yet, within feminism, the attributes and expressive habits culturally associated with Jewish ethnicity—such as being raised to speak our minds, to trade on education and eloquence when there is no other currency, to interrupt or else be interrupted—contradict the ideal of (Quaker meetinghouse turn-taking) sisterhood.

Jewish stock types also present extra problems in feminism. For instance, the Jewish Mother epitomizes the self-sacrificing, maternal role that many feminists vocally repudiate.

Pauline Bart of Chicago is troubled by this:

My Jewish qualities are as discriminated against in the lesbian movement as a height requirement would discriminate against Puerto Ricans in the fire department.

The ideal dyke personality is in direct conflict with my socialization as a Jew. The acceptable dyke is a jock. She's into mechanical things like fixing cars or carpentry. She's tough, unemotional, non-monogamous. In short, the model for the ideal dyke is an adolescent, working-class Gentile male—right down to the body build, the cap, and the butch jacket. There's no way I can fill that role.

The Jewish American Princess (JAP) stereotype—a materialistic child-woman, indulged by her parents and educated to lure a husband—runs dead against the feminist ideal of a strong, up-front, self-supporting radical who demands her rights and makes her own life. (In 1971, *Off Our Backs* ran a comic strip lampooning "a Jewish Princess named Felicia" who had a nose job, a lawyer father, a dentist husband, three children, a split-level house in Jersey, a powder-blue Mustang, and played bridge every Thursday.)

A third stereotype, the Exotic Jewess, is usually portrayed as dark, voluptuous, close to "animal" sexuality, and privy to carnal mysteries. This feminized version of the "dirty Jew" stereotype gave the Cossacks an excuse to rape women of the shtetl; it is useful to pornographers, sexual sadists, and even to the Christian mainstream in which Eve, the Old Testament temptress, is cast as inventor of Original Sin. Diane Gelon, the administrator of Judy Chicago's artwork, *The Dinner Party*, says she often heard comments like, "It must have been done by Jewish women; it's so blatantly sexual."

Add to these distinctly female stereotypes the old "classics," the Jewish Intellectual and the Jewish Moneymaker, and there is no room for us to be *anything* without triggering someone's preconception.

Gloria Greenfield's experiences illuminate the point:

As publisher and treasurer of Persephone Press, I get a lot of heat. When negotiating the financial terms of a contract, I've been accused of being "cunning," a "cheap Jew," or of "Jewing someone down." When Evie Litwok and I gave financial workshops, several women said we were only into money because we're Jews. They reduced our revolutionary strategy for women's economic self-sufficiency to a Jewish business.

As for the intellectual put-down, a lot of feminists see women's studies as an organizing tool; when I say I see it as serious research, I'm called a bourgeois Jewish intellectual. Bourgeois! My parents are Russian immigrants. Neither of them went to high school. My mother is a janitor; my father works as a cab driver and a hospital worker. Feminists could try to understand what education means to someone like me.

Andrea Dworkin has altered her behavior to defy the stereotype:

I keep quiet at meetings more than I should because I don't like feeling singled out as the Jew with the words.

I grew up poor in Camden, New Jersey, where Jews had to stay on our own block. For us, reading and writing was the only thing they couldn't take away from us. Even though I was a girl, my family encouraged me to become literate. And now, in the Women's Movement, I am made to feel self-conscious about being "an intellectual."

As feminists should know well, stereotypes often originate in group survival techniques and coping mechanisms that have been flattened into caricature. Stereotypes are also barriers to intimacy because they deny individual complexities. They add insult to injury, transforming group pride and survival strengths into cause for shame. And they hurt.

Internalized oppression. Both Inge Lederer Gibel and Cynthia Ozick reminded me of the words of Rosa Luxemburg, the German Communist leader who had this response to a letter about the atrocities and pogroms against the Jews in Eastern Europe: "Why do you pester me with your special Jewish sorrows? . . . I cannot find a special corner in my heart for the ghetto."

Luxemburg, a Jew, went on to speak movingly of suffering Africans, Asians, and Indians—which at the time prompted one historian to marvel at the phenomenon of a group so capable of compassion for others but only of contempt for its own. Of course, the overall record of Jewish philanthropy to other Jews disproves that generalization, but it is true enough in its particulars to rankle. (And to give me the chills, for not one Jew in Rosa Luxemburg's Polish ghetto was left alive by the Germans in World War II.)

If today's women also slough off our "special Jewish sorrows," it is because many of us have internalized anti-Semitic views of everything Jewish—including our own suffering—adding a double unworthiness for being both female and Jewish. Self-hatred and denial of a part of oneself or one's origins is a kind of *invisibility imposed from within.*

Oddly enough, internalized oppression is a luxury. Like the Queen Bee, the "only Jew in the club" functions best when denial of one's group is possible and assimilation is permitted. As factual oppression worsens, assimilated Jews have historically been forced to rediscover their Jewishness one way or another. (Although under most conditions Jews can choose to pass where blacks cannot, Hitler proved that a society that wants to can rout out its Jews regardless of their denial or disguise.)

I think the current rebirth of Jewish identity among feminists—or at least the desire to confront anti-Semitism—is a repudiation of that internalized oppression that kept us so closeted.

It is no accident that this Jewish "coming out" process has in many feminist communities been spearheaded by lesbians. Having opened the windows on one secret identity and not only survived but flourished, lesbians seem less willing to live with another part of their identity repressed—and more willing to brave the consequences within feminism for calling attention to those "special Jewish sorrows."

No matter how "un-Jewish" we are, no matter how unobservant, atheistic, disconnected to the Jewish community or the State of Israel, more and more women who were *born* Jewish are coming to believe they must deal with what that identity means to them and how they feel about other Jews and Jewish issues.

On January 11, 1981, at the San Francisco Women's Building, 350 Bay Area feminists showed up for a forum on "Anti-Semitism in

the Women's Community." Fifty had been expected. The women
who organized the event—Sharone Abramowitz, Marsha Gildin,
Chaya Gusfield, and Pnina Tobin—filled the program with a history
of anti-Semitism, a short skit on women resistance fighters in the
Warsaw Ghetto, a presentation on Jewish women in the labor movement, another on anti-Semitism in the early suffrage movement, and
a listing on a blackboard of all the Jewish stereotypes called out by
women in the crowd. But it was the speak-out on "passing" that
brought forth visceral pain and dammed-up tears.

Rising from the audience, woman after woman told of how she
hated her "Jewish nose" and had it "fixed"; how she straightened
her despised, kinky "Jewish hair"; how she allowed herself to be
mistaken for Italian or Puerto Rican; how hard she worked to get rid
of her "Jewish accent" or to force herself to stop talking with her
hands; or how inevitably she preferred to identify as a civil rights
worker, a Marxist, a veggie, a radical feminist—anything but a Jew.

Tobin felt that the forum was important to build Jewish awareness
and strength in the face of the rise of the right. She, too, had been
denying her roots. "In the 1960s, I tried to be a hippie mother—
white Anglo Southern California mellow," says Tobin.

*Only now am I reclaiming the positive qualities of the Jewish mother
in me: the strength, the warmth, the characteristics of the shtetl.
They may seem outmoded here, but when children's lives are in
danger, like in the pogroms, it's important for women to hover and
protect. Also I was finally able to admit that the feminist format for
consciousness-raising (taking turns speaking in order) is not right for
me; it's frustrating for anyone whose training is to get excited, interrupt, argue within the* mishpacha. . . *[family], and expect enough
love and warmth to absorb it all.*

Another common symptom of internalized oppression is described
by Maxine Feldman:

*As a kid, I was the only Jew on my block to keep my own nose, and
in the movement's early days, I was the only one to keep my own
name. Women were changing their names if they had a "man"
ending. They said it was to deny the patriarchy, but they were also
denying their Jewish identities. Feldman is a Jewish name, not a*

male name. When they asked why I didn't change it, I answered, "Why don't Margie Adam and Cris Williamson *change theirs?"* *(Margie and Cris are singers and feminist cult heroines.)*

Pianist-composer Davida Goodman uses the name Ishatova, which is "good woman" in Hebrew. She chose to identify as a Jewish woman for the first time at the West Coast Women's Music Festival at Yosemite. To a hushed audience she talked about her pianist mother, a survivor of Auschwitz; she played the same Chopin piece that her mother played in the concentration camp and read a poem about her mother.

Said Goodman:

People came up to me crying. They told me, "I'm Jewish" or "I live with a Jew" or tried to make some connection. Since then I have a feeling of "my people" with Jewish women.

For the poet and writer Louise Bernikow, the absence of negativism is enough of a positive:

I came from a lower-class Jewish family and I had an image of a Jewish girl locked in the attic with the Nazis outside her door. I obliterated my own Jewishness. Most of my friends were Christian. The night I went to the New York feminist seder was the first time I'd ever been at an organized Jewish women's event. I was deeply moved by the ceremony, but more so by the fact that Gloria Steinem was there talking about her Jewish grandmother and identifying as a Jew when she is half-Jewish and had the choice not to.

This business of *identifying* was posited in a new way by a Gentile friend: "Would you say to your c-r [consciousness-raising] group 'I'm a Jew' or 'I'm Jewish?' " she asked. "Why does 'Jew' seem to be a racial slur, and 'Jewish' the polite liberal term?"

Her questions made me realize that almost all the women I interviewed had called themselves "Jewish"; few had said, "I'm a Jew." Is this a clue to our self-hatred? Do we avoid the noun as too strong an embodiment, too central an identity? (Jewish woman is as bland in its way as working woman, Democratic woman, Southern woman.) Have we absorbed the anti-Semite's invective use of "Jew" to the point where we cannot speak our tribal name without fear?

PROBLEM 4
Religion, Gods, and Goddesses—
The 5,000-Year-Old Misunderstanding

There is a morning prayer in which every Orthodox Jewish man thanks God for not creating him a woman. "I wish I had a nickel for every time a feminist has quoted that prayer to argue the supreme sexism of the Jewish faith," says Pnina Tobin. "That prayer has probably been spoken more often by anti-Semitic non-Jews than by Jewish worshipers."

Several years ago, Leonard Swidler wrote an essay that has become the basic catechism for Christian feminists. In it he argued that "Jesus was a feminist" because he broke with many Jewish customs that mistreated women. However comforting this thesis may be for some (especially in view of the misogyny of the religious right), it leaps over all the Christian sexism perpetrated in Jesus's name, from the masculinist liturgy to the lack of women Apostles, to the Catholic refusal to ordain women priests—and it has been used to make Judaism the heavy among patriarchal religions. In fact, a major focus of attention at the December 1981 convention of Catholic, Jewish, and Protestant Feminists of Faith was the disconcerting trend toward anti-Semitism in the writings of some Christian feminists.

"The more negative they can make Judaism," explains Professor of Religion Judith Plaskow, "the more feminist Jesus appears for veering away from it."

When asked if she was flatly denying the sexism in Judaism's origins, Plaskow replied:

Obviously Judaism is patriarchal. This hurts us deeply. Yet it's one thing when we articulate it in our terms and another when it is taken up by Christians as evidence that Jews are more patriarchal than any other people. Just as Jews have been called more Communist, or more stiff-necked, or more whatever, this kind of projection of humanity's ills onto one group has been used against women. It is what we as feminists are committed to destroy.

Speaking of projection, a feminist who believes menstrual blood is sacred told me flatly one day that Jews killed the pagan glories of the female religion by inventing the patriarchal God of Abraham. As I listened to this spiritualist "sister," the commonality of our menstrual blood disappeared. It was my Jewish blood that ran cold. We who have been called "Christ-killers" had become "Goddess-killers." Feminism or not, how far have I progressed if I am still called murderer?

Author Miriam Schneir points out that ancient Judaism was against polytheism, rather than against women, and that it took Christianity to articulate the rabid woman-hating that culminated in church-led witch hunts. Yet Judaism takes the rap for the death of the female deity in several Spiritualist/Matriarchist books, most notably *The First Sex* by Elizabeth Gould Davis (Putnam, 1971), and *A Different Heaven and Earth*, by Sheila D. Collins (Judson, 1974).

Plaskow says of those authors: "They overlook the fact that many goddess-worshiping cults were themselves patriarchal, also that the Goddess was being dethroned long before Judaism came along."

Goddesses may have become important symbols to many feminists for whom both Christianity and Judaism are beyond the pale. But, warns Cynthia Ozick,

Let's not romanticize them. Their purpose was often human sacrifice. Babies were killed to appease them. Mothers were brainwashed to want their children chosen for death.

And author Tillie Olsen insists:

The present feminist spirituality movement wipes out the fact that for its time, Judaism was a tremendous step forward. The old religions were terrible. And who needs goddesses anyway? Why not dignify ourselves with the actual achievements of real women: shelter, food gathering, the invention of language. Why let men's definition of religion be the source of our spirituality?

PROBLEM 5
Black-Jewish Relations

If parallels between women and Jews are sometimes missed, parallels between Jews and blacks are almost too obvious—so close, in fact, that rather than inspire coalitions, they incite what Susan Weidman Schneider calls "a competition of tears."

I think the reason we often fail to identify together is the same for both black women and Jewish women: we do not always have the ability to be feminists *first*. Right now, for example, I feel more vulnerable in America as a Jew than as a woman.

Many black women have suffered more for their race than for their sex. Many Jewish women, from biblical times through the Holocaust, have been slaughtered not because they were female but because they were Jewish. As a result, both groups have often chosen to stand in solidarity with their men against a hostile world rather than explore shared circumstances and synthesize an analysis that includes racism, sexism, *and* anti-Semitism.

Black women have been criticized by some white feminists for putting race ahead of sex. From my new perspective and with my sense of Jewish vulnerability, I understand this propensity and I wonder whether the feminist worldview needs to be expanded to recognize that there are times when sisterhood must bow to "peoplehood" for blacks and Jews.

Instead we do little more than compare burdens and police one another's privileges. Historically, we have been pitted against each other: in ghetto slums as the poorest housing passes to the lowliest newcomer group; in competition for liberal philanthropic dollars; in transitional neighborhoods and suburbs; in schools and jobs where a finite number of slots is reserved for all non-WASPs to divide amongst themselves. That this game of blacks versus Jews is continued in the Women's Movement is one of the gravest failures of feminism.

Many Jewish women specifically resent that, for years, they have talked openly about "confronting" their racism, while with a few noteworthy exceptions black women's anti-Semitism has been largely unmentionable.

My interviews suggest this is changing. Jewish women are asking their black sisters to deal with the fact that they (like other Gentiles) stereotype, scapegoat, and stigmatize Jews—not just because we are white, but because we are Jews. Don McEvoy of the National Conference of Christians and Jews puts it succinctly: "Being anti-Semitic is one way for blacks to buy into American life."

Jewish women I interviewed mentioned certain grievances more than once. For example, this passage from Iva E. Carruthers's "War on African Familyhood," an essay in the anthology *Sturdy Black Bridges* (Anchor, 1979):

Today one of the most serious assaults to African familyhood is being forged by the white feminist movement the theory for which is emerging from a predominantly Jewish elite group. . . .

Carruthers goes on to identify "Aryan intrusion" as the means by which Jewish feminists destroy African familyhood; the grating irony of equating Jew and Aryan is evidently lost on her.

Also cited by some Jews as deeply offensive were two poems in the journal *Conditions 5*, the issue focusing on racism. In Carole Clemmons Gregory's poem "Love Letter," a black Delilah suggests that the Jewish Sampson would use his God-given strength to kill black people. And these lines from Judy Simmons's poem "Minority" seemed gratuitously divisive:

> mine is not a People of the Book/taxed
> but acknowledged;
>   their distinctiveness is
> not yet a dignity; their Holocaust
>   is lower case.

That "competition of tears" foolishly pits slavery against Nazi genocide, as though inhumanity was a zero-sum phenomenon and there was only so much moral outrage to go around.

"Over and over again I heard blacks complain that the *Holocaust* miniseries on television was the Jews' way of stealing the spotlight from *Roots*," said a black friend.

The average black is not sympathetic toward any white person who is brutalized or discriminated against. A lot of black women resist the Women's Movement because they think it's full of pushy Jewish women who have nothing to do but complain; but when the going gets rough they have their men to protect them.

Barbara Smith, the black feminist writer and activist, said:

I think it's important for Jewish women to claim their oppression but acknowledge their white-skin privilege. At the same time I understand why women of color find it hard to accept that anyone with white-skin privilege can be oppressed. It is necessary for both groups to make an effort to comprehend each other's situation.

Renee Franco runs workshops on black-Jewish issues in Boston and Atlanta. "Anti-Semitism from minority groups, as well as from people in general, is based on misinformation about Jews," she maintains. "Women say to me, 'You don't look or act Jewish,' and when I challenge them they say they mean I'm not loud or rich and I don't have a Jewish accent." Franco is a Sephardic Jew who was raised in the American South.

Inge Lederer Gibel spent most of her adult life in the civil rights movement. At a retreat organized to discuss sexism and racism, Gibel raised the problem of elderly Jewish women living in poor neighborhoods. "If they have been mugged and robbed by black teenage boys and they are now afraid of black males, do we tell them they are racists?" she asked. Gibel reported that one black woman fliply answered: "Nobody gets mugged unless they're looking for trouble."

"I said, 'I don't think mugging old woman is funny,'" Gibel continued.

The black woman yelled back at me, "That's why you people have always been in trouble, and are always going to be in trouble." I asked her, "What do you mean by 'you people?'" She snarled, "You know what I mean," called me a racist, and suggested I go into the next room with her and fight it out physically. Some people see white racism as the only evil on earth, but ignore anti-Semitism, which is the oldest form of racism.

In 1979, when United Nations Ambassador Andrew Young resigned after admitting he had met secretly with a PLO representative, many blacks blamed his ouster on "the Jews." Among those heard from were several important black women. Esther E. Edwards, director of the Regional Office of the National Black Human Rights Caucus, said, "Young was used as a scapegoat to appease Jewish ethnics here and in Israel. . . ."

Sherry Brown, president of the Frederick Douglass Community Improvement Council of Anacostia, told the *Washington Post*:

We have to understand who our true enemies are. Jews have historically profited as slumlords and merchants from the suffering of black people.

Most disturbingly, Thelma Thomas Daley, then president of Delta Sigma Theta, a predominantly black sorority of some 100,000 members, took off from the Young affair to accuse Jewish groups of "subverting affirmative action programs." She showed no awareness of the great numbers of Jewish *women's* groups that have worked for affirmative action from the very start.

In an interview in *The New York Times*, Daley said of Jews:

We have been patient and forbearing in their masquerading as friends under the pretense of working for the common purpose of civil rights. . . . Their loyalties are not compatible with the struggle of black Americans for equal opportunity under the law. Indeed, we question whether their loyalties are first to the State of Israel or to the United States.

Of course, while our groups remain divided, our violent enemies continue to see us as one and the same. According to Klanwatch, a project of the Southern Poverty Law Center, men and women in the KKK are "prepared to kill black people and Jews in the 'race war' their leaders say is coming." And pornographers, sadists, and rapists make interchangeable use of black women and Jewish women as the ultimate sexualized victim. As Susan Brownmiller points out, "the reputation of lasciviousness and promiscuity" is black women's and Jewish women's historic common bond. Unless we ourselves forge a healthier, more life-enhancing bond, we leave it to our enemies to tell us who we are and what we have in common.

Some readers may be relieved that this report corroborates their own experiences. Others may feel disheartened and wish for some hopeful proposals for dealing with anti-Semitism in the Women's Movement so that it doesn't divide us. I'm sorry to say I have no such proposals. Instead, I feel suddenly akin to the many black women I know who have refused to take responsibility for curing white racism. I feel angry and sad and I find myself agreeing with Cynthia Ozick who once said:

It is for decent persons to come forward and sound that note of hope, either through self-repair or through declarations of abhorrence for anti-Semitism. We Jews can't get rid of anti-Semitism by ourselves.

Since that long-ago day on the beach in Winthrop when I discovered my parents' lies, nothing has left me feeling quite as shocked and vulnerable as the discovery of anti-Semitism among feminists whom I had regarded as clear-thinking allies and crusaders for social justice. Even worse, in a way, was the overwhelming evidence of *Jewish* denial, *Jewish* self-hatred, and the flight from Jewish identity that I had uncovered in my interviews with feminists who were Jews by birth.

I began to recognize in many Jewish activists the Rosa Luxemburg syndrome—the tendency to ignore our "special Jewish sorrows" as if they are somehow too self-serving. I too began to question what accounts for the phenomenon of a group so capable of compassion for others but only of contempt for its own. In this respect, Jews in general closely resemble women in general. Traditionally, both women and Jews have been reluctant to confront our persecutors: women are afraid to rile the men in our lives; Jews, to provoke the Gentile. We are good at self-criticism. We are better at fighting for the rights of others—workers, children, Central Americans, boat people, other minority groups—than standing up for "our own."

What happened with the *Ms.* readers' letters is a good case in point. Of the twenty or so that were critical of my article, several were from women who took issue with me for singling out blacks, a few were from spiritualists defending the goddess-worshipers, one or two promoted anti-Zionism or the Palestinian cause, and a few were from Movement loyalists who faulted me for breaking ranks and publicly criticizing the Movement. My editorial colleagues decided to print three letters which they introduced with the following editors' note:

Letty Cottin Pogrebin's article ... drew one of the largest reader responses of any article ever published in Ms. *The overwhelming majority of the letters expressed support of Letty Pogrebin for taking on a topic of such complexity, gratitude for an analysis that challenged their own assumptions, and relief that someone had named for them a problem that had brought pain to their own lives. ... For the anti-Semitism forum, we have chosen to expand the discussion by publishing three longer letters expressing points of view challenging arguments in Pogrebin's analysis. We hope that these critiques will serve the original purpose of a continuing dialogue on this important issue.*

This troubled me. *Ms.* had never initiated a "continuing dialogue" on racism, nor had we felt the obligation to publish disproofs of black women's claims of racism, but somehow the existence of anti-Semitism was open to argument. The first letter was a rebuttal from novelist Alice Walker; the second was from the spokeswoman of a Palestinian Rights Organization. But the third published letter was the most disturbing. It was a group effort signed by ten *Jewish* academics and it began: "We do not wish to deny the validity of others' experiences, but we suspect that the charge of anti-Semitism in the Women's Movement is exaggerated." After acknowledging that "anti-Semitism in any form is impermissible" and "anti-Semitism did taint" the U.N. Conference, and "a couple of Pogrebin's examples from Third World women's literature do support her argument," the professors concluded, "We see these examples as atypical." They excused the debacle of Copenhagen as a phenomenon of "international diplomacy, where imperialist and anti-imperialist politics prevail over autonomous feminist discourse." And they asked that the anti-Semitism of black feminists be understood in the light of "the relevant history [of] the contradictory and sometimes tormented relationships of Jews and blacks in the United States."

Men and women also have a long history of "tormented relationships," yet feminists do not soft-pedal our critique of male sexism or let "understanding" of our shared history dictate a tolerance for misogyny. I am well aware of the historical relationship but rather than excuse black anti-Semitism because of it, I believe that our shared history results in higher expectations on both sides.

Finally, the group letter accused Jewish women of "disproportionate concern with anti-Semitism in the Women's Movement," attrib-
uting it "to the recent focus on racism." In other words, they claimed
Jewish women were playing me-too with black women: "An assertion
of Jewish identity and a focus on anti-Semitism allows many Jewish
feminists to participate in the politics of the oppressed."

For ten first-rate Jewish intellectuals to interpret other Jews' testi-
monial evidence as a bid for attention—or for that matter, for any
feminist to ignore another woman's felt experience of humiliation and
ridicule—struck me as selective feminism, or Rosa Luxemburg–ism at
its worst. Would the academics have charged "exaggeration" had
eighty Asian-American women recounted their experiences with anti-
Asian bigotry in the Women's Movement? Would Japanese, Chinese,
Korean, Filipino, and Vietnamese women be accused of asserting their
ethnic identity just to get in on "the politics of the oppressed"? Or
wouldn't they have been heard—and wouldn't the women's community have responded with mea culpas from every quarter? That ten
Jewish women had refused to hear the special Jewish sorrows of other
women struck me as a danger signal.

I picked up similar signals in some of the unpublished letters from
other Jewish women who beat up on themselves and other Jews
rather than engage the anti-Semites. One condemned her fellow
Jews as Philistines and capitalist oppressors, never crediting the Jewish social reformers who pioneered in the settlement house movement, labor union movement, civil rights movement, antiwar
movement, not to mention the Women's Movement. Some letter
writers said they had grown up believing Jews to be uniformly over-
privileged; they didn't seem to know there are Jewish working
classes or Jewish old people living in poverty, not country clubs.
They thought Jewish suffering had faded away like the photographs
of their immigrant ancestors on the Lower East Side. Even sophisticated political activists were ignorant of how recently Jews
had been banned from restricted communities, victimized by Jewish
quotas in universities, corporations, and law firms, and attacked by
"respectable" anti-Semites on the radio and in public life. They
never wondered (or noticed?) why such a disproportionate number
of political activists are Jews, or what might have impelled so many
Jews to work in social justice movements, and especially in feminism. Could it be something in their Jewish upbringing or heritage

that led them to doggedly pursue justice for women? With all the energy devoted to feminist theory and analysis, these movement women seemed uninterested in how the Jewish ethical system, with its profound emphasis on justice, might have informed their politics.

Most troublesome, in my view, were the many admissions of Jewish collaboration or silent complicity in the face of personal experiences with anti-Semitism. Like many of the women I had surveyed for my article, the Jewish letter writers revealed their ethnic shame, or should I say lack of ethnic pride. Feminists who felt ashamed had chosen to dissociate themselves from the negative stereotypes firmly imprinted in their minds. Rather than identify as Jews, they had preferred to count themselves as feminists, anarchists, leftists, Marxists, civil rights workers, defenders of minorities and oppressed peoples. They did not recognize in their own denial of Jewish oppression proof of the impact of anti-Semitism. Nor did they perceive the irony of feminists struggling to fortify one dimension of their being, the female, while leaving another dimension, the Jew, repressed, and humiliated.

Things have changed since my article was published in 1982. An affirmative Jewish feminism has flourished in secular contexts about which I shall say more in the next chapter. But while thousands of women have claimed or reclaimed their Jewishness in proud, positive ways, Jewish negativity and shame are also flourishing. At this writing, some women shy away from Jewish identification in order to distance themselves from the Israeli government's sometimes brutal repression of the *intifada*. More commonly, others want to dissociate themselves from the JAP stereotype, and its pernicious by-product, "JAP baiting," a form of hate speech, which has lately inspired menacing outbursts of anti-Semitism, especially on college campuses.

News reports document a growing number of incidents of virulent JAP baiting directed at Jewish women by men and women, non-Jews and Jews. JAP baiting is the one hate crime of which men are never the victims. It takes many forms, from vulgar jokes to verbal assaults to symbolic acts of violence, but the target is always female. At schools in what some call the "Oy Vey League"—Syracuse, Boston, American, Cornell, Miami, Ithaca, George Washington, Maryland, and Pennsylvania universities—whole stadiums shout "JAP! JAP! JAP!" while shaking their fingers at well-dressed Jewish women in the stands at sporting events. Slogans like ZAP-A-JAP or SLAP-A-

JAP are scrawled on walls or emblazoned on T-shirts. Catcalls and graffiti say, "JAPs suck!" and "Frigid JAP bitch." At American University, two male students sponsored a contest to find the "Biggest JAP on campus." At Syracuse, areas where Jewish women students live are called JAP havens. The SDT sorority is translated "Spend Daddy's Trillions." Other schools label certain locations "JAP-Free Zones" or "Bagel Beach" (where the JAPs get their tans).

Much of JAP baiting is sexually denigrating; some of it implies sexual and physical violence. One T-shirt says, MAKE HER PROVE SHE'S NOT A JAP; MAKE HER SWALLOW. Another asks, HAVE YOU SLAPPED A JAP TODAY? Posters mimicking the Ghostbuster symbol show a diagonal line through a woman holding a Visa card and a can of Tab soda, under the headline, BACK OFF BITCH. I'M A JAP-BUSTER! The Cornell University "humor" magazine published a chilling feature called "JAPS-B-GONE: A Handy Info Packet for the Home Exterminator," which instructs users on how to kill a JAP.

Logically, there's no difference between "Kill a JAP" and "Kill a Jew" since women who are called JAPs are also Jews, yet few Jewish people react to JAP "joking" with anything like the horror and outrage that would accompany the first T-shirt that said HAVE YOU SLAPPED A JEW TODAY? or BACK OFF YID, I'M A JEWBUSTER!

The young Jewish women who have been under attack have reacted with understandable humiliation and fear. Some say they have been so stigmatized and denigrated by JAP baiting that they are often considered—and consider themselves—unworthy of a Jew's love or a Gentile's friendship.

"At Passover, I always wanted to ask 'The Fifth Question: How come my brothers don't go for Jewish girls?'" said a Los Angeles woman who is quoted in *The Invisible Thread*, Diana Bletter's book of interviews and personal profiles.

A student from a Jewish community on Long Island admitted in another interview how painfully self-conscious she has become about her appearance, origins, and ethnicity:

When I attend college next year, I plan to dress conservatively. But I'm worried that even if I wear well-tailored, nonflashy clothes, people might still label me as a JAP. . . . I'm nervous that when I walk into the dorm, my future roommate might look at me and think, "Oh, no, a Jewish girl from Long Island."

Some defenders insist that what is under attack is the JAP "image," a certain way of dressing or speaking that can describe a Jew and a non-Jew alike. But the point is that the image or condition under attack is being defined *as* Jewish. Constant usage of this negative association desensitizes people to the power of name calling and creates a seemingly "rational" excuse to defame or harm Jews. Not so long ago we saw chilling evidence of where this excuse can lead: JAP hatred provided a Jewish man with his murder defense. Steve Steinberg claimed that his wife, Elana, was a "spoiled, overindulged brat—the stereotypical Jewish-American Princess." He said her excessive shopping drove him crazy, so he stabbed her twenty-six times. In 1981, an Arizona jury acquitted him.

Sexism and anti-Semitism are interactive hatreds. That JAP baiting is as hurtful to Jews as to women remains true even though JAP caricatures often are created by Jews and joked about by Jews—including Jewish women. The JAP idea seems to be the dumping ground for a lot of garbage from everybody with a problem—non-Jews who hate Jews, men who hate women, Jewish men who hate Jewish women, and Jewish women and men who hate themselves. Male novelists, screenwriters, comedians, or "innocent" tellers of JAP jokes seem to be projecting their own Jewish self-hatred onto the JAP character. By attacking Jewish women, they can believe they are attacking *women* and not the Jewishness they despise in themselves. The woman who collaborates in this game may unconsciously hope to deflect attention from her own Jewishness or femaleness onto the JAP target, thereby asserting that she is a better class of Jew or woman—as if to say, "That girl is one of them, but I'm not."

Jews who JAP bait, and Jews who trivialize JAP baiting, reveal that they do not consider an attack directed solely and specifically at Jewish women to be an attack on The Jews. Yet JAP harassment has been a climate-setter for other kinds of anti-Semitism, from Nazi regalia at fraternity parties, to vandalized campus sukkah structures, to Holocaust denial, to anti-Semitic speakers like Louis Farrakhan being invited to many universities, to the physical intimidation of Jewish students.

Most Jews who laugh at JAP jokes have little understanding of the cumulative impact of incessant negative imagery on a Jewish woman's sense of herself, and on the whole culture's view of Jewish women. But sociologists are beginning to document how JAP bash-ing contributes to Jewish intermarriage by influencing more and more Jewish men to disdain and avoid Jewish women. Psychologists have begun to chart its corrosive effect on the self-esteem of Jewish girls. And Jewish feminists are hammering home the idea that the JAP stereotype is driving Jewish women away from their identity and their community.

"I grew up thinking that being Jewish meant shopping in malls, hating nature, and talking about non-Jews as 'the goyim,' " says a Jewish woman from Virginia in *The Invisible Thread.*

> *I thought that being a young Jewish woman meant being a Jewish American princess, and being an older Jewish woman meant marrying a short dumpy man and playing Mah-Jongg. Since I didn't feel like either kind of woman, I thought there was no place for me among Jews. Those stereotypes chased me away from Judaism.*

Such sentiments—and I hear many of the same things when I speak before Jewish audiences—leave me more concerned about the impact of *Jewish identity resistance* on the Jewish future than about the long-term effects of Christian anti-Semitism. In 1989 there were 1,432 incidents of anti-Semitic vandalism, harassment, threats, and assaults, the highest level in the United States since the Anti-Defamation League first began compiling statistics eleven years before. But while the ADL counts incidents of swastika graffiti and bomb threats, they do not keep track of the number of Jewish women who are being damaged, and "chased away from Judaism," by the deprecations of the JAP stereotype. It is not enough for Jews to be *anti*–anti-Semitic, we must also be pro-Jewish—and that means being pro–Jewish women.

12

Why Feminism
Is Good for
the Jews

WHEN I WAS IN THE THIRD GRADE MY PARENTS ENROLLED ME AT THE Yeshiva of Central Queens, where we had a full Hebrew school curriculum in the morning and "English school" until four in the afternoon. I remember little of my two years at the Yeshiva other than a teacher named Mrs. Young who wore bright red lipstick and eyeglasses to match, and the way the boys fidgeted with their tzitzit, the biblically prescribed tassel fringes that hang out from the waistline of men's pants. And I remember one particular Talmud session . . .

We were reading about Rabbi Akiba who insisted on studying the Torah regardless of a Roman decree forbidding it. When a friend asked him why he took such a risk, Rabbi Akiba answered with a parable about a fox on a riverbank watching fish run in a stream.

"Why do you run so?" asked the fox.

"Because we fear the fishing nets," replied the fish.

"Well," said the clever fox, "why not come up on dry land and live with me in safety?"

"Because if we are not safe in water which is supposed to be our home, how much less safe will we be on land where we shall surely die?"

Rabbi Akiba was talking about Jews.

"The Torah is our life," he explained to his friend. "We may study it and be in danger from our enemies; but if we give it up, we would disappear and be no more."

When the teacher, a visiting rabbi, finished telling the story, I raised my hand. "There must be other possibilities besides the fox or the fishnet," I insisted. "Why should Jews have the choices of a fish?"

"Oy!" moaned the rabbi, palms to the sky. "Who needs a girl with a boy's head?"

Maybe he meant it as a compliment, the way people say "She thinks like a man" with the intention of flattering a woman. But when I was nine years old, I thought he was saying there was something wrong with me. My father reassured me that my head was just fine and that the rabbi obviously thought I had asked a smart question. But since there isn't much place for smart women in Judaism, what he really meant was, "Who needs such a brain to be *wasted* on a girl?" The rabbi was telling me that I could be a brain or a girl, but not both.

In the Jewish world, as everywhere else, I am still hearing smart women labeled unfeminine when all they want is the right to think. Women who speak up on their own behalf are called "strident" when all they are asking is "What about us?" Women who work on women's issues are treated as traitors to Jewish solidarity when all they are saying is "We are Jews too." Women who challenge male supremacy are accused of betraying Jewish men, when all they are doing is refusing to be, in the words of Isaac Bashevis Singer, "a man's footstool." A Jewish feminist is nobody's footstool.

However, Jewish women are forced to make choices not required of Jews who aren't women, or women who aren't Jews. Specifically, we often are asked to choose between two movements that represent both aspects of our double identity—Judaism and feminism. Pressured to declare a priority, I feel like a child who is given the impossible task of selecting a preferred parent, or like a prisoner allowed food or water but not both. It makes no sense to ask me to side with only one half of my self interests, yet at times both camps—organized Judaism and organized feminism—expect just that. They yank and pull until I feel like the rope in a tug-of-war, frayed and frazzled both as a Jew in the women's movement and as a feminist in Judaism.

In this chapter, rather than assume we all understand the term "Jewish feminism" the same way, I want to explain that I use it to summarize a whole system of moral and political commitments. Feminists dissect privilege. We deconstruct and examine the way gender plays out in power relations, political agendas, and economic contexts. We ask, "Who benefits? Who hurts?" *Webster's Dictionary* defines feminism as a doctrine advocating the legal, economic, and social equality of the sexes. *Jewish* feminism is all that plus a doctrine advocating unmitigated chutzpah within the Jewish community.

The Jewish feminist analysis begins at the beginning with Judaism's male favoritism. "The world cannot be without sons and daughters," said Rabbi Judah the Prince, who compiled the Mishnah, "yet happy is he who has sons and woe to him who has daughters." The ancient tradition of son preference continues today: nearly 92 percent of American Jewish couples say they want their firstborn to be a boy. In Israel, when a woman has just given birth to a daughter, a common response is *"Banot simon le banim"* ("Having a girl is a sign you will have a boy next"). In other words, next time you'll get it right.

To Jewish feminists, this rudimentary sexism is symptomatic of a world in need of repair. Indeed, if *tikkun olam*—the repair of the world—is an assignment Jews are supposed to take seriously, Jewish feminists add to the repair kit not just the tools of Jewish ethics but the equity blueprints of feminism. We start with Judaism's core mandate to do *tzedakah*—the Hebrew word meaning charity, caring, and "right action" whose linguistic root, *tzedek*, means justice—and we apply that mandate to gender. Although Judaism is not an egalitarian system, we believe that the theological injunction to "pursue justice" must lead ethical Jews to challenge the gender double standard. We test the fairness of a statement or policy by substituting the word "woman" wherever it says "Jew," or "Jew" wherever it says "woman." When we find inhumanity to women, we say "custom" is no substitute for decency, and when we find less justice for Jews than non-Jews, we expect reparations.

Jewish feminists believe that women should not only perform *tzedakah* and *gemilut hesed* (acts of lovingkindness), but also receive them. We ask that the Jewish community, which is so generous to the poor and hungry, be generous to women, who are spiritually impoverished and hungry for power over their lives. But we do not limit our purview to women who are victims. We celebrate women of intellectual boldness and worldly achievement. We believe that the Jewish woman who refuses to be a footstool for a man is also fortifying herself so that if need be, she can refuse to be a footstool for a Gentile.

In the United States, Jewish feminism has become almost as specialized as the field of medicine. Religious feminists target injustice in the synagogue and repair that world with new rituals and a new inclusiveness. Secular feminists monitor the world outside the synagogue, but do it with a Jewish heart and a broadened definition of "our issues."

Homelessness, for example, is both a women's and a Jewish issue. It's a women's issue because more and more mothers and children are living on the streets, and because many women are just one man away from homelessness themselves. It's a Jewish issue because, whether or not Jews are personally affected, relieving human misery is a moral imperative and acting morally is what *makes* us Jews. This is not a tautology. In Leonard Fein's words, "It is the right way to live whether or not it promotes Jewish continuity or anything else outside itself."

Some Jewish feminists do their caring in the world outside the Jewish community. Every Saturday morning, for instance, a group of women wearing prayer shawls and *kipot* on their heads meet in front of an abortion clinic and say a prayer to help each other endure the day ahead. They are volunteer escorts who will stand between taunting, shrieking "Operation Rescue" bullies and the frightened pregnant women who come to the clinic to exercise their right to reproductive choice.

Other Jewish feminists direct their caring to the struggle for disarmament and environmental sanity, to the sanctuary movement, to antiracism work, gay and lesbian rights, the national campaign for child care, hunger projects, and AIDS activism—and they bring their feminist values and their Judaism with them wherever they go.

In Natan Sharansky's autobiography, *Fear No Evil*, one splendid passage describes the way a developed Jewish identity can expand rather than contract one's political commitments:

> *While my own focus was on Jewish emigration, I was also active on behalf of people from many national and religious groups whose rights were brutally violated by the Soviet regime, including Pentecostals and Catholics, Ukrainians and Crimean Tatars. . . . My interest in helping other persecuted peoples was an important part of my own freedom— a freedom that became real only after I returned to my Jewish roots.*

Sharansky's next paragraph (absent the masculine pronouns) could have been written by a young Jewish feminist:

For the activist Jews of my generation, our movement represented the exact opposite of what our parents had gone through when they were young. But we saw what had happened to their dreams, and we understood that the path to liberation could not be found in denying our own roots while pursuing universal goals. On the contrary: we had to deepen our commitment, because only he who understands his own identity and has already become a free person can work effectively for the human rights of others.

There are also Jewish feminists who choose to focus their efforts on the needs of Jews. They help Jewish institutions establish child-care centers, parenting classes, support groups for Jewish lesbians, social programs that break the Noah's Ark syndrome and welcome Jewish singles one by one. They promote lectures, films, and courses that reflect feminist perspectives on issues of concern to Jews—like the environmental crisis, or the morality of surrogate motherhood. They introduce nonsexist books and biographies of achieving Jewish women into Hebrew schools. They collect women's oral histories so that female reality will be part of the Jewish master story for future generations.

Along with a wider definition of "our issues," Jewish feminists also broaden the concept of *tzedakah*. They support not just traditional Jewish causes like Hadassah Hospital or Yeshiva University, but progressive social justice groups like New Jewish Agenda, American Jewish World Service, New Israel Fund, the Shalom Center, the Jewish Fund for Justice, and projects that specifically benefit women—such as *Lilith*, the magazine of Jewish feminism; or the Israel Women's Network; or the battered women's shelters here and in Israel. Traditional Jews have no trouble contributing to Hadassah Hospital or Yeshiva University, but if Jewish feminists do not support women's empowerment projects few others will.

When it comes to philanthropy, I have begun to ask my audiences to take a cue from our mothers' warning that we had better wear clean underwear in case we get hit by a truck. I ask that we look at our checkbook stubs instead. If you got hit by a truck, and someone found your checkbook, what would it tell the world about you and your values? Are you buying too much clothing, jewelry, vacations, more pleasures than you need? Are you giving only to "safe" causes like the library, symphony, cancer, or heart disease? Or are you developing the habit of *feminist* philanthropy—giving independently of your husband if you have a husband—and are you funding change, not charity, especially for women?

Of the eight degrees of *tzedakah* described by Maimonides, the highest is that form of assistance we give to enable the weak to raise themselves. Likewise, feminism's goal is not to "help" but to permanently strengthen women by developing their self-esteem and marketable skills and reducing their dependence on men or social services. Feminists search out projects that directly benefit and empower *women,* because we see women as both the subject and the instrument of our efforts.

Jewish feminists also serve as watchdogs within the community. We complain when other Jews subvert women's issues. We fuss when Jewish men treat child care, parental leave, domestic violence, or sexual harassment as trivial sidelines to the main battles on the Jewish agenda. We fault the men who have opposed affirmative action—who worry about its impact on Jewish *men* and ignore the fact that many Jewish women lawyers, doctors, engineers, students, and executives have affirmative action to thank for their education or their job. We criticize Jewish agencies because more than half their staffs but only 2 percent of their executive directors are women. We protest when the Jewish establishment makes politically pragmatic alliances with Evangelical Christians and right-wing conservatives, selling out women's rights in return for lip service to Israel's security. We want our agenda to be a priority for Jewish men too, and we deplore those whose loyalty to Israel becomes an excuse for bedding down with the reactionaries.

In the 1980s, we could not understand why Jews supported Ronald Reagan, why they were not only willing to overlook his AWACs sellout and his visit to Bitburg but also the many ways that he was shamelessly anti-woman. Reagan was the first American president to oppose the Equal Rights Amendment. He would have given a fetus more rights than the woman in whose body it exists; he wanted to criminalize even those abortions that would save the life of the pregnant woman. During his tenure, he appointed three Supreme Court justices whose decisions now threaten our reproductive freedom. Yet there are Jews who loved him *just because he was pro-Israel.*

On the same basis, many Jews joined forces with right-wing Christian fundamentalists, despite their antipluralist actions: censoring textbooks, denigrating Jewish prayers, ridiculing Jewish noses, opposing shelters for battered women and children, imposing "God-given sex roles"—meaning dominant men and submissive women. Jewish feminists expect all Jews to choose better political bedfellows.

In the personal sphere, we want girl babies and boy babies to be greeted as equally precious Jewish lives and we want those lives to be made equally meaningful and satisfying. We are not happy when parents spend more money to celebrate a Bar Mitzvah than a Bat Mitzvah. We ask friends of the family to choose an appropriate coming-of-age gift to give to both sexes, rather than codify sex-specific rituals by giving a boy a kiddush cup or a prayer book, while a girl gets a *challah* knife or candlesticks. We scowl at people who buy Jewish girls "JAP-in-training" necklaces. (If it were up to me, the JAF—Jewish-American Feminist—would replace the JAP as our *positive* paradigmatic female.)

Jewish feminists talk back. We are not always polite. We make other Jews uncomfortable. We openly rebuke a wide variety of Jewish men—the comedian who gets laughs at our expense; the liberal man who boasts of being a supportive mate and "letting" his wife work, but never makes it any easier for her by doing the laundry; the screenwriter who blames his mother for everything; the novelist who makes Jewish women unlovable; the mythographer who glorifies only the *ayshet chayil* (the wife who "watches her family's comings and goings") and not our activist heroines.

That's a pretty wide-ranging definition of Jewish feminism, but let's assume you go along with it. Okay, feminism is good for women, you say, but you're still worried. Is it good for the Jews? you ask. To this I would respond talmudically by posing a question of my own: What do you mean by *the* Jews?

We've seen that feminism's preeminent goal is to grant full humanity to the female of the species from the moment when the doctor says, "It's a girl!" Can full humanity for the other half of the Jewish people be bad for "the Jews"?

Feminism envisions a world in which women can be more in control of the forces that affect their lives. How can that be bad for "the Jews"?

Feminists are also challenging the equation of masculinity and dominance, trying to enlarge men's capacity for emotional expression and family caregiving, and to expand children's options regardless of their gender. Is it possible that greater opportunities for children, more loving men, and more competent, confident women could *not* be good for "the Jews"?

If we understand the word "feminism" in this way, the original question loses all possible logic unless—*unless* the flaw lies with one's concept of "the Jews." Jewish feminists define women as Jews, but some others define us only as Jewish *women*. To them, "Jews" means *men* the way "everyone" means men in the New Square Talmud class.

For instance, when the media quote "American Jewish reaction" to Yasir Arafat's latest pronouncement, they do not quote the presidents of B'nai B'rith Women, National Council of Jewish Women, Federation of Temple Sisterhoods, or Amit Women. They quote the chair*men* of the boards of the Conference of Presidents of Major Jewish Organizations, or the male heads of B'nai B'rith, American Jewish Congress, or American Jewish Committee. For the most part, "Jewish opinion" is the opinion of Jewish men. (Amazingly, as this book went to press, the Conference of Presidents has just elected its first woman chair, Shoshana Cardin, and the new president of the World Jewish Congress is a woman named Evelyn Sommer.)

The same male bias holds true in that much-publicized entity called "the Jewish vote." Commentators make it sound as if all Jews vote the same, yet our gender gap is as wide or wider than the difference between men's and women's political attitudes in the general population. For instance, in the 1988 Bush-Dukakis race, 50 percent of all women and 41 percent of all men voted for Dukakis, a 9 percent difference. Among Jews, the gender gap was 10 percent—73 percent women and 63 percent men voted for Dukakis. In 1980, Ronald Reagan won 55 percent of men's vote and 47 percent of women's, an 8 percent gender gap that held firm among Jews even though proportionately far fewer Jews cast Reagan ballots—39 percent of the men and 31 percent of the women.

Similar gender disparities have shown up in attitudes toward economic and environmental issues, nuclear disarmament, capital punishment, military spending, gun control, and the entry into the war in the Persian Gulf. Jewish women tend to be far more liberal on those issues, yet men's opinion is treated as a synonym for *Jewish* opinion. When people say things like "The Jews have become more conservative" or "The Jews were better off under Reagan than Bush," the Jews they are referring to are not *us*.

Which leads me back to my point: when critics say feminism is bad for the Jews they mean bad for Jewish men. They are really saying that independent-minded Jewish women can be inconvenient, annoying, or threatening to Jewish men or institutions. Otherwise, whatever makes Jewish women stronger would be seen as adding strength to "the Jews."

In Cynthia Ozick's phrase, Jewish women want not just equality as women with men but "as Jews with Jews." We are tired of being what Rachel Adler called "peripheral Jews." We want to move to the center. We want to be valued not just because we are devoted wives, or mothers of the Jewish people, but because we ourselves *are* the Jewish people. Anyone who agrees that Jewish women are Jews with Jews ought to accept that feminism is good for "the Jews." But if something is still troubling you, maybe the question you meant to ask in the first place was, Is feminism good for Jewish *survival*?

That strikes closer to the bone. That is the question most Jews have on their minds when their minds are on feminism.

We Jews monitor the prospects for our own survival as a people by taking measurements of three social phenomena: anti-Semitism, assimilation, and affiliation.

We monitor the incidence of anti-Semitism to ensure that Jews are physically safe and free to live our lives.

We monitor the rate of assimilation—and the proliferation of intermarriages and conversions—because we want to promote generational continuity.

We monitor the degree of Jewish affiliation—membership in a synagogue and Jewish communal organizations—because we want to perpetuate Jewish cultural identification, religious practices, and community responsibility.

As one who shares these concerns, I've asked myself quite seriously, *Does feminism threaten any of those elements of Jewish survival?* And the answer still is a clear, flat *No.*

First let's examine whether feminism has any impact on anti-Semitism. While there are Jew haters in the Women's Movement, no one would claim that feminism *made* them Jew haters. Fighting for the autonomy and civil rights of women does not inspire bigotry or imperil Jewish safety. Promoting equal household responsibilities and shared parenting has no effect on Gentile attitudes toward Jews. The feminist attack on machismo does not put Jews in any danger; in fact, our well-being has not depended on men's fighting prowess since biblical times. Therefore, Jewish masculinity paradigms that honor intellect and success, not size and brawn, are well served by feminist campaigns for a more flexible definition of manhood.

Is feminism a threat to Israel's survival? I see no connection. When people who identify themselves as part of the women's movement argue for a Palestinian state but against a State of Israel, they are engaging in selective nationalism, not feminism. As for the impact of feminism in Israel itself, I have already suggested that a strong dose of equality might improve that nation's security. The disparate treatment of women in the Israeli army is not just an occupational inequity but a strategic error; it wastes human resources that would be useful in defense emergencies.

After the issue of Jewish safety come questions of assimilation and Jewish continuity. Is the Women's Movement responsible for the shrinking Jewish birthrate, dwindling traditional families, and the increasing incidence of intermarriage and conversion?

For the birthrate, in part; only in the sense that feminism has helped women to see themselves as more than just breeders. But should that be cause for blame or cheers? Instead of calling a woman's personal growth "selfish" because it may result in her choosing to have fewer children, the Jewish community should applaud women achievers and lobby for family enhancements like child-care assistance, flexible work schedules, parental leaves, and other policies that would make child rearing less isolating and privatized. Then too, if we want to encourage Jewish women to have children, we should encourage Jewish men to be more participatory fathers. And we should reward Jewish mothers by giving them power in the Jewish community, not just in the kitchen. We should make it easier for women to do as men have always done—develop both a family persona and an independent self.

The claim that feminists denigrate the family is simplistic to the point of distortion; what we actually do is denigrate family patriarchy, challenge the politics of gender roles, elevate women's status, and create a climate in which women can feel entitled to pursue not just their domestic duties but their own aspirations.

Few women can be pressured into childbearing by apocalyptic scare rhetoric about Jewish extinction. Quoting Scripture won't convince us to breed nor will turning back the clock on reproductive choice.

The only way Jewish women will want to have more children is when the toll on our lives is lessened and the responsibilities of motherhood are equaled by the responsibilities of fatherhood. That is the feminist challenge to the Jewish community.

To those who say feminism exacerbates gender warfare and is thus divisive to the Jewish community, I would quote Harry Brod, the editor of the anthology, *A Mensch Among Men: Explorations in Jewish Masculinity*:

> *I find this view backwards. The Jewish community is already divided along gender lines and damaged by sexism. Feminism offers the only hope of uniting us on a firm foundation.*

To those who insist that feminism undermines the Jewish family by "promoting" lesbianism, one can only point out that most people do not cut their sexuality to fit their politics, but more often do the opposite. The Jewish community would be ill served by coercing lesbians into marriage (assuming it could be done). Moreover, if we're really worried about Jewish continuity and the declining Jewish birthrate we should help Jewish lesbians who want to adopt a child, or be inseminated; we should support lesbian mothers who are threatened with the loss of custody of their children; and we should make alternative families feel welcome in our synagogues.

So much for feminism's supposed effect on assimilation. Now, as for the problem of intermarriage, which accounts for one-third of all Jewish marriages, the people to blame for this are not feminists but Jewish *men*, who marry Gentiles four times more often than do Jewish women. In his recent American Jewish Committee study of mixed and converted couples, Dr. Egon Mayer points out that intermarriage is a consequence of life in an open society—and if intermarriage is ever stopped, it will be the anti-Semites, not the Jews, who stop it. As Jews approach equality and become more integrated into American society, we become more acceptable as marriage partners. If being successful predicts marrying out, and men are more successful than women (which is still the case), no wonder it is men who do most of the intermarrying.

Mayer's studies show that children of mixed marriages are most likely to consider themselves Jewish when the father is the Jewish parent. Notice the paradox. Halachically, a Jew is someone with a

Jewish mother, but in actual practice, a Jewish mother by herself does not seem able to pass on the legacy of Judaism to her children. On the other hand, while having a Jewish father is not enough to make a person Jewish by law (except in Reform Judaism), because of the higher status of men in Jewish life or because men have traditionally been more Jewishly knowledgeable, fathers carry the power to pass on their Jewish heritage to their children even when the mother is a Gentile. In this light, intermarriage situations prove that we need a sex-role–resistant Judaism, and strong, assured, educated Jewish women who can hold their own as Jews whatever the religious or ethnic pull of the other parent.

The same applies when divorce transforms a Jewish couple into two single parents. If they only know rigid Jewish sex roles, single parents or intermarried parents cannot by themselves offer their children more than the male or female half of Judaism. I'm thinking of the single father who had to learn to make *latkes* (potato pancakes) for Hanukkah and children's costumes for Purim when he no longer had a wife to fulfill the domestic half-life usually reserved to women. And, more typically, I'm thinking of the single mother who had better do more than make *latkes* and sew costumes if she is to communicate the full meaning of Jewish life to children who have no in-house father to do it. (And even to those who do.)

"You've all gone to college," said Arthur Hertzberg to a convention of the National Council of Jewish Women. "If I asked you to write a paragraph about Saint Thomas Aquinas, how many of you could?" Many women raised their hands, having taken the history of philosophy. "If I asked you to write on Maimonides, how many of you could?" Hertzberg continued. Only six women raised their hands, and three of them were wives of rabbis.

If a woman cannot teach substantive Judaism to her children, "the Jews" may lose those children forever. If we care about Jewish survival, we need to care about educating women so that by themselves, if need be—in mixed marriages or as single mothers, in the home and in the world—they can be the sole carriers of the Jewish heritage. We cannot leave women "Jewishly naked," to borrow a phrase from Max Brod, the biographer of Franz Kafka. We must teach them Hebrew, Jewish history, literature, and theology; encourage them to be fully involved in religious ritual; accept them in positions of influence in Jewish organizations and then heed their counsel. In other words, strange as it seems, we must adopt the feminist agenda, and empower Jewish women *for the sake of Jewish survival.*

I don't mean it to sound hostile, but a large dimension of the empowerment of Jewish women involves the disempowerment of Jewish men. The stereotype of the gentle male scholar doesn't hold true in Jewish organizational life. It is the arrogant, domineering Jewish man, and not feminism, who stands in the way of that third prerequisite for our survival as a people—affiliation with the organized Jewish community. From personal experience I know that when Jewish institutions fail to acknowledge and respect a woman, she will find other arenas in which to contribute, express her social concerns, and exercise adult autonomy.

To encourage more Jewish women to affiliate with Jewish communal organizations, men will have to redress women's grievances. They will have to give up the mystique of male authority, to move over and make room for new leaders. It's not going to be easy. Secular men defending their prerogatives in Jewish organizations are essentially the same as the black hats defending their turf at the Western Wall. Lawyers and businessmen may not throw chairs, but they throw their weight around to perpetuate one another's hegemony. Notice who gives whom 95 percent of the seats on every commission, board, or foreign delegation. When it was decided that "six Jews" would go to Geneva to meet with Nelson Mandela before his historic U.S. visit, all six were men.

"A group of wealthy, assimilated Jewish men dominate the Jewish community and speak in our name. Who elected them?" asks journalist Aviva Cantor. She also points out that $2 billion is raised each year in the Jewish community, and women have very little say in how it's spent.

"Remember the ladies," wrote Abigail Adams to her husband John when he and his friends were drafting the United States Constitution. "Remember the women," Jewish feminists keep telling Jewish men and we want more than John gave Abigail. We want men to stop speaking on our behalf—particularly when the subject is women. We want to be put forward as representatives of *all* Jews, not just Jewish women. We are not afraid to speak out and we don't need "a boy's head" to do it. Unfortunately, however, it's still the rare man who treats a woman as if she had a head on her shoulders at all.

The sound of benighted male supremacy can be heard in the voice of Irving Howe, author of *World of Our Fathers*, writing in *The New Republic*:

> *Traveling around the country recently, I encountered middle-class Jewish ladies intent on discovering their family genealogies. I suggested to them, not very graciously, that if they were serious they would first try to learn their people's history and then they might see that it hardly mattered whether they came from the Goldbergs of eastern Poland or the Goldbergs of the western Ukraine.*

Underlying Howe's contempt and obtuseness is his failure to understand that when "their people's history" is rendered as the world of their *fathers*, women might feel somewhat disenfranchised. With the world of our mothers in shadows and nothing else to go on, why wouldn't a woman start small trying to tease her origins out of the tangle of family artifacts and hearthside myths. It makes sense that "middle-class Jewish ladies" might try to connect with their Goldberg foremothers because they cannot connect with Bar Kochba or Samuel Guggenheim.

What self-respecting woman would want to affiliate with the Jewish community if it means battling with men who desert women's interests or men who think like Irving Howe? However, in all honesty, when we consider affiliating with organized Jewry, men are not our only problem. We also have our female Uncle Toms, described as follows by the late Annette Daum:

> *The male power structure uses "Tante Tovahs" to oppose those who are feminists. No matter what issues the Jewish women's movement chooses to address—whether liturgy, ritual, halacha, religious education, research, family relations—the most vocal opposition to change comes from other women who are still dependent on the protective image of God the Father.*

Traditional women often fight change because they fear losing the status they have as wives; they cannot imagine anything better than the women's auxiliary. "Many wives of establishment Jews are organized into relatively powerless but status-granting organizations," says Phyllis Chesler, who feels saddened "by how contemptuous they are of each other, how jealously they guard their own little pseudo-fiefdoms (much like men do); by their harem mentality."

The Tante Tovahs and harem wives tend to come from the same generation that spawned those selfless don't-worry-about-me volunteers who are dying off and are no longer reproducing their numbers. Many have daughters who disdain Jewish voluntary organizations and rebel against their mothers' causes. As a result, few Jewish groups have experienced a membership growth proportionate to the size of the daughters' generation.

Lately, when I speak before Jewish women's groups—whether it is Federation, NCJW, Israel Bonds, or a Jewish community center—I've been counting the women who appear to be under forty. Rarely do they amount to more than 20 percent of the audience, not enough to ensure that group a vigorous future. Younger women predominate in college Hillel audiences, of course, and in some peace groups and Business and Professional Women's meetings, but otherwise, sad to say, the future is largely absent from the present. Where are the young Jewish activists? The young philanthropists? The young idealists? Have they all left town for other movements, or are they joining nothing at all?

Because of these many concerns, I want us to bridge the gap between secular women who don't realize that being *Jewish* matters, and organizational women who don't realize that being *female* matters. Traditional Jewish organizations can start by actively recruiting feminists who happen to be Jewish. Besides their numbers, many feminists bring to their activism special sensitivities and talents. They tend to be women who are combining family and work, and who understand firsthand what the problems are. In their Women's Movement activities, many have developed a sophisticated grasp of complex political agendas. They may offer fresh advocacy techniques. Many of them are students of ethnicity and culture. Others are feminist scholars who would greatly enrich the intellectual life of Jewish women's groups. (Such groups might have to change the currency of acceptance from check writing to willingness to fund-raise—or even suspend that requirement for academics who have no money and poor friends.) Best of all, experienced feminists tend to be less afraid of *power* than is the average Jewish woman, and power is the ultimate weapon when the name of the game is How *Not* to Be a Footstool as a Woman or a Jew.

Too many Jews have not seen the connection between woman-power and Jewish-power because they have not seen women as Jews. When they do, the empowerment of the Jewish woman and the battle against sexism will become more central to the Jewish community. It is the mission of Jewish feminism to hasten that change. But Jewish feminists also have a second mandate on their second flank, and that is to change the misperceptions that exist about Jews in the Women's Movement. Unfortunately, our problems work both ways: antifeminism exists among Jews; and anti-Semitism exists among feminists. Besides reporting on other women's experiences, I too have been a witness to feminism's occasional insensitivity to Jewish interests. The all-female staff of a philanthropic foundation spent two days at a retreat where the goal was to "understand the connection between the various forms of oppression." They covered the oppression of race, class, ethnicity, sexual orientation, age, disability—but not anti-Semitism. When a Jewish staff member said she did not identity herself as white but as Jewish, no one picked up on her testimony, and it never surfaced in the final report.

I've heard a women's studies professor ignore Jewish historical figures while being solicitously attentive to the heroines of other minority groups. I've watched conference organizers get testy when a Jew suggested they not schedule a meeting on Saturday since observant Jewish women would not be able to participate. I've seen women resist including Jewish spirituality under the feminist banner, as if only Wicca worshipers are authentically spiritual, as if religious women might corrupt the Marxists in the movement, as if belief in God (as we define God) proved us weirdos or dupes. I've heard feminists critique Israel and patriarchal Judaism in noticeably stronger terms than those they use for the Vatican and patriarchal Christianity, or for Iran and patriarchal Islam. And I've heard put-downs of "New York middle-class women" that sound suspiciously like parodies of Jewish women.

Such behavior is far from the monopoly of Gentiles. Jewish women, or at least women who were born Jewish, have committed similar indignities or, more typically, have disowned the Jewish label and assumed the posture of the Neutral. Since it took me so long to discover that being Jewish "matters," I cannot condemn other feminists, most with far less Jewish background than mine, who find no reason to identify as Jews. Still, it troubles me that in their commitment to alleviate suffering—an impulse that is quintessentially feminist *and* quintessentially Jewish—they do not see fit to include one or two "special Jewish sorrows." And it hurts to see so many Jewish women putting their energies into secular groups when we desperately need some more feminist heads and tactics in American Jewish organizations.

The situation in both camps fills me with questions. I turn first to my Jewish side and ask:

Why aren't we Jews more upset about all the female talent and leadership that have been concentrated in secular feminism and lost to the Jewish community? An anonymous philosopher once said, "If you're one step ahead of your times, you're a genius; if you're two steps ahead, you're a crackpot." Feminists are one step ahead but it looks like two because the Jewish establishment is at least a step behind. Might that explain why so many Jews have failed to honor their feminist geniuses? How many activist women might have chosen to affiliate with organized Jewry if they hadn't thought they would be treated like crackpots? Could it be that Jewish communal groups are just as glad *not* to have to put up with heavy-duty troublemakers ruffling men's feathers and stirring up trouble among "the ladies"?

Are some Jews using the existence of feminist anti-Semitism to justify the existence of Jewish sexism, as if one evil canceled out the other? I ask this because Jewish groups that showed no interest in having me as a speaker when I was lecturing on Jewish sexism suddenly became eager for me to be their speaker *after* I published my essay on feminist anti-Semitism. Did the essay give Jews a convenient new excuse to put down the Women's Movement? Has it been used to dissuade "nice Jewish girls" from the feminist sisterhood?

After posing these questions on the Jewish side of my seesaw, I shift to the feminist side and ask: How come so many sister feminists seem defensive about the number of Jewish women in visible leadership positions? Do they secretly believe that the Women's Movement is part of some "international Jewish conspiracy"? Or are they worried that too many Jewish leaders might declass the Movement?

Why do feminists nod approvingly when I criticize sexism in Jewish life but not when I ask the Women's Movement to investigate its anti-Jewish bias?

Why was I placed on a feminist conference panel as a representative of white women, and not Jews, when women with the same skin color as mine were invited to represent Hispanics or working-class ethnics? In other words, why do Jews remain unseen in our particularity when women from other groups are honored in theirs?

If slavery is an acceptable historical reference or feminist metaphor, why is any mention of the Holocaust treated as melodrama or hyperbole? If people of color are allowed to get angry at racism, why are Jews who get angry at anti-Semitism called paranoid and divisive? If Movement groups are so exercised about what's happening in Israel, how bad does it have to get in Libya, Iraq, Syria, Panama, Colombia, China, or Saudi Arabia before Movement women start picking on *them*?

Such questions have a way of pointing to their own answers. They suggest that much consciousness-raising and hard political work remains to be done among both Jews and feminists. And they make it clear that asking a Jewish woman to choose between her two identities is like asking her to abandon Judaism to the misogynists, or feminism to the anti-Semites. Neither community can afford to lose its Jewish feminists because we have crossover consciences; we look both ways; we keep each constituency alert to the other's needs.

Single-issue diehards will insist that Jewish feminists are by definition neither good Jews nor good feminists because we cannot be wholehearted in our advocacy. "What happens when you're faced with competing interests?" they ask in the same tone I hear Gentiles use when querying American Jews about their "dual loyalties" to the United States and Israel.

The answer is, if it really comes down to a situation where we must choose, then we will choose. In Mexico City or Copenhagen, the Jewish feminist steps forward as a Jew. At the Wall in Jerusalem, she steps forward as a woman. But most of the time, the choice itself is false and demeaning. Most of the time, we act as both because we *are* both. Moreover, because we are both, our commitment to pursue justice is enriched by the values that undergird both philosophical systems, Judaism and feminism.

In the midst of this closing paean to Jewish feminism and ethnic advocacy, some disclaimers are called for. Although I am committed to reconciling my two worlds, and although I believe Jewish identity can coexist with feminist ideals, I am aware that linking feminism with any form of ethnicity is not a risk-free activity. In fact, when *non*feminists try to sell ethnic revivalism to women, it's usually time to load the cannons. Sentimental calls to "go home to one's roots" frequently mask a reactionary antifeminist agenda that would redomesticate women, not redeem us.

In the Jewish context, for example, those heart-tugging images of Mama making chicken soup can become subliminal commercials for sex-role conformity. There is a sorry tendency among some Jews to suggest that a woman who does not make chicken soup is not a real woman. While I recognize the talents of my female ancestors, and while I may choose to continue making their recipes, I may not want to replicate all their behaviors. This does not mean I am rejecting the Jewish past, it simply means I am rejecting certain past roles.

Of course, ethnic revivalism need not inspire retrograde role playing or male chauvinism; it can empower a woman by linking her to her people, her history, and her resources. Those who are in doubt as to which kind of ethnicity is being enshrined in their community should study its propaganda; if it praises a variety of the ethnic group's women heroes, the revivalism is probably positive; if it trots out the same old heroines, idolizing virtue, chicken soup, and self-sacrifice and bemoaning the decline of womanhood since the good old days, watch out.

One more warning: because women and men experience the same culture differently, it is important to assess *how ethnicity interacts with gender*. At a folk festival, I praised a couple who had performed an ethnic dance in their native costumes. "I haven't had so much fun in years!" enthused the man. "Sure he has fun," said the woman peevishly. "He just shows up to dance; I've been making these costumes for months."

Wash away the nostalgia, and you may discover that the good old days were not equally pleasurable for women and men. If you were to ask my eighty-eight-year-old uncle to describe a "Jewish home," he would most likely focus on the parlor or porch of his house where he sat reading, talking, and watching television, or the dining room where he enjoyed so many fine Jewish meals and holiday celebrations. Meanwhile, to my eighty-six-year-old aunt, the words "Jewish home" might bring to mind an entirely different set of images from the same sixty-two years of married life: a backward-reeling film of endless table setting, serving, clearing, scrubbing, cleaning, cooking; millions of dishes and pots; billions of spills and stains; six decades of hard labor that culminated in her husband's memories of a nice "Jewish home." She too loved her home, but for her it was also a work site.

Again, double vision is a useful adaptive trait. If looking at Jewish tradition through women's eyes can so radically change one's perspective, it's no surprise that looking at women through Jewish eyes also offers new insights.

At first, feminism had trouble acknowledging Jewish eyes at all. Itself a dissenting movement, it could tolerate neither dissent nor difference within its ranks. We put all our stock in the ideal of female solidarity and the belief that sisterhood is more powerful than other claims on women's loyalty. Over time, however, we realized that uniformity is not necessary for solidarity. Ignoring real differences among women was as misguided as old liberal attempts at "color blindness," which resulted in neglect of the special circumstances of people of color. All cultures make distinctions based on gender, class, and race. Feminists have to examine how these categories interact in each woman's life, and with what results. While retaining our basic analysis of the female condition, we are learning to be sensitive to individual circumstances that are as personal as a genotype—which means we no longer speak only of "women" but of Jewish women, and sometimes even more specifically of Jewish women who are disabled, *agunot*, rural, poor, lesbians, widows, or otherwise defined as "different."

Of course, the concept of difference can become as reified as the concept of sameness. We must not subdivide into so many special-interest categories that the category Woman is lost in the fragments, while we also must not pretend that all women have the same vulnerabilities or the same dreams.

In other words, some of all women are Jews and half of all Jews are women, and those of us who are both cannot always be single-issue advocates. Jewish women may not be able to support a pro-choice candidate who is anti-Israel, any more than African-American women could support a pro-choice candidate who fails to protest apartheid. Rather than espouse a utopian universalism, today's feminists must make room for ethnic and cultural priorities. The Women's Movement's political comfort zone must widen so that Jewish women can be female-identified when it comes to fighting male domination in B'nai B'rith, and Jewish-identified when it comes to marching with our brothers against the convent in Auschwitz.

Because I want to be able to march in both directions, I continue to insist that forced choices are false choices. No Jewish woman can let herself be divided either by other women or other Jews. She cannot emancipate the Jew within and leave the woman shackled, any more than she can emancipate the woman within and leave the Jew at risk—for no human being can exist in one body, part slave and part free. I reject freedom in half measures. I've come a long way from the third grade of the Yeshiva but I still refuse the limited choices of a fish.

13

From *Marjorie Morningstar* to *Dirty Dancing*

Finding Myself at the Movies

IN JUNIOR HIGH SCHOOL, MY GIRLFRIENDS AND I USED TO PLAY A game we called "Choose or Die."

"If you had to give up one of your five senses, which would it be?" we asked each other.

"Suppose there's a nuclear attack and Serkin and Katz, the two worst teachers in school, are the only ones left. Who would you pick for homeroom?"

"Who would you marry if you absolutely *had* to choose between stupid handsome Bobby and smart geeky Ben?"

Such agonizing hypothetical exercises prepared young women for a world of narrow choices, limited social roles . . . and Hollywood movies.

I remembered Choose or Die when I started thinking about how much motion pictures have influenced my life. Until recent years, when I took the trouble to educate myself about Jewish women, I had been exposed to so few religious or historical heroines that movie characters found their way into my psyche with little competition from grander or more mythic personages. Movie women entered, good and bad, with their grating voices and their funny lines, their kind eyes, round bosoms, and oversized gestures; skittish women, brown-haired usually, women with the contours of a cello; screamers and whiners, women who give the anti-Semites plenty to write home about, and women who could have been my grandmothers.

Other than life experience, nothing left a deeper imprint on my formative self than the movies. They took me out of the hothouse of my family, beyond the confines of the Jamaica Jewish Center, and away from the neighborhood where I grew up believing that everyone was either Jewish or Catholic and another word for Catholic was Protestant. Except for a few of my father's conventions, one trip to Miami when I was a baby, and another when I was ten, my parents took me no farther from Jamaica than the Catskills, and until I went away to college I took myself no farther than my cousin's apartment in the Bronx. Hollywood was my bridge to the outside world.

I went to the movies almost every Saturday after shul. My friends and I walked to 175th Street and Jamaica Avenue, to the Loew's Valencia, a three-thousand-seat "atmospheric" movie palace (now the Tabernacle of the Prayer for All People) which in itself was a fantasy world. The interior was a vivid recreation of a Venetian Moorish courtyard at twilight, its vaulted heaven a rival to the Hayden Planetarium. Projected against a cerulean sky were a moon, twinkling stars, and a continuous procession of filmy white clouds. Along the walls was etched the dark silhouette of a medieval skyline with parapets and turrets, crenelated rooftops and Spanish archways, and up front at the center of it all was the movie screen, the bridge to Anywhere.

Woody Allen wasn't the only child of my generation who dived headlong into the world according to Hollywood. I *loved* the movies. I loved anything with Bogart or Gable, Fred Astaire or Cary Grant, and my favorite women—the wholesome blond Bettys—Hutton and Grable—the waterlogged Esther Williams, the terminally cute June Allyson, and also Vera Ellen, Doris Day, Ruth Roman (who was rumored to be Jewish), and the peerless Hepburns, Katharine and then Audrey. These stars taught me what was expected of Americans; but the films I loved best were those that taught me what was expected of Jews. As a child, I used the movies as a litmus test and lesson plan to guide my growing up; and later, as an escape from my impacted religious rebellion into the open field of cultural Judaism where I found something of an alternative identity. I studied the Jewish women: Is that how I'm supposed to behave? Is she what I can hope to become? Am I like that? Is anyone? Above all, the movies helped me define the Jewish women I did *not* want to be.

Recently, to revisit these images, I became the best customer of the local video store, renting two or three cassettes a day to refresh my recollection of films with Jewish characters. Why this sudden desire to saturate myself with movie memories? No doubt the same impulse that has contributed to my writing this book: a need for answers to the most obscure questions of my identity. A search for how I formulated my ideas of Jewish womanhood; a search for coherence in my past that might even include the movies. As I watched one film after another, I discovered that no matter how good the movie might have been artistically, the female characters left me feeling bad. Not one of them could be considered a complete Jewish heroine, a fully realized, positive, well-balanced, successful, or admirable Jewish woman. Not one aroused in me that uncomplicated "Gee I'd like to be her" fantasy that scores of male film characters activate in the male imagination. Instead, the best I could find were women who made the least intolerable trade-offs, those who did not have to pay too high a price for being themselves.

For instance, Choose or Die: *If you had to live your life as Marjorie Morningstar or Yentl, which would you be?*

If you choose Marjorie, be prepared to give up your identity. You'll be pampered, praised, educated-but-empty—a slate on which men write their dreams and project their inadequacies. But choose Yentl and you'll have to give up love and family; pay for your spirituality by disguising or renouncing your sexuality; pretend to be a man so that you may be a scholar; discover that the only way to be true to yourself is to live a lie. Take your pick: Marjorie's bourgeois subordination or Yentl's lonely rebellion. Some choice!

Again, Choose or Die: *If you had to be the mother in* Marjorie Morningstar *or the mother in* Portnoy's Complaint, *what's your pleasure?*

Here, it's six of one and half a dozen of the other. Both are caricatures, but if you were up against the wall in the forced-choice game, you'd probably opt for Marjorie's mother on the grounds of class. At least she lives on Central Park West, while Mrs. Portnoy hangs her apron strings in a Brooklyn walk-up.

Most films with Jewish characters seemed to have very little human complexity. What I found instead were four debilitating stereotypes, two familiar ones—the Jewish-American Princess and the Jewish Mother—and two that I call the Jewish Man's Burden and the Jewish Big Mouth. By deconstructing these stereotypes and examining how they function in some of the most memorable films of the past thirty years, I began to see where I and my generation got our ideas about Jewish-American womanhood and why we had so much to unlearn before we could claim a proud Jewish female identity.

To begin with, let me establish some thumbnail definitions of these four stereotypes as the culture sees them:

The Jewish-American Princess is a spoiled, materialistic, vapid, demanding, self-absorbed brat who twists Daddy around her little finger and stalks a husband who will support her in the style to which her father has made her accustomed. She's trendy, sexy-looking, but, alas, frigid. She's tired, she has a headache, sex is inconvenient; she prefers shopping. She's a clotheshorse, an inveterate home decorator, a collector of furs, jewelry, and vacations. She loves to entertain but hates to cook. "What does she make for dinner?" asks the Jewish comedian. "Reservations." What's on her bumper sticker? I BRAKE FOR BARGAINS.

Several movies of the last thirty years have helped mold the JAP image. *Marjorie* started it all in 1958, *Goodbye, Columbus* fleshed it out in 1969, *Private Benjamin* took it into parody in 1980, and in the past decade, *Flamingo Kid* and *Down and Out in Beverly Hills* updated it by inventing a significant subgenre, the middle-aged Jewish-American Princess.

The second familiar stereotype, the Jewish Mother (J.M.), comes to life on the screen as a loving Yiddishe mama (like Sara in *The Jazz Singer*), hard-working shtetl wife (like Golda in *Fiddler on the Roof*), or repellent shrew (like Aunt Gladys in *Goodbye Columbus*, the tush-kissing Momma in *Where's Poppa?* and the humiliating Hovercraft mother-in-the-sky in Woody Allen's *Oedipus Wrecks*, from the trilogy *New York Stories*).

At the loving end of the spectrum, the J.M. is a nurturant, self-sacrificing character of warmth and dignity—the 1950s television character Mollie Goldberg, say, or an Old World sage like the grandmother in *Crossing Delancey*—or else a crusty martyr like the mothers in *Brighton Beach Memoirs*, *Radio Days*, and *Beaches*. Either way, you laugh at her but you love her.

Love is out of the question when it comes to the shrill harpy at the other end of the spectrum. This Jewish Mother is a world-class guilt-tripper. Her every word sets your teeth on edge. She is crass, bullying, asexual, *anti*sexual, and of course a food fetishist. She emasculates her husband, infantilizes her sons, overprotects her daughters, over-feeds everyone, and obsesses about digestion and elimination.

For instance, take Sophie Portnoy. *Please!* Her turf: the kitchen. Her job: standing with an ear to the bathroom door. Her definition of sin: eating *chazerai*. Her conversational style: "Alex! What is it with those bowels?"

Take your choice: Long-suffering mothers or mothers who made other people suffer. Some choice!

The third stereotype found at the movies is the one I'm calling the Jewish Big Mouth. While the Princess demands her privileges, the Big Mouth demands her rights. Often an Ugly Duckling, she is so bright, funny, accomplished, and confident that people forget her looks. But she has one major problem: she acts like a person. She lets everyone, especially the men in her life, know who she is and what she thinks. If she wants something, she goes for it. A nonconformist, she won't play her assigned role—either as a Jew or as a Woman.

This character is best exemplified in Barbra Streisand's Jewish trilogy, *Funny Girl*, *The Way We Were*, and *Yentl*. Although these movies were released years apart, watching them more recently in sequence revealed the Achilles' heel, if you will, of the endearing Big Mouth. Although she still appeals to me above all other character types, and holds great promise for self-respecting Jewish women, she comes with a curse: she is not allowed to have it all. She has to pay a price for her independence, and the price is love.

The fourth category, the Jewish Man's Burden, parallels the convention that once described Third World blacks as the White Man's Burden. The Jewish Man's Burden is the Jewish woman whom he views as primitive and underdeveloped. She is an embarrassment to him, like the new immigrant wife in *Hester Street*. She's a drag on his social climbing, like Tina Balzer in *Diary of a Mad Housewife*. She's an albatross, like the bride with egg salad on her face in *Heartbreak Kid*, or the shallow, whiny Bette Midler character in *Ruthless People*. The Jewish Man's Burden stands between him and the American dream. She is an unwanted "too Jewish" reminder of his origins and an unendurable obstacle to his advancement.

These stereotypes operate on different levels depending on whether a film is *implicitly* or *explicitly* Jewish. Implicitly Jewish movies are those in which the character's Judaism is incidental or is implied only by context or cultural reference markers—which is very different from movies in which a character's Jewishness is explicitly stated, intrinsic to the theme, or integral to the story's tension or conflict.

A film is explicit when it is about being Jewish the way *Diary of Anne Frank*, *Portnoy's Complaint*, *Hester Street*, and *Yentl* are about being Jewish. Anne Frank's life in hiding during Hitler's reich is a uniquely, unmistakably *Jewish* story. Portnoy blames his complaint, his impotence, on his Jewish mother and his self-prescribed cure is avoidance of all Jewish women. *Yentl* and *Hester Street* draw on halachic imperatives and Old World texture to explore the tension between Jewish tradition and women's changing roles and aspirations.

In contrast to these sharply focused Jewish plots, other films have casual, offhand Jewish references. *Hello Dolly!*, for example, is not *about* being Jewish, it is about a woman who happens to be Jewish. It is a story of the time-honored nonsectarian pursuit of a husband, yet it communicates information about Jewish women by implication. The syllogism is subliminal: (a) We know Dolly Levi is meddlesome and manipulative; (b) We know Dolly Levi is Jewish; therefore (c), women who arc Jewish are meddlesome and manipulative.

Never mind that Dolly's Judaism has absolutely no bearing on the plot and no relevance to the other characters, all of whom seem to be Gentile. We're not talking logic here, we're talking stereotypes. The minute there is a whiff of Jewishness in the air, the associations are set in motion.

The whiff is weak in *Dolly*, *Mad Housewife*, and *Flamingo Kid*; somewhat stronger in *Funny Girl*, *The Way We Were*, and *Dirty Dancing*; and overpowering in *Morningstar*, *Heartbreak Kid*, *Private Benjamin*, and *Beaches*. But there's a subliminal syllogism in every one of those films, and because the negative byproduct is so much less conscious than that put out by the explicit *Yentl* or *Portnoy*, its impact may be more pernicious.

Jewish film characters, male or female, no matter how vaguely drawn, seem to be emblematic of Jews in a way that non-Jewish film characters—with the possible exception of Italian Mafia types—are rarely emblematic of a group of Christians. As soon as we know that we are watching Jews, we engage in a circular dynamic. We ascribe weight to these stereotypes because of the power of the film image, and then those weighty character traits become prescriptive. They function as a form of social control, or role modeling by innuendo. For Jewish women, certainly for me, this dynamic has created a choose-or-die game of limited moves.

Looking back at the power of Hollywood's messages, *Marjorie Morningstar* seemed to be my starting point. Ostensibly a love story about a young woman who goes away from home and falls for the wrong man, it is also a Jewish family saga and an ethnic message movie. By including scenes involving a Bar Mitzvah, a family seder, and a Jewish wedding, this movie clearly establishes its ethnic roots. Therefore, the behavior of Rose and her daughter, Marjorie, is seen as unambiguously Jewish feminine behavior. And here is what it says about us.

Rose, the mother, is a climber. "An ordinary Bar Mitzvah wasn't good enough for you," complains her husband. "Ever since we moved from the Bronx, nothing is good enough." Rose buys Marjorie a new outfit for every occasion so her princess can attract the right kind of husband. Rose nags, schemes, is sexually repressive and given to odd monetary references. Faced with Marjorie's rising libido, Rose says, "Save those feelings. Put them in the bank." She sends Uncle Sampson to guard what is "more important than Fort Knox," meaning Marjorie's virtue which is under siege by Noel Airman (formerly Ehrman), the handsome, older theater director at the Catskill resort.

Even though Noel is Jewish, he's not husband material. We deduce that through coded messages. His black outfits, Christianized first name, and Americanized last name establish that he is disconnected from the faith, a luftmensch, an insubstantial, free-floating "air man," a nothing. "A man has to be something," Rose proclaims.

A woman, however, can be nothing. Marjorie Morgenstern takes a job in Noel's summer theater but proves untalented as an actress. Wasp-waisted, whiny, eternally awed, apologetic, and virginal, all she wants is "someone to love." Noel dubs her Marjorie Morningstar, as if changing her name will free her from Jewish moral constraints. But she herself admits she wants excitement without risk. "I'm afraid to break the rules," she says.

For Marjorie—and all of us Marjories of the 1950s—it was a no-win situation: If she rejects Noel's advances, she remains Daddy's little girl, patriarchy's virgin, and Judaism's daughter. But giving in to the apostate in black would mean defying her parents, heritage, and gender imperatives. When she chooses Noel, Marjorie (like the Jews in mid-twentieth-century America) allows herself to be seduced by rebellion and assimilation. With an air man, she is doomed to be as evanescent as a morning star. It's all there in the names.

Hollywood's symbol of second-generation Jewish manhood is not a lawyer, doctor, or businessman, but the precursor of bad boy Philip Roth, the sort of man who describes Jewishness as the antithesis of freedom. Noel ridicules Marjorie for resisting his brand of liberation. He calls her a "Shirley"—his nickname for a Jewish tease who trades sex for matrimony. He predicts Marjorie will end up married to a doctor with a practice in New Rochelle—a prophecy that will be fulfilled thirty years later in another Catskill movie, *Dirty Dancing*, in which the main character has a doctor father and a mother named Marjorie but, significantly, this time the daughter has big plans to be a somebody.

In a line drenched with disdain, Noel says the destiny of a Shirley "was charted by five thousand years of Moses and the Ten Commandments."

Such statements trotted home with me from the movie house on the back of another subliminal syllogism: (a) Marjorie is Jewish; (b) Marjorie is a Shirley; therefore (c), Jewish girls are Shirleys. Shirley, of course, was the first JAP, but not the last.

"Marjorie, you *are* your mother," says Noel, compounding the insult, warning us that JAPs become Jewish Mothers and Jewish mothers raise new JAPs who become again like their mothers. So goes the gospel of Jewish continuity according to Wouk, Roth, Mailer, and other literary princes who created this modern mythology to deal with their own renunciation of their pre-American past.

The concept of the Jewish woman as a reminder of a man's origins is played out more overtly and with varying degrees of offensiveness in movies about The Jewish Man's Burden.

Hester Street opens on the Lower East Side in 1896. Jake has been living here for a few years and feels like a full-fledged American. He speaks English, goes to dance halls, dates the thoroughly modern Mamie. "Here a Jew is a mensch," he says. "In Russia, I was afraid to walk ten feet near a Gentile." When his wife, Gitl, arrives from the Old Country with their son, she threatens to pull Jake back to the old ways. He despises her immigrant habits and superstitions. He wants his son to have a baseball in his pocket, not salt to protect against the Evil Eye. And he wants Gitl to give up her *sheitel*, the wig worn by married Orthodox women to cover their hair from men's view.

Gitl refuses. "I won't be a *goya* even for my husband," she says. Jake demands a divorce so he can marry Mamie. Before Gitl will agree, she makes the happy couple fork up $300, all of Mamie's savings. You want to get rid of your burden? this frankly antiassimilationist film seems to be warning us. Okay, but it'll cost you.

Diary of a Mad Housewife is as vague in its ethnics as *Hester Street* is explicit. But the husband Jonathan Balzer (ballsy?) carries the whiff of Jewishness to anyone who buys the stereotype of the insufferably demanding, upwardly mobile lawyer with an apartment on Central Park West. Along with his maniacal pursuit of brand names and the "right" friends, Jonathan wants his wife, Tina, to be a status object as well. He complains about everything from her hair, to her four-minute eggs, to her shyness.

"Don't hang onto me," he tells her at a party. "Circulate."

He accuses her of holding him back in his career. In the end, when *he* has made a complete mess of their lives, *she* goes into therapy.

Until I saw her again on my VCR, I had forgotten how much the Jewish bride (Jeannie Berlin) in *Heartbreak Kid* had embarrassed me. Rather than deal with my feelings at the time, I laughed at the revolting Lila along with everyone else in the audience. Seeing the film again recalled my sense of passive degradation as I watched the groom, Lenny (Charles Grodin), find fault with Lila immediately after their wedding, ridicule the way she makes love, the way she keeps talking about the next fifty years, the way she sings and eats egg salad and goes to the bathroom and gets hideously sunburned. Oh yes, and she can't swim. For God's sake, every American kid knows how to swim, but not the disgusting Lila. Lenny's view of Lila humiliates *us*.

Three days into his honeymoon, Lenny meets Kelly Corchran (Cybill Shepherd), the golden *shiksa* from Minnesota, blond, rich, spoiled, a JAP in WASP clothing. Kelly *can* swim. Kelly and Lenny swim *together*. You can almost hear *America the Beautiful* playing in the background when he tells her, "I've been waiting for a girl like you all my life." He divorces Lila—his Jewish burden, his Jewish past—and with knavery and pretense, succeeds in marrying Kelly. In the last scene of the movie, surrounded by small talk and Midwestern wedding guests, Lenny sits dazed and lost amid alien corn. He got his wish; now he has to live with it.

Because of that devastating final scene, I can't say whether Jewish men took the movie as pro-*shiksa* or anti-*shiksa*, but I am sure that no Jewish woman felt good about hailing from the same tribe as the pitiful, loathsome Lila.

The wife in *Ruthless People* (Bette Midler) is a different sort of loathsome and also a transitional figure—a kind of JAP gone gross. She starts out fat, vulgar, and self-indulgent. Her husband married her for her money and now he wants to dump her for his Gentile mistress. He gets rid of *his* Jewish burden by refusing to pay the ransom when she's kidnapped. As for the Jewish wife, captivity brings out the best in her. She makes friends with her kidnappers, loses weight, and discovers she has talent in the *shmatte* game. Which only proves that one man's burden is another man's chief executive officer.

The JAP's capacity for change is developed best in *Private Benjamin*, which is why I ended up liking this movie quite a lot. By the time she was eight, Judy Benjamin knew her heart's desire: "All I want is a big house, nice clothes, a live-in maid, and a professional man." Her wish comes true in the person of her second husband, Yale Goodman. (Again, check out the name: the assimilated Ivy League Jew is a good man to find.) Yale is a sharp, successful lawyer whose sexual artistry ranges from a forced blow job in the back seat of a parked car, to a near-rape on the bathroom floor, both of which Judy tolerates as familiar indignities, that is, until she realizes that he has not just come but gone.

Is his untimely death a warning that a JAP can be fatal to a Yalie? That may be stretching it, but prior to the stunning denouement on the bathroom floor, other unambiguous aspects of the JAP stereotype have already been established. Judy has forcefully reprimanded her upholsterer for using the wrong mushroom-colored fabric on her ottomans, proving herself adept at handling domestic crises. Like Marjorie, Judy has also shown herself to be a skilled Daddy's girl— oriented to the man of the house from whom all bounty flows, but not expecting much more from him than money. On her wedding day, Daddy gives Judy a hefty check, then turns back to his TV. Marjorie's father realized too late, "Maybe I should have spent more time with you; I've been neglectful." Judy's father doesn't know how old his daughter is and doesn't care.

Widowed after six hours of marriage, Judy moans, "I've never not belonged to somebody. If I'm not going to be married, I don't know what to do with myself."

So she joins the army. Too stupid to see through the recruiter's lies about boot camp luxuries, she arrives at basic training asking, "Where are the yachts?" She files her nails, bitches about her fatigues—"Is this the only color these come in?"—and is personally offended by her sleeping quarters. When she realizes this is army life, she wants to revoke her enlistment and go home.

Daddy comes to the rescue, scolding, "How could you do this to your parents? Haven't we given you everything you wanted? Didn't I get you into college? Bail you out of your first marriage? Why are you punishing us? You were never a smart girl. You are obviously incapable of making your own decisions."

This recitation sounds like an indictment of Jewish princesses and their royal families when in fact it could be applied to millions of non-Jews, including the golden Kelly Corchran and her white-bread parents. Yet the movie makes the Benjamins' behavior seem uniquely Jewish—as if only a Jewish daughter is supposed to fulfill certain roles and expectations, as if only Jewish parents take it personally when a child diverges from their teachings, as if only Jewish parents have ever tried to make life easier for their children, or kept a daughter too weak to take care of herself.

When I first saw *Private Benjamin*, I defended against the stereotype from the point of view of its target, the young Jewish woman. This time, I found myself objecting from the perspective of Judy's parents. I had crossed the generational line, but the scene did not get any easier to watch. To me JAPs are no joke.

Private Benjamin didn't find the image funny either. After her father's insulting harangue, she decides to stay in the army despite its hardships, and proceeds to distinguish herself as a soldier of considerable courage and intelligence.

I confess to feeling a tad squeamish about the implied syllogism here: (a) former JAP finds self-respect in the army; (b) the army stands for America; therefore (c), for a young Jewish woman to become self-respecting she must join the American mainstream. This message is not so great either for Jews or women. It takes the position that female emancipation and Jewish culture are incompatible; that to choose personhood, a woman must necessarily renounce peoplehood.

Rather than accept such a bifurcation, I wanted to see the army as a kind of Outward Bound program for Judy and not a metaphor for her assimilation. But the movie wouldn't let me off the hook.

To drive home its point, Judy falls in love with a French-Jewish gynecologist. If the army represents assimilation into mainstream America, the new lover represents the next best thing, assimilation into aristocratic Judaism. But gradually, we watch the gynecologist— symbol of both the adored Jewish professional man and all male experts who presume to know more about women than we do ourselves—become unfaithful and belittling, and we watch Judy backslide into domesticated JAPdom. Then, just as they are about to exchange marriage vows, she sees the light. She challenges the doctor (imagine *that!*) when he makes the mistake of calling her stupid. She throws a punch at him, tosses off her wedding veil, and strides into the sunset—presumably to a new life as a strong-willed, self-assured Big Mouth, a breed that, despite its problems, yields Hollywood's most admirable female film characters.

As long as we have to put up with stereotypes, let's admit that some stereotypes are better than others. Just as most Jewish men would rather be denounced as the smart, industrious Jew than the stingy, clannish Jew, I would rather identify with a Jewish Big Mouth than a JAP.

In all the films I reviewed I found only one unlikable Jewish Big Mouth: Naomi, the strident, hypercritical Israeli in, what else, *Portnoy's Complaint*. "I went with a Jewish girl and I can't get it up in the state of Israel," says Alex, reconvinced that Jewish women are his problem.

Other than Naomi, the Jewish Big Mouth is the closest thing to a winner that we've got in films. From *Anne Frank* to *Funny Girl* to *The Way We Were* to *Dirty Dancing*, the character of the clever, outspoken Jewish girl has become a film convention that empowers everywoman. Most important, films portraying the Ugly Duckling who rises above her appearance have assured girls with big noses and frizzy hair that they too can invent their own kind of terrific and leave Miss America in the dust. Jewish women could take comfort in the triumph of wit and brains over conventional beauty. We may not be able to do much about the WASP ideal and its judgmental view of "ethnic" looks but we could try to get a little smarter every year.

The progenitor of the Jewish Big Mouth character was none other than thirteen-year-old Anne Frank. As powerful as the diary was to read, seeing the film's Anne function despite many confinements—the confinement of her Amsterdam hiding place, of her traditional Jewish family, and of the suffocating Nazi juggernaut—left me with an indelible image of her bravery and spunk. "I'm living a great adventure," Anne says. "I want to write . . . I want to go on living even after my death." "I don't want to be dignified," she tells Pater, the boy whose family shares the attic. "I want some fun."

Anne Frank serves as a shining rebuttal to the insipid anti-fun *Marjorie Morningstar*, released the previous year. Anne herself, representing the new Jewish woman, directly challenges the other three female archetypes in her story:

She challenges her own Jewish mother—"Mother and I have nothing in common. When I try to explain my views, she asks me if I'm constipated." She challenges her docile sister—"I won't have them walk all over me like Margot. I've got to fight things out for myself. Make something of myself." Though Margot is supposedly the pretty one, Anne outshines her as a bonfire outshines a streetlamp. And she challenges Pater's mother, another middle-aged JAP figure, played by Shelley Winters, who talks of little else but her fur coat and her father, who gave her "the best money could buy."

In contrast to these women, the headstrong, rambunctious Anne sends an electrical charge through the attic, disturbing the peace. "You need an old-fashioned spanking," says Mr. Van Dam, Pater's father, who loses patience with her big mouth. "A man likes a girl who'll listen to him. A domestic girl who likes to cook and sew. Why do you show off all the time? Why not be nice and quiet like your sister Margot?"

"I'll open my veins first," shouts the glorious Anne. "I'm going to be remarkable."

And so she is. By the film's end, when the Nazis barge in, we have seen glimpses of the extraordinary woman she would have become. We see it best in the way she welcomes and comes to terms with her burgeoning sexuality. Thumbing her nose at propriety and defying the realities of confinement, Anne creates a magical romantic separateness, majestically dons a shawl and gloves, and visits Pater alone in his room as if it was an elegant rendezvous rather than a few square feet of space at death's door. Their hours together are filled with palpable sexual energy, good conversation, and mutual respect, a paradigm of friendship and love.

You can't do much better than that. Except of course to survive.

But we've never been able to have it all. Something's got to give. In the best of the Jewish Big Mouth films—the Streisand trilogy, *Dirty Dancing*, and *Beaches*—strong Jewish women don't lose their lives, but they lose their loves.

In *Funny Girl*, Fanny Brice loses Nick Arnstein because her success unmans him. The same scenario is played out in *Beaches* when Bette Midler's character, C.C., a singing star very like herself, loses her John. In *The Way We Were*, Katie (Streisand) loses Hubbell (Robert Redford) because her passion and commitment disturb the calm of WASP stability and confidence. *Yentl* loses Avigdor, her friend, soul mate, and Talmud study partner, because the sources say one cannot be all that, and a woman. And in *Dirty Dancing*, Baby loses Johnny, because a member of the Painters and Plasterers Union is no match for a girl who's planning to change the world.

Compared to other romantic losses in traditional American films, these girl-loses-boy deprivations are oddly, gratefully unhumiliating. That is because all five women are deeply loved in the leaving. It is the *situation* not the woman that is judged to be impossible. It is patriarchy, Orthodoxy, or classism that causes the impasse, each a condition that is not immutable, a condition we can hope to change. Fanny and Nick, and C.C. and John, would be fine in a society that accepts a wife's public prominence as readily as a husband's. Katie and Hubbell might be together if women activists were viewed as heroes, not troublemakers. Yentl and Avigdor could pursue their passion for Talmud *and* each other, if Judaism did not so vengefully guard its gender ghettos. And Johnny and Baby might have made it if our culture didn't demand that women marry up.

Besides being well-loved, all five female protagonists share another positive quality. When her guy is gone, each woman has something left: Fanny and C.C. have their spectacular careers, Katie her antiwar protests, Yentl has Talmud, and Baby has her whole life ahead of her. The point is, when things don't work out each woman still knows who *she* is.

"I'm a bagel in a place full of onion rolls," proclaims Fanny, who felt destined to be a star, despite her American Beauty nose. "I'm a natural hollerer," she says. She won't let Ziegfeld tell her what to sing, and she refuses to compete with the beautiful Follies showgirls; she comes onstage as a pregnant bride, and wins the spotlight through laughter. Her personal life is not so controllable. Nick wants to be the head of the family and Fanny wants to be a Sadie, a married lady (which I suppose is a grown-up Shirley), but she's not good at faking deference or subordination.

Yentl won't fake it either. After Avigdor learns that his brilliant little study partner is really a woman, he proposes that she be his wife and that he do the thinking for both of them. But Yentl cannot deposit her brilliance in a stewpot. She cannot squelch her passion for Talmudic discourse or overcome her ineptness at the traditional female role. While living with Hadass, a model Jewish wife, she has come to understand the seductive appeal of female solicitousness—the peace in it for a man, the flattery, the comfort. But Yentl can never be a Hadass. "I want to study with you, not darn your socks," she protests. Avigdor insists being his wife should be enough. Echoing Freud's famous question, he asks, "What more do you want?" Yentl answers for millions of us: "More."

In *The Way We Were* and *Dirty Dancing*, the love theme contains an important difference: the object of the woman's affections is a Gentile and the theme is Jewish Big Mouth Wins Gorgeous Goy by Being Her Intense Natural Self. Since we know by now that stereotypes symbolize much more than themselves, we could translate that to read The Jewish People Finally Make Good in America. However, in both movies, girl loses boy, *willingly*. To me, these movies are warning Jews not to sell our souls for a piece of the American dream.

Ultimately, I took *The Way We Were* and *Dirty Dancing* not as antiassimilation stories but as subtle films of Jewish pride in which the ethical standard is upheld by a female. Both are *women's* films. The sex scenes are tuned in to female fantasies and in one or two encounters the women are the sexual initiators. Jewish women *kvell* (beam with pride) watching Barbra Streisand and Jennifer Gray, with their frizzy hair and non-pug noses, win the love of Robert Redford and Patrick Swayze. We tell ourselves, "If she can do it, I could do it—if I wanted to."

At the same time, we understand that neither union can last because each woman in her way is too Jewish to compromise; and also because each woman is a cut above her man—and in this culture, that's not allowed; the masculine rules of hegemony hold fast.

Katie Moroski, a working-class woman who fights to save the world from fascism, red-baiting, and nuclear war, is the moral superior of Hubbell Gardner, the Beekman Place Adonis, star athlete, and dashing naval officer, who wrote about himself, "He was like his country;

everything came easy to him." *The Way We Were* is about *not* doing it the easy way, not compromising, not selling out your principles, not laughing at Eleanor Roosevelt jokes or ironing your kinky hair, or naming names for the red-baiters.

Dirty Dancing continues what was begun in the Catskills with *Marjorie Morningstar*; in fact, the two stories bracket the thirty-year development of the Jewish female protagonist in American film. *Dirty Dancing* is both a message movie and a showcase for message stereotypes: there's Baby, the Jewish idealist who's "gonna change the world"; Lisa, her JAP sister, who's "gonna decorate it"; Daddy, the doctor who fixes everything; the Jewish Mother, here a quiet background figure but mischievously and symbolically named Marjorie; the waiters, all Jewish Princes—law students, medical students, and egomaniacs—and Johnny Castle, the new royalty, the working-class idol who attracts Jewish women with his decency and his dirty dancing.

Here, ethnicity's stock characters are flipped on their heads. Gentile Johnny is a kind, sweet, hard-working guy who is exploited by Jewish employers and sex-starved Jewish women. Lest we cry anti-Semitism, Baby redeems the Jews: she wants to send her leftovers to Southeast Asia; she helps people, tells the truth, plans to major in the economics of underdeveloped countries in order to enlist in the Peace Corps. In such a future there's no place for a guy like Johnny Castle.

The movie suggests that for achieving Jewish women, hot sex is as off-limits as working-class Gentiles; there are more important things in life than pleasure. Johnny understands what Noel didn't—that he is a man for one season, a summer fling. He knows Baby is beyond him. At the last big event of the summer, he honors her publicly as "the kind of person I want to be."

You've come a long way, Baby. Thirty years separate Marjorie's Catskill movie from Baby's. In that time, Jennifer Gray, a Jew, has replaced the non-Jewish Natalie Wood in the starring role, and the male love interest is no longer a man in black who calls her a Shirley, but a man in black who calls her his hero. From that summer to this, the Jewish woman has gained a self and a future.

But Baby hasn't come *all* the way. Today, she's going to *be* somebody—but she may not be *with* somebody. The forced choice is still there. Choose or Die. Either/Or. A great love or a full life. In the movies of the next thirty years, I'll be looking for both.

PART FOUR

Living with a Feminist Head and a Jewish Heart

14

Ain't
We Both Women?

Blacks, Jews, and Gender

I HAVE THIS FANTASY, OR MAYBE IT'S A DREAM:

I am sitting in the audience at a huge feminist conference, listening to an increasingly rancorous debate between African-American women and Jewish women. Suddenly I rise, take to the stage, and deliver an extemporaneous oration about black-Jewish understanding that echoes the cadences of Sojourner Truth's celebrated "Ain't I a Woman?" speech at the Women's Convention of 1851. Described at the time as having a "magical effect on the gathering," Truth's haunting, hard-hitting words challenged white suffragists and abolitionists to see slave women *as women*. My remarks, delivered in the twilight of the twentieth century, ask black and Jewish feminists to see *one another* as women, to stop arguing about men's politics and to build on the commonalities that outweigh our differences.

When I finish (remember this is fantasy), my words also have a magical effect. They inspire the founding of a pluralist coalition that foments a feminist revolution comparable to the democracy revolutions that swept Eastern Europe in 1989.

I admit to this messianic fantasy only because it reveals how frustrated I feel about the growing rift between Jews and blacks in America. According to a Yankelovitch poll, in the last quarter century, anti-Semitism has declined among whites but increased among blacks. Now, blacks are twice as likely as whites to hold significant anti-Semitic attitudes and, even more alarming, it is younger and better-educated blacks who tend to be the most bigoted.

By the same token, although a 1990 poll done by the National Opinion Research Center found that Jews have more positive attitudes toward blacks and a greater commitment to equal opportunity than do other white Americans, the poll also found that a majority of Jews do not favor government help or government spending to benefit blacks. Worse still, a Harris poll found that Jews are more likely than other whites to be upset if blacks move into their neighborhood; and 20 percent of Jews said they did not want their children to attend school with blacks, as compared to only 14 percent of other whites.

With such depressing statistics, no wonder my fantasy life turns for relief to imaginary scenarios and magical thinking. But magic won't bring back that simpler time before all the "troubles" that split our communities: the Ocean Hill–Brownsville teacher-neighborhood confrontation, the Bakke affirmative action case, the forced resignation of U.N. Ambassador Andrew Young, Jesse Jackson's "Hymietown" statement, and the advent of Louis Farrakhan, the black nationalist extremist. Magic won't recapture those years when blacks and Jews worked together for a goal called freedom, when Jews composed more than 50 percent of the young volunteers during the Mississippi Summer of 1964, when Chaney, Goodman, and Schwerner became our shared martyrs, when Jewish and black clergymen linked arms in the front lines of massive civil rights marches and everyone sang "We Shall Overcome"—and when in the 1970s feminists of all colors dreamed of combating bigotry through sisterhood.

In 1980, when a black friend refused to sign the petition protesting the Zionism-is-racism resolution in advance of the U.N.'s Copenhagen conference, I was forced to recognize that the politics of identity had displaced the ideology of universal sisterhood in the Women's Movement. It would take years of black-Jewish dialogue for me to understand how dramatically identity politics had altered black-Jewish relations. In the process, I had to come to terms with some bitter truths: No longer can blacks and Jews be drawn together simply because other Americans hate us both. No longer can we expect each other to agree on what constitutes racism, anti-Semitism, or institutional barriers to equal opportunity. No longer can a single speech or slogan move us to march together. Now, we often march in opposite directions or face each other across an abyss. Now, our two communities clash regularly over issues of power, priorities, competitive oppression, and conflicting self-interest. Finally, I have to give up my fantasies and settle for real life, which means arguing, negotiating, and struggling with blacks to find common ground within our changed circumstances and new suspicions. Now I know that black-Jewish coalition building takes work and leaves scars.

I can hear my critics asking, Why does she keep singling out African-Americans? It only exacerbates black-Jewish enmity. Why perpetuate the idea that blacks and Jews have special problems when the basic difficulties exist between blacks and all other races, and between Jews and all non-Jews?

To me, that's like saying, Why single out husbands and lovers when all men give women a hard time? I single out blacks and Jews because, like women and their husbands or lovers, when we give each other a hard time and it hurts more because we once were very close. (The humorist Calvin Trillin captures our former closeness by recalling an apocryphal headline in a New York newspaper in the good old days: COLD SNAP HITS OUR TOWN. JEWS, NEGROES SUFFER MOST.) For decades, Jewish-Americans and African-Americans suffered often and sometimes suffered together. We had comparable experiences of dislocation and loss; we had a special empathy for one another which we expressed openly in our politics and our friendships. Because of these historic connections, we continue to approach each other with higher expectations than either of us brings to any other group. Likewise, our disappointments inflict sharper wounds. I've felt the pain—and learned the most—from confrontations with my black friends on several issues of interest to both communities, women in particular.

I S S U E
Race vs. Gender

It was a summer evening in 1984, the day after the Democratic National Convention nominated Geraldine Ferraro as Walter Mondale's vice presidential running mate. I couldn't have been happier if my mother had been commemorated on a postage stamp. A woman vice president! In our lifetime! What a triumph! After work, I bounded up to Donna Shalala's apartment for a get-together of our black-Jewish women's group. I could hardly wait to share my ecstasy with my pals.

The longest-lasting of four black-Jewish dialogues in which I've been involved, this all female one meets for dinner in each of our homes several times a year, pledged to discuss anything and everything relating to race and gender. The evening's host provides the meal or organizes us to bring potluck dishes, and there is always lots of wine to lubricate the gears of revelation.

It's hard for me to imagine any group of men doing what we do—laughing, crying, confessing anger and weakness, letting our hair down. As in feminist consciousness-raising groups of the 1970s, we try to focus each meeting on a particular subject—how it felt to grow up black or Jewish; how we deal with the sexism in our own community; our reactions to controversial news events. South Africa and Israel have taken a good chunk of our time, as have Ed Koch and Louis Farrakhan. Blacks offer candid impressions of Jews and Jews give our uncensored impressions of blacks—and each of us tries to speak the truth and whatever else is on her mind at the moment. For example:

A Jewish woman arrived at one of our sessions complaining that a black cab driver had called her a "kike" when he thought her tip inadequate. "That's nothing," a black woman answered. "Usually I can't get a cab to pick me up at all."

Another time, a black woman admitted how much she resented white women, and especially Jewish women, who date black men. "If whites are dating blacks, why make it a *Jewish* issue?" asked one of the Jews in our group. "Because," a black woman replied, "Jews make up fifty percent of the white partners of blacks and almost all of them are Jewish *women* dating black men." "Well then," said a Jewish member, "maybe this proves Jews more than other whites see blacks as equal human beings. What's bad about that?"

"What's bad is that Jewish women are siphoning off educated black men who might otherwise be available partners for black women whose dating options are already severely limited by a dwindling pool of black males" was the reply.

The Jewish women listened to the facts: homicide is the leading cause of death among young black men; black men die ten times more often than whites of hypertension disease; men in Harlem are less likely to survive to age forty than men in Bangladesh. Suicide, drug addiction, AIDS, and imprisonment account for another large drain; the male prison population has grown by 80 percent since 1970, and now there are more college-age black men in prison or on parole than in college. More black men than women drop out of school, which explains why at some colleges there are twice as many black female as black male students. Add to all this the average rate of homosexuality and it's clear that marriageable, healthy, heterosexual, educated black males are an endangered species. So when a white woman claims a black husband, it is a deeply felt loss. The Jewish women, presented with these facts, understood.

In another discussion, one of our Jewish members said she resented black women's reluctance to join integrated feminist organizations. An African-American replied that groups like the National Organization for Women and the National Women's Political Caucus are dominated by middle-class whites with an elitist agenda. The Jewish women insisted that would cease to be the case only if black women joined up and altered the agenda from within. This chicken-and-egg argument was a draw.

Such exchanges have taught us that our two constituencies see events quite differently in more ways than we had imagined, and that on certain subjects, it takes a concerted effort just to hear each other out. After the black teenager Yusef Hawkins was killed in Bensonhurst merely for wandering into an Italian neighborhood, the black women insisted that Jews should have expressed more public outrage. We Jews just wanted to stay out of the spotlight; we were thankful it wasn't Jewish kids who did it. And after the "wilding" attack on the Central Park jogger, the Jewish women wanted more condemnation from the black community. One black woman answered it was white society that needed condemning: "If you treat our kids like animals long enough, you can't suddenly blame them for acting like animals."

While we diagnose our differences mercilessly, we also try to acknowledge our commonalities: for instance, the fact that both Jews and African-Americans seem to have problems accepting strong women. On the one hand, women are said to be the backbones of our families and the mainstays of our churches or synagogues. On the other hand, these same talents elicit accusations that we are suffocating (Jewish mothers) or domineering (black mothers), and that, as a result, Jews and African-Americans are "feminized" peoples.

Many black women object when African-Americans' concern about male weakness translates into hostility toward female strength, or compensatory formulas calling for black women's subjugation. The black "manhood problem," they say, can only be solved through massive structural changes—assistance to black families, public school reform, emergency programs to combat drug abuse, job training, and leadership development. Black men can't build their self-esteem on the backs of self-abnegating black women, and shouldn't kid themselves that machismo is the path to human dignity.

The Jewish "manhood problem" has a similar outcome but a different genesis. It can be traced to the biblical phenomenon of the weaker, smaller son—Isaac, Jacob, Joseph, David, Solomon—being God's or his mother's favorite, though not initially admired in the world. It plays out in the Eastern European stereotypes of anemic shtetl scholars, of husbands and fathers who could not protect their families from the Nazis, emaciated Jewish men going like "lambs to the slaughter," and more recently, American-Jewish men who are called henpecked, eggheads, nerds, or bleeding-heart liberals. As an antidote to these "feminized" images, Jews have fallen in love with a macho substitute—the Israeli soldier who takes no crap from anyone. For years after the Six-Day War, the Jewish fighter was a source of enormous pride, but lately he sometimes seems to be a savior gone mad, a military Golem who is helping to destroy the moral system he was created to defend.

It is the nature of manhood problems to play themselves out in the lives of women. When a black man or a Jewish man is subjected to racism or anti-Semitism, his antidote of choice very often is sexism; that is, he processes the defamatory or discriminatory treatment not solely as an attack on his race or religion but as emasculation. To compensate for being treated as an inferior he lords it over *his* perceived inferiors, "his women." Or he projects his self-loathing onto the women of his own group and then rejects them in favor of women of the dominant majority, as if he can prove himself the equal of white men or Christian men by taking "their women" away from them. Or he emulates his culture's current male heroes—for Jews it may be the scions of Wall Street or the Ariel Sharons of the battlefield who prove their manhood through wealth and power; for blacks, men like Malcolm X, who demanded that black leaders "stand up and fight like men instead of running around here nonviolently acting like women," or Farrakhan, who promotes Muslim sex-role orthodoxies and fuels black pride with Jew hatred.

Such are the subjects we've tackled in the six-woman black-Jewish group that Harriet Michel and I founded in 1984 when we became frustrated with the proceedings in the forty-person New York City Black-Jewish Coalition to which both of us belonged. This larger assemblage—which was organized around the issues of the presidential campaign and composed mostly of male religious, business, and community leaders—had been effective defusing Jewish anger at Jackson's "Hymietown" slur, and black anger at a full-page ad headlined JEWS AGAINST JACKSON, but most of the men seemed incapable of going further talking personally, exposing their vulnerabilities, and making real human connections.

After one power-posturing, speechmaking session, during which Harriet and I had been grimacing to each other across the room, we decided to convene a small women's group that would try to approach black and Jewish issues more honestly and from a woman's perspective. Harriet, then director of the New York Urban League, chose two other black participants—Bernice Powell, then president of the New York Coalition of 100 Black Women and now executive associate to the president of the United Church of Christ, and another prominent black woman, who prefers that I protect her privacy and not use her name. I chose two Jewish women—Marilyn Braveman, who was the director of education and women's issues for the American Jewish Committee, and Jacqueline Levine, past chair of the National Jewish Community Relations Advisory Council (NJCRAC) and vice president of the American Jewish Congress. Because we had no idea how confrontational our conversations might become, we also asked someone to join us who was neither black nor Jewish (but who, we laughed, could pass for either)—Donna Shalala, a Lebanese Christian who was president of Hunter College and is now chancellor of the University of Wisconsin. Donna agreed to serve as our mediator just in case there were stressful moments.

These then were the women sprawled around Donna's living room that summer evening after Geraldine Ferraro made history at the Democratic convention. We toasted her, bubbling with enthusiasm as we reviewed our impressions of her acceptance speech, the prospects for the ticket, and the pitfalls of a male-female candidacy. (When they greet one another, should Ferraro and Mondale embrace or shake hands? How would Ferraro's husband relate to Mondale's wife? and so on.) After a few minutes, I noticed that the black women in the group were not bubbling quite as effervescently as the Jewish women.

"How come you three aren't so excited?" I asked them. "Is there something wrong with Ferraro?"

I wasn't being rude: directness is one of our ground rules.

"She's white," answered the blacks, almost simultaneously.

"But she's a woman, like you, like us," said one of the Jews.

"But she's white."

"Yeah, she's also a Catholic and not a Jew, but I still feel her achievement as my own," said a Jewish woman. "I think to myself if an Italian Catholic woman can do it, maybe someday a Jewish woman can be in the White House."

"It's a big leap from a white Catholic woman to a black of any kind," said another African-American.

"Shirley Chisholm was black but her 1972 candidacy was only symbolic," replied a Jewish member. "Angela Davis was black but it made no dent when the Communist party put her up for president. But this is the real thing; it's a tremendous breakthrough for the American political system. If Gerry can be the candidate of a major party, *you* could be too."

"Not so!" was the reply. "And that's the point. The woman in me is glad for Gerry but the black in me has no greater political possibilities today than last week. Gerry's success won't help my people one bit."

In the midst of my celebratory raptures, my African-American friends forced me to change my angle of vision, to alter my strictly feminist orientation and acknowledge a critical difference between black women's marginalization and mine. Whereas it depends on the political and social climate of the moment as to whether I feel more vulnerable as a Jew or a woman, for black women the oppression of color and class *always* outweighs the oppression of gender or religion. In a white-run society, racism is the overriding injustice; it does not allow invisibility, or passing, or a strictly feminist orientation.

Jewish women, with our white skin privilege, are allowed to feel like women first; thus Marilyn, Jackie, and I could identify with the success of another woman, even though she was not Jewish. But our African-American counterparts are always blacks before they are women, so it would take a black victory to clear the way for them.

Turning the facts around, I could prove their point for myself. If a Jewish *man* had been nominated as Walter Mondale's running mate, I would have felt pleased and proud but I would not have been popping my cork. Jew or not, I would have seen it as a *man's* triumph and thus familiar. His victory would not have greased the track for a Jewish woman, or *any* woman. Likewise, Ferraro would not ease the way for *any* black, male *or* female.

If our women's group works harder at deciphering causes and delves deeper into the realm of feelings than the other dialogue groups I'm familiar with, it's because we all consider ourselves feminists as well as advocates of our own communities. We are interested in one another not just as blacks or Jews, but as women. We start with women-things in common and we explore the problems females share—sex discrimination, street hassles, dealing with condescending men, raising nonsexist sons, being role models for younger women, adjusting to the aging process.

While we are not afraid of confrontation, we are more devoted to female-style communication, down-and-dirty mutual self-disclosure and emotional honesty. Fortunately, we spent our first few sessions speaking about our personal histories, so that by the time we tackled the tough, divisive issues, we were well-enough acquainted to trust that expressions of anger would not break us apart. By then, we knew a good bit about each other's parents, husbands, or boyfriends, bosses, children, bad habits, and sore points. We could imagine each other as little girls. We had a sense of each other as political women. We knew who were the mystical ones and who were the resident skeptics. We knew who had job troubles and who had man troubles. We knew and felt known.

When one of our members moved away in 1987, the group worried that we'd have to backtrack and lose our intimacy to accommodate her replacement. But we hadn't counted on the special sensitivity of Jualynne Dodson, a sociologist and former assistant dean of Union Theological Seminary, who fit in as if she'd been with us from the start. And now that another black member has left New York, the group is taking this opportunity to expand: we're adding two black women and another Jew for a total of eight. We never did replace Donna Shalala when she moved to become Chancellor of the University of Wisconsin. We couldn't think of anyone who could fill her shoes. Besides, we no longer need a mediator. We've become friends.

Respect for these women's privacy prevents me from saying more about them except that I now carry their stories around inside of me as part of my "master story," and whenever I get involved in black-Jewish coalition building, I am no longer surprised by the explosive nature of the endeavor for I've had my dry run in the confines of our intimate group.

Here, I have learned that although I see myself as a Jewish woman, blacks see me as a white woman. Here, I have had to admit that I see blacks as black before I think of them as Christian. Here, I have bounced back after hearing some of the infuriating opinions blacks have of Jews, and I've gotten off my chest some racial hostility I wouldn't have dared to confess anywhere else. At times, I have sided with my African-American colleagues against positions taken by my Jewish sisters, yet not felt disloyal. I have discovered that after hours of wrangling and fueding, we can still look forward to the next meeting and leave each other with a hug.

ISSUE
Jesse Jackson

At the victory rally the night David Dinkins won the 1989 New York City mayoral primary, Jesse Jackson made a speech that contained a number of gratuitous Christian religious references. The next day I asked a black friend, "Since Jews supported Dinkins in greater proportions than any other group of whites, don't you think all that Jesus talk was pretty insensitive of Jackson?"

The black woman's face closed tight. "You're not gonna get me to speak against Jesse," she said flatly. Jesse Jackson is our Israel. Even if he embarrasses us or says the wrong thing, he's the best we've got and I'm not going to bad-mouth him—just like you're not going to bad-mouth the Jewish State."

Her analogy made so much sense that I took it a step further in my own thinking. I've been saying that uncritical support of Israel threatens the integrity of Israeli democracy and the Jewish ethic. Following my friend's analogy, I want to insist that blacks' uncritical support of black leaders who are insensitive to Jews or who are outright anti-Semites can be just as corrosive to the integrity of African-Americans. This is so whether the leader in question is Jackson, who not only called Jews "Hymies" but once claimed that he was "tired of hearing about the Holocaust," and who embraced Yasir Arafat years before the PLO renounced terrorism. Or Farrakhan, who said Hitler was "a great man," Jews have "abnormal power," Judaism is "a gutter religion," and Israel "an outlaw act." Or Steve Cokely, the former mayoral aide in Chicago, who claimed that an international Jewish conspiracy controls the world, and Jewish doctors are infecting blacks with AIDS.

I'm not saying Jackson is comparable to Farrakhan or Cokely, but that blacks should understand why added together their remarks confirm Jewish fears that anti-Semitism is more malignant (or at least more publicly acceptable) among African-Americans than among other groups, an idea that arouses enormous anxiety among Jews who are anxious under benign circumstances. Cumulative insults, plus polls showing rising black anti-Semitism, plus black criticism of Israel, have coalesced for some Jews into an irrational fear of Jesse Jackson, simply because he is the most prominent representative of black sentiment. Because I feel it important to distinguish Jackson from more virulent black voices—and because women's issues are at stake here too—I want to deal with Jackson first.

When evaluating any politician regardless of race or religion, I test his or her views against my own interests as a woman and a Jew. I will not support anyone who ensures the freedom and safety of Jews but does not simultaneously ensure the freedom and safety of women. And vice versa.

Given these criteria, I would no sooner choose to be ruled by Louis Farrakhan than by Muammar Qadaffi, Saddam Hussein, King Fahd, or the latest ayatollah—all of whom, by virtue of their attitudes toward Jews and their treatment of their own culture's women, would keep me about as oppressed as a female as I would be as a Jew. Incidentally, the same litmus test works in Israel too: Jewish religious extremists and ultraright nationalists are coincidentally antiequality and antipluralism; they are neither sympathetic to women's interests nor tolerant of *all* Jews. They throw chairs at women who pray at the Western Wall and stones at Jews who drive their cars on the Sabbath. They have divided Israelis, fomented violence, and undermined the moral and ideological foundations of Zionism.

Compared to "enemies" like Farrakhan, Qadaffi, or the ultra-extremist rabbis, I find Jesse Jackson less troublesome and more complicated. While a 1988 American Jewish Committee poll showed that

59 percent of Jews believe Jackson is anti-Semitic, I would argue for a more tolerant attitude toward Jackson and a more vigilant monitoring of the ultraright.

Jackson's main public role has been to promote voter registration of young people, poor people, and minorities and to articulate social-justice concerns that centrist Democrats have been neglecting (and that closely match the liberal Jewish agenda). In contrast, ultraright fundamentalists use their TV pulpits and fund-raising networks to advance their reactionary aim of Christianizing America and eradicating church-state separation, which would be the death knell for pluralism and Jewish integrity.

Jackson's "anti-Israel" reputation rests on two positions: his willingness to talk to the PLO (which the U.S. State Department, the Israeli left, and many American Jews also have been willing to do), and his call for a mutually negotiated two-state solution in the Middle East, a notion espoused by many political moderates the world over. "I support Israel's right to exist with security within internationally recognized boundaries," Jackson told *The Jewish Week* in January 1990, adding, "My position is clear: the present relationship between Israelis and Palestinians is one that is destroying both peoples"—a statement with which no reasonable Jew would disagree.

In contrast, the supposed "pro-Israel" reputation of the Christian fundamentalists rests on the scriptural prophecy that requires a Jewish presence in the Holy Land as a prerequisite to the Second Coming of Christ and the subsequent conversion of the Jews. This is hardly authentic pro-*Jewish* advocacy. Therefore, I found it strange indeed when Prime Minister Menachem Begin refused to see Jesse Jackson, but did meet with Bailey Smith, the Baptist minister who declared that God does not hear the prayers of a Jew.

I agree that at times Jackson has been insensitive to Jews and insufficiently respectful of Jewish historical experience (imagine how he would react if whites said they were "tired of hearing about" black oppression), but I do not believe he has demonstrated disregard for Jewish interests. On the contrary, I think we have reason to take heart from many of his gestures of support: his appearance in the pulpit of the Skokie synagogue prior to the announced Nazi march, his public apology at the 1984 Democratic Convention, his stirring remarks at a Holocaust memorial service, his interceding with Mikhail Gorbachev on behalf of Soviet Jews, and his participation in a 1988 Kristallnacht remembrance. Such actions have persuaded me that Jackson is capable of sensitization and change.

The evangelical right and the ultraconservatives, on the other hand, are rigid, ruthless proponents of public policy that threatens pluralism (meaning the rights and free expression of Jews and women, among others). Their nativistic anti-Semitism, though more subtle, is also more far-reaching than anything Jackson has said or done. They have introduced Christianity into the schools with their "Equal Access" law, won several crèche cases, banned books like *The Diary of Anne Frank* from schools and libraries, opposed abortion even in the case of rape and incest, firebombed family-planning clinics, and forced into the Republican platform the requirement of a religious test for the appointment of federal judges. They have made no secret of their moral imperialism: they intend *by law* to "Christianize America," impose prayer in the public schools, revitalize family patriarchy, and proscribe reproductive freedom.

Conservatives—and for that matter, "mainstream" Republicans like Patrick Buchanan—have proved their enmity to Jews *and* women by word *and* deed. Why aren't we on the warpath against those reactionaries? Why are we so focused on Jesse Jackson, a man whose commitments on the Jewish question are still evolving and have yet to be fully tested? Moreover, if his progress on women's issues can be taken as a bellwether, Jackson has the capacity to grow and change. Remember that he moved from antichoice to pro-choice on reproductive rights, and from the male-supremacy line of the black power movement to a spirited advocacy for women's needs. I believe he can be similarly sensitized to Jewish needs. I take his overtures toward Jews as a sign of his potential for empathy and self-education. Unless he shows clear evidence of backsliding, I see no purpose in the continued attacks on him, especially as long as he remains a strong advocate for women.

Using the Jackson/Israel analogy of my black friend on post-Election Day, I believe that Jews who want the world to give Israel the benefit of the doubt despite her errors and flaws can work harder to understand the gigantic significance of this African-American leader, flaws and all, and should give him the benefit of the doubt as well.

I S S U E
Hate Speech

Despite my willingness to overlook Jackson's past insults, I do believe that words are weapons and when deployed with lethal intent, they demand a response. Lethal intent is what Jews discerned in the words of Farrakhan, the Black Muslim extremist, and Cokely, the Chicago political hack. Jewish reaction to their slander was swift and wrathful. We demanded an immediate apology and expected to hear a chorus of condemnation from the black leadership. When neither was forthcoming, we were stunned, and when some blacks countered by criticizing our demands, we were devastated.

Although Jackson finally distanced himself from Farrakhan, it was not without obvious reluctance. Moreover, many Jews still do not believe he meant it, while many blacks are still offended that he was forced to capitulate to "Jewish pressure." For similar reasons, it took a week for Chicago's black mayor to fire Cokely for his libelous comments about Jewish doctors and such. Long afterward, some black and Jewish spokespersons continued trading barbs while responsible leaders worked hard at damage control.

For Jews, the problem is not what any single extremist says but the reluctance of mainstream blacks to repudiate their anti-Semites instantly and unequivocally. The response of African-Americans is often a barrage of tough questions: "Why should each of us have to represent the entire black race?" "If I don't blame you for Ed Koch or Meir Kahane, why do you insist I answer for the behavior of one or two black fanatics?" "Besides, you have power; we're powerless, so why do you care what a few of our extremists say about you?" "How come the only time we hear from Jewish people is when you want us to denounce one of our own?" "Where are you when we need you to *support* us?"

At a black-Jewish dialogue weekend in Racine, Wisconsin, Gary Rubin, an American Jewish Committee expert on race relations, pointed out that culturally and historically, blacks and Jews have learned to respond to insults quite differently. Experience has taught Jews to take anti-Semitism seriously; we know that what begins with insulting words can end in the ovens. What's more, our talmudic legacy schooled us to believe that an aggrieved party has a right to demand a retraction and obtain redress. On the other hand, African-

Americans' experience with slavery and oppression has taught them that insults must be ignored, that in a sense, ignoring an affront invalidates it. Strategically, blacks have had to let today's abuse roll off their backs since tomorrow they may have to work with the abuser in the interests of black advancement. In short, Jewish culture puts the burden on the insulter to retract. Black culture puts the burden on the insultee to *not* respond.

David Shannon, a black minister from Atlanta, agreed with Rubin's analysis: "If we'd permitted ourselves to respond to every insult, we'd all have been dead by 1619."

"We don't even criticize our own for what they do to *us*," added Bernice Powell of the United Church of Christ. "When Mayor Wilson Goode dropped a bomb on black people in Philadelphia, not one black spoke out."

On the issue of Farrakhan's anti-Semitism, the women in our small black-Jewish group battled for months to change each other's minds. The argument sounded something like this:

Black Woman: "Since we have so few spokesmen who can engage the attention of the whole community, we have to protect our leaders, not censure them. Even if I disagree with Farrakhan, even if I think Cokely's a fool with no following, I'm not going to denounce them. I'm not going to attack any African-American just to make the Jews feel better; and I'm certainly not going to attack Farrakhan, who's been such a positive influence on our youth. We're trying to develop living symbols of black aspiration; we're tired of reciting the same old list of dead heroes."

Jewish Woman: "But Farrakhan's hate message should *invalidate* his hero potential. Would you have ignored the fact that Mussolini dropped poison gas on Ethiopia just because he made the trains run on time? Real leaders send the message to their followers that bigotry is unacceptable. Real leaders aren't afraid of denouncing injustice, whoever its targets or perpetrators."

B.W.: "Maybe Jews feel strong enough to go around undermining other Jews, but we have to worry about exacerbating the tensions that already divide the African-American community—tensions between the black middle class [now a quarter of the black population] and an increasingly entrenched underclass; tensions between moderates like David Dinkins and crazies like Al Sharpton [a media spokesman for black defendants, who is known for his antiwhite remarks, and crowd-

rousing demonstrations, particularly in defense of Tawana Brawley].
When Farrakhan endorsed Jackson, blacks were overjoyed because until then he had preached black separatism and counseled his followers
not to participate in political elections. Now we have this glimmer of
new unity, and you want me to criticize the man who reached out his
hand to Jackson and brought in thousands more black votes! If I did
that I'd lose my own credibility."

J.W.: "I know you're in a tough spot but by not making a statement
you *are* making a statement. Or as someone once said, the best way
for evil to triumph is for good people to do nothing."

B.W.: "Some of our moderates *have* protested black anti-Semitism,
but others feel they're in a double bind: if they don't speak out,
they're unacceptable to Jews whose votes or support they need; and
if they do speak out, much of their own rank and file dismiss them as
traitors to black solidarity and puppets of the Jews."

J.W.: "Jews aren't pulling anyone's strings. We have a *proven*
record of supporting black leaders. Los Angeles, Chicago, Philadelphia, and New York wouldn't have elected their black mayors if not
for Jewish voters who supported them in far greater proportions than
did other whites. The same is true for Doug Wilder, the governor of
Virginia. And in Jackson's second run, after he modulated his rhetoric, he got nine percent of the total white vote but *ten* percent of the
Jewish vote, up from four percent in 1984. So Jews are there for
blacks when it counts."

B.W.: "If you really were there for us, you'd stop harping on Farrakhan. Only one percent of American blacks are members of the
Nation of Islam. There are millions of white anti-Semites. Isn't it
hypocritical to keep throwing Farrakhan in our faces?"

J.W.: "On the contrary: the fact that we keep raising Farrakhan is
a measure of our respect for black leadership. It's precisely because we
believe in black empowerment that we cannot ignore these hate messages. We pay attention to what your extremists say about us because
we believe these men and their protégés may someday become leaders
of the larger community and have power over everyone's lives."

B.W.: "Well, to us Farrakhan's anti-Semitism is nothing but rhetorical excess. It's completely irrelevant to his main message which is
a Jewish-style message of economic independence, self-help, and mutual support. What you do for your community is what Farrakhan
wants African-Americans to do for our community. Because of the

federal deficit and cuts in social services, self-help is our only hope. Farrakhan goes to jails and reclaims our drug addicts and promotes black entrepreneurs. But whenever he speaks in public, the press reports only what he says about Jews."

J.W.: "Why not point that out to him? Maybe if he edits out the Jew hating, the press will notice his economic program. No one's going to pay attention to the "main message" as long as it's surrounded by malice. And how can you be sure that his anti-Semitism is rhetorical? Maybe he consciously *uses* it to gain attention. Anyway, Jews have learned from experience that no expression of anti-Semitism is just rhetorical. Every pogrom starts with a hate campaign. Why not just admit it's wrong?"

B.W.: "Because the Al Sharptons of the world would interpret it as kowtowing to the Jews. People like Sharpton gain their following by stirring up the frustrations of the underclass and making them suspicious of traditional black leadership. Poor blacks are so disaffected with the system that they're quick to identify with anyone who challenges it. Middle-class, educated, moderate African-Americans like us are running to keep up with them. Our leadership is too precarious. We can't afford to look weak."

J.W.: "Would it be seen as weakness to issue a principled statement like "We will not denigrate another people in order to achieve our own self-esteem."? Maybe women like yourselves could say it if the men are too hung up on face saving."

B.W.: "We can't do it. Look what happened to Laura Blackburn [a prominent lawyer and specialist in conflict resolution] and Hazel Dukes [president of the New York State NAACP]. When they spoke out, Sharpton and Alton Maddox [a black lawyer often allied with Sharpton] called them Uncle Toms."

And so it goes, hour after hour, meeting after meeting. We circle around each other. Neither side seems able to win a point. Even in our intimate group, where there is a will to understand, we spent five or six sessions on Louis Farrakhan and finally declared an impasse.

ISSUE
The Politics of Survival

At about the same time that Harriet Michel and I started our small dialogue group, I helped to found a thirty-member black-Jewish women's group whose purpose was to prepare our two communities to play a constructive role at the Nairobi U.N. Conference. Although it continued meeting after the conference was over, this group petered out within two years. At first, I attributed its failure to waning black interest.

"Why do you think so many black women stopped coming to our dialogue meetings even though we started out with an equal representation?" I asked a black friend who had been part of the group.

"You Jews have to stop acting like God's chosen people," she barked, her eyes hard and angry. "The world doesn't revolve around you. Relations with Jews are not a priority for most African-Americans; our main concern is *survival*."

The differences between blacks and Jews are rarely more obvious than when each group speaks about its own "survival," a word that both use frequently but with quite dissimilar meanings. For blacks, survival means actual physical endurance, staying alive in the face of violent crime, drugs, hunger, homelessness, and infant mortality rates that are more than triple that of whites; it means surviving as a viable community when 30 percent of the adults and 75 percent of the young live in poverty, when 44 percent of black seventeen-year-olds are functionally illiterate, and black unemployment is twice the white rate. For Jews, survival means keeping a minority culture and a religion alive against all odds, guarding against anti-Semitism and the slippery slope that could lead from hate speech to the gas chambers, and helping to guarantee the security of Israel.

In other words, blacks worry about their actual conditions and fear for the present; Jews worry about their history and fear for the future. Black survival is threatened by poverty; Jewish survival is threatened by affluence, with its temptations of intermarriage with the more privileged majority, assimilation, and moral corruption. Racism is a bacterium, potentially curable but presently deadly; anti-Semitism is a virus, potentially deadly but presently contained.

My friend's point about black priorities was well taken, but her words hurt. By now, I thought, she should understand what I had explained many times before: that fear motivates Jews the way economics motivates blacks. Intergroup dialogue is the Jewish response to our deep-seated insecurity. We invest in dialogue as a form of insurance against anti-Semitism. Although safe and relatively prosperous right now, Jews are a people whose vulnerability is seared indelibly into our collective unconscious. We are congenitally afraid that tomorrow will be worse. After the Babylonian exile, four Roman wars, the Christian Crusades, the Spanish and Portuguese Inquisitions, the tsarist pogroms, Stalin, Hitler, and five Arab attacks on Israel (six including Saddam Hussein's), we must be forgiven our obsession with victimization.

"In America, though permitted to be rich, Jews are not permitted to be comfortable," asserts writer Leonard Fein. When those who make us uncomfortable are black—for instance, Spike Lee, whose film *Mo' Better Blues* included the gratuitously stereotyped nightclub owners Joe and Moe Flatbush; or the rap group Public Enemy whose best-selling record called Jews "Christ killers" and whose "minister of information, Professor Griff," said, "Jews are responsible for the majority of wickedness that goes on across the globe"; or talk-show host Oprah Winfrey, who benignly accepted the claim of a guest that Jews murder children for religious ritual; or Nobel laureate Bishop Desmond Tutu, who lectured Jews on forgiving the Nazis for the murder of the Six Million—we Jews somehow feel more threatened and betrayed, expecting better from our former allies. The color of the perpetrator does not determine the degree of our safety, only the degree of our surprise.

A totally assimilated Jewish friend of mine says he can never relax as long as a swastika is painted on even one wall in America. Another friend has researched which countries in addition to Israel are most hospitable to Jews, in case anti-Semitism ever forces her to leave the United States. I have a recurrent dream in which my children and I are being herded into cattle cars en route to Auschwitz. Every Jew remembers that our people were powerful and well-off in the 1930s in Berlin and Prague and Warsaw, but their prosperity didn't save them. We remember how quickly Jews and Israel were scapegoated in the United States during the gas shortages of the 1970s and the farm crisis of the 1980s. We notice that no matter how few we are, Jews are blamed for the slightest economic reversal in the Soviet Union, Eastern Europe, or France. In 1991, we heard whispers that the war in the

Gulf was the fault of the Jews. So, regardless of what we have accomplished in life we continue to fear the swastika and smell the smoke. In fact, the more we flourish, the surer we are that the anti-Semites are out there begrudging our success. As the old joke would have it, paranoids have enemies too.

My cattle-car dream takes me unawares every few years, like a dormant parasite that eats away at the intestines with no apparent provocation. I have toured the Dachau concentration camp near Munich but that was long before I had children. I lost relatives to the Nazis but my own immediate family, spawned in the 1960s, has never been in danger. Still, I dream that dream. I tell this to my black friend with the angry eyes. I want her to remember that in her lifetime and mine, one out of every three Jews in the world was slaughtered.

"Even if never personally threatened, you would need constant reassurance if one-third of your relatives had been murdered," I tell her.

My friend listens but she still doesn't get it. She grew up in a neighborhood where Jews collected the rent, ran the shops, employed black domestic workers, checked up on welfare clients, and taught black children. She works now in New York City where every Jew she sees is thriving. She points out that 30 million American blacks have only twenty-four congressional representatives and no black senators, while 6 million American Jews have thirty-one Jewish members of the House and seven Jewish senators. Through her eyes I see how it might seem unbelievable that a people so affluent, powerful, and *white* could possibly be quaking at the summit.

How very differently our two out-groups view the world. To blacks, America is the nation that enslaved them and continues to deny them opportunities. To Jews, it is a promised land that made good on its promises. Blacks worry that their (bad) situation will never improve—therefore their issues are fundamental issues like affordable housing, better education, and affirmative action. Jews worry that our (good) situation will never last—therefore our issues are safety issues like freedom of religion (separation of church and state), freedom of emigration (Soviet Jews, Ethiopian Jews), and a secure Israel. To summarize these complex differences in an oversimplified statement, African-Americans need relief in the form of practical economic assistance; Jews need relief in the form of normalized group and individual acceptance.

Assistance. Acceptance. Clearly these needs are not comparable, but they can be experienced with comparable intensity and they can lead people to the same place. Thus, blacks enter into dialogue in the hope it will result in action to address their needs, while for Jews, dialogue *is* the need: if blacks are still talking to us, we think, maybe the liberal alliance is not dead, maybe we don't have to stand alone, maybe we can feel a little safer in America.

Dialogue has taught me that each group inaccurately perceives the negative power of the other. Blacks are not really in a position to hurt Jews, but because of their superior numbers and a few high-profile anti-Semites, Jews fear them. Jews are not really in a position to hurt blacks, but blacks believe we are determined to keep them down. African-Americans are saying, If we're supposed to be brothers and sisters, how come you're doing so well and we're in the streets? Jews are saying, If we're supposed to be friends, how come you keep picking on us?

Maybe Jews and blacks lock horns more than other groups because we are the only ones who take each other seriously, the only minority groups who still seem to believe that our destinies are interwoven. (There are innumerable black-Jewish dialogues, but where are black-Italian or Irish–African-American conclaves?) Or maybe we are encouraged to fight in public as surrogate combatants for the bigots in the dominant culture. As the media magnifies every black-Jewish clash, other Americans can let off steam vicariously while avoiding the anger that might otherwise be directed at them. Meanwhile, blacks and Jews get hooked on the oldest scam in the world: divide and conquer.

I refuse to let that happen. While I had been hurt by my friend's angry words, talking with her clarified that I was the one who had not understood. I had suggested that there was something wrong with African-Americans for dropping out of the dialogue, when in fact there was something wrong with the dialogue for failing to serve the needs of its black participants. Because the Jewish agenda—creating alliances—was being fulfilled, Jews kept showing up at the meetings. But the black agenda—cooperative activism—had stalled, so some black women had stopped coming. It was as simple as that. Beneath her fury, my friend was really saying, "Stop complaining. Your needs are being met and mine are not." She saw Jews getting what they craved (acceptance) while what blacks craved (assistance) wasn't forthcoming.

Given their survival emergencies, the African-Americans in many of these dialogue groups have become impatient with the Jewish need for feel-good talk about the old civil rights alliance—tired of hearing how Rabbi Stephen Wise, reformer Lillian Wald, and other Jews helped found the NAACP, and how 75 percent of the money for SNCC, CORE, and SCLC came from Jews; fed up with references to Goodman, Schwerner, and Chaney; resentful of Jewish nostalgia for past "unity," which blacks remember not as peer collaboration but as patronizing Jewish "help." Our African-American dialogue partners want to be seen as equals. They want to focus on today's realities. They want us to regard the underclass as a human problem, not a black problem, and black advancement as a moral imperative, not a quid pro quo for black-Jewish friendship. They want us to stop telling them what we have in common and start listening to black assessments of our differences. They want us to use our political and economic power to get some action.

Blacks are asking Jews to go beyond tension reduction into practical, nitty-gritty activism and advocacy work. They want biracial teams to organize and lobby for economic and social programs in the areas of affordable housing, child care, health, dropout prevention, improved education, and drug treatment. They want us to mount joint press conferences, petition campaigns, conferences, demonstrations, vigils, and fact-finding trips. They want public education projects, guest columns in each other's newspapers, pulpit exchanges in each other's churches and synagogues, black-Jewish pairs speaking in the schools, Jewish intellectuals promoting books by and about African-Americans, career internships for black students. They expect us to work together monitoring police prejudice, hate crimes, media distortions, vandalism, harassment. They want Jews to "interrupt" racism whenever we see or hear it. And they want financial support for black self-reliance projects—they want white resources put into black hands for programs that African-Americans control.

African-Americans may not realize it but what they are asking Jews to do, in my opinion, is to *act Jewish*. How we each practice religious Judaism is a private matter, but the practice of moral Judaism is something I believe Jews must express publicly through our commitments. That's why I was glad I could help to found a group called Jews for Racial and Economic Justice, made up of progressive New York Jews dedicated to an action agenda. Our first act was to put our money where our values are. Thirty of us fund-raised like mad and in one month collected $30,000 in small donations from hundreds of Jews for the African National Congress. In the name of the Jewish community (we *too* are the community, not just the big organizations), we presented the check to Nelson Mandela during his visit to Manhattan. Regardless of his opinion of Arafat, Qaddafi, or Castro, we wanted to help Mandela continue the fight against apartheid in South Africa. We also wanted to stand in solidarity with black New Yorkers, and to establish that Jewish people care about more than our own self-interest.

Remember, to be morally Jewish requires doing *tzedakah* and *gemilut hesed* and these are actions, not just talk. The pursuit of justice is one definition of activism. It is also, as I've said, what makes and keeps us Jews. If we lose our purpose, we lose our peoplehood and become no more than an odd collection of folks with common ancestors, unique religious laws, and an uncanny potential for victimization. That's not Jewish enough for me.

ISSUE
Israel, Affirmative Action, and South Africa

I have been trying to persuade black friends that Zionism—the commitment to keep Israel alive as a Jewish state that gives Jews automatic citizenship—is not racism any more than goals and timetables for black hiring are reverse racism. I believe that anyone who can understand why history entitles minorities and women to affirmative action ought to understand why history entitles Jews to safe space and preferential immigration policies. And just as legal remedies are justified in reparation for racism and sexism, the Law of Return is justified by worldwide religious persecution and anti-Semitic bigotry.

I often have to remind black friends that although 70 percent of the American public is against affirmative action, the majority of Jews, and especially Jewish women, are for it—and that when some Jews object to quotas, it is because they remember when quotas were used to exclude Jews from jobs or universities, not because they wish to impede black advancement. Few blacks are aware that virtually every American Jewish leader has spoken out in behalf of affirmative action and that some organizations even favor the use of quotas to remedy past inequities when there is a court finding of race discrimination in a particular case. I want blacks to know that many individual Jews support quotas that establish a floor but not a ceiling—quotas that set forth minimum goals without putting a cap on a given group's numerical representation.

In the "good old days," Golda Meir was an early supporter of black African equality and a vocal critic of apartheid. By the same token, many of yesterday's most prominent blacks, such as W. E. B. Du Bois, Paul Robeson, and Ralph Bunche, supported the national liberation movement called Zionism, and in 1967, Israel's victory in the Six Day War was hailed by senior black leaders including Martin Luther King, Jr. Over the last two decades, however, sympathies have shifted, largely because many blacks (including Jesse Jackson and Nelson Mandela) have posited a parallel between Palestinians in the occupied territories and blacks in South Africa. Black-Jewish disputation on international issues first surfaced in the headlines when Jimmy Carter dismissed Andrew Young from his position as U.N. ambassador for secretly meeting with the PLO. Many blacks blamed Jewish pro-Israel lobbying for his ouster. More recently, due to its treatment of Palestinians in the occupied territories, Israel has lost its underdog status and now appears to blacks to be as powerful on the world stage as Jews appear in the United States. (Even the Scud landings didn't change Israel's image for the blacks.) African-Americans cannot identify with Goliath; they cast their lot with the Palestinians whom they see as David—a Third World political ally and a beleaguered people of color.

Another major irritant between blacks and Jews has been Israel's supplying guns, water cannons, electronic border fences, and other military equipment to the government of South Africa, training its soldiers and police, and even (rumors report) nuclear collaboration, all of which implicated Israel as an accessory to the crimes of the apartheid regime. Although Jerusalem claims to have stopped all *new* arms agreements, it has refused to nullify those already in effect, giving black militants justifiable cause to whip up anti-Israel sentiment. The double-standard argument—that other countries, including twenty-three black African nations, Saudi Arabia, Germany, and France, have similar ties with Pretoria—swings no weight with my black friends. I can't blame them for expecting more from a *Jewish* state (I do myself), or for bringing up a double-standard question of their own: Why should Israel's relatively well-off 4½ million people get $3 billion dollars in aid (much of it military) when all of black Africa, with its ½ billion poor people, gets less than $1 billion? Given the U.S. budget crisis, they say, some of the money earmarked for Israel might be redirected to developing African nations, black Caribbean islands, and the Third World within our own borders: Harlem, the South Bronx, Detroit, Watts, and the South Side of Chicago. They question whether U.S. resources should go to an Israeli government that so brutally represses its Palestinian minority. They wonder whether American aid might have been transferred from African famine programs to finance the rescue of Ethiopian Jews. They are not happy to see Jews favored at home and abroad.

Many of these issues trouble me as well, but I see them in a different light. Firstly, I agree of course that Israeli arms sales to South Africa cannot be justified even though other countries did similar business and even though Israel, a victim of trade boycotts, badly needed to increase its export income. Neither excuse carries any moral weight given the abhorrent apartheid policies of the importer. Furthermore, if it is true as some have suggested that the Israeli government, private arms dealers, and ex-Army specialists assisted South Africa in the development of offensive nuclear technology and internal security expertise, which had the effect of sustaining human rights violations, I would be the first to denounce the perpetrators in the strongest terms.

By the same token, however, I cannot understand those who were silent when the United States supplied AWACs, missiles, and guns to the brutal feudal monarchy in Saudi Arabia, or when the United States, France, China, and Germany sold weapons (chemical or otherwise) to Iraq, or when the Soviet Union armed the savage Syrian forces to the teeth. Rather than selectively condemn Israel, I choose to challenge the worldwide proliferation of advanced weaponry and the scandal of public and private profiteering from it.

Secondly, I resist the facile comparison of the Palestinians with the black population of South Africa. Equating them would be like watching one person drown and another person die of thirst and saying that their predicaments are similar because both are having a water problem. Although each resistance group suffers egregious human rights violations and breaches of due process, it is important to acknowledge that their situations have profoundly different origins and that they, as peoples, have different long-term objectives.

The Palestinians' situation originated in their own intransigence— the dreams of glory that fueled their former unwillingness to accept partition of the land. Remember that the Jewish majority rules over an occupied minority not because of an offensive action or invasion but because the Palestinians, who several times had the option of being an independent nation, chose war and terrorism rather than political and territorial compromise. Black Africans, on the other hand, have been offered no such political choice and are subjugated simply because they are black. In contrast to Israel, in South Africa, the minority rules over the majority, the issue is racism not nationalism, and the possibility of equality has yet to be offered on a national scale.

As to the difference in objectives, the way I see it is since 1988 when the Palestine National Council formally endorsed a two-state solution, the goal in the Palestinian-Israeli conflict has been to separate the two populations and allow each to govern itself. In the South African conflict, the goal is to integrate the black, white, and colored populations and allow them to govern the country together.

Thirdly, when my African-American friends criticize the amount of U.S. foreign aid to Israel, I insist they can demand more for Africa without deleting Israel's allotment. I also point out that, as opposed to African nations, Israel is surrounded by many powerful enemies whose declared intent is to eradicate the state and who have been armed for Armageddon by Western and Soviet leaders. As long as this hostility continues, I believe Israel's defense spending is essential to ensure that she remain militarily superior to the combined strength of her adversaries.

Although the United States has traditionally claimed Israel both as a strategic and democratic ally in the Middle East, the Gulf War and the American demand for Israel to maintain a low-profile has proved that her strategic utility is limited by the complexities of petro-politics and shifting U.S.-Arab alliances. That makes it all the more vital for Israel's democratic credentials to be reaffirmed and strengthened for the sake of its institutional and ideological commonality with the West as well as for the nourishment of its own soul. Therefore, I would argue for a portion of U.S. aid to be earmarked for expenditures that enhance Israeli democracy and advance Jewish-Palestinian coexistence. Such a commitment from the United States would pressure the Israeli government to spend more equitably on education, land development, water and power projects, village infrastructures, and on establishing an equal system of justice for Arabs in Israel and the occupied territories.

I understand that money is fungible and that targeting funds for peaceful purposes frees up other resources to be spent on guns and tear gas. I also know that foreign aid is supposed to have no strings attached. Still, I believe it important for the United States to send a message with our money. Surely it is not unreasonable to insist that American dollars be spent to prepare for peace, not just for war.

And finally, while advocating continued aid to Israel, I also favor increased assistance to poor people whether they live in Africa, Antigua, or Atlanta—and I don't see why one commitment should detract from the other. Humanitarian aid must not be a zero-sum game. Moreover, it is naive to claim that what now goes to Israel—or for that matter to Egypt, the second largest recipient of U.S. foreign aid—would otherwise be directed to hungry and destitute people of color. Let's not kid ourselves: If our leaders wanted to help poor people and poor nations, they would find a way to do so. They always find money for what matters to them, to wit, the savings and loan bail-out, the rescue of ailing corporations like Penn Central and Continental Bank, and the overkill defense budget.

During that brief window of opportunity after the end of the Cold War and before the Gulf Crisis, when it looked as if the U.S. Treasury might enjoy a windfall from reduced defense spending, I looked for some massive public clamoring for the "peace dividend" to be spent on human emergencies whether in Africa, Latin America, the Caribbean, or American inner cities. But no such mobilization took shape. It disturbs me to hear the clamoring only in the context of comparing Israel to Africa. I ask my African-American friends to stop blaming "the pro-Israel lobby" for what is, at root, a deep-seated *American* disregard for Third World suffering. The disregard is reprehensible but it is not a Jewish plot.

Despite growing antagonisms between African-Americans and Jews, I draw hope from surveys that show our two communities still are the most politically compatible groups in the country. Some observers insist that to most blacks, Jews are just white people. But Jewish opinion and Jewish commitments tend to match those of blacks, not whites. Our voting patterns are more alike than those of any other racial or religious categories. We share a common vision of justice. The Congressional Black Caucus and the Jewish members of Congress vote together on most issues including those affecting Israel, Soviet Jews, and South Africa. In our electoral habits, we are perverse in similar ways: Although Jews have experienced great economic success, we still vote our consciences, not our pocketbooks. Although blacks have experienced great economic stress, they still vote their consciences, not their resentments. It's up to us to build on this compatibility, bring it beyond the statistics and make it work for us.

ISSUE
Slavery and the Holocaust

"I'm not saying that blacks don't care about the Holocaust, only that most of us don't think about it," said a black friend around the time of the fiftieth anniversary of Kristallnacht. "And when we do think about it, in all honesty, it makes us mad that Jews are able to lay claim to a debt from the Nazi period and we are not owed that same debt for two hundred years of slavery in our own country."

Competitive suffering. Comparative victimology. Some blacks seem to see our two horrors as part of a zero-sum game: if the Holocaust wins, slavery loses. And some Jews seem more concerned with staying number one in the catastrophe ratings than with the feelings of other human beings. And when you add to the contest the particular misery of women—the rape of women slaves and women concentration-camp inmates; the unspeakable cruelty of separating black mothers and Jewish mothers from their children—then the tournament gets really tough. How did we come to this? Aren't there enough tears to go around? Can't we agree that both of us have known horrific tragedy and leave it at that?

Apparently not. If you recall my interviews for the anti-Semitism piece, some black women insisted that the *Holocaust* TV series was a conscious Jewish move to steal the spotlight from *Roots*—presumably engineered through Jewish "control" of the networks. Rather than critique the series as a weak, inaccurate rendering of Jewish experience, or as a case of copycat commercialism similar to *Rambo II* or

Godfather III, blacks saw conspiratorial racism in the fact that it was broadcast at all.

Recently, some African-Americans (including two City University of New York professors, a psychologist, a psychiatrist, and several journalists) have suggested that AIDS and crack are weapons with which whites are carrying out their genocidal plan against blacks—just as systematically as the ovens and the gas chambers exterminated Jews. "It reminds me of Nazi Germany," said psychiatrist Dr. Frances Welsing on Ted Koppel's program. Asked for documentation, she answered, "Black people don't have the details just like Jews didn't have the facts."

In an interview in *Tikkun*, the liberal Jewish opinion journal, Jesse Jackson called South Africa the Fourth Reich and equated Hitler and Prime Minister Botha. A Jewish respondent, David Twersky, countered, "Without apologizing for the abhorrent racist policies of South Africa, I find the comparison rather disturbing. . . . There is no planned systematic program of race extermination in South Africa."

Continuing this macabre competition, some blacks have expressed resentment of the $150 million National Holocaust Memorial scheduled to open in 1993 on the Mall in Washington—as if its construction funds were taken directly from coffers set aside for some future National Slavery Memorial. I have real problems with the building of another Holocaust museum in the United States (there are already more than 150 museums, resource centers, and research institutions, including the Simon Wiesenthal Center in Los Angeles and the Museum of Jewish Heritage in New York), but my objections relate to Jewish community values, not to blacks or anyone else. I see no reason why an institution commemorating Nazi slaughter should be located in the shadow of the Washington Monument on land donated by the government of this country where Jews have found an unparalleled welcome. I think a major Holocaust museum belongs where it is, at Yad Vashem in Jerusalem where a new society has arisen from the remnants of European Jewry, or at Buchenwald, Auschwitz, or Dachau, where the blood-soaked earth has been covered with bucolic grass, the meadows of amnesia.

I would have preferred to see the money that Jews have raised to commemorate death be used to enhance life. Imagine what $150 million might have done to help resettle Soviet Jews, rescue more Ethiopian Jews, improve Jewish education for young people. In the wider society, the money could have been dedicated to AIDS research, low-income housing, and child health programs. It could have honored the Six Million by alleviating six million children's hunger and poverty. In the name of each of our dead, we could be keeping someone else alive. Instead, we are encasing the Nazi horror in concrete, building a monument to their madness as much as to our survival. It makes no sense.

On the other hand, I believe a museum commemorating the black experience *does* make sense and does belong on the Mall in the nation's capital. White America should not be allowed to forget that it kept Africans in captivity for two centuries and that black people have gone on to contribute so much to our collective culture. Since the black community cannot afford to divert its own resources to such an institution, I am glad a bill calling for a national museum of African-American heritage has been introduced in Congress by sixty-seven co-signers. Jews should support it.

Finding fault with the decision to build a massive Jewish mausoleum in a land where Jews have prospered does not mean I want to forget or let others forget the ultimate, absolute evil of the Shoah. So immediate is my identification with the generation that perished in the camps that I sometimes feel the weight of a shroud beneath my clothes.

I remember especially my mother's cousin Isaac, who came to New York immediately after the war and lived with us for several months. Isaac is my connection to dozens of other family members who were murdered in the concentration camps. Because he was blond and blue-eyed, he had been chosen as the "designated survivor" of his town; that is, the Jewish councils had instructed him to do anything to stay alive and tell the story. For Isaac, "anything" turned out to mean this: the Germans suspected his forged Aryan papers and decided he would have to prove by his actions that he was not a Jew. They put him on a transport train with the Jews of his town and then gave him the task of herding into the gas chambers everyone in his trainload. After he had fulfilled that assignment with patriotic Germanic efficiency, the Nazis accepted the authenticity of his identity papers and let him go.

Among those whom Isaac packed into the gas chamber that day, dispassionately, as if shoving a few more items into an overstuffed closet, were his wife and two children.

The "designated survivor" arrived in America at about age forty, with prematurely white hair and a dead gaze within the sky-blue eyes that had helped save his life. As promised, he told his story to dozens of Jewish agencies and community leaders, and to groups of family and friends (which is how I heard the account translated from his Yiddish by my mother). For months he talked, speaking the unspeakable, describing a horror that American Jews had suspected but could not conceive, a monstrous tale that dwarfed the demonology of legend and gave me the nightmare I still dream to this day. And as he talked, Isaac seemed to grow older and older until one night a few months later, when he finished telling everything he knew, he died.

I share the Jewish community's desire to perpetuate the memory of all our Isaacs, but I become distinctly uncomfortable when our remembering feels automated, or choreographed by a "Holocaust industry," or overtaken by what Arthur Hertzberg calls "Holocaust glitz," or when Jews seem more intent on retaining the title of World's Foremost Victim than on using our experience to fight all forms of racism. Because we have known genocide, the ultimate fruition of racism, Elie Wiesel's definition should be the last word: "Not all victims were Jews, but *all* Jews were victims." We needn't force blacks, Armenians, or Russians of the Gulag to admit that their nightmare was less than ours in order to know that ours was absolute. We must use our nightmare for something more constructive than the reification of nightmares.

I try to honor each group's experience without either ranking our agonies or blurring our distinctions. I do not expect my black friends to "think about the Holocaust" any more than I can be expected to feel the immediacy of black slavery. But I do expect us to respect one another's grim obsessions.

The white cop in the movie *Driving Miss Daisy* acknowledged our shared "otherness" when he muttered, "An old Jew woman and an old nigger goin' down the road together. Ain't that a sorry sight." Racist rednecks lump us together; neo-Nazis lump us together; the Klan lumps us together; Posse Comitatus, Skinheads, the Aryan Nation, and the National Association for the Advancement of White People lump us together. If we were less competitive and more politically savvy we would lump ourselves together, become a lump in America's throat, a pebble in the redneck's shoe, a pea under the mattress of royalty. We would make life uncomfortable for those who hate us.

Together African-Americans and Jewish-Americans make up 15

percent of the population. History has taught us that the fate of each out-group is inevitably linked to the destiny of the others and an assault on one presages an attack on the other. Therefore, we can be each other's early warning system; we can blow the whistle on threats to the democratic pluralism that protects all ethnic, gender, and racial outsiders. It should not take a burning Torah or a flaming cross to make us form a bucket brigade.

My attempts to live life with a feminist head and a Jewish heart often culminate in pragmatic idealism, an attempt to distill something constructive out of a morass of difference and disputation. Where black-Jewish relations are concerned, I find my Women's Movement experience instructive. In the early years of the Second Wave, as I've noted, millions of disparate women accentuated female commonalities in order to create a unified feminist movement. This period was analogous to the time when blacks and Jews accentuated their common dream of justice in order to create a unified civil rights movement.

Now, however, feminists are acknowledging that each woman comes from a different place and has different needs. Likewise, racial and ethnic groups have had to face up to their unique circumstances, which give rise to different demands and solutions. Our challenge is to respond to each group's special situation without degenerating into warring factions.

My utopian self regrets that the politics of identity have replaced the politics of commonality. But the pragmatist in me accepts the necessity and inevitability of special-interest advocacy, group cohesion, and self-affirmation through solidarity. Without it, we've seen how easy it is for the dominant powers to overlook us. Today, blacks and Jews and other outsiders insist on being let "in" (wherever "in" is) without having to pay the price of conformity—without having to melt or blend or prove ourselves "just like everyone else." Given this clamoring for ethnic and racial honor (as well as gender consciousness), the only way to avoid internecine competitiveness is for each group, while affirming itself, to acknowledge each other's uniqueness. And the only way to acknowledge a people's distinctions is to know them—not necessarily agree with them or join their cause, but know them well enough to understand what winds them up and makes them tick. So, my final effort in this chapter will be to write a brief prescription for mutual knowledge, a formula neither elaborate nor profound, only urgent and basic:

We must get together. Not because we will ever see the world the same way, but because we must keep trying to understand how and what the other sees. The barriers between us have been growing more opaque, preventing us from looking into each other's eyes. Even if we find hatred in those eyes—and sometimes there *is* hatred there—we must get close enough to challenge it and hope that our opponents, in turn, will see our humanity regardless of whether they can see our point.

Stereotypes, distance, and isolation are our greatest enemies. No longer does contemporary life routinely bring blacks and Jews together. Without a middle-income housing mix, there is de facto neighborhood segregation. Without the social-welfare programs of the Great Society, there are far fewer official interactions between Jewish and black community-service organizations. Without a strong federal commitment to equal opportunity, there is not enough school or workplace integration. College students who major in women's studies, black studies, or Judaic studies rarely cross over to attend each other's classes. Blacks and Jews who work in the same job categories rarely do so in a corporate culture that encourages real friendship. Therefore, apart from some dialogue groups that have been ongoing for years—I'm thinking of those in New York City, Atlanta, Washington, D.C., Chicago, and New England—most Jews and African-Americans have no regularized opportunities for linkage.

Because we have been isolated, each group has developed an attitude of moral absolutism about the other, and an abysmal ignorance about its people. That's why few Jews know which black leaders denounced Farrakhan, and few blacks know which Jews have fought for affirmative action. We don't really know each other's heroes. Other than the superstars of rock or sports, how many of the other group's political up-and-comers can you name? How about their community organizers? Advertising geniuses? Promising first novelists? We have no idea whether our kids sing the same lullabies or have the same dreams. We don't know each other's sensitivities, insecurities, vulnerabilities, or aspirations. We think we do, but we don't.

The fact of our physical separation has persuaded me that, simple as it sounds, getting together is our most immediate imperative. If we do not live in the same communities, mix in school, or work in close enough proximity, we must *create* opportunities for contact and collaboration; we must find each other, make our own way from our separate spheres, start the dialogues, take on the action projects, do what needs doing to bridge the chasm.

I'm not saying it's easy. Sometimes, the other person is suspicious or rejecting, or just doesn't respond to your efforts with commensurate enthusiasm, or accepts your invitations but doesn't reciprocate. Sometimes it's uncomfortable to be the constant initiator. Most of us are accustomed to the "exchange model" of interpersonal relations; we're most comfortable with giving and getting in return. But this is not about comfort or social symmetry; this is about justice.

Although I do not read the Scriptures literally, I have chosen to take seriously the moral authority of the account of the Israelites' flight from Egyptian bondage, which has provided the narrative framework for virtually all liberation ideologies from Cromwell's revolution in seventeenth-century England, to the American Revolution of the eighteenth century, to the Zionist movement of the nineteenth century, to the modern civil rights movement—each of which utilized Exodus language and imagery to arouse a people's social conscience and inspire political action.

We respond spiritually and symbolically to Exodus references because they instantly evoke three basic human themes: suffering, struggle, and redemption. To be sure, these themes weave throughout the story of the Jewish passage from Hitler—the ultimate Pharaoh in the quintessential Egypt—through the DP camps and the flight to Palestine to the realization of the State of Israel. And they weave throughout the story of the Women's Movement, which in effect posits international patriarchy as an Egypt with many pharaohs (male supremacists, antichoice extremists, men who rape and batter, ultraright conservatives, and fundamentalists of every faith) and puts forth a promised land of equality and dignity.

Given my connection with these Jewish and feminist Exodus experiences, I'm not surprised to feel myself responding in deep ways to the African-American Exodus story, which seems to me the furthest from closure, the furthest from freedom in full measure. With its roots in slavery, its leaders and preachers demanding "Let My People Go," its protest pilgrimages through Southern towns and Northern cities, and Martin Luther King's moving, Mosaic plea to be "Free at Last," it is the black liberation struggle that arouses my feelings as a Jew. One sentence from Exodus (23:9) provides the link:

> *You shall not oppress a stranger, for you know the feelings of the stranger, having yourselves been strangers in the land of Egypt.*

To me, that commandment is not some scriptural anachronism, but an ongoing moral prescription for the whole Jewish people.

I believe the reason why Jews throughout the world repeat the Exodus story at every seder, and thank God for our liberation from Egypt in so many prayers throughout the year, is that liberation is the core event of Jewish history. It is the experience that *defines* us as a people. It tells us who we are and what we are supposed to do.

Most people who have been oppressed try to forget it; Jews insist on remembering it, for a reason that becomes a mandate: *to stay connected with human suffering even after we ourselves have ceased to suffer.* Before we can celebrate our liberation, or speak of the Promised Land, we are instructed to recollect where we came from. At the seder, the Feast of Freedom, we remember slavery.

And the formula for remembering is quite extraordinary. We do not just say that our ancestors were slaves, but that we *ourselves* were slaves. We are commanded: "In every generation you must regard yourself as if you personally came forth from Egypt." You must reexperience the sins of subjugation in order to better appreciate freedom.

This immanent "you" appears in verse 23:9 with the immediacy of the present tense: "You shall not oppress a stranger, for you know the feelings of the stranger. . . ."

I think of this as God's commandment to empathize.

It is here that emotion enters history, here that personal experience dictates compassion and justice, here that all excuses for evil behavior disappear in the intimate truth of known human pain. We are told to act justly not because it is right according to some moral abstraction, and not because God says so and will punish us if we don't, but because we know what it feels like to be treated otherwise.

A code of behavior in a single verse: You've been there, so you know better. *Remember the pain.* Remember how it feels. And then take that ritual of empathy one step further. Besides repudiating the role of the oppressor, resolve to identify with the oppressed—and to act with them and for them.

We in the here-and-now are instructed to enter into the experience of the Exodus—to feel the feelings of the alien, the minority group, the outsider; to remember the weight of the lash, taste the bitterness of oppression, suffer the cruelty of domination. We are commanded to relive this bondage so that we will never do to others—or allow to be done—what was done unto us.

No longer an impatient child, I now welcome the seder's repetition of this ritual of empathy as a reaffirmation of the Jewish people's commitment to justice.

The mandate is deceptively simple: *Imitateo Deo*. Imitate what God did for us and do it for others. How do we imitate God? By relieving suffering. By helping to free the oppressed. By undertaking the ritual of empathy and the search for justice as commitments of our own. Thus does the theology of hope inspire the politics of social change.

Ideally, many Jews might want to normalize our relationship with African-Americans and forge unself-conscious friendships with their peers. But if we don't work at parallel desks or live next door—if our life circumstances do not allow for organic friendship—there is nothing wrong with making a *conscious* effort to create justice if not camaraderie. Sadly, it's not hard to find the strangers, the out-groups, the alienated. We don't have to look far to see homeless families huddled in doorways and feeding off garbage, people dying of AIDS, women trapped in poverty, people of color anchored to second-class citizenship, babies who are born addicted to crack, twelve-year-olds who can't read, runaway kids and pregnant teenagers, incest survivors trying to blot out their trauma, men and women on drugs; hungry people, sick people, and old people who live and die alone.

There is a Third World here in America. There is an Egypt right here in the middle of our Canaan. Whatever our personal goals and wherever our promised land takes us, we can commit ourselves to choose just one piece from the jagged puzzle of human misery and try to make it better. We can join advocacy groups and work together to combat hate and promote pluralism. We can organize, fund-raise, lobby, volunteer our time, speak out, fight for fairer allocation of public resources, give our own money, work in a soup kitchen, demonstrate—yes, even march together once again.

I didn't form my opinions about blacks from media stories or other Jews, but from working with women of color on feminist issues, making black-Jewish dialogue one of my priorities, quarreling over the issues one by one, refusing to walk away when offended, staying to listen and demanding to be heard.

Disdain and disengagement solve nothing. Talking to one another and doing social-justice work together can be redemptive. Constructive interaction is our only option. We may not agree on everything (or anything), but unless blacks and Jews sit at the same table in the same room at the same time, we will never achieve even our most modest goals.

This truism is best illustrated by a story told to me by a black father:

> *Graffiti appeared one morning on the big double doors of my daughter's public school. Someone had scrawled "Nigger" on one door and a swastika on the other. My child never noticed the vulgarities but my wife and I were so upset we decided to enroll her in a private school. After three days, she came home with a little Jewish girl named Emily who soon was her constant companion. A few weeks later, she asked me, "How come you and Mommy aren't friends with Emily's parents?"*

Noxious graffiti had no meaning to the child, but the absence of human contact made an impression. In real terms, in the long run, estrangement is more telling than insult. We must get together. Whether it is men with men, women with women, or mixed groups; whether we have a fixed agenda or a freewheeling discussion; whether our style is to posture and pontificate or to bare our souls—whoever we are, whatever we do, wherever it leads, however it hurts, we *must* get together to talk, struggle, and work through our differences.

It is bad enough for blacks and Jews to be combatants. It would be intolerable for us to be strangers.

15

The International Jewish Feminist Conspiracy

IN THE WINTER OF 1988, I WENT TO JERUSALEM AS ONE OF 320 delegates to the First International Jewish Feminist Conference. Our purpose was to identify issues of concern to Jewish women *as* women all over the world, regardless of our cultural or national differences. The meeting was sponsored by the American Jewish Congress, the World Jewish Congress, and the Israel Women's Network, with the ultimate goal of establishing a global network of Jewish feminists who would commit themselves to mutual support.

It took two years to make this conference happen. During the planning phase, I served on the outreach committee which was charged with inviting appropriate delegates from as many countries as have sizable Jewish populations. By "appropriate," we didn't mean just any Jewish women, but Jewish *feminists*, and we didn't mean support troops, but leaders. In each country, we were searching for women who operate either in the Jewish community with some feminist awareness, or in the secular women's movement with some Jewish identity—in other words, women who've noticed that male Jews often forget the needs of women, and Gentile women often forget the needs of Jews. We also hoped to find women who are comfortable with the term "feminist" and who affix the label to themselves as a shorthand way of describing their priorities, or who've had the label pinned on them by others.

I thought of our ideal delegate as standing on a sturdy three-legged stool: one leg would be Jewish communal pride; one leg, commitment to women's equality; and one leg, ability to knowledgeably represent her country. If any of those legs was weak or short, the stool would not support our delegate.

In the United States, thousands of Jewish women answer to that description—from grass-roots organizers, to employees of communal agencies, to educators, professionals, and members of synagogue social action committees. Off the top of our heads, we could think of public figures like Bella Abzug and Liz Holtzman; scholars like Paula Hyman, Cynthia Epstein, and Evelyn Torton Beck; organizational leaders like Mimi Alperin of American Jewish Committee, Jacqueline Levine of American Jewish Congress, and Judith Stern Peck of UJA-Federation; psychologists like Phyllis Chesler and Naomi Weisstein; artists like Judy Chicago, Bea Kreloff, and Edith Isaac-Rose; and scores of writers such as Betty Friedan, Blu Greenberg, E. M. Broner, Lilly Rivlin, Fran Klagsbrun, Anne Roiphe, Aviva Cantor, Susannah Heschel, Susan Weidman Schneider, and many more.

In fact, there were so many outstanding Jewish feminists in the United States that our outreach committee had a hard time paring down the list of American invitees. Our counterparts in the Israel planning committee also faced a dizzying oversupply of strong candidates, veterans of the battle against economic and legal discrimination on Golda's home turf. In other countries, however, locating Jewish feminists turned out to be harder than finding practicing Mormons in downtown Detroit. This was not because the women we were looking for don't exist, but because they have yet to identify themselves.

I would propose four explanations for this: First, in countries with either overt religious persecution or particularly harsh forms of male supremacy, few Jewish women would be likely to risk the condemnation associated with high visibility either as Jews or as feminists. Jewish women reflect the condition of both Jews and women in their own societies, and most nations marginalize their Jews and promote traditional sex roles for their women. The Jewish world within those countries likewise rewards conventional feminine behavior. In such an atmosphere, it would be difficult for women to surface in leadership positions, except in "do-gooder" women's organizations that pose no threat to male power, either secular or Jewish. To self-identify as a feminist in such an environment would be an admission that one was a troublemaker on two fronts. So we had to be on the lookout for quiet revolutionaries.

The second reason why women in some countries had not become self-defined feminists is that they had no *movement* with which to identify.

In the United States, in the 1960s and 1970s, "women's liberation" described a fusillade of personal epiphanies, media events, and legislative victories that dramatically altered gender relations and gave women a sense of having *collectively* brought about change on each other's behalf. The early consciousness-raising, street-demonstrating, arm-in-arm stage of feminism was an organic part of the emancipation process—the part that converted anger into understanding, understanding into action, and social upheaval into a coherent movement. As a result of having lived through that phase together, millions of American women had a sense of "we" that stood us in good stead when conservatives and fundamentalists began striking back and it became obvious that we would have to spend the rest of our lives defending our gains. To meet this long-term challenge, we were able to transform the radical, showy, street feminism of the past into pragmatic, multifaceted *feminisms* in which millions of women now work day after day, year after year, on the issues that concern them most—child care, pay equity, reproductive rights, women's economic development, sexual violence and militarism, equality in organized religion, labor unions, and college faculties—to name just a few. Today, American feminism is so broadly based, so omnipresent, so thoroughly woven into the fabric of our lives, that we don't always see it.

One vibrant expression of these femin*isms* can be found among Jewish-American women committed to the dual agenda that I've been exploring throughout this book. In the United States—although we have no official umbrella organization—Jewish feminists feel themselves part of a growing ideological movement with its own rhetoric, polemics, literature, theory, theology, women's studies programs, prayer groups, ceremonies, films, art, music, and even scholarly disputes. I wish we could export a simple template of our diversity, a pattern that Jewish women everywhere could press into their own soil, like a child's sandbox mold. I wish we could send them a list of suggested activities and resources, a how-to kit for revisionist rituals, a membership card in a movement that should know no boundaries. But I know better. Cultural imperialism—no matter how admirable its intent—is doomed to fail. Every woman must be the author of her own emancipation.

But in countries without an indigenous women's movement, authorship is a lonely business. Working alone, Jewish women with problems far more extreme and pressing than ours have been less willing to name their grievances *as* women's issues, and the naming is a prerequisite for unifying women around common complaints. Without unified action and shared political consciousness, there is no entity from which leaders can emerge and be recognized. Absent an organized movement, it is left to a few hardy individuals to sustain the battle alone. Each functioning within her own vacuum, isolated from the universality of women's struggle, pays a personal price in exhaustion and economic sacrifice. Many fold when they are stigmatized as "self-hating Jews" or "man-hating malcontents." Some burn out. But there are always a hardy few—the prophets without honor, conductors without an orchestra, heroines without a name—who keep up the fight. They were the women we were looking for.

The third reason why Jewish feminists may be hard to find outside the United States has to do with the vulnerability of the Jewish woman in the non-Jewish world. Several times during the planning effort, when someone proposed that an invitation go out to a prominent woman in a particular country, someone else on our committee would say, "Are you sure she's Jewish?"

In most societies, a public Jewish persona is still incompatible with career success. As a result, many Jews choose to protect their job security by remaining silent about their Jewishness and by presenting themselves in the most neutral way possible (say, by avoiding Jewish causes or overt holiday observances). But the effect of that silent neutrality is to keep each Jew unaware of other Jews around her, and to retard public recognition of the contributions Jewish women are making to public life in each nation.

After many delicate inquiries, our committee was able to confirm that a number of "neutral" women—a banker, a TV personality, a businesswoman, and a social reformer—were in fact affirmatively, though privately, Jewish. Away from their work context, they seemed delighted to be "found out" and to connect with their international peers who have the same perceived need to blend in.

The final reason why I think Jewish feminists remain a largely hidden constituency is the fact that many European and Third World women suffer from a fear of the "F" word. They shy away from the term "feminist" because of the negative valence it has acquired in the international media. Rather than be considered "radical," or part of a special-interest group (as though half the human race is a "special interest"), or as unladylike, strident, or tough—especially in the eyes of Jewish men—they resist identifying themselves as feminists regardless of their true sympathies.

This is not just a linguistic matter. A summary label—whether it be Democrat, environmentalist, or vegetarian—allows us to recognize and affiliate with like-minded people. By failing to take possession of the term "feminist," and by allowing those who are threatened by gender equality to use *our* word against us, we become collaborators in their divide-and-conquer strategy.

Despite these four stumbling blocks and several wild-goose chases and dead-end streets, we did eventually locate more than three hundred extraordinary women to participate in our conference. But before everyone ended up together in Jerusalem, we in the planning committees had to endure more Sturm und Drang than any good soul should have to bear.

I grew up in an argumentative family. My father and mother quarreled almost daily. My grandparents split along Litvak/Galitzianer (Lithuanian/Polish-Austrian) lines. My relatives fought about communism, labor Zionism, halacha, Henry Wallace, the Rosenberg case, and the Jewish War Veterans. This background taught me that: (1) certain issues are serious enough to fight about; (2) relationships between people can survive their differences; and (3) to be Jewish is to be argumentative. Jews argue because we care. Or as my father might have put it, "I yell, therefore I am."

Yet, despite my familiarity with disputation, nothing prepared me for the altercations that dogged this particular family of women from the beginning of the two-year planning phase until the last day of the conference itself. Committees wrangled over which speakers from which countries should speak on what subjects. We fought about whether there were too many organizational women involved and not enough independents. We struggled with the program—how to keep a balance between secular feminist issues, like rape, and Jewish feminist issues, like job rights for women cantors. We almost came to blows about how to accommodate radical feminists and grass-roots peace groups who wanted to discuss the effect of the *intifada*, the Palestinian uprising, on women.

I argued strongly for a plenary session on the Israeli occupation of the West Bank, an issue that seemed to me to deserve place on a program that purported to cover *all* of Jewish women's concerns. Lilly Rivlin (one of my seder sisters) also was a forceful advocate during those months of rancorous debate. She was in touch with representatives of the peace groups in Israel who had hoped to be part of our proceedings. However, most of the other conference planners felt such a session would give a platform to Israel's enemies, and the whole conference could be tarred with the media attention that one session would attract. After many long and brutal arguments, it became clear that the subject was so controversial, some women's fear of the establishment so paralyzing, and the funders of our conference so conservative, that there would be no conference at all if those of us in favor of including the issue made it a do-or-die proposition.

Women who had links to the people who held the purse strings told us the American Jewish and World Jewish Congresses would withdraw their money and sponsorship if the subject of the occupation was added to the agenda, which in effect meant the conference would be canceled. Rather than torpedo the whole event, Lilly and I settled for an "academic" session entitled "Women, War, and Peace," at which two researchers would present their findings on women's attitudes toward military solutions to conflict. We took this compromise as a victory, since so many of the organizers had wanted to avoid the subject altogether. I'll confess, however, that when I agreed to the compromise, it was in the belief that, after the presentations by the two scholars, local Israeli peace activists and other sympathetic delegates would politicize the session and move us from the academic to the flesh-and-blood realities of the occupation. I did not anticipate the explosion of right-wing rage that was to steamroll the session and muzzle the peace advocates altogether.

As if we didn't have enough rancor here at home, the New York and Jerusalem planning groups also crossed swords more than once. By fax and phone, we argued about speakers, about how much emphasis should be given to religious issues, about the paucity of Sephardic delegates, about how to publicize the conference, and how to ensure that it would be truly international despite its U.S.-Israel sponsorship.

All together, this punishing advance work prepared me for the problems that would unfold on the scene as the conference geared up and got underway. Finally, on November 24, 1988, our conferees began arriving in Jerusalem. At that very moment, Israel's political forces were engaged in one of their now-familiar protracted efforts to form a government, and the religious parties were trying to barter their votes in return for a change in the Law of Return, which guarantees automatic Israeli citizenship to every Jew, but does not precisely define Who Is a Jew. (I love Rabbi Harold Schulweis's formula: "A Jew is someone who, after four thousand years of history, is still asking 'Who Is a Jew?' ") The Orthodox were proposing to narrow the definition to "a person born of a Jewish mother, or converted by an Orthodox rabbi."

All of diaspora Jewry was monitoring the crisis. A change in the Law of Return would challenge the legitimacy of conversions performed by Conservative and Reform rabbis and thus the legitimacy of Conservative and Reform Judaism as practiced by the majority of Jews the world over. It would change Israel's open-door policy which, for many, is a bulwark of Zionism and the raison d'être for Israel's existence in a post-Holocaust world. In order to prevent the politicians from capitulating to the Orthodox on the Who Is a Jew issue, dozens of organizations from many nations had sent their top officials to Jerusalem to petition party leaders Yitzhak Shamir and Shimon Peres not to cave in.

Several of our women who had arrived in Jerusalem early decided to mount a demonstration outside Prime Minister Shamir's office. Since we were already there, it made sense for us to add our voices to the international protest.

It made sense to many but not to all. When a group of about thirty of us met to plan the demonstration for the next morning, one woman insisted we had no business mixing in Israeli affairs; another said the question of Who Is a Jew should be left up to the rabbis; a third opposed the demonstration on the grounds that the feminist agenda was being eclipsed by Israel's political machinations. The dissenters were outvoted.

I spent the evening helping to make placards—DON'T PLAY POLI-

TICS WITH JUDAISM, WE ARE ALL JEWS, KNESSET GET OFF OUR BACKS, WOMEN FOR PLURALISM—and helping Bella Abzug, our designated spokeswoman, think through what she would say to the press. The next morning, some two dozen of us spread out across a plaza facing the prime minister's office building, held up our placards, and chanted our slogans. Media coverage was extensive and when we returned to our hotel, the women who had stayed behind were upset that the coverage had not made clear that our demonstrators represented the American Jewish Congress and not the International Jewish Feminist Conference.

Dear God, I thought, if we can't stand together on the Who Is a Jew issue, what other weird disunities lie in wait?

One answer came immediately in the form of an Open Letter slipped under the door of every delegate's hotel room. It was from "SHANI—Israeli Women Against the Occupation," and it objected to the omission of the occupation and the *intifada* from the official conference proceedings:

> *Some SHANI members and other women working against the occupation will be attending the AJC conference with the intent of raising the issue of the occupation. We urge you to talk with them. We want to be sure that you hear the Israeli voice of dissent against the continuous abuse of human rights by the Israeli government.*

That evening, the conference we had worked so hard to make happen finally opened. About eight hundred people—official delegates and observers from Israel and elsewhere—packed the large hall in which we would conduct all our plenary sessions. But just as the first speaker was being introduced, a long line of peace activists pressed into the room carrying a huge banner identifying them as ISRAELI FEMINISTS AGAINST THE OCCUPATION. They snaked through the crowded auditorium passing out flyers describing Israel's human rights violations, discriminatory treatment of Oriental Jews and Israeli Arabs, and the violence suffered by Palestinian women in the occupied territories. Boos and cheers accompanied their somber parade through the aisles. Some audience members stood in support of the protestors and I joined them, hoping that those women in the planning committee who had been in mortal fear of this issue would not be foolish enough to try to evict the demonstrators.

Fortunately, the protest was unimpeded and eventually the marchers left as peacefully as they had come. I was counting on them reappearing at our "compromise" plenary session on "Women, War, and Peace," not as silent marchers but as audience participants who could appeal to our delegates with Israeli logic and moral suasion. (I noticed during the next three days that the peace demonstration seemed to have had a salutory effect on the whole conference. Surfacing the issue on that first night made the occupation a valid subject for concern, rather than the unspeakable time bomb it had been in the planning committee. It emboldened several speakers to mention the occupation and the *intifada* whenever these issues were relevant to anything else on the agenda.)

The peace demonstration, however, wasn't the only incendiary incident of the evening. Minutes later the first speaker, South Africa's Helen Suzman—veteran of a forty-year battle against apartheid, and the evening's keynote speaker—was booed by about a dozen women when she tried to justify Israel's trade with South Africa, and to argue against divestment. Undaunted, she said she was no stranger to controversy; back home, she informed us, her opponents shout either "Go back to Russia" or "Go back to Israel," depending on whether they consider communist or Jew the greater insult. When she finished, most of the audience gave Suzman a standing ovation; a few women stayed in their seats, their arms folded.

Bella Abzug put us on the high ground with a stirring review of Jewish women's achievements throughout history and a reminder of the work we were there to accomplish. But when, in passing, Bella acknowledged that the Palestinians had a right to a homeland, one audience member shouted, "Move here and let your sons die fighting Arabs." More boos, more cheers, more chaos.

The dissension we'd seen in the planning committee was mirrored in women's reactions to the opening session. Some complained that the Palestinian conflict was being "sidestepped." Others insisted the conference was getting "too political."

"We're here to talk about women," said one group. "Let's not let men's political issues divide us."

"Don't be naive," said the opposing camp. "War and peace *are* women's issues. The *intifada* and any future Arab-Israeli confrontation will affect us as much as men."

With such disparate approaches, it was no surprise that everyone's whipping girl was that infamous panel on "Women, War, and Peace."

The speakers were Galia Golan and Naomi Chazan, professors at Hebrew University, who presented in the most apolitical, academic terms possible the results of three separate surveys on women's attitudes toward conflict and peace-making. They had found that 70 percent of women but only 50 percent of Israeli men favor direct talks with the PLO. Religious women tend to be more hawkish than religious men; secular women are more dovish than secular men. Better-educated women are more dovish than those less educated.

Throughout their formal presentations, harsh murmurings could be heard, and when the speakers finished, pandemonium broke loose. Right-wing women were furious that both Golan and Chazan hailed from the peace camp, and their research findings seemed to buttress their private political position. To even the score, the Likud women rushed to the floor microphones and monopolized them until well after midnight, using the time to attack the "one-sided" panel and to promote their anti-Arab, militaristic, territorialist points of view. In short, the evening was a fiasco.

A few days later, on December 2, after the International Jewish Feminist Conference adjourned, a concentrated all-day "postconference conference" would be held in Jerusalem organized by the Israeli peace groups and entitled "Occupation or Peace: A Feminist Response." This was the program that Lilly and I had lobbied to have included in our conference, and I'm still convinced that our delegates would have profited from exposure to the views and experiences of Israeli women who were on the front lines of the Israeli-Palestinian peace movement. Clearly, it had been absurd to imagine that we could keep off our agenda the hostilities that were on the front page of every newspaper. (However, I'm also convinced that, in view of the paranoia of the other planners, Lilly and I were right to back off. It had been no small miracle to get funding in the first place from mainstream Jewish organizations for an international meeting convened under a feminist flag. Pressing the issue of the occupation against the wishes of the majority would have had a disastrous effort. Given the alternatives of the moment, we chose compromise to cancellation.)

Although the war-and-peace issue was the most volatile, it was far from the only controversial topic at the conference. There were grumblings of every kind from every quarter: You should have planned more sessions for religious feminists. No, the conference was obsessed with Orthodoxy. One panel couldn't possibly do justice to issues affecting lesbians, widows, single women, and childless women. No, the conference had paid far too much attention to these "fringe issues." The status of Sephardim (or Soviet Jews or Ethiopians) didn't belong at a feminist conference. No, no, women should be contributing fresh thinking to whatever problems confront the Jewish community.

We were too radical. Too mainstream. Too middle-aged. Too middle-class. Too Western. Too feminist. Maybe, I thought, if *nobody* was happy, the conference had been fair to *everybody*. Or maybe the whole thing was a big mistake.

I myself had few complaints. In fact, I found many of the sessions quite illuminating. The workshop on "The Single Woman in a Coupled World" stays with me because of the heartrending honesty of every speaker: the woman who was made to feel like a freak in Jewish communities that assume all Jews come in pairs, like socks; the woman who said she respects those who are single by choice, but she herself yearns to meet Jewish men and wants the Jewish community to help her do it; and the Israeli lesbian who took the microphone and in a brave, tremulous voice declared, "I am not a nice Jewish girl. I am a dyke."

Another provocative session, "Jewish Women in a Non-Jewish World," became unforgettable when Liliane Shalom, an American who was born in Morocco and speaks with a husky French accent, abandoned her text and gave an extemporaneous cri de coeur on behalf of the forgotten, oppressed Sephardim in Israel.

Despite these high points, the cacophony of complaints had dampened my spirits, and by the last day of the conference I felt utterly defeated. That afternoon, I was to deliver the closing speech, "A Call to Action." I couldn't imagine how I could hope to motivate so many cranky factions to form an international network that was supposed to be founded in sisterhood. I lingered in my room in despair, then decided to get some exercise, just a walk around the hotel. Meandering through the halls and lobbies, I stopped eight or ten delegates at random to take a reading of their mood. "How do you feel about the conference so far?" I asked. "Do you think we're getting anywhere?" To my amazement, the answers were all upbeat.

They had met inspiring women. They had been moved by other wo-men's stories and therein found themselves. They had crossed the boundaries of culture and nationality and found remarkable com-monalities with women who lived thousands of miles from their doors. Other women had given them great ideas they could use back home. They had felt the contagion of courage. They had made new friends.

Maybe the new surge of positivism was inspired by the experience of praying at the Western Wall at dawn that day. Or maybe their complaints had been put into perspective by that morning's session. Renee Epelbaum, founder of Mothers of the Plaza de Mayo, who focused world attention on Argentina's state terrorism and the plight of the "disappeared," had brought the audience to tears when she said, almost as an afterthought, that her own three children had been kidnapped and murdered. Refusenik Ida Nudel had talked about her years in Siberia and her struggle on behalf of Soviet Jewish "prisoners of conscience." Shulamit Aloni, a Member of Knesset, had illustrated the rising power of the ultra-Orthodox by describing how, instead of opening the Knesset session in the usual way, with a mixed chorus singing "Hatikvah," Israel's national anthem, the Orthodox members insisted on having a male cantor sing it, because "listening to wom-en's voices is like infidelity." And the Knesset voted to accept the change.

Maybe hearing about *real* problems made crankiness seem self-indulgent. Whatever the reason, the delegates were now a booster squad. They were high on each other. A comment by a delegate from Canada summarized the sentiments of many:

> *This is the first feminist conference I have ever attended at which the embrace of feminism has been so inclusive. Painful, but inclusive.*

Inclusiveness is the hallmark of Jewish feminism—and the reason for the pain. Each woman wants to be accepted for the person she is; she refuses to carve herself to fit any mold, even a feminist mold. So maybe it was for the best of reasons that we had such a tough time working things out together at our first International Jewish Feminist Conference.

Precisely because we were so inclusive, our proceedings demanded great leaps of tolerance. And empathy. And patience. International diplomats could take a cue from us. No one walked out. No one refused to sit in the same room with her opponent. Hearing each other and trying to reflect all points of view did not always lead us to consensus, but it did bring about a sharpened understanding of our differences—and no small amount of pride in the fact that we had exposed the magnitude of those differences and still remained together, arguing, listening, compromising.

The way we handled conflict in Jerusalem helped me appreciate both the seductiveness of reconciliation and the dignity of a standoff. Instead of hiding our disputes, we aired them. Instead of feminine agreeableness, we exhibited passionate partisanship. And it was all to the good, because those disputes were not petty ego outbursts but expressions of deeply held values honed in the diversity of our national experiences.

I think my family was right: certain issues are serious enough to fight about; relationships between people can survive their differences; and often to be Jewish is to be disputatious.

Jews argue because we care. And Jewish feminists argue even more because we have even more to care about.

I did issue my call to action that last afternoon of the conference, and together we founded an International Jewish Feminist Network that was to function across national boundaries as a support system, information and referral service, and political action corps to assist any aggrieved member. And we began to forge a detailed Jewish-feminist agenda with these double-edged goals:

• To increase the representation of Jewish women in every arena *while* transforming the value system in many of those arenas to reflect feminist ideals.

• To enable Jewish women to participate fully in religious and communal life while *also* ensuring that Jewish men participate fully in the domestic and family sphere.

• To expose the truth about long-denied problems of *agunot*, Jewish alcoholism, drug addiction, and domestic violence (and the myth that Jewish men always make the best husbands), while *also* honoring the warmth and strength of Jewish family life.

• To ensure Jewish women's sexual and reproductive freedom in the face of rabbinic controls while also safeguarding *all* women from sexual and reproductive abuse.

• To attack negative stereotypes of Jewish women while also publicizing those inspiring foremothers whom Bella catalogued for us at the opening session of the conference.

• To build on the experience of those delegates who prayed with *talitot* and Torah at the Western Wall, while also respecting secular Jews who choose nontraditional ways to express their spirituality.

• To fight anti-Semitism, racism, and poverty in our respective national cultures while also policing the sexism institutionalized within Judaism in every land.

• To defend Israel in the world while also defending democracy in Israel.

• To guarantee the survival of Israel, as a state and a state of mind, while also acknowledging the humanity, dignity, and peoplehood of the Palestinians.

In other words, we established an agenda for Jewish feminism that is as wide and deep as the reality of Jewish women's lives. But we did something beyond that: Despite cataclysmic disputes among the conference planners and widespread disagreement among the delegates, most of us left Jerusalem feeling empowered by our pride in each other.

In a world of hyperbole and false firsts, this conference was a real first. Sure, there had been other international gatherings of Jews, women, and feminists of all stripes. But never before had there been this particular coalition of women leaders who function, consciously or not, at the nexus of Judaism and feminism.

Even after we sent out our invitations, I wondered who would make the trip. No woman active in Jewish life anywhere on earth *needed* another meeting. And no feminist who had lived through any part of the previous twenty years was looking to start the struggle all over again on a global scale. But 320 women leaders came to Jerusalem anyway because, although no one needed another conference, everyone needed each other.

And it had been intoxicating to find each other. From the remarkable array of delegates, I will never forget: Helen Suzman, the South African anti-apartheid activist who seemed too small and soft-spoken to have survived the many hate campaigns against her. Renee Epelbaum, who found the strength to keeping going after losing three children to the Argentine murder squads. Mona Williams of New

Zealand—a black Jew from a family that has been Jewish for generations, lecturer in English literature, political lobbyist, active Zionist—who described New Zealand as "a land of sixty million sheep and three million people of which only five thousand are Jews," and who said that her nation elected a Jewish prime minister, was the first nation to grant women the vote, banned all nuclear warships, yet also has its share of anti-Semitic graffiti and everyday sexism. The inspiring Bella Abzug, who reminisced about her upbringing in the Bronx where her father owned the "Live and Let Live" meat market and her mother raised her to believe she could do anything. Cathy Gelbin—the young founder of Feministisher Schabbeskris, a Jewish feminist prayer group in East Germany—who recounted her coming out as a Jew and as a lesbian in equally painful terms. Brazil's Celia Szterenfeld, a feminist psychotherapist and organizer of an egalitarian minyan, who told us about her country's first woman rabbi and the first woman mayor of São Paolo in equally prideful terms. Ora Namir, five times elected member of the Israeli Knesset and author of the nation's report on the status of women, who insisted that peace was Israel's most important issue—and so was the rising power of Orthodoxy, and so was the neglect of women's issues in the last national elections, and so was . . . everything.

Plus women from Yugoslavia, France, Australia, Belgium, England, India, Russia, Canada, Tunisia, Italy, Sweden, and more, whose words took me into their lives.

But now I have to ask, *So what?* Writing this recollection two years after the event, I am sorry to say that there have been few concrete byproducts of the First International Jewish Feminist Conference. Nor has there been a Second. The only worldwide feminist organizing that grew out of our Jerusalem experience is the International Committee to Support the Women of the Wall, whose actions—initiating prayer groups, raising money to purchase a Torah, supporting legal action in the Israeli courts, making a return visit to the Wall—I described earlier.

But the World Jewish Congress and the American Jewish Congress, the major conference sponsors, have done little follow-up. It's as though they put everything they had into the wedding and then couldn't care less about married life. When we all returned home, individual American delegates spoke to local groups about our experiences at the conference and then let the ball drop and did little more to activate the agenda we passed at the conference. The AJC established a subcommittee of its Commission on Women's Equality (CWE) to oversee the International Jewish Feminist Network, but has given it no special budget and almost no staff time. The success of the conference and the establishment of the Network seems to have elicited little palpable enthusiasm from the WJC and AJC boards or administrations.

The CWE has sponsored a few meetings with visiting Israelis who updated us on pending cases of special feminist interest, but CWE did such things before there was a Network. CWE has neither organized a pilgrimage of Jewish women from other countries nor helped American Jewish feminists to fan out into the world. There is no administrative mechanism to facilitate such communications between and among our delegates. The directory that is to contain biographical information about all those who attended the Jerusalem meeting is still in the works. If and when it is finally published, it will allow us to connect with one another by mail, or link up when we travel to each other's countries. Presumably, occasions will arise when one member of the network, or any Jewish feminist from Oshkosh or Okinawa, might want to call upon someone in the directory for the promised "mutual support" and "shared resources," but by the time the directory appears will we all remember who each other is and what we meant to accomplish?

It is easy to blame the individual women: if we could spend two years organizing the conference, if we were creative and assertive enough to pull it off, why couldn't we do the same in the follow-up phase? Because during the planning stage we had institutional support and now we don't. It's that simple.

Without financial firepower and organizational resources, the Network will never be more than a great idea that got off to a flashy start and died aborning. In Jerusalem, we said the Network would mount a program of international activities, but even if we had the directory, 320 women from twenty-three countries, many of them economically deprived, cannot run an organization out of their offices or kitchens. In Jerusalem, we agreed that the Network would sponsor regional conferences to enlarge our outreach into every geographical area and to gather more specific testimony of Jewish women's problems, region by region. We can't do that without an administrative staff and a decent budget. In Jerusalem, we said we would host a major international seminar on feminist approaches to Middle East peace. We can't plan such an event on our home phones or employers' fax machines. We need Jewish organizational backup. We need the clout of the Establishment. We need "the Jews" behind us.

The whole experience strikes me as an unfortunate paradigm for the marginality of Jewish women. With the Jerusalem conference we accomplished the first part of what we set out to do, and in the process attracted a flurry of official endorsements and lots of good press for the American Jewish Congress and the World Jewish Congress. They were visionary enough to launch us. Now, with shrinking funds and new priorities, they've dropped us and moved on to other causes. Our issues were trendy; now they're expendable. But what women learned at those meetings in Jerusalem is not expendable. We learned how hard it is to be a Jewish woman in virtually every country of the world. We learned that thousands of Jewish women are isolated, poor, undereducated, disenfranchised, victimized, and forgotten. If our communal agencies can raise millions to help oppressed Jews called Soviet Jews, Syrian Jews, Albanian Jews, or Ethiopian Jews, they can rescue an even larger category called Women Jews.

With all our best intentions, Women Jews cannot do it alone.

16

———————————

And Finally,
the "P" Words

Palestinians and Peace

I WILL ALWAYS REMEMBER THE FIRST TIME I MET A PALESTINIAN. IT was Tuesday night, March 7, 1978, in a meeting room at Jerusalem's King David Hotel. She had come there at my invitation to speak to our *Ms.* tour group on the subject of the Israel-Palestinian conflict. Her name was Raymonda Tawil.

Journalist, political organizer, and mother of five, Tawil had fascinated me from afar, and why not? She was a feminist who confronted Arab patriarchy, and a Palestinian nationalist who openly supported Arab-Jewish coexistence.

Three months earlier, when reached by phone at her home in the West Bank town of Ramallah, Tawil said she would accept my invitation because she was a fan of *Ms.* magazine, but she wanted me to know that she was putting herself at great risk by meeting us, especially inside the Green Line (Israel's pre-1967 borders). Both authority structures had something against her. The Jews considered her a dangerous subversive—for presenting herself to foreign journalists as a PLO spokesperson; for reporting on matters they said endangered Israeli security; and for organizing Palestinian tax revolts, women's groups, student demonstrations, and hunger strikes on behalf of detainees, deportees, or prisoners. Just the year before, she herself had spent four months under house arrest, and she still was under surveillance.

Her own people also were monitoring her behavior. She had begun her activist career by organizing a jazz concert in the West Bank that was attended by both sexes, a revolutionary concept. Since then, she had become more political and quite controversial. Many Palestinian officials condemned her advocacy of a two-state solution—a flagrant contradiction of PLO policy, which at the time called for the destruction of "the Zionist entity" and the creation of a secular, unified Palestine. Others criticized her campaign for Arab women's equality, her insistence on wearing Western dress, her habit of traveling alone, and her autonomous contacts with Western journalists. While the top ranks of the PLO excluded women, Tawil was rumored to be close enough to Yasir Arafat for it to be tacitly assumed that he approved of her politics, including her meetings with Jews when dialogue with the "oppressor" was distinctly unpopular. In the previous month, however, the Palestinians had killed four of their own for collaboration. They could turn against her at any time, she told me, yet for the sake of feminist solidarity, she would meet with us; and given the impracticality of transporting fifty-odd people to Ramallah, she would take the risk and come to Jerusalem.

I was grateful. I liked the sound of her voice. I liked her forthrightness. I thanked her profusely. Then, as we were saying good-bye, she asked if I was aware of the irony of my request.

"You have invited a member of a so-called terrorist organization to speak at the King David Hotel," she said cryptically. It took me a moment to make the connection: In 1946, when England was blocking the open immigration of Jewish refugees into pre-state Palestine, a Jewish underground (some would say "terrorist") organization known as the Irgun blew up the King David Hotel which housed British military headquarters. Many employees—Brits, Jews, and Arabs—were killed or injured in the explosion and the hotel was gravely damaged.

"Yesterday's terrorist is today's prime minister," said Tawil, obviously referring to Menachem Begin, the former commander of the Irgun who recently had been elected Israel's prime minister. I heard a smile in her voice as she added, "And today's terrorist will be tomorrow's president of Palestine."

As I hung up the phone, I felt a tremor of fear. Was I getting *Ms.* in too deep? What if the PLO decided the hotel should explode again? Maybe I should limit our itinerary to feminist issues and leave the minefields of nationalism to others. Maybe I was asking for trouble. And yet, I thought, if feminists can't talk about macropolitics, aren't we in even bigger trouble? I reminded myself that the region had been relatively quiet lately (it would be nine years before the start of the *intifada*); President Anwar Sadat had just completed his historic visit to Jerusalem, and the Egyptian-Israeli peace treaty was in the works. It seemed like a good season for dialogue.

I decided not to worry about the PLO. In fact, I would flesh out the Tuesday night program by teaming Raymonda Tawil with another radical, Leah Tsemel, Israel's answer to William Kunstler. A lawyer specializing in Palestinian civil rights cases, Tsemel is an Israeli Jew and an outspoken anti-Zionist; she opposes not just Israel's occupation of the Territories but the very concept of a Jewish state. Although I disagreed with her, I wanted our group to meet a Jewish woman who spent her life defending poor people and political rebels.

At the time, I regarded Palestinians as troublesome political insurgents who deserved justice but little compassion. They were the enemy within. Sometimes I hated them for hating Israel; other times, I scorned them for allowing themselves to be made pawns of the Arab states; occasionally I noticed their dreadful living conditions, caught the anger smoldering beneath their obsequiousness, considered how I would chafe under military rule—and pitied them. Yet, even with my pro-Israel biases, I was bothered by reports of infringements on Palestinian rights; I wanted our group to hear about the realities of second-class citizenship for Arab-Israelis, and life under occupation in the West Bank and Gaza. My faith in the merits of Israel's position was secure enough to allow the other side an opportunity to present its grievances.

Our side, it seemed to me, had made its case beyond the shadow of a doubt. The Holocaust had proven the urgency of establishing a homeland for Jews, and the logical place for such a state was the turf of our biblical ancestors—"a land without a people for a people without a land." I'd heard that slogan all my life. I had also learned that where the land was previously owned by Arabs, it had been purchased with hard cash by the Jewish pioneers—socialist revolutionaries with no agricultural talents who went on to make the desert bloom. That those early settlers were periodically slaughtered by Arab marauders was known to me both as a historical and a family fact: remember—they had murdered my grandfather.

Everything seemed simple to me then. Whether it was a raid on Tiberias in 1939, or the massacre of Israeli athletes at the 1972 Olympics, events had shown the Arabs to be treacherous anti-Semites who wanted to destroy Israel and didn't care how many they killed to achieve their goal. History was simple too: the Jews had always been willing to share the land but the Arabs refused to give an inch. With all-or-nothing arrogance, they defied the U.N. partition plan of 1947 which would have assigned them the lion's share of the area, and declared war on the fledgling Jewish state. When the shooting stopped, Israel had gained more territory. What the Arabs retained, Jordan annexed, keeping its people in political limbo awaiting some future full-scale conquest rather than underwrite a small but independent Palestinian state whose existence would have implied a de facto acceptance of the state of Israel.

Furthermore, rather than resettle the 800,000 Palestinians made homeless by partition and combat, Arab authorities purposely kept them in refugee camps where their wretchedness could be exploited to arouse international sympathy. War erupted again when Egypt mobilized its troops against Israel in June 1967. This time the Arabs lost everything in a humiliating Six Day War that resulted in Israel's occupation of the Sinai Peninsula, Golan Heights, West Bank, East Jerusalem, and the Gaza Strip, and the creation of more than 400,000 new refugees. Although the PLO was founded in 1964, the national rights of the Palestinians did not figure into the Middle East conflict to any significant degree until after the defeat of the Arab states which gave new impetus to the guerrilla movement. Then Black September 1970, the October War of 1973, and the upsurge in PLO terrorist attacks from bases in Lebanon fully confirmed the majority Jewish view that Arabs could not be trusted and would not be satisfied with anything less than everything.

Raymonda Tawil was a rare exception—someone working for Palestinian nationalism who also accepted Israel's right to exist—and a feminist heroine to boot. On the phone, she sounded like one of us. And when I saw her that Tuesday night in Jerusalem, my first thought was, she *looks* like one of us, a common reaction when Jews and Palestinians meet. I imagined that with her and her colleagues we might found a coalition of Jews and Arabs working for peace and women's liberation. I had high hopes for our evening together and for our shared future.

Leah Tsemel spoke first. Her charges against Israel began with Jewish exploitation of Palestinians for cheap labor, then escalated to descriptions of preventive detention without due process, home demolitions, deportations, and the assertion that the army uses electric shock torture to elicit information. I was stunned. Throughout her talk, I watched the audience murmur and squirm; they too weren't ready for this. If even half of what she says is true, I thought, we Jews must pay attention. I flashed on an old maxim: "Some are guilty, but all are responsible."

When it was Raymonda Tawil's turn to speak, she did so with the vocabulary of feminism and the cadences of a preacher:

> *Although Arab women suffer more gender discrimination than any other women in the world, it is impossible to ask us to care about the sexual revolution when the individual Palestinian is dehumanized, when there is a conspiracy against the realization of our human rights, when our being is threatened, when our identity is denied and when we have no home.*

"First I want my national identity," she said, her eyes turning dark.

> *I must be a free person before I can be a free woman. The Israelis have taken my lands and the identity on my passport. They changed the name of my village to a Hebrew name. They changed the books with which they teach my children at school. They do not let me say the word "self-determination." My people live in tents. We starve. We suffer double oppression—dehumanization from Israel and discrimination from our Arab brothers.*
>
> *We had a culture in Palestine for centuries. We knew English, German, French, music, art. We were a light in the desert. Now we have lost everything. We are a people without a country. We are the Jews of the Arab world.*

My tape recording runs out here, but I have no trouble remembering what happened during the question period. The audience challenged Tawil's presentation on grounds that have since become familiar arenas of battle: our disparate views of history and of terrorism. One

American after another insisted that Tawil take some blame for the current situation, reminding her that Jews had always been willing to share the land while the Arabs left no room for compromise. The audience accused her of lies, revisionism, "selective amnesia." A black woman charged her with crimes against Africans because the Arabs had kept slaves. "No Jew has ever kept a black under the lash," the African-American yelled. Several women wanted Tawil to disavow Arafat and renounce terrorism before they even looked her in the eye. They demanded that she answer for the PLO hijackings and terrorist attacks—especially the horrific massacres at Kiryat Shmonah, where guerrillas machine-gunned eighteen men, women, and children; and at Ma'alot, where twenty teenagers were killed, most of them girls.

"What about Israel's role in all this?" Tawil shot back. "The Israelis drive us to it. We have no alternative. We're powerless. We have to defend our dignity and self-respect."

"There's no excuse for all this bloody violence," replied one Jewish woman, who could not let go of the terrorism issue.

"What about *your* violence?" Tawil insisted. "You should answer to me for the Jews who bombed this hotel. And the Jews who massacred 250 Palestinians at Deir Yassin. We have children too."

A chorus of voices shouted out of turn, accusing her of bad faith and bad feminism. "How can you equate those few examples of Jewish violence with your PLO butchery?" demanded an American.

"Armed struggle is a form of resistance," she seethed. "It's the only way frustrated people can get the world's attention."

Her words frightened me. I had believed she was different but here she was, a feminist defending terrorism. I felt sorry for her—being on our playing field and vastly outnumbered—but in my fear, I lost control of myself and the meeting.

"Killing innocent people isn't armed struggle, it's murder!" I heard myself bellow, breaking out of my moderator's cage. At that, Tawil slammed her fist on the table, stood up, and roared, "There is no place for the Jew in the Middle East!" With Leah Tsemel close behind, she turned on her heel and stalked out.

We sat in our seats like shell-shocked soldiers, almost surprised to find ourselves breathing. I realized how naive I had been to think we could have a polite exchange of views and then make common cause in the struggle for women's equality. I had a lot to learn. The evening's stumbling blocks—our incompatible historical memories and our differences on the issue of terrorism—would prove to be mountains between our two communities from that night until today. Hearing Arab and Jewish versions of events leading up to the present impasse is like venturing into the world of Pirandello or *Rashomon,* so different are each group's views of the same facts. The complexities of Palestinian partisanship, the tension between national liberation and women's liberation, the question of seesawing priorities and competing loyalties, would occupy my thoughts throughout the following decade. But my political education began with Raymonda Tawil.

Five days later, on Saturday, March 11, our tour bus was tooling along the main coastal highway between Caesarea and Tel Aviv when we came upon a squad of Israeli Defense Forces (IDF) spread across the road. One of the officers told us that a bus—an Egged bus like ours—had been ambushed by Palestinian guerrillas just a few miles up ahead. Some people had been killed; nobody knew how many, or whether the terrorists had been caught.

An IDF soldier carrying an Uzi submachine gun climbed on board to escort us to Tel Aviv. Despite his presence, drumrolls of adrenaline beat against my chest as we crawled forward in the glut of traffic. Some women on the bus responded with nervous bravado: alumnae of women's self-defense classes promised to karate-chop the guerrillas to shreds; a few jocular types composed parodies of the obituaries our friends would read about us back home (UPPITY JEWISH FEMINISTS SILENCED AT LAST). One New Yorker quipped, "And I thought the *subway* was dangerous!" But most of us sat there silent as stones, staring out into the unknown where each roadside bush loomed like a nest of hidden vultures and every turn of the tires sounded like footsteps scurrying toward us in the gathering dusk.

I was thinking about how tempting our bus might appear to a cadre that had escaped from the earlier gunfight, or a kamikaze loner itching to kill for his cause. For a split second, I even worried about rape.

Then suddenly, a question pressed against my temples. "What did Raymonda Tawil know and when did she know it?" Could our speaker possibly have been involved in planning this action? Or, when she met with us, was she aware it was going to happen? What if our bus had been a little farther down the highway? Blind luck and a few precious miles had saved us from death. What if *we* had been the next innocent victims of her "armed struggle"? What would Raymonda Tawil say to us now?

In Tel Aviv, we heard that roadblocks were being set up everywhere and the army had posted a nationwide curfew. The evening event that I'd scheduled on our itinerary months before was a meeting with Israeli feminists at the Tel Aviv Women's Center. Now, more than ever, we needed community; we needed to be with other women. So even though we would be out beyond the curfew deadline, our group decided to proceed with the plan. As we journeyed cautiously through streets abuzz with news of the bus attack, I wondered if our Israeli counterparts would make it past the roadblocks or break the curfew, or if the center would be open at all. But we arrived to a full house.

During the meeting, I noticed that the Americans kept asking their hosts about Israeli abortion law, consciousness-raising groups, and sex discrimination, rather than grapple with the lunacy of random violence. Maybe we were reluctant to talk about our one frightening experience when these women live in a perpetual state of fear. Or maybe we felt impotent before the enormity of terrorism as the details of the carnage became known.

Thirty-seven people had been killed that day, including six of the eight seaborne Fatah commandos whose leader had been an eighteen-year-old Palestinian woman named Dalal Mughrabi. Another woman's name also forever would be associated with the tragedy: Gail Rubin, an American-born nature photographer who had been alone on the beach when the commandos landed. Years before, Rubin had fallen in love with the Israeli landscape, and enjoyed spending long solitary hours trying to capture its wildlife on film. She was taking pictures of seagulls and spoonbills when she was shot. Her book, *Psalmist With a Camera* (Abbeville Press, 1979), would remain for me a poignant memorial to her life's work, and a paradoxical reminder of how she died.

The next day, as our plane took off for home from Ben Gurion Airport, I felt mixed emotions: relief to be able to escape from the pressure cooker of vulnerability, and regret that I could not stay to be part of the healing process and the struggle to bring peace. I also tried to carry with me the dream that women could break down barriers that men have erected between peoples. I forced myself to focus on Raymonda Tawil's pain, her passion for justice and hunger for national dignity, rather than on her final apologia for terrorism or her outburst banishing "the Jew" from the Middle East. I wanted to believe that her justification of violence was merely the rhetoric of revolution; that she *had* to defend PLO actions because she was being watched, but that if she had real power, she would never have condoned the attack on the tourist bus. She would have chosen women's ways of resolving conflict—dialogue, negotiation, compromise.

Then I remembered that Tawil, a woman, had slammed the door on other women long before any of us got anywhere near dialogue, negotiation, or compromise, and that we who had ganged up on her were also women. I remembered it was a woman who led the death squad onto the beach, and that women had been part of many previous PLO hijackings. Three years earlier in Mexico City, women had engineered the Zionism Is Racism equation (and two years hence, in Copenhagen, it would be women who would mimic masculine expressions of power and hatred).

Perhaps feminism would be *an* answer, but it would not be *the* answer to an ideological split as deep and complex as this ancient enmity, which some trace to the U.N. partition, others to the Balfour Declaration, the Ottoman Empire, the Muslim conquest of 636, or to the time 3,800 years ago, when Abraham's wife, Sarah, and his Egyptian concubine, Hagar, gave birth respectively to Isaac and Ishmael, progenitors of the Jewish and Arab peoples. Clearly, gender fealty—no matter how politicized—could not by itself supersede a woman's primal loyalties to family, tribe, faith, and nation.

A few weeks later, I heard that Raymonda Tawil had been arrested on March 23. Reading her book, *My Home, My Prison*, published in 1980, I discovered that the arrest had been on charges of "terrorist activity"—subsequently changed to "causing public disturbances." She spent two weeks in solitary confinement, was interrogated and beaten, then put under administrative detention until her release on May 7. After that I lost track of her, but I remember something she wrote—that the hardest questions she faces are how to relate to an enemy as a human being and how to relate to a human being as an enemy. Her answer to both was dialogue.

Not for years did I dare to dream again of dialogue with Palestinian women. In the interim, the political situation had worsened and Israeli public opinion had turned to the right. Orthodox Jewish chauvinists and secular territorial maximalists had gained political legitimacy. People began saying aloud such formerly unspeakable words as "annexation" (of the Territories), "transfer" (mass deportation of the Arabs), and "Greater Israel" (a euphemism for Jewish rule from the Mediterranean to the Jordan River). Under the approving eye of the Begin government, religious and ultranationalist Jews had established some forty new settlements in the West Bank, exacerbating Palestinian rage and complicating the task of future geographical disentanglement. Islamic fundamentalism, boosted by Khomeini's ascendancy in Iran, was gaining a foothold in the Territories. The PLO had rejected the Camp David accords, which would have established a "self-governing authority" during a transition period within which the IDF would be withdrawn and the parties would begin talks on the final status of the West Bank and Gaza. Although Camp David did not give the Palestinians their own flag, its timetable would have put them and the Israelis at the negotiating table by the early 1980s. Instead they were at war.

"Operation Peace for the Galilee" had escalated into an all-out Israeli offensive against PLO strongholds in Lebanon. The world was shocked by the massacres in the Palestinian refugee camps at Sabra and Shatila, and even more outraged when subsequent investigations revealed that the horror was perpetrated by anti-Palestinian Christian Phalangists with the passive approval of Israel's General Ariel Sharon. Thousands of Israelis took to the streets to protest. Israel's indirect responsibility for the slaughter ignited brushfires of anti-Semitism everywhere. It also inspired collective soul-searching among Jews who suddenly felt adrift from their ethical moorings. At the same time that the war in Lebanon (temporarily) destroyed the PLO's state-within-a-state, it also undermined Arafat's influence, and allowed extremist Palestinian hard-liners to capitalize on the chaos. Ultraterrorist Abu Nidal murdered Issam Sartawi, the foremost architect of Palestinian moderation. With metaphorical symmetry, Meir Kahane, the racist Jewish fanatic, won a seat in the Knesset.

The time seemed ripe for transformative, visionary politics, and the U.N. Women's Conference scheduled for the summer of 1985 in Nairobi seemed to me to offer a meaningful impetus for action. Most likely, it would once again focus disproportionate attention on the Israel-Palestinian conflict, but this time, because the conference was the culminating event of the Women's Decade, and because of the disastrous experiences of Copenhagen and Mexico City, many of us hoped the feminist community would feel obliged to improve on its previous performances.

To help write a new script for Nairobi, I decided to do some advance work. In the spring of 1984 I began to organize meetings among Jewish women leaders from the World Jewish Congress, B'nai B'rith Women, National Council of Temple Sisterhoods, International Council of Jewish women, and others to discuss ways we might make this conference less explosive and more directed to women's issues such as economic development, sexual violence, and reproductive freedom. During the summer, I made contact with someone from the Feminist Arab-American Network which was based in East Lansing, Michigan, but after one exchange of letters, efforts to start a dialogue group with them ground to a halt. Early that autumn, however, I did help start the thirty-member Black-Jewish Women's Dialogue mentioned earlier, whose objective was consensus building for Nairobi. They jumped into the morass of issues and soon devised practice scenarios of confrontation and conflict resolution. I wished I could have added Arab-American women to the Black-Jewish group, but at the time I did not know even one Arab personally and didn't trust myself to make cold calls without understanding the political spectrum of the American Palestinian community.

The following spring Reena Bernards, then executive director of New Jewish Agenda, asked me to help convene still another Nairobi planning meeting, this time one that would include Jewish, black, *and* Arab-American feminists. Reena, too, was concerned that the upcoming conference would see an instant replay of old clashes unless we could develop new habits of discourse. She invited the Jewish participants (who included Bella Abzug, author Christie Balka, and filmmaker Lilly Rivlin), I helped identify black women to invite, and Gail Pressberg, then director of Middle East programs at the American Friends Service Committee, brought in the Arab-Americans, among them several Palestinians, an Egyptian, and a Lebanese, all members of FAN, the Feminist Arab Network, or the Arab-American Anti-Discrimination Committee. Reena asked me to serve as moderator.

That's how I found myself in a conference room at 777 United Nations Plaza on April 9, 1985, entering a mirror image of the meeting in Jerusalem seven years before. Barely had we finished the go-around of introductions when the onslaught began. It was, as Yogi Berra once put it, déjà vu all over again—the same bile-bubbling fury that I remembered from the King David Hotel, except this time the attack was launched by the Palestinians and the woman in the hot seat was me.

I was taken completely by surprise, as were Reena and Gail. None of us had realized that, after my report on the Copenhagen conference was published in *Ms.*, I had become anathema to the Arab feminist community who contended that, by giving voice only to the experience of Jews, I had made the oppressor into the underdog and turned American feminists against the Palestinians.

"The article didn't claim to be a balanced view of the Middle East conflict," I reminded them. "It reported on the harassment *of* women *by* women at a feminist event, and the plain fact is that the Arabs were the harassers in Copenhagen, not the Jews."

"But it's not that simple," one woman shot back. "You should have traced the causes of our anger."

My article grew from the premise that anti-Israel sentiments cannot be allowed to take the form of anti-Semitic torment, and that women who buy into that villainy should be exposed. The Palestinian women couldn't see my point, and back then I couldn't see theirs. They insisted the American press never tells the story from their perspective. They said that by letting the Jewish delegates complain in print I had portrayed Palestinians as bullies, not freedom fighters. They couldn't understand that Jewish women would never be receptive to Palestinian freedom if its cost was danger to Israel or the Jewish people. Nor could they see that bullying reminds Jews of millennia of persecution and that fighting back is one of the ways we guard against history repeating itself.

"Don't talk to me about Jewish persecution when Israel is oppressing us and you Jews support Israel," shouted one of the Arabs.

I reminded her that some Jews support *two* states, Israel and Palestine, side by side, and that I had taken that position in print as long ago as 1982.

"Do you also support the right of return?" someone barked.

"Yes, of course," I answered, thinking she meant the right of all Jews to emigrate to Israel and become citizens. But she meant the right of Palestinians to return to the homes their families left behind in 1948 or 1967, homes in Haifa, Jaffa, and Jerusalem that now are inhabited by Jewish families. I had never considered this question. I paused. Even if it was morally defensible, was it reasonable to expect Jews to abandon houses they'd lived in for decades; and was it politically wise to displace a whole new generation even in the act of undoing an old injustice? I could see the Palestinian demand for their right of return escalating into a controversy as divisive between Jews and Arabs as affirmative action has become between Jews and blacks.

I ventured an answer: "Maybe the right of compensation could substitute for the right of return to specific places."

This satisfied no one. Questions came hurtling at me like hardballs from a hyperactive pitching machine—questions about Jewish settlements, about why Palestine should be a demilitarized state and not Israel, about trust, fairness, justice.

I tried to answer each salvo, but just as Raymonda Tawil could not persuade her audience, nothing I said could mollify the Arab women. Rather than slam out the door, however, I just stopped talking. Eventually, the shouting died down and I was able to redirect the group's attention to the agenda—which was to create strategies for dialogue in Nairobi. Everyone agreed that what we had just endured did not bode well for the process, but they wanted to try again, and they did meet twice more prior to their July departure.

Apparently everyone's advance work paid off. I had to stay home that summer to deal with the book I was writing, but dozens of returning delegates told me that women from our pre-Nairobi task forces had been instrumental in making this conference far more productive than the previous meetings, and that much of the difference was due to the way these women faciliated dialogue.

Gail Pressberg, a fifteen-year veteran of Middle East friendship efforts and a gifted political analyst, interprets the particular dynamics of Jewish-Palestinian dialogue this way:

> *Palestinians worry that Jews might try to whitewash the issues or suck them into something that would dilute their right to self-determination. Jews worry that Palestinians will try to win their case at the expense of Israel. Nairobi was successful because women created a different way to talk to each other.*

This became possible partly because maverick leaders—Jews and Palestinians—had been meeting with one another openly in Israel, the West Bank, and elsewhere. (In fact, in 1989, Nabil Sháʼath, chairman of the Palestine National Council's political committee, revealed that secret friendships with Jews such as Philip Klutznick, past president of the World Jewish Congress, helped Palestinian leaders to finally defy their own rejectionists and publicly endorse a two-state solution.) News of these dialogue initiatives had filtered through the Palestinian women's groups and as a result, many of their conference delegates were more amenable to compromise and less bound by the adversarial politics of the past.

The pre-Nairobi dialogue groups had learned the key to avoiding polarization: *start* by affirming both peoples' right to self-determination; acknowledge the fears, needs, and humanity of The Other; *then* speak your mind. It is this lesson—confirmed by the experience of my black-Jewish consciousness-raising group—that gave me so much faith in dialogue as a first step to bring people together, whether they be women seeking a common ground within feminism, or Arabs and Jews facing the future they are condemned to share. Statesmen (and they are *men*) will negotiate where to mark the boundaries, but ordinary people must prepare the ground for peace by tilling the soil of compromise, and weeding out as many differences as we can. The tilling and the weeding are the labor of dialogue.

Until 1985 I had involved myself in Israeli-Palestinian issues only when they intersected with feminism, but during the next two years, I felt my interest broaden and deepen in the Middle East. What mobilized me were three major developments: the political paralysis of the Israeli government, the growing tendency of American Jews to confuse devotion to Israel with loyalty to the government of the moment (whose policies may not correspond with the best interests of the state), and the outbreak of the grass-roots uprising known as the *intifada*. I began to read books and periodicals relating to the conflict, attend lectures, and generally immerse myself in the issues. I also agreed to serve on the boards of the International Center for Peace in the Middle East (ICPME) and Americans for Peace Now (APN), two groups that carefully educate their members for activism.

ICPME brings together community and political leaders, academics, policymakers, lawyers, and writers to hear noted speakers—such as Abba Eban, former Israeli foreign minister; Boutros Boutros-Ghali, the Egyptian deputy foreign minister; Yehoshafat Harkabi, Israel's leading expert on Arab relations and former chief of military intelligence; or any number of army generals and Knesset members—

discuss events in the Middle East with the expressed hope that we "opinion makers" will lecture, write, and work for peace. Drora Kass, our executive director and a remarkable catalyst for Arab-Jewish dialogue, also has arranged for us to meet in the United States and abroad with a wide array of Palestinian leaders whose temperate positions, intelligence, and seriousness of purpose have persuaded me that there is indeed "someone to talk to on the other side."

Although the main mandate of ICPME is peace education and political strategizing in Israel and the United States, its most celebrated contribution to the peace process was the December 1988 meeting with Yasir Arafat that Kass and board members Rita Hauser and Stanley Sheinbaum initiated in Stockholm. I would have been with them had not the meeting date conflicted with my twenty-fifth wedding anniversary and the party to which our children had invited more than a hundred of our friends and family. Never have my public and private selves clashed more painfully than when Rita Hauser called on a Sunday morning and invited me to be one of the five delegates to Stockholm. Ultimately, of course, the private side won; others could go to Sweden but only my husband and I could be the guests of honor at our own silver anniversary.

The meeting with Arafat resulted in his first clearly articulated willingness to fulfill the three preconditions set forth by the United States before it would open a dialogue with the PLO: recognize Israel's right to exist, endorse U.N. Resolutions 242 and 338, and renounce terrorism. The previous month in Algiers, the Palestine National Council (PNC—the PLO's parliament in exile) had issued its declaration of statehood and its acceptance of the *principle* of partition, but with many attendant ambiguities. It took the Stockholm meeting for push to come to shove. Contrary to those who criticized ICPME for "interfering in Israeli affairs" and meeting with the nemesis of the Jews, I felt that the Stockholm mission was utterly appropriate: it was an effort by *American* Jews to get the *American* government to meet with Israel's adversary and move them toward the peace table. The United States can be both a powerful agent for peace *and* an advocate for Israel, but only when we are actually engaged in the labor of peacemaking. Influencing the American government to be more involved in a foreign crisis is a legitimate activity for U.S. citizens who have a vested interest in the resolution of that crisis. And, in fact, that interest was furthered, at least for a while, when the breakthrough in Stockholm led the PLO chief to make his concessions official one week later at a press conference convened after the special session of the U.N. General Assembly in Geneva. Shortly thereafter, diplomats from the United States and the PLO opened their dialogue in Tunis.

Unfortunately, in June 1990, after Arafat failed to unequivocally condemn Abul Abbas's aborted attack on a Tel Aviv beach, President Bush ordered the talks suspended on the ground that the no-terrorism pledge had been violated. I deplore the Abul Abbas operation, but I cannot see how any purpose was served by reinstituting silence between Tunis and Washington. Thankfully, the PNC did not withdraw its endorsement of a two-state solution after cancellation of the talks—or in response to the Gulf crisis. They made the misguided, politically disastrous decision to take Iraq's side in the war. But whether or not the PLO "behaves" is not the point. As long as they represent the Palestinians, and as long as the Palestinians are Israel's enemy, the road to peace must pass through PLO headquarters.

While ICPME directs its American efforts toward political elites, Americans for Peace Now (APN) is a populist organization. I work with both groups because I feel both approaches are necessary. Founded in 1978 by 350 reserve officers, applauded by Golda Meir just months before she died, and since endorsed by many Knesset members and security experts, Peace Now favors the exchange of land for peace and opposes Israeli settlements in the Territories. In Israel, it organizes public demonstrations, trains political activists, monitors Jewish settlement activity in the Territories, and initiates democracy education projects and coalition-building among immigrants, Jews in poor development towns, Israeli Arabs, and Palestinians.

Since its massive protests against the Lebanon War, Peace Now's most remarkable accomplishment was to organize a human chain in December 1989 in which more than 30,000 Jews, Christians, and Muslims—kids and grown-ups, Israelis, Palestinians, and others—wearing T-shirts, cut-off jeans, kaffiyehs, clerical garb, and traditional Arab dress—joined hands around the walls of the Old City of Jerusalem chanting, "We Want Peace!" No recent event has had as much impact because the human chain made visible for the first time the national and religious diversity of the peace movement. Jews saw that Palestinians were willing to stand up openly for a two-state solution, and Palestinians saw that Israelis were willing to get teargassed side by side with them.

Not only does APN support its Israeli namesake, but its Washington office keeps the American public and elected officials informed about events in Israel that are not always represented fairly by the Israeli government or the American Jewish establishment, and its grass roots educational efforts help to clarify why the land-for-peace formula is Israel's best chance for long-term security. In both countries, the preeminent goal of Peace Now is to get the parties to *talk now*—without further loss of life or hope.

Whether through these organizations or other social or professional affiliations, I've met a number of Palestinians in the last five years who have left indelible impressions, and whose words have informed my most deeply held political beliefs. Since politics are rather like a second religion to me, these encounters have been as memorable as epiphanies of the spirit.

I'm thinking of Suad Joseph, a Palestinian-American anthropologist, whose analysis of the sexual politics of the Muslim world resonated so fully with my view of women's status in traditional Judaism that I felt myself crossing an invisible line, and I was suddenly able to perceive us both, Arab and Jew, as Middle Eastern women. She helped me understand why Palestinians often resist identifying with American feminists, even in the interest of peace: because past Western influences, for instance in dress and sexual attitudes, that at first appeared to emancipate Arab women often backfired and aroused more repression. Also because Arab women who put gender issues before issues of class, imperialism, and national liberation tend to be condemned as bourgeois or trivial.

If feminism can be said to undermine women's loyalty to nationalist goals, then I could see why, conversely, nationalist movements might inhibit the development of an autonomous women's movement, and why, as Suad put it, "women can be political actors without benefiting themselves as women." She gave me a new reason to support Palestinian statehood: it would free Palestinian women to be as demanding as we Jews.

At an event that had nothing to do with the Middle East—a publication party for Mary King's book about civil rights—I met a soft-spoken Palestinian-American named Odeh Aburdene, then an officer of the Arab Bank and now executive vice president of the First City Bank in London. For hours that evening and in subsequent talks, he infused me with his gentle but irrepressible optimism. He insisted that once a political solution was achieved, our two peoples would overcome our past bitterness and not just coexist but prosper together. He knew this, he said, because of experiences he and his extended family had had with American Jews in recent years, and with Jews in the Middle East before 1948, and he assured me—long before official PLO policy changed—that moderation would be the wave of the future. Odeh quoted the words of one of the founders of Hasidism, Reb Nachman of Breslov: "As your answers have become my questions, perhaps my questions may become your answers."

When someone embodies sweet reason, his or her cause seems reasonable. In their separate ways, Suad and Odeh personified the human face of Palestinian nationalism; they breathed life into this effigy that had been all menace and no heart; they melted its frozen jawline, and gave it a voice I could both listen to and hear. After Suad and Odeh, I was able to hear other Palestinians too. My receptors no longer shut down in anticipation of attack, nor did I feel obligated to counterattack or defend everything Jews have ever done. I realized that if I had been born a Palestinian, I too would be demanding liberation, self-determination, and freedom in just those words—for I have used the same words to argue on behalf of women and Jews.

Because I was beginning to hear Palestinians did not mean I accepted everything they said. But I could allow myself to feel less threatened when they had logic on their side. I knew that listening to them did not mean I had closed my ears to Israel. In fact, *understanding the Palestinian perspective could be a service to Israel*, and talking to the "enemy" a kind of Jewish patriotism. Before 1977, the Palestinians were the hard-liners and the Israelis the moderates; then it flip-flopped and the moderates took over the Palestinian helm while the hard-liners began to dominate in the Israeli government. My fear is that this symmetry will be corrected in the worst way—giving us extremist leadership on both sides. Talking to moderate Palestinians and helping to legitimate their views may bring us closer to the permanent peace without which Israel may not survive into the twenty-first century. Not talking and not listening get us nowhere.

There is a huge gap between the feelings Jews report to pollsters and what they say in public. Here and in Israel, most Jews believe the status quo is untenable but offer no practical alternative. I stand with those who advocate an alternative: open dialogue, negotiated settlement, two states for two peoples—and security through peace. Among the voices that speak similarly are those of some well-known Palestinians whose very effectiveness has put them in peril. Mahdi Abdul-Hadi, president of PASSIA (Palestine Academic Society for the Study of International Affairs) once said of his fellow moderates:

> *The Israeli public must know that we exist and be exposed to our point of view, but please call us nationalist figures, not leaders; it is suicide for any activist to be described as a leader.*

Palestinian moderates are always at the mercy of Palestinian assassins, but this time he meant *political* suicide and he was referring to the travel restrictions, administrative detentions, house arrests, and deportations visited by Israel upon many Palestinians who rise above the crowd and speak in favor of a two-state solution. Indeed it appears as if the government of Israel cracks down on the very people who offer a real possibility of alternative leadership—as if to deny such talent to the Palestinian cause and eliminate such spokespersons from the roster of potential interlocutors at the peace table. Included in this roster is Faisal Husseini, the preeminent West Bank nationalist and the man some say would be president of a future Palestine were Arafat and other diaspora figures disqualified as candidates. Yet Israeli authorities seem to find this potential statesman as threatening as any terrorist. From 1982 to 1987, Husseini was under house arrest, restricted to the confines of Jerusalem. Since then, for various periods, he has been interrogated, held in administrative detention, or barred from travel to the Occupied Territories or abroad.

Between travel bans, he has been at several meetings where I've had the opportunity to be impressed by his cautious but deeply committed advocacy of mutual recognition, peace, and coexistence. He once described himself this way:

> *In 1967, for the first time, I met Israeli people, not just the army. I began to see that this enemy is like us—some are strong, weak, wiser, more foolish. I saw children like my own children. I started to think differently. I decided if we want real peace, both peoples will have to set aside two things: our dreams and our nightmares.*

The dreams, of course, were the maximalist visions on both sides, and the nightmares were the specters of past suffering and fear of the demon Other.

Lately, this son of Abed Khader Husseini, a prominent Palestinian commander in the war of 1948, has been a speaking partner of Yael Dayan, daughter of the late Israeli war hero General Moshe Dayan. The symbolism of their team effort as well as the substance of their message argues for optimism. However, I've also heard Faisal's pessimism, for instance when Israeli prime minister Shamir reneged on his own election plan for the Territories even after the Palestine National Council fulfilled Israel's criteria.

"Whatever we give they want more," said Faisal. Like many others, he thinks Israel's strategy is to undermine Palestinian moderates and incite the extremists, thereby discrediting the viability of the entire cause. Yael Dayan agrees but says there are two spoilers: "The closer we get to a peace breakthrough, the more extremists on both sides will try to undermine it." After reports of yet another Arab attack on an Israeli bus and another random shooting by Jewish settlers, Yael said, "This kind of horror is exactly what moderates on both sides are going to have to fortify themselves against *together*."

One of the most impressive moderates on the Palestinian side is Ziad Abu Ziad, a West Bank lawyer and journalist with whom I met in New York and Jerusalem. Years ago, he admitted that although "self-determination" was the code word for an independent state, once Palestinians have self-respect and international recognition, they may well vote for confederation with Jordan or some other political arrangement. "It is the self-respect that matters most," he said.

As I write this, Israel is holding Ziad in administrative detention. Those of us who know of his peace advocacy have sent telegrams of protest. If they keep putting reasonable men like Ziad Abu Ziad and Faisal Husseini in prison, Israel will end up having to negotiate with arch-terrorists like Abu Nidal and Abul Abbas.

Another woman who helped alter my angle of vision is Hanan Mikhail-Ashrawi, dean of humanities at Bir Zeit University, who became a celebrity after her appearance on that memorable Ted Koppel program when a physical barrier was placed between the Israeli and Palestinian guests. The steely gaze and stately eloquence Hanan exhibited on television are softened in conversation as she describes her husband as "one of the few liberated Palestinian men." Hearing about her fear for her daughter's safety as she leaves for school each day, or her current conundrum, whether to devote her political energies to making the occupation less onerous or to ending it altogether, has made Hanan a very real person to me.

I've heard her worry aloud that, despite their good intentions, Jewish peace groups have the negative effect of disarming the Palestinian resistance by suggesting that there are more sympathetic people in the Israeli camp than is actually the case. Nevertheless, she counsels Palestinians to keep talking with Jews and working for peace:

> *We should not make any further political concessions but we should persist in what we're doing, and keep repeating our message. Education is a long process. The public needs to hear it over and over again: we want two states for two peoples; there is no alternative to the PLO; and Jews and Palestinians don't have to love each other, we just have to understand each other.*

When asked if Mahatma Gandhi and Martin Luther King might have something to offer her cause, she said that passive resistance had been tried and failed when Palestinian women stood quietly, holding up pictures of their children in jail, but were met with Israeli gunfire and tear gas. "At least, throwing stones lets people vent the frustration of freedom denied."

It was over dinner at the American Colony Hotel in East Jerusalem that a few of us from ICPME first met the editor of *Al Fajr*, Hanna Siniora, another determined Palestinian "peacenik." Hanna and his wife Norma speculated with us about the positive consequences of the *intifada* which had broken out just five weeks before. They agreed that if Palestinian violence remained limited to stone throwing, it would provide daily proof that the status quo is intolerable, but not enough reason to justify harsh repression. It would force Jews and others to bury the illusion that everything is okay in this corner of the world, or that Palestinians are content because they have it better under Israeli domination than they did before 1967, or because they may be better off than other Arabs. Hanna hoped that images of IDF brutality and other bad press might drive the Israelis to the peace table. The effort to coordinate the uprising and the general strikes might teach Palestinians to govern themselves, a necessary prerequisite for statehood. Maybe the young people who began the *intifada* would prove themselves viable future leaders; maybe these kids from the West Bank and Gaza would be more pragmatic than the PLO Old Guard in Tunis. Maybe ... maybe ...

"Maybe if you get self-determination, you won't need Yasir Arafat," I muse.

"Arafat will be our Moses," says Hanna. "He will lead us to the Promised Land but once inside, there will be new leaders."

After coffee, Norma agreed to accompany me to a nearby shop where earlier in the day I had fancied a small antique carpet. Thanks to her charm and her Arabic, I was able to bargain with the proprietor until he would accept a price I could afford. The carpet is rolled out now like a welcome mat in the entry hall of my home. Someday, I hope, Norma and Hanna will see it.

Driving from Jerusalem to Gaza City, I scribbled my impressions in a notebook: "Orange trees, cactus, palms. Border police question us as if to say, What are nice folks like you doing in a place like this?"

Inside the Gaza Strip my notes describe:

> *Soldiers on rooftops, soldiers on street corners, guns pointing at us from every direction. There are 650,000 people in 350 square kilometers and they're living on top of one another. Garbage in the streets. Arab women carrying loads of grass on their heads. Donkey carts. Crushed oil drums. Tin roofs. Rusted Mercedes-Benz taxis, circa 1965. Mud. Kids playing on hills of rotting vegetables and broken glass. Peeling paint. Barbed wire. The only saving grace in Gaza is the sea.*

The law office of Fayez Abu Rahme, head of the Gaza Lawyers Association, is situated above a butcher shop on a dusty, bustling street. I was eager to meet the man who once told the press that he wanted peace so badly, he didn't care if the Palestinian state was demilitarized and its police unarmed. "If necessary, they can be barefoot and in bathing suits," he added. Fayez Abu Rahme means "victorious father of mercy" and the name seems to fit this man whose almost Victorian dignity could not mask an ineffable sadness. I sensed how tired he was of explaining his cause and yet he did so to me and three other visiting Americans with patient determination—and despite growling interjections from Yusra Al Barbari, the white-haired president of the Palestine Women's Union of Gaza, who sat at his side like a Bad News

Bear. She reminded me of the old joke: What's the difference between a Jewish pessimist and a Jewish optimist? The pessimist says, "Oy, things can't get any worse." And the optimist says, "Oh, yes they can." This leader of Palestinian women in Gaza was as negative as any "Jewish optimist" about the prospects for peace.

"Our Mrs. Barbari is tougher than Chairman Arafat," laughed Dr. Haider Abdal Shafi, president of the Red Crescent (like our Red Cross), who was the third Palestinian in the room.

We sat on plastic chairs in Fayez's long, narrow office, his desk at one end, gauze curtains whispering at the windows, ancient law books lined up on the shelves. We drank tea from glasses set on floral china coasters. Bowls of pretzels and Oreo-type cookies sat on the table before us, untouched.

"Mubarak had ten points, Baker had five points, I have one point: direct negotiations," said Fayez. He talked about how peace is a precious thing and friendship would add more to Israel's security than its whole army. He envisioned full cooperation and freedom of movement for citizens of both states. Warning systems, yes, but open roads, open skies.

> *Without testing us, they can't say they have no faith in a demilitarized Palestinian state. Right now, there are more soldiers between Israel and Gaza than between twelve European states. It makes no sense. One day there will be no borders between any of the states in the Middle East, including Israel and Palestine.*

How would Gaza fit into the new Palestine? we asked.

> *We could negotiate a corridor to connect it with the West Bank and that would be Palestinian territory. Of course, if Israel insists the 1967 borders are not negotiable then this would be impossible and we're at an impasse.*

Fayez accompanied us to the Beach Refugee Camp about a mile from his office. My notes say:

> *45,000 residents. Camp under curfew. Dirt streets. Warm sunny day. Blankets on windows. Children's voices audible everywhere but no children outside. Only garbage and soldiers, a few goats, and young*

Arabs whitewashing political graffiti with IDF guns at their backs. Islamic University closed. Health clinic pitifully underequipped. Nurse says last night Israeli soldiers broke into main medical facility seeking files to help identify rebels wounded in a demonstration. Richard Larsen, UNRWA director, says average 70 people a week shot in Gaza.

When we bid good-bye to Fayez Abu Rahme, he smiles: "We must be optimistic," he says. "We must get rid of the obsession with power and keep fighting for friendship."

Unknowingly, all these people—each in her or his own way—renewed my belief in peacemaking and prepared me for the intense experiences I've had in The Dialogue Project, a series of weekend retreats involving American Jews and American Palestinian women. The Jewish side of the equation was born in the spring of 1988 when women leaders from mainstream Jewish organizations gathered in homes in seven cities in the United States to hear Alice Shalvi, the Orthodox feminist who chairs the Israel Women's Network, speak about conditions in Israel since the start of the *intifada*. Distraught at the violence in the Territories and its reverberations in Israeli society, Alice let her tears flow as she told the forty of us who had gathered to hear her in New York City: "We are killing our youngsters physically, metaphorically, morally. We are killing our own future."

After her moving presentation, many women in the audience confessed feelings of anguish, impotence, and ignorance. They wished they knew more about the Palestinian revolt. They wanted to hear honest debate about it in the Jewish community but they said the Middle East conflict rarely appears on the agendas of Jewish women's organizations. They wanted advice on how to utilize their leadership to get their members involved. Some women realized they had been taking refuge in avoidance, or had just assumed that men would handle the crisis for them. Others admitted they hated what was happening in the Occupied Territories but were reluctant to criticize Israel. Alice Shalvi begged them to get involved, for Israel's sake:

The only hope I can see is that U.S. Jews who care about Israel help us to find a way out. Work with us. Don't listen to the Israelis who say you have nothing to say. You have everything to say. You are us. Am Yisrael Echad. Am Yisrael Arevim ze Ba'ze. The people of Israel are

one; the people of Israel are responsible for one another. We have to
work together. . . .

  One of the ways is to persuade our government and your adminis-
tration that they've got to stop saying we cannot talk to the Palestin-
ians. We've got to talk to the Palestinians because they're there. We
have to recognize their existence. They are our partners in dia-
logue. . . .

  You've got to help us. . . . We've got to identify those Palestinians
who are moderate. . . . We have to enter a process of bargaining, of
sitting together. There has to be mutual recognition and dialogue. . . .

  And I really believe that women have something to teach men about
achieving consensus, about giving in a little in order to ultimately win
a lot. . . .

Hearing Alice inspired about a dozen of us, with the help of the
intrepid Reena Bernards, who had organized that pre-Nairobi meeting, to found the Jewish Women's Consultation whose goals are as
follows: to help women become part of the decision-making process
in the Jewish community; to empower them to express their political
opinions without "peer fear"; to contribute to the peace process
through educational initiatives addressed specifically to the Jewish
mainstream where there is similar confusion; and to organize dialogue with moderate Palestinians, a constituency that many Jews do
not believe exists. By our actions the Jewish Women's Consultation
hopes to answer the question that most bedevils our community:
What role should American Jews play in the Israeli political situation?
The answer is, when a family member is in trouble, it is a moral
responsibility as well as a loving act to tell them what we think. If
concerned American Jews feel free to speak out on what's happening
in Nicaragua or South Africa, certainly we cannot be expected to
remain silent about Israel. Moreover, silence is not neutral; it is in-
terpreted as support. Therefore, unless we agree with the actions of
the Israeli government, or anything else that affects world Jewry, we
are obligated to make our feelings known. When the "Who Is a Jew"
issue threatened to undermine Israel's Law of Return, American Jews
registered their objections unambiguously and decisively. When the
Orthodox parties threatened to restrict access to abortion, American
Jewish women showered the Shamir government with protests. And
as long as the Palestinian conflict threatens the security of the state,

we must be just as outspoken. Regardless of the rigid judgments of a good part of the American Jewish community, diversity is not disloyalty. The Jewish Women's Consultation—a creation of women with unquestionable loyalties and impeccable community credentials—has expanded the definition of a "friend of Israel" to include one who *advocates dialogue, negotiation, two states, and coexistence with the Palestinians as the best route to a safe and moral future.*

After several months of trying to bridge the extremes in the Jewish spectrum, we were ready to become partners with Palestinian women in the aforementioned Dialogue Project, the first attempt in this country at informal but organized contact between the established leadership of both communities. Unlike that ill-fated meeting at 777 U.N. Plaza, this group was convened by a joint planning committee of Jews and Palestinians who met several times to conceptualize the project, agree on ten participants from each side (we each invited one woman from the Middle East), and plan the agenda for the first session—a foundation-funded weekend in the country at a retreat called Stony Point; no press, no fanfare, no men. For three days in June 1989—and on subsequent weekends in February 1990 and April 1991—Palestinian women active in national Arab-American organizations and Jewish women with comparable affiliations talked deep into the night, battled over the issues that divide us, and wept together more than once. By protecting the identities of the participants, I can offer a composite of the extraordinary experiences we've shared.

The goals of The Dialogue Project were set forth in advance: we wanted to get to know one another as leaders in our respective communities, understand each other's perspectives, discuss ways of resolving the Israeli-Palestinian conflict, define areas of agreement and disagreement, discuss possible actions to support the peace process, and build relationships for future work. But before any of this could happen we would have to cease being The Other to one another; we would have to connect as human beings and, more important, as women.

We arrange our chairs in a circle, careful not to bunch up Jews on one side, Palestinians on the other. Once again I am struck by how many faces advertise our common Semitic origins. We could pass for a cousins' circle, a family reunion. Each woman in her turn offers a miniautobiography—family details, schooling, work life, religious and political identity, personal concerns. To varying degrees, all of us identify as feminists, and for me and others this gathering recalls our consciousness-raising groups of the 1970s. We take seriously the model of sisterhood; we move quickly from uneasy cordiality to tentative self-disclosure. We open up to each other, offering anecdotes, self-exposure, sorrow. Clearly, the feminist axiom "The personal is political" is to be our roadmap to intimacy. This first night, we do not grapple with Zionism or Palestinian nationalism. We talk about ourselves.

When introducing herself, a Palestinian remembers meeting one of the Jewish women at another conference to which the Jewish woman was late arriving:

> *You told us you were delayed because your daughter got her period for the first time. We all digressed to talk about when we first got our periods. The men in the room didn't understand that this was important to us as women.*

In general, the Jewish women mention their religion more often, while the Palestinians say more about their politics. (Earlier I was amused to note that each side had put a pamphlet in our conference packets: the Jews' contribution was a "Service for Shabbat"; the Palestinians' handout was the text of their 1988 Declaration of Statehood.) The Jews keep harking back to the Holocaust, the Palestinians to their 1948 diaspora—the *nachma*, the dismemberment. The Jews talk about the children they have; the Palestinians, about the children they *were*. In all three retreats we've had women who were born in Nablus, Jerusalem, Hebron, Jaffa, Safed, Acre, and Lebanon, Texas and New Jersey; born into families they describe as "Pan-Arabist," "very political," "stigmatized," "uprooted," "humiliated," "idealistic." The American Palestinians now live in or near Washington, New York, Minneapolis, Chicago, Salt Lake City, Seattle, San Francisco, and small towns in Virginia, Maryland, and North Carolina. Half are Muslims, half Christians, but all call themselves "secular nationalists." They are single, married, or divorced; most have children—a five-year-old who is "terrified of Israeli soldiers," a ten-year-old whose best friend is the son of a rabbi, two grown-up feminist daughters, a teenager who has "problems with his Arab identity."

"It's a challenge to bring them up proud *and* tolerant," sighs the professor from Chicago.

We Jews are underachievers compared to these women. Nearly every one has a Ph.D. There is a physicist who was a Fulbright scholar; a social worker associated with a Palestinian think tank; a political scientist who teaches women's studies and Middle Eastern affairs; a research librarian (whose brother is a well-known PLO official); a bookkeeper; two historians; a sociologist, a journalist, and a pride of professors. The personal concerns they share with us cover human rights, women's issues, anti-Arab discrimination, curing cancer, "teaching Palestinian women how social change affects female consciousness," "yearning for a homeland," and "working at dialogue."

The professor from Utah speaks movingly about her "assimilation period"—when she put all her energies into American politics, especially the feminist movement—and what happened when she went back to the West Bank and saw what was happening to her people and decided to stop running away from her identity. Her journey strikes a familiar chord. In fact, in all the Palestinians' stories, I hear Arab-esque echoes of my own double agenda—the struggle to reconcile my commitments as a woman and a Jew.

I am most taken with a Minneapolis woman who tells us about her Palestinian-Jewish dialogue group back home, a story that strikes me as both a prophecy and a warning:

We met once a month for two and a half years. Initially, it was very rewarding. As we got to know each other, we could feel the barriers breaking down. We lingered at this stage longer than we should have because it was so comfortable. Finally came the moment of truth. We started talking about history.

It was incredible how totally different our realities were. Each group tried hard to convince the other that its version was the right one. It was impossible to reconcile the two. When the Palestinian women dwelled on 1948, homelessness, suffering, the Jewish women said let's move on. When the Jewish women dwelled on the Holocaust and anti-Semitism, the Palestinian women said let's move on. But we didn't move on. Neither side could let go.

Then came the intifada. *Everyone was upset about it but for different reasons. The Jewish women talked about human rights, Jewish values, and Israel's public image. Our women wanted to hear affir-*

mation of Palestinian self-determination and nationhood. The Jewish women agreed to say it, but the words stuck in their throats.

Meetings became too stressful and the process began to disintegrate. What killed it was impatience. Our expectations were too big. We thought we could solve the whole Israeli-Palestinian conflict. We needed smaller objectives so we could have a sense of accomplishment step by step.

I'm frustrated because we failed. Still, I have moved beyond despair. I'm no longer afraid to speak out. I know Jews and Palestinians must come together or there's no future for either of us. The dialogue must have had a positive impact because here I am ready to start all over again. In hindsight, I know how I'd do it differently: When you reach a stumbling block, you just have to let it be.

Stony Point is well named: there are stumbling blocks throughout our program and being forewarned doesn't stop us from tripping over them. The next day begins with a session in which we establish the ground rules for dialogue: mutual respect, trust, confidentiality, honesty, a commitment to listen. We'll have a couple of formal presentations and several opportunities for each group to caucus separately, but the rest of the time will be spent together just talking. And of course, nothing said here will leave this room.

At this, one of our more prominent Jewish women confesses great anxiety. "Just being here might have repercussions for me," she says.

If it means the Jewish community can dismiss me as part of a radical fringe, this dialogue could have big political costs for me. It could endanger the rest of my agenda including my feminist work. Maybe I should quit now.

Two or three other Jews concur. They're afraid of the consequences, afraid of how what is said here may be distorted. Further discussion ensues until the Jews are reassured that no publicity will be released about who is in the dialogue or what is said here unless the parties give their permission.

One of the Palestinians admits she is surprised at this:

I would understand if our group wanted to hold the dialogue in a closet. We used to be afraid that meeting with Jews would hurt our

image in the resistance movement. But why should you be worried
about meeting with us? Your pro-Israel politics are so well established.

The Jewish women smile. How could we explain to an outsider that
one Jew's idea of pro-Israel politics is another Jew's idea of treason?

The Palestinian misinterprets our smiles as suspicion. "I want to
assure you that none of us are PLO officers or PNC members," she
says very kindly, adding, "although of course we all accept the PLO
as our legitimate representative."

In the next session, one speaker from each side gets equal time to
formally present her people's version of the conflict. Both sides are
well prepared for the *Rashomon* effect; all of us know this is a
boulder-size stumbling block, yet we cannot stop ourselves. Rather
than move on to the next session, "Options for the Future," we
spend the afternoon arguing over the past—debating whether biblical mandate or international law is the greater entitlement,
whether the Arabs owned 70 percent or 20 percent of the pre-state
land, or the Crown did, or whether the Western concept of land
ownership is totally irrelevant; one-upping each other's miseries, re-
hashing each other's crimes.

Someone reminds the group that we're here to create *new* history,
that we must move forward. But at the session on the future, it's hard
to see beyond our present differences; sometimes it's hard to see at all
through the tears. For instance, all hell breaks loose when the Jewish
women demand support for the revocation of the U.N.'s Zionism Is
Racism resolution. We call Zionism the national liberation movement
of the Jewish people; Palestinians see it as the force that swept them
from their homes and mutilated their peoplehood. We consider the
U.N. resolution a libelous international lie; they say it's true as long
as Israel continues to grant Jews rights and privileges not available to
other groups.

Discussions also hit the wall on the question of Soviet immigrants.
The Jewish women see them as the miracle aliyah, the last great
migration of our history, and the ultimate proof that Israel is the one
reliable haven from anti-Semitism; what we worry about is where to
put them all, what kind of Russians are coming, hawks or doves, and
which political parties will get their votes. The Palestinians couldn't
care less about the Russians' politics; they only see more soldiers for
the Israeli army and more Jews spilling over into the West Bank. They

remember that between 1918 and 1946 they were demographically disenfranchised when the Jews increased tenfold and the Palestinian population only doubled. We Jews insist the Israeli government will keep its word and not settle the Soviet immigrants outside the Green Line. The Palestinians do not believe it. They are worried about *their* aliyah. Where will they put all the Palestinians who will return to *their* new state if the Territories are overrun with Jewish settlers (now up to 100,000) and Soviet immigrants, who are estimated to top off, finally, at 1 million?

The Palestinian "right of return" is another detonator for our group. Mainstream Jews cannot imagine the region being swelled by 2 million Palestinians. Jewish leftists prefer to talk about compensation for the refugees who cannot return. They want Israel and Jordan to form an economic confederation with the Palestinian state to buttress its underdeveloped infrastructure and prevent the discontented and unemployed from flooding into Israel. Regardless of the practicalities, Palestinians cannot imagine a new state that excludes their brothers and sisters who have been trapped in refugee camps or scattered to the winds. They want to reunite divided families. We say Palestinians who are doing well in America, France, or Morocco will probably behave like the Jews in our Diaspora: they will stay put. But the Palestinian women insist the option of return should be there for them if they need it, as Israel is there for the Jews.

Sparks fly as we touch on other tender spots and incendiary controversies. Jews fault Palestinians for the violence of the *intifada,* for the summary execution of collaborators, and for supporting Saddam Hussein. Palestinians fault Israelis for their collective punishments, for commuting the sentences of Jewish militants who have been convicted of maiming and murdering Arabs, and for leaving them no hope, thus driving them into the arms of Saddam. We debate the impact of Islamic and Jewish fundamentalism on the region (20 percent of the Palestinians in the territories are religious fundamentalists; 18 out of 120 members of Knesset are ultra-Orthodox Jews). We argue about the final status of Jerusalem; about U.S. foreign aid to Israel; about the PLO covenant, which does not recognize Israel's right to exist (in contradiction of the PNC's recognition statements of 1988); and about how the feminist movement relates to the nationalist struggle.

"If we're supposed to be building a new future," says a Palestinian woman, "maybe we can at least start by affirming both peoples' right to self-determination."

"That's fine with me," a Jewish woman answers instantly. Then her face clouds over. "But I don't want your state to threaten my state."

Self-determination means power, and at this point some Jews cannot imagine Palestinian power without Palestinian violence. I cannot imagine continued Palestinian *powerlessness* without its leading to more violence, and, in any case, I believe in separating the problem of terrorism from the right to statehood. I do not think Israel should deprive a whole people of their homeland in order to punish the viciousness of a small minority.

The Palestinian woman's reply shows respect for Jewish fears:

> You must understand that we've changed; we've moved from total denial, to armed resistance, to the realization that there must be co-existence. We don't deny our past attacks on noninvolved third parties; however, we no longer justify it; it cost us morally and in pragmatic terms. I'm not proud of our terrorism and I'm glad the PNC has disavowed it. But we had to engage in bloodletting before we could come back to our senses.

Then she asks for Jewish understanding of what it took to come this far.

> Our moderates began accepting U.N. Resolution 242 back in 1974 but it was a long process to get the majority to abandon the maximalist position; it didn't just happen in Algiers in 1988. It took fifteen years for us to sell it to our public. Don't forget there was a lot of anger out there . . .

The same history that reminds Jews of their vulnerability reminds Palestinians of their anger. "What if someone barged into your house and dispossessed you?" burst out another Palestinian.

> For years, you live in misery and shame while you try to get your house back every way you can. Finally, for the sake of peace for your children, you give up the whole house and agree to live in less than half of it. Haven't we given the Jews enough?

"But we don't accept that the whole house was yours to begin with!" says a Jewish woman—and we're off again, fact-wrestling with the monsters of memory. Donna Jenson, one of the facilitators, offered a perfect simile:

> *Strange as it sounds, Jews and Palestinians are like partners in an arranged Catholic marriage. Neither partner would have chosen to marry the other, but they can't get a divorce. They're stuck with each other, so for the children's sake they have to learn to make the marriage work.*

At some point in every weekend we ill-matched partners finally tackle the agenda for the future. We decide to set aside our sticking points and prepare a draft of our Points of Agreement, not for the media but for our own guidance. Both groups go into caucus, come up with their proposed list, then respond to the other side's items and emerge with fifteen points that converge. Next we summarize the project's purposes—to replicate, educate, and activate—and then go on to discuss future ventures: more weekend retreats, seminars, reading packets; Jewish-Palestinian speaking teams that go out into both communities to describe our work and help people begin their own dialogues; joint writing and lobbying efforts on our Points of Agreement; coordination with Israeli and Palestinian peace groups; and a fact-finding trip to the Middle East for which Jews plan the itinerary in Israel and Palestinians determine what the delegation will see in the West Bank and Gaza.

When we break into subcommittees, there's some backsliding: the women writing the Points of Agreement argue over how to distinguish the *intifada* from terrorism; the subcommittee planning the fact-finding trip argues about tourist sites versus propaganda sites—and I stand up to do some deep knee bends.

Dialogue is an exhausting, emotionally draining experience. At moments such as this I feel like a mouse in a maze, barreling around the track to the sound of a broken record, hitting this blind alley, that dead end, trying again and again to find a way out of an endless old labyrinth. In this dialogue, cultural differences are not a problem. We enjoy each other's sense of humor. On feminist ideology, I often feel more in tune with the Palestinians than with my Jewish sisters. We're comfortable together as women, comfortable enough to exchange career tips and family stories. Religious differences create no tension; in fact, we Jews invited the Palestinians to our Sabbath service, and the following day at the dialogue session, a Christian woman proudly sang "Adon Olam" to me, albeit with an Arabic accent. Months later, she sent me a Passover card.

We are decent women with good impulses, but cross-cultural ecumenism cannot paper over polar differences on such issues as history, land, security, sovereignty, identity, suffering, competing rights, and comparative misery. As I learned long ago at the King David Hotel, and at 777 U.N. Plaza, disputes of this magnitude cannot always be subordinated to feminist solidarity. And no matter how hard we try, not all of our differences can be settled; sometimes we have to end a debate by agreeing to disagree—agreeably. (A few women have personalized their one-on-one clashes and serious repair work has been needed to protect the group process.) I know it's important not to isolate myself from people whose minds I cannot change, but sometimes, the hardest thing of all is just to sit and listen respectfully to the painful things the other side says.

Nevertheless, there have been dazzling moments of reconciliation: for instance, when we realize that unconsciously, we have seated ourselves around the conference table in perfect alternation: Palestinian-Jew-Palestinian-Jew. Or when the conference facilitators set up a display of about twenty pictures—photographs of Jews and Palestinians, the Jerusalem hills, the Galilee, a military cemetery, women weeping, a peace demonstration, women embroidering, soldiers with children—and we're told to walk around in Jewish-Palestinian pairs and discuss them and then to choose the most affecting images, and my Palestinian partner and I unbeknown to one another pick the same three pictures.

"Can you imagine two men doing what we did for the last hour—discussing their feelings about photographs?" she asks.

"No," I reply. "They'd be saying, 'I bet this was shot at F4.5 at 1/500 shutter speed with a tripod.'" And we laugh together.

Or when I am suddenly overwhelmed with feeling for a Palestinian woman who clearly cannot speak the word "Zionism" without breaking down—and I try to imagine how a word I grew up with, a word of Jewish honor could elicit such anguish. And weeks later, I read an essay by one of our Palestinian participants who confesses similar empathic feelings:

*When I saw one of the American-Jewish women fighting a battle
within herself . . . wanting to be objective yet afraid to betray her
people by doing so, I was reminded of myself. I could see deep into her
very heart. . . .*

Or when, just after Iraq invaded Kuwait I feel free to pick up the
phone and call halfway across the country to discuss my fears with a
Palestinian friend. We had different "takes" on the situation but both
of us were afraid—both of us have draft-age sons.

This same friend once quipped, "If you don't have knots in your
stomach, then you're not really doing dialogue." But the real question is, why bother doing it at all? If it's not group therapy to make
each other feel better, and we know it is no substitute for direct
action or negotiation, why do we put ourselves through this meat
grinder? The reason, I think, is wonderfully, humanly paradoxical:
we endure these excruciating hours of disputation and tension in
order to create their opposite—ordinariness and normalization in
our relationships with The Other. Change comes through action
and process, not just politics and warfare. Twenty women at Stony
Point can't make peace in the Middle East, but we can humanize
the enemy and create a new vision of coexistence. We can remind
the world that all the dead on both sides have not settled our differences, so now it is time for the living to renounce violence as a
means of solving this conflict. We can model equality of rights for
two peoples, and feminist modalities for intimacy, and we can give
each other the gift of understanding.

Although we have not solved the big problems, at least both sides
know what Reena Bernards calls "the don't-do part"; we have learned
that the win/lose strategy is what keeps Jews and Palestinians in
that eternal maze, and win/win is the only way out. So we try to
remember:

• Not to argue about who deserves the land more, but to agree that
both peoples deserve a homeland.

• Not to argue about who suffered more, but to agree that both
people have experienced tragedy.

• Not to argue about who's to blame, but to agree that both peoples have made mistakes.

• Not to argue about who has more reason to distrust, but to agree that while both peoples have reason to distrust, both need peace more.

• Not to argue about who killed more, or got killed more, but ensure that there is no more killing.

When I am asked what I've learned from the dialogues with Palestinians, I mention those "rules." I also mention the fundamental contradiction that has yielded such unexpected rewards: I went into the project afraid that it might erode my commitment to my own people, but what happened was the reverse: dialogue inspired me to dig down to my roots and feel more firmly grounded in the Jewish past; it made me a better-informed spokesperson for what I believe should be and can be a better kind of Israel.

After spending so much time talking and thinking about Israel, Palestinians and peace, I'm almost surprised to find that my conclusions can be summarized in a few paragraphs:

• The history that seemed so simple to me back in the 1970s has become complicated by my understanding of Palestinian perspectives. And while I retain my strong Zionist belief in Israel's right to exist, I can now appreciate the frustration of another people who see Jewish national liberation as Palestinian national obliteration. I can see why, *in their view,* making them share the land with the Jewish people was as untenable as it would be for me to take two of your four children so that I too can have a family.

• Understanding their perspective does not lessen my commitment to Israel but it does allow me to acknowledge how far Palestinians have come in accepting at last that the Jewish people also deserve to have a family—and that *in our view,* those two children have been ours all along. This Palestinian acceptance is what Jews have been waiting for since 1948 and yet now, ironically, in Abba Eban's words, it is the Israelis who "will not take Yes for an answer" and who have steadily retreated from the idea of compromise.

• In this era of global transformation, only Israel stagnates. She is the only Western democracy that controls another people against its will. She should give up the Occupied Territories—not just to fulfill her democratic principles, and not just to do right by the Palestinians, but *for her own sake.* Never before have the Jewish people dominated anyone and those who have dominated us have been vanquished. Why emulate them?

• A nation's security is determined by much more than its military power; security is measured in the substance and texture of everyday life. Policing the Territories—the daily obscenity of school closings, censored news, house demolitions, and blood-soaked children—has been rotting the foundations of the Jewish ethos. It has polarized Israeli society and poisoned the morale of what once was a proud citizens' army. The occupation and the *intifada* have wreaked havoc on Israel's economy, which is racked by inflation under benign circumstances. The military budget sucks up a third of Israel's resources, including shekels needed to solve social problems. Those who suffer most are Oriental (non-European) Jews who make up 56 percent of the population, Israeli Arabs who make up 17 percent (but get only 3 percent of the state's development funds and less than one-third of its welfare allocations), and especially the women and children of both groups.

• All social strata are affected. Newlyweds cannot find housing. Hotels are half empty and the tourists who come are afraid to walk around in certain areas in broad daylight. Native-born Israelis are leaving the country even as the international spotlight shines on the country's struggle to accommodate its rising waves of Soviet immigration. While her leaders are obsessed with politics, and her resources committed to the military, Israel has been inept at absorbing these new citizens whose arrival has engendered demographic and religious celebration but not enough housing or jobs. Charges of racism, favoritism, and corruption besmirch the absorption effort. And the hostility between Jews and Palestinians creates a threatening, inhospitable environment rather than a vibrant, welcoming homeland. No wonder that a surprising number of Soviet Jews are settling in Germany rather than seek refuge from anti-Semitism in the Jewish state. Aware of the chilling historical irony represented by this choice, one Russian refugee told *The New York Times*: "Israel is a militarized state. We have lived under pressure for too long. We want to be in a peaceful country like Germany."

• Israeli militarization also takes its toll in heightened social violence and diminished democracy. A Van Leer Institute study found that two-thirds of Jewish high school students favor curtailing the civil rights of Israel's Arab citizens. Observers have documented increased hostility in language, public discourse, and children's games (kids play *intifada* and several have been killed in street roulette). A few storekeepers have been displaying signs that say NO ARABS WORK HERE. Sociologists have noted a strengthening of racist and patriarchal attitudes in the popular culture, from commercial advertising to hard-core pornography. Rape and domestic violence are on the increase among both Arabs and Jews. Abuses of police and army power have become more frequent and egregious. Jewish-Arab belligerence has spread like a stain inside the Green Line and the nightly newscasts attest to an upsurge in random knifings, sniper shootings, and outbreaks of fundamentalist-sponsored terrorism that are as frightening in their way as Scud missile attacks on Tel Aviv. Not only did the government issue a gas mask to every Jew and Arab because of fear of Iraqi chemical attacks but more and more average folks are applying for pistol permits because of fear of each other. In sum, the Jewish state has become an armed camp in the midst of the armed camp of the Arab world. Or as Israeli novelist David Grossman puts it: "We are like a giant with very muscular arms and legs but no internal organs at all."

"The dilemma for me is not the Palestinian problem but how can Jewish people live like this?" says an Israeli friend. Other Jews insist the internal problems are nothing compared to the hostility of the surrounding Arab states. Yet Syria, Jordan, Iraq, Saudi Arabia, and Lebanon all have declared that they will not make peace with Israel until she comes to terms with the Palestinians—by which they mean negotiate with the PLO. Moderate Palestinians are beginning to panic as the Hamas fundamentalists unseat the PLO in the *intifada* leadership and in the hearts of a desperate people. They warn that they—and we—may end up with an Islamic dictatorship in the West Bank and Gaza, unless Israel accepts Arafat now.

So the Palestinians *are* the problem—as Gershom Sholem put it, blood flows toward the wound—and they are the solution. They are everyone's trump card. Israel could take the card away from the Arabs by playing it herself. Just imagine how altered events would have been if Shamir was already at the negotiating table on August 2, 1990, when Saddam Hussein invaded Kuwait. George Bush's carefully crafted international coalition against Iraq would have been far less vulnerable to Arab slippage and the arrow of "linkage" would have been missing from Saddam's quiver.

When Israel and the PLO make peace, the other Arab countries will lose their main excuse not to. When Israel and the PLO make peace, the Palestinians will be too busy consolidating their strengths and building a state to let themselves be used to divide or realign the Arab world. When Israel and the PLO make peace, the two states might even unite for their mutual protection against a madman like Saddam Hussein—a scenario no less imaginable than the unlikely coalition between the United States and Syria less than two years after Syria assisted in the terrorist explosion of Pan Am flight 103 over Lockerbie, Scotland.

In politics, everything can change overnight. In ethics, however, certain standards remain immutable, Jewish standards even more so. There can be no ethical justification for continued Jewish domination of 1.7 million Palestinians. There is no way for Jews to "transfer" Arabs and still remain moral human beings. Euphemisms won't mask the fact that annexation, expulsion, and deportation are fascist tactics. During centuries of dislocation and powerlessness, we kept our soul. Now, we have a homeland and an army but our soul is in mortal danger. Power corrupts, and what's worse, power has not made Israel safe. Only peace can make her safe. Even the good book counsels us to beware of the role of the oppressor (see Exodus 22:20 and 23:9).

Above all others, we Jews should know that a people with a nationalist mission and a coherent sense of themselves *as a people* will never give up their struggle for self-determination, just as we never gave up ours. David Ben Gurion was right; Golda Meir was wrong: Palestinians exist. And, as is becoming tragically more apparent, Israelis will either deal with them or die with them. Peace activists favor dealing with them now, and living with them in future harmony.

Virtually every poll shows that the majority of Israelis think it is worth trading land for permanent security; they accept the notion of an independent Palestinian entity, although they do not trust the Arabs, especially the PLO. Eventually, they will have to accept that nations do not negotiate with friends but with enemies (it would be pleasant to talk peace with the Swedes but where would it get them?), and that trust need not figure into the equation as long as the final settlement nails down all the loopholes and guarantees internationally monitored safeguards.

According to Professors Galia Golan and Naomi Chazan at Hebrew University, Israeli women are significantly more dovish than Israeli men: 70 percent support direct talks with the PLO, compared to 50 percent of the men. Since the beginning of the *intifada*, more than 150 new peace and protest groups have been formed, and women play a highly visible role in all segments of the movement. This is because, Chazan says, women tend to make no distinction between the battlefront and the home front. Their lives are sapped and strained by violent conflict and their children are in danger, whether from stones or rubber bullets. Women's political opinions are less dogmatic; they don't lose the forest for the trees. Once mobilized, they are consistent and persistent; they don't burn out as fast as men.

For feminist-minded women, the themes of the *intifada* resonate with feminist ideals of equality, independence, and dignity. Rather than let economic inequity, social malaise, immigration, or sexism divert attention from the peace issue, feminists help Israelis to see the connection between worsening social problems and the *absence* of peace. This connection was understood by the women who started the American antiwar movement that forced our troops out of Vietnam (remember Women Strike for Peace). It is well understood by Palestinian women to whom the *intifada* has given more active roles in the resistance to occupation, which in turn has given them more power in their own communities. It is understood by increasing numbers of Israeli women who are at the cutting edge of the Middle East peace movement. And sometimes, understanding the connections brings Palestinian and Israeli women together in joint peace actions that bear a distinctly female stamp.

As one woman explained:

Feminists in Israel have been confronting the links between the militarization of Israeli society and the subordination of women. War creates pressures for having many children. It prioritizes men, and emphasizes macho values. In addition, many women have concluded that there is a relationship between the oppression of Israeli Jewish women and the oppression of Palestinians, and that the continued Israeli military occupation of the West Bank and Gaza, and the condition of almost permanent warfare, is not in their interest or that of Israel as a whole.

The Women and Peace Coalition, an umbrella for eight groups, organized a march of 5,000 women from West to East Jerusalem, followed by a conference entitled "Women Go for Peace," both of which included Palestinians who support the goal of coexistence. (There are four Palestinian Women's Committees in the Occupied Territories, some more active than others in the peace effort. The committees devote most of their time to running community institutions and working for women's advancement within their own infrastructures. Still, many of them fear the effect of rising fundamentalist power upon women's freedom and they worry about suffering the same fate as Algerian women, who shared in making their revolution but showed few gains in its aftermath.)

The best-known partner in the Coalition is Women in Black, an ad hoc group of Israeli and Palestinian women who stand at busy intersections every Friday at one P.M. in some thirty locations all over the country. Like a somber line of mourners, they wear black clothing to symbolize the tragedy of both peoples. I had heard that Israelis routinely subject the demonstrators to physical assault—throwing eggs, spraying them with bug repellent, trying to run them over—as well as heavy sexual harassment. Women are called "whores"; their male supporters win the expletive "faggots." Hawks like to cast aspersions on male virility, as if it were less courageous to risk peace than wage war—and on female purity, as if to coexist with Palestinians is to fornicate with them. When last in Jerusalem, I stood with Women in Black in French Square carrying a sign that said END THE OCCUPATION. A man leaned out of a passing car, spat at me, and shouted something in rapid Hebrew. The woman at my side translated: "He just asked you how many Arabs you fucked today."

Also in the Women's Coalition are:

• The Bridge (Gesher), Israeli women from diverse religious and ethnic backgrounds who run lectures and conferences on Arab-Jewish relations.

• Tandi, a joint Jewish-Arab women's movement dedicated to peace and women's rights.

• Shani: Israeli Women Against the Occupation, which organizes parlor meetings, visits the Territories, and protests against school closings, house demolitions, and other manifestations of the occupation.

- Women's Organization for Women Political Prisoners, which fights against illegal arrests, censorship of information about those arrests, the use of women as hostages to pressure male relatives—and provides aid and legal counsel to women who are in detention for political activity or whose health is endangered in prison by violence, maltreatment, or sexual abuse.

- The Peace Quilt project, to which more than 5,000 Jewish and Arab women contributed small squares of fabric embroidered with personal peace messages that were pieced together to make a symbolic ceremonial cloth for the negotiating table. (The cloth also has been wrapped around the house of the president of Israel.)

During the Gulf crisis, the Women and Peace Coalition issued the following statement:

> *We women refuse to accept war as a solution to solve conflicts no matter how complicated they may be. Especially in this period of crisis, there is a need to persist in the principle of dialogue and in finding peaceful solutions.*

A somewhat more centrist women's group, the Reshet (Women's Network for the Advancement of Peace), was formed at the close of a historic meeting in Brussels in May 1989 attended by leading Arab and Jewish women who overcame their mutual suspicion and, after long debate and painstaking compromise, agreed on common goals for achieving a durable peace. Back home, the Reshet women circulated a summary of the Brussels Declaration, and thousands of supporters signed on to its principles. Since then, they have worked to influence public opinion and help both sides get to know "the faceless enemy" on human terms. They sponsor meetings in living rooms where women listen to an Israeli and a Palestinian engage in dialogue on subjects ranging from "How do you feel about amniocentesis?" to "Is there a difference between an Arab terrorist knifing people on a bus, and the militant Rabbi Levinger shooting innocent Palestinians outside their shops?" Reshet's Jewish women tell me that getting to know Palestinian women like Rana Nashashibi, a psychologist from East Jerusalem, or Zahira Kamal, president of the West Bank Union of Palestinian Women's Work Committees, has made it no longer possible to talk about "them" as if Palestinians were a monolith instead of real people with families, work, worries, dreams, and lives of their own.

Those lives come clearly into focus during Reshet-sponsored day trips into the Occupied Territories. After one such trip to a Gaza refugee camp, an Israeli woman reported:

> *It's odd, the details that strike you. In the Jabaliya camp we heard all sorts of disturbing things from doctors in the medical center. But what really impressed me most was a visit to . . . a kindergarten for more than thirty children . . . with almost no toys. You know, a box with three pieces of Lego in it for thirty kids. . . . That did something to me. Its effect was completely different from the reports of violent clashes.*
>
> *After we left Gaza, we stopped in a shopping center at Yad Mordechai. I sat and watched the Israelis. . . . A well-dressed father taking his well-dressed kids out to buy ice cream . . . choosing between ten different flavors. I felt like I had just come from another planet. . . . Will that feeling change me? Will it change the situation? I don't know.*

Almost in direct reply, another Reshet member added:

> *I think of those three young women who run the kindergarten. They were so proud to show us how active they are in taking charge of their lives as women. I can't describe how touched I was. And how, in the midst of this dreadful reality, it helped me personally to get over some of my tremendous fear.*

The Reshet, the Women and Peace Coalition, and the women's dialogue groups differ from the rest of the Israeli peace movement in that they bring a conscious feminist perspective to their work. In the United States, Jewish feminists try to add a similar dimension to the myriad "co-ed" groups working on peace issues, groups like the American-Israeli Civil Liberties Coalition, Americans for Peace Now, Jewish Peace Fellowship, the Jewish Peace Lobby, New Jewish Agenda, The Road to Peace (a resource service), Project Nishma (Hebrew for "Let us listen"), Interns for Peace, the New Israel Fund, the International Peace Union, or the U.S. Interreligious Committee for Peace in the Middle East.

Esther Cohen, one of the two women who organized the "Road to Peace Conference," cosponsored in New York City by *New Outlook*, a liberal Israeli magazine, and *Al Fajr*, the Palestinian newspaper, describes the sort of problems women encounter:

> *It took us a while, as organizers, to realize that it was easier for Israeli men and Palestinian men to recognize one another's significance as legitimate power players than it was for either side to recognize the crucial role of women in the Middle East peacemaking process. We fought and fought for women to be represented. However, only one-third of the Israeli delegation were women . . . and the Palestinians had an even smaller number. To emphasize the crucial role of women organizing dialogues for peace, we created a "Women and Peace" workshop at the conference, one of the most successful workshops because women explained how their capacity to listen has encouraged talk and action.*
>
> *As another way of emphasizing the centrality of women to the peacemaking process, we created an evening also called Women and Peace, the only part of the [conference] that was open to the public. Held at B'Nai Jeshurun, a synagogue in Manhattan, the event attracted an audience of over 700. For all of the Palestinian speakers, this was their first time in a synagogue. For most of the Jews in the audience, this meeting provided their first exposure to the Palestinian side of the Middle East story. While Palestinian and Israel women have been working together in the Middle East, this effort is only now beginning in any significant way, in the United States. Women in the audience attributed the power of the evening to the honest expressions of fear and hope the speakers were able to articulate so directly.*

Some women prefer not to navigate the shoals of sexism within the broader peace movement and instead choose to work in single-sex groups such as the Jewish Women's Committee to End the Occupation. One of the most effective of the American leftist-feminist peace groups, JWCEO holds monthly demonstrations in several U.S. cities in support of Israel's Women in Black, organizes meetings and lectures around emerging Middle East issues, and publishes "The Jewish Women's Peace Bulletin," which publicizes women's peace efforts in Israel, and lists contact persons for local women's groups in the United States and Canada.

Finally, there are ongoing colloquies between Jewish- and Palestinian-Americans all over the country, some private or even secret, others wide open; some convened through churches and synagogues, others made up of Jewish and Arab professional people, academics, neighbors; and some, like The Dialogue Project, organized by women for women, according to feminist principles of honesty, empathy, and mutual respect. (In a female environment, I find, women speak out when they have something to say. In mixed groups, women are more likely to let men do the talking.)

None of this ferment existed thirteen years ago when I met my first Palestinian. Recently, I picked up her book again, and noticed that it was dedicated "to the young generation of Palestinians and Israelis in the fervent hope that they will live side by side in dignity and peace." These past thirteen years, a new generation has come of age in a worsening climate of fear and alienation. But in the same period, people like myself have traveled from anger to activism, from silence to dialogue, from passivity to protest.

I wanted Raymonda Tawil to know the role she played in my journey. I decided to search for her, and on December 14, 1990, the seventh day of Hanukkah, I found her in Washington, D.C.

She remembers me well, she says on the phone—and also our night at the King David.

"Quite honestly, I had expected the *Ms.* group to understand Israel's oppression of Palestinians in the same light as men's oppression of women. I thought Americans who supported women's liberation would support our liberation," she says, echoing my own faith in feminism's unifying power. "I felt betrayed."

"We felt betrayed too," I tell her. "Our bus was on the coastal highway that day."

She knows exactly what day I mean. "Oh, no!" she cries. "Thank God you were saved."

"Raymonda"—my voice is tentative—"did you know in advance that a bus was to be hijacked?"

"Of course not! How could you think that?"

"Because you justified terrorism to us."

"I *explained* terrorism to you," she corrects me. "I warned you that frustration forces people to lash out. The odd thing is, after the bus attack, I thought of you. I was in jail at the time. I wanted to tell you that I didn't agree with this tactic but I hoped you could hear the message of the bus tragedy as the message of young people begging the world to listen to them."

"The world listens to a peacemaker's words better than an outlaw's bullets," I insist. I spend a few minutes describing my work in the peace movement and in dialogue. "Terrorism had hardened my heart, but what turned me around were words—especially the words and feelings of Palestinian women."

"You move me," she sighs. "Thank you for telling me this."

Then she fleshes out her story. After being released from prison in 1978, she lectured to young people in kibbutzim arguing for a two-state solution. The military authorities stayed close at her heels. Then she started the Palestine Press Services but the government closed it down, she says. One day in 1984, she found a bomb in her car that she believes was planted by Palestinian collaborators at the behest of Israeli Intelligence. She left the country and since then has been living in Paris and Washington D.C. where she operates a branch of the Jerusalem News Service. Her fondest wish is to return to Ramallah but the danger is too great. While home for a visit in 1987, her car was blown up. A caller, speaking in Arabic, warned that within three days she would be assassinated. U.S. Consul General Morris Draper helped speed her escape.

> He told me, "Better a living woman than a dead hero." But I am in great conflict. I want to go home but I am afraid. Not just of death but of character assassination. People suggest that I have affairs; they create the idea that I am not clean, not a good mother, not an ideal nationalist. I am a feminist but this attack is devastating to me, my husband, and my children.

Raymonda says the campaign against her has emanated from the Israeli military government which regards her as a malevolent propagandist for peace; and from Arab men who cannot bear to see a woman in the Palestinian leadership. Both groups know they can destroy her if they destroy her image in the eyes of conservative Arab society.

"It's not fair to do this to me when my only crime is to speak and write about peaceful coexistence."

I feel it appropriate to say to Raymonda what she said to me: "You move me. Thank you for telling me this."

"Let's try to get together the next time you're in Washington or I'm in New York," she says. "We have much to talk about."

I agree. Yes.

So much to talk about.

Chapter 1 of this book began inside my family, where first I acquired the Jewish values and "gendered" experiences that would inform so much of the story you have just read. Now, I bring these pages to a close about as far away from family as one can get—"in the presence of mine enemy"—and yet not so far away as it seems, for those Jewish values and female experiences have made it possible for me to arrive at this place. My belief in Israeli-Palestinian reconciliation is very Jewish; my method of choice, dialogue, is very feminist; and although beliefs and methods do not always work in practice, the desire to root one's goals in a continuum larger than one's own numbered days is what keeps life mindful and meaningful.

Because unmitigated chutzpah (nerve, guts, gall) is indispensable to revolution, my having participated in the American Women's Movement turned out to be uncanny training for the Middle East peace movement, a struggle that seems destined to occupy my energies well into the twenty-first century. Feminism's challenge to discrimination and hierarchical male-female relations could be a template for the ideal of equality and justice in Jewish-Palestinian relations. It's no wonder that, in times of war or crisis, women's movements *become* peace movements—as has been happening in Israel and among Jewish women's groups in the United States, Europe, and elsewhere. As national priorities are skewed to favor the needs of armies before people, and democracy is sacrificed at the altar of security, women discover that peace is the prerequisite for everything else we care about, especially equality and justice.

Writing this, I realize how easily words like "equality," "justice," and "peace" blur into abstractions unless they are made real in thought and action. Activism reifies them. For me, making peace is a physical act of creation, like writing a book that never existed before, or giving birth to a child. None of these "products" just happens; each takes work. Peacemaking is perhaps the hardest work of all and, if you'll excuse a touch of sanctimony, it is the culmination of everything I believe in as a woman and a Jew.

In the Sixties and Seventies, I got used to being called a "women's libber," "man-hater," or worse; usually I walked away from the insults rather than debate with fools. Now, like others in the Jewish peace camp, I have to accustom myself to being attacked as naive, a self-hating Jew, even a traitor. But in this case, I do not let the insults go unanswered. Because I am devoted to Israel and believe her survival is at stake, I view such confrontations as opportunities to proselytize for peace. I refuse to leave the fate of that country in the hands of the Orthodox black hats and Ariel Sharon. I believe Palestine must exist in order for Israel to exist. I say the status quo is untenable. But far from being a gratuitous critic I do have a positive vision. I want a smaller, safer, sweeter Israel. Often, what I find among the self-styled Israel-chauvinists is no vision at all but just a knee-jerk loyalty that amounts to a mindless defense of one political interest group (Shamir and the Likud party). Usually their idea of the best interests of the Jewish State is whatever AIPAC, the American Israel lobbying group, decrees. They say they want peace in Israel when what they really want is quiet.

Furthermore, those people who ridicule the ideal of coexistence or call doves "self-hating Jews"—*they* are the ones who have betrayed their heritage, for nothing is more fundamentally, quintessentially Jewish than the search for peace. In *The History of the Jews*, Paul Johnson writes,

> *The idea of peace as a positive state and noble ideal which is also a workable human condition is a Jewish invention and one of the great motifs of the Bible.*

Proverbs tells us that wisdom's ways are "ways of pleasantness and all her paths are peace." Deuteronomy 16:20 commands us, "Justice, justice shalt thou pursue." For Jews, it is even "more important to promote peace than to do nominal justice," says Johnson, adding that, "One of the great functions of Jewish scholarship was to use the law to promote peace."

In the Talmud, we read, "The whole Torah exists only for the sake of peace." And again, "Three things sustain the existence of the world: justice, truth, and peace."

Hillel said, "Love peace and strive for peace."

Three times a day, observant Jews are obliged to say a prayer for peace.

And the sages promised that the first act of the Messiah will be to declare peace.

I do not think the Jewish people and the State of Israel can afford to wait for the Messiah. Where Jews and Arabs are concerned, we must do it ourselves—and where Jewish and Palestinian *women* are concerned, we will do it together.

Bibliography

HISTORY, ANALYSIS, ESSAYS

Balka, Christie, and Rose, Andy. *Twice Blessed: On Being Lesbian, Gay, and Jewish*. Boston: Beacon Press, 1989.

Baum, Charlotte, Hyman, Paula, and Michel, Sonya. *The Jewish Woman in America*. New York: Dial Press, 1976.

Beck, Evelyn Torton, ed. *Nice Jewish Girls: A Lesbian Anthology*. Trumansburg, NY: The Crossing Press, 1982. (Revised and updated, Boston: Beacon Press, 1989.)

Belth, Nathan C. *A Promise to Keep: A Narrative of the American Encounter with Anti-Semitism*. New York: Schocken, 1981.

Berkovits, Eliezer. *Jewish Women in Time and Torah*. New York: KTAV Publishing House, 1990.

Biale, Rachel. *Women and Jewish Law*. New York: Schocken Books, 1984.

Birkland, Carol J. *Unified in Hope: Arabs and Jews Talk about Peace*. New York: Friendship Press, 1990.

Bletter, Diana, and Grinker, Lori. *The Invisible Thread: A Portrait of American Jewish Women*. New York: The Jewish Publication Society, 1989.

Bourne, Jennie. "Homelands of the Mind: Jewish Feminism and Identity Politics," *Race and Class*, vol. 29, no. 1 (1987).

Briffault, Robert. *The Mothers*. New York: Atheneum, 1977.

Brod, Harry. *A Mensch Among Men: Explorations in Jewish Masculinity*. Freedom, CA: The Crossing Press, 1988.

Broner, E. M. *Her Mothers*. New York: Holt, Rinehart and Winston, 1975. Bloomington, IN: Indiana University Press, 1985.

———. *A Weave of Women*. New York: Holt, 1978. Indiana, 1985.

Bulkin, Elly, Pratt, Minnie Bruce, and Smith, Barbara. *Yours in Struggle: Three Feminist Perspectives on Anti-Semitism and Racism*. Brooklyn, NY: Long Haul Press, 1984.

Christ, Carol P., and Plaskow, Judith, eds. *Womanspirit Rising: A Feminist Reader in Religion*. San Francisco: Harper & Row, 1979.

Daly, Mary. *Beyond God the Father: Toward a Philosophy of Women's Liberation*. Boston: Beacon Press, 1973.

Deen, Edith. *All of the Women of the Bible*. New York: Harper & Row, 1955.

Dworkin, Andrea. *Pornography: Men Possessing Women*. New York: Perigee, 1981.

Eckardt, A. Roy. *Black-Woman-Jew: Three Wars for Human Liberation*. Bloomington and Indianapolis, IN: Indiana University Press, 1989.

Erens, Patricia. *The Jew in American Cinema*. Bloomington, IN: Indiana University Press, 1984.

Falbel, Rita, Klepfisz, Irena, and Nevel, Donna. *Jewish Women's Call For Peace.* Ithaca, NY: Firebrand Books, 1990.

Feldman, David. *Marital Relations, Birth Control and Abortion in Jewish Law.* New York: Schocken, 1974.

Freedman, Marcia. *Exile in the Promised Land.* Ithaca, New York: Firebrand Books, 1990.

Geller, Laura. "What Kind of Tikkun?" *Tikkun,* vol. 1, no. 1 (1986).

Goldfield, Anna. "Women as Sources of Torah." *Judaism,* vol. 24, no. 2. (Spring 1975).

Greenberg, Blu. *On Women and Judaism.* Philadelphia: The Jewish Publication Society of America, 1981.

Haut, Rifka, and Grossman, Susan, eds. *Daughters of the King: Women and the Synagogue.* New York: Jewish Publication Society, 1991.

Henry, Sondra, and Taitz, Emily. *Written Out of History: Our Jewish Foremothers.* New York: Biblio Press, 1983.

Hertzberg, Arthur. *The Jews in America.* New York: Simon and Schuster, 1989.

Heschel, Susannah, ed. *On Being a Jewish Feminist.* New York: Schocken Books, 1983.

Katz, Jacob. *From Prejudice to Destruction: Anti-Semitism, 1700–1933.* Cambridge, MA: Harvard University Press, 1980.

Kaufman, Jonathan. *Broken Alliance: The Turbulent Times Between Blacks and Jews in America.* New York: Charles Scribner's, 1988.

Kaye/Kantrowitz, Melanie, and Kelpfisz, Irena, eds. *The Tribe of Dina: A Jewish Women's Anthology.* Montpelier, VT: Sinister Wisdom Books, 1986. (Expanded, Boston: Beacon Press, 1989.)

Koltun, Elizabeth, ed. *The Jewish Woman: New Perspectives.* New York: Schocken Books, 1976.

Lippman, Beata. *Israel the Embattled Land: Jewish and Palestinian Women Talk about Their Lives.* New York: Pandora Press, 1988.

Marcus, Jacob Rader. *The American Jewish Woman, 1654–1980.* New York: KTAV Publishing House, 1981.

Mazow, Julia Wolf, ed. *The Woman Who Lost Her Names: Selected Writings by American Jewish Women.* San Francisco: Harper & Row, 1980.

Meiselman, Moshe. *Jewish Woman in Jewish Law.* New York: KTAV, 1978.

Meyers, Carol. *Discovering Eve: Ancient Israelit Women in Context.* New York: Oxford University Press, 1990.

Mirian, Selma. "Anti-Semitism in the Lesbian Community." *Sinister Wisdom,* 19, 1982.

Morgan, Michael L. "Overcoming the Remoteness of the Past: Memory and Historiography in Modern Jewish Thought." *Judaism,* vol. 38, no. 2.

Najjar, Orayb, and Warnock, Kitty. *Portraits of Palestinian Women.* Salt Lake City, UT: University of Utah Press, 1992.

Newman, Leslea, ed. *Bubbe Meisehs by Shayneh Maidelehs: An Anthology of Poetry by Jewish Granddaughters about Jewish Grandmothers,* Santa Cruz, CA: Herbooks, 1990. (Herbooks, P. O. Box 7465, Santa Cruz, CA 95061.)

Palgi, Michal, et al. *Sexual Equality: The Israeli Kibbutz Tests the Theories.* Pennsylvania: Norwood Editions, 1983.

Phillips, John. *Eve: The History of an Idea.* San Francisco: Harper & Row, 1984.

Plaskow, Judith. *Standing Again at Sinai: Judaism from a Feminist Perspective.* San Francisco: Harper & Row, 1990.

———, and Christ, Carol P. *Weaving the Visions: New Patterns in Feminist Spirituality.* San Francisco: Harper & Row, 1989.

Priesand, Sally. *Judaism and the New Woman*. New York: Behrman House, 1975.

Reuther, Rosemary. *Sexism and God-Talk: Toward a Feminist Theology*. Boston: Beacon Press, 1983.

————— and Ellis, Mark, eds. *Beyond Occupation; American Jewish, Christian, and Palestinian Voices for Peace*. Boston: Beacon Press, 1990.

Russell, Letty M., ed. *Feminist Interpretation of the Bible*. Philadelphia: The Westminster Press, 1985.

Schneider, Susan Weidman. *Jewish and Female: Choices and Changes in Our Lives Today*. New York: Simon and Schuster, 1984.

Stern, Geraldine. *Israeli Women Speak Out*. Philadelphia and New York: Lippincott, 1979.

Swidler, Leonard. *Biblical Affirmations of Woman*. Philadelphia: The Westminster Press, 1979.

Swirski, Barbara, and Safir, Marilyn P. *Calling the Equality Bluff: Women in Israel*. Elmsford, NY: Pergamon Press, 1991.

Tawil, Raymonda Hawa. *My Home, My Prison*. New York: Holt, Rinehart and Winston, 1980.

Teubal, Savina J. *Hagar the Egyptian: The Lost Tradition of the Matriarchs*. San Francisco: Harper & Row, 1990.

—————. *Sarah the Priestess: The First Matriarch of Genesis*. Athens, OH: Swallow Press, 1984.

Trible, Phyllis. *Texts of Terror: Literary Feminist Readings of Biblical Narratives*. Philadelphia: Fortress Press, 1984.

Wegner, Judith Romney. *Chattel or Person? The Status of Women in the Mishnah*. New York and Oxford: Oxford University Press, 1990.

Welch, Susan, and Ullrich, Fred. *The Political Life of American Jewish Women*. New York: Biblio Press, 1984.

Wenkart, Henny, ed. *Sarah's Daughters Sing: A Sampler of Poems by Jewish Women*. Hoboken, NJ: KTAV Publishing House, 1990.

Willis, Ellen. "The Myth of the Powerful Jew: The Black-Jewish Conflict, Part II." *The Village Voice*, September 3, 1979.

PRAYER, RITUAL, AND MIDRASH

Adelman, Penina V. *Miriam's Well: Rituals for Jewish Women Around the Year*. New York: Biblio Press, 1986.

Aschkenasy, Nehama. *Eve's Journey*. Philadelphia: University of Pennsylvania Press, 1986.

Bal, Mieke. *Lethal Love: Feminist Literary Readings of Biblical Love Stories*. Bloomington, IN: Indiana University Press, 1987.

Cohen, Sharon. "Reclaiming the Hammer: Toward a Feminist Midrash." *Tikkun*, vol. 3, no. 2.

Falk, Marcia. *The Book of Blessings: A Feminist-Jewish Reconstruction of Prayer*. San Francisco: Harper & Row, 1989.

Frymer-Kensky, Tikva. *Motherprayer*. Boston: Beacon Press, 1989.

Lefkovitz, Lori. "When Lilith Becomes a Heroine: Midrash as Feminist Response." *The Melton Journal*, Spring 1990.

Reifman, Toby Fishbein. *Blessing the Birth of a Daughter: Jewish Naming Ceremonies for Girls*. New York: Ezrat Nashim, 1976.

Seid, Judith. *We Rejoice in Our Heritage: Home Rituals for Secular and Human-*

istic Jews. Ann Arbor, MI: Kopinvant Secular Press. (Kopinvant Secular Press, 910 Arbordale, Ann Arbor, MI 48103.)

The Shalom Seders: Three progressive Haggadot for Passover. (From New Jewish Agenda, 64 Fulton Street, Suite 1100, New York, NY 10038, $12.95 plus $1.50 postage.)

Spiegel, Marcia Cohn, and Kremsdorf, Deborah Lipton, eds. *Women Speak to God: The Poems and Prayers of Jewish Women.* San Diego, CA: Woman's Institute for Continuing Jewish Education, 1987. (See below.)

Stein, J. *A Jewish Lesbian Chanukah.* 2nd printing. Cambridge, MA: Bobbeh Meisehs Press, 1984.

Torah in Motion: Creating Dance Midrash. Denver, CO: A.R.E. Publishing, Inc. (A.R.E. Publishing, Inc., 3945 South Oneida Street, Denver, CO 80237.)

Umansky, Ellen. *Piety, Persuasion and Friendship: A Sourcebook of Modern Jewish Women's Spirituality.* Boston, MA: Beacon Press, 1991.

———. "Females, Feminists, and Feminism: A Review of Recent Literature on Jewish Feminism and the Creation of a Feminist Judaism." *Feminist Studies,* 14, no. 2 (Summer 1988).

Wenig, Maggie, and Janowitz, Naomi. "Siddur Nashim: A Sabbath Prayer Book for Women." *Lilith,* 1978.

The following publications are available from:

The Jewish Women's Resource Center, 9 East 69 Street, New York, NY 10021:
- *Resource Center Birth Ceremonies Guide,* $8.00
- *Blessing the Birth of a Daughter,* $6.00
- *Ketubot,* $3.50
- *Rosh Chodesh Ceremonies,* $4.50
- *Weaning Prayers,* $1.50
- *Tu B'Shevat Feminist Haggadah,* $3.50
- *Passover Feminist Haggadah,* $3.50
- *Menstruation Prayers,* $1.50
- *Top Jewish Women's Source Books,* $1.00

The Woman's Institute for Continuing Jewish Education, 4079 54th Street, San Diego, CA 92105 (619) 442-2666:
- *Taking the Fruit: Modern Women's Tales of the Bible, A New Edition.* Twenty-three interpretations of Biblical texts by contemporary Jewish women writers.
- *Midlife, A Rite of Passage,* by Irene Fine
- *The Wise Woman: A Celebration,* by Irene Fine
- *Educating the New Jewish Woman,* by Irene Fine
- *Women Speak to God: The Prayers and Poems of Jewish Women* by Marcia Cohn Spiegel and Deborah Lipton Kremsdorf
- *On Our Spiritual Journey: A Creative Shabbat Service* edited by Jacquelyn Tolley
- *Taking the Fruit: Modern Women's Tales of the Bible* edited by Jane Sprague Zone

PERIODICALS, SPECIAL ISSUES

(Addresses have been included for currently available periodicals.)

Amit Woman, 817 Broadway, New York, NY 10003. Five issues per year. (Orthodox women's concerns)

Big Mama Rag, July 1982.

Bridges, "A Journal for Jewish Feminists and Our Friends," P. O. Box 18437, Seattle, WA 98118. Two issues per year.

Dyke, Issue 5, 1977.

Genesis 2, March 1981.

Hadassah Magazine, 50 West 58 Street, New York, NY 10019. Monthly, published by Hadassah, the Women's Zionist Organization of America.

Jewish Women's Newsletter, P. O. Box 335, Berkeley, CA 94701-0335.

Lilith: The Jewish Women's Magazine, 250 West 57 Street, New York, NY 10019. Quarterly.

Ms., June 1982, August 1987. 230 Park Avenue, New York, NY 10169.

Na'amat Woman Magazine, January/February 1990. 200 Madison Avenue, New York, NY 10016.

New Outlook, "Women in Action," June/July issue, 1989. Also request the magazine's most current "Guide to Peace Networking," which is updated and expanded annually. 301 East 87 Street, Apt. 21C, New York, NY 10128.

Off Our Backs, February 1972, April 1982, August 1982.

On the Issues, vol. xi, 1989 and Summer 1990 (special reports on women at the Wall).

Plexus, September 1982.

Response: A Contemporary Jewish Review, Summer 1973. Summer 1980. Spring 1983.

Sojourner, August 1978, July 1983.

Tikkun, progressive Jewish journal with occasional essays of feminist interest. 5100 Leona Street, Oakland, CA 94619.

Womanews, December 1981.

Women's American ORT Reporter, 315 Park Avenue, New York, NY 10010. Quarterly.

BIBLIOGRAPHIES AND OTHER RESOURCES

An Annotated Bibliography of Writings by Lesbians of Color and Jewish Lesbians (1980–1987), by Diane M. Spaugh. 412 Foerster Street, San Francisco, CA 94127.

Jewish Women's Call for Peace: A Handbook for Jewish Women on the Israeli-Palestinian Conflict. Resources and essays on Middle East peacemaking. Firebrand Press, 1990. Available from Jewish Women's Committee to End the Occupation, 163 Joralemon Street, Suite 1178, Brooklyn, NY 11201, $4.95.

Cantor, Aviva. *The Jewish Woman 1900–1985: A Bibliography.* New York: Biblio Press, 1987. (Revised edition.) Biblio Press, Box 22, Fresh Meadows, New York 11365.

International Committee for Women of the Kotel, 1356 Coney Island Avenue, Suite 130, Brooklyn, NY 11230. Membership fee of $25 includes newsletter. Donations are requested to assist Israeli women's legal expenses and educational outreach to support the right of women to pray aloud, as a group, with Torah and tallit at the Western Wall.

Women's Peace in the Middle East. A half-hour documentary film on Isareli, Palestinian, and American women working for peace. From the producer-director, Suli Eschel, 3600 North Lake Shore Drive, Chicago, IL 60613. (312) 868-4140.

The following publications are available from:

The American Jewish Committee, 165 East 56th Street, New York, NY 10022:
• *Alternative Families in the Jewish Community: Singles, Single Parents, Childless Couples and Mixed Marrieds,* $4
• *Single and Jewish: Communal Perspectives,* $2
• *Jewish Views on Abortion* by Rabbi David M. Feldman, $1.50
• *Skinheads: Who They Are and What to Do When They Come to Town,* send self-addressed stamped envelope. Free.
• *Beyond Conflict: Black–Jewish Relations—Accent on the Positive* (1980). $2
• *Bibliography on Black–Jewish Relations, 1980–1990,* $1.50
• *Face to Face: Black–Jewish Campus Dialogues* (1989), $5
• *Women's Issues: Program and Resource Kit* (1987). Free.

The American Jewish Congress Commission on Women's Equality, 15 East 84th Street, New York, NY 10028:
• *International Jewish Feminist Directory* (in progress)

The International Jewish Peace Union, Box 20854, Tompkins Square Station, New York, NY 10009:
• *Organizing Teach-Ins for Middle East Peace.* Includes list of peace organizations plus bibliography.

The Israel Women's Network, POB 3171, Jerusalem, 91031, Israel:
• *The Status of Women in Israel* (1988), $15.00
• *Jerusalem Directory of Women's Health Services* (1989), $8.00
• *Networking for Women,* $15.00 per year (quarterly)
• *Women in Politics* Fact Sheet, $3.50

The Institute for Palestine Studies, P. O. Box 25301, Georgetown Station, Washington, DC 20007:
• *Journal of Palestine Studies,* $24 per year
• *Toward Coexistence: An Analysis of the Resolutions of the Palestine National Council* (1990), $3.95, paper
• *Israel, Palestinians and the Intifada* (1990), $29.95
• *United Nations Resolutions on Palestine and the Arab-Israeli Conflict, 1947–1986* (1988), three volumes, $29.95 each
• *American Jewish Organizations and Israel* (1986), $12.95, paper

The Jewish Women's Resource Center, 9 East 69 Street, New York, NY 10021:
• *Bibliographies* on "Abortion—Jewish Perspectives," $2; "Megillat Ruth," $.50; "Ordination of Women Rabbis," $3; "Sarah the Matriarch," $1.50.
• *Proceedings of the Conference on Feminist Judaism,* December 3, 1989, on cassette audio tapes—$20 per session or $175 for full set. (Write for plenary and workshop titles.)

The National Council of Jewish Women, 53 West 23 Street, New York, NY 10010:
• *Facts About Volunteers*

The New Jewish Agenda, 64 Fulton Street, Suite 1100, New York, NY 10038:
• *Lesbian and Gay Liberation: A Bibliography for the Jewish Community*, $.75
• *Nairobi Report—of NJA's participation in the U.N. Decade for Women Forum, 1985*. $5.
• *Report of NJA's National Speaking Tour: Israeli Arab and Jewish Women in Dialogue*, featuring Mariam Mar'i and Edna Zaretsky, January 4–20, 1989.

The Religious Action Center, Union of American Hebrew Congregations, 2027 Massachusetts Avenue, Washington, DC 20036.
• Publishes a guidebook to creating bridges between Black and Jewish communities, as well as legislative updates and action alerts on such issues as discrimination, reproductive choice, lesbian rights, and violence against women.

WOMEN'S PEACE GROUPS*

Israel

Gesher (The Bridge), POB 9041 Haifa
Gesher L'Shalom (Bridge to Peace), POB 11567, Tel Aviv
Shani: Israeli Women Against the Occupation, POB 9091, Jerusalem
Tandi, POB 29501, Tel Aviv
The Peace Quilt, POB 36448, Tel Aviv
Women in Black, POB 61128, Jerusalem
Women in Black, c/o Isha l'Isha, 88 Arlozorov Street, Haifa
Women's Organization for Women Political Prisoners, POB 8537 Jerusalem

United States

Jewish Women's Committee to End the Occupation, 163 Joralemon Street, Suite 1178, Brooklyn, NY 11201

Canada

The Jewish Women's Committee to End the Occupation, c/o Lois Fine, 540 Dovercourt, Toronto M6H 2W6

For locations of local peace organizations, consult the bibliography in *Jewish Women's Call for Peace: A Handbook for Jewish Women on the Israeli-Palestinian Conflict* (bibliographic listing above).

*See descriptions in chapter 16.

Index

ABOUT THE AUTHOR

LETTY COTTIN POGREBIN is a founding editor of *Ms.* magazine and the author of *Among Friends, Family Politics, Growing Up Free, Getting Yours,* and *How to Make It in a Man's World.* She is also the editor of *Stories for Free Children* and the co-developer with Marlo Thomas of *Free to Be You and Me* and *Free to Be a Family.* She and her husband live in New York City.